Lincoln's White House Secretary

LINCOLN'S
WHITE HOUSE
SECRETARY

The Adventurous Life of William O. Stoddard

Edited by Harold Holzer

Southern Illinois University Press / *Carbondale*

Copyright © 2007 by the Board of Trustees,
Southern Illinois University
All rights reserved
Printed in the United States of America

10 09 08 07   4 3 2 1

Library of Congress Cataloging-in-Publication Data

Stoddard, William Osborn, 1835–1925.
  Lincoln's White House secretary : the adventurous life of William O.
Stoddard / edited by Harold Holzer.
    p. cm.
  Includes bibliographical references and index.
  ISBN-13: 978-0-8093-2753-9 (cloth : alk. paper)
  ISBN-10: 0-8093-2753-8 (cloth : alk. paper)
  1. Stoddard, William Osborn, 1835–1925. 2. Presidents—United
States—Staff—Biography. 3. Secretaries—United States—Biography.
4. Lincoln, Abraham, 1809–1865—Friends and associates. 5. Lincoln,
Abraham, 1809–1865. 6. United States—Politics and government—
1861–1865. 7. United States—History—Civil War, 1861–1865—Personal
narratives. 8. Washington (D.C.)—History—Civil War, 1861–1865—
Personal narratives. 9. Journalists—United States—Biography.
10. Stoddard, William Osborn, 1835–1925—Homes and haunts—New
York (State) I. Holzer, Harold. II. Title.

E664.S85A3 2007
973.7092—dc22
[B]   2006028604

Printed on recycled paper. ♻

The paper used in this publication meets the minimum requirements of
American National Standard for Information Sciences—Permanence of
Paper for Printed Library Materials, ANSI Z39.48-1992. ∞

For Eleanor Stoddard
Who touched the hand that touched the hand . . .

Contents

CONTENTS

Illustrations

Acknowledgments

oth Eleanor Stoddard and I are grateful beyond measure to Southern Illinois University Press for its longstanding and unflagging enthusiasm for this project, during the long wait before an edited manuscript could be delivered. John F. "Rick" Stetter, former SIU Press director, first signed the project back in 1995, with the enthusiastic endorsement of SIU Carbondale history professor John Y. Simon, executive director of the Ulysses S. Grant Association, editor of the multi-volume *Papers of Ulysses S. Grant*, and a treasured friend. We thank them both for their encouragement and patience. More recently, SIU editor Sylvia Frank Rodrigue took on the project and handled it with her usual expert guidance, and design and production manager Barb Martin did much to take the old typescript and turn it into a computer-age manuscript on CD-ROM. Kathleen Kageff served ably as project editor, and Louie Simon was an excellent, eagle-eyed copy editor.

The Stoddard story unfolded not only in his own unpublished manuscript, but also in his many other published books, articles, and interviews, and a number of libraries around the country generously made their archives available to the editor in the search for these documents. I thank my many friends at the Lincoln Museum in Fort Wayne—especially CEO Joan Flinspach, and her able staff, including Carolyn Texley, Cindy VanHorn, and Sara Gabbard, for their considerable assistance and support. Over the years, Thomas F. Schwartz and Kim Bauer generously made additional documents available from the old Illinois State Historical Library in Springfield, later incorporated into the Abraham Lincoln Presidential Library and Museum. And Samuel Streit of the John Hay Library at Brown University opened the files of William O. Stoddard's correspondence with John M. Hay.

Most of all, I am grateful for the opportunity to work over the years with the inspiring Eleanor Stoddard. Her knowledge, her editing ability, and her willingness to conduct additional, unending research to check and re-check facts in her grandfather's story, elevated this project from a work of research to a labor of love.

Even if she had been nothing more than a figurehead—the keeper of the family book (and she was of course so much more)—I would still treasure knowing her. For, among other rewards, she has given me the unforgettable opportunity on more than one occasion to begin a lecture by saying there was someone in the audience who had touched the hand of someone who had touched the hand of Lincoln—his private secretary's granddaughter. Those announcements invariably elicited gasps of surprise, the turning of heads, and appreciative applause. I second the emotions.

Harold Holzer
Rye, New York
November 6, 2006

Introduction

Most students of the Civil War era know the name of William Osborn Stoddard (1835–1925). The young newspaperman served from 1861 through 1864 as the so-called third secretary in the original triumvirate of principal assistants who loyally served President Abraham Lincoln in the wartime White House.

But few modern readers know much about Stoddard's life *after* the Lincoln era—when he became a dazzlingly prolific writer of reminiscence, history, biography, and children's literature—or of his fascinating early years in a host of vocations, including student, clerk, lecturer, messenger boy, collector, peddler, salesman, marksman, editor, farmer, frontiersman, hunter, fisherman, pig-butcher, and soldier. Stoddard belonged to a remarkable generation of future statesmen, soldiers, ministers, writers, and artists who grew up in the 1830s and 1840s in Central New York and, in many cases, migrated westward in search of experience, fame, and fortune. They were smart and well educated, intoxicated by ambition, inspired by notions of unbridled possibility, and ultimately inflamed by the horrors of slavery and war.

Fortunately, Stoddard was never at a loss for words, and in addition to the valuable articles and books he later wrote about life behind the scenes in the Lincoln administration,[1] he also personally typed a comprehensive, largely unpublished, 767-page autobiography rich in incident, character study, and atmosphere, which, according to its original subtitle, he conceived as a permanent record of his long life for the exclusive enjoyment of his children.[2] This major contribution to our understanding of nineteenth-century social, political, and military history has somehow evaded the attention it deserves for more than a century and a quarter. Though the text is at times self-congratulatory, its rediscovery and publication rescue a priceless treasure trove of first-hand recollection by a brilliant observer and masterful storyteller, thus shedding considerable light on a lost era.

It is difficult to believe that the prolific Stoddard did not also mean at least some of his "private" manuscript for professional publication, wide distribution, and public consumption. For though it is occasionally repetitive, and from time to time confiding in tone—as if the author is reading out loud, chapter by chapter, to a wide-eyed audience of children at bedtime—it is so richly detailed, particularly in describing eastern town life in the 1840s, western frontier existence in the decade that followed, and of course the heady excitement of Washington during the Civil War, that it is hard to believe that Stoddard did not envision it also as a well-published book. Who knows? He lived so long, he might have imagined it as a silent movie, too.[3]

His story would have been well worthy of cinematic adaptation. Stoddard enjoyed—and vividly recalled—a joyous childhood of church-going, boyish mischief, thrilling excursions into woods and on lakes, encounters with Indians, and frequent family relocation to new towns in then-rural upstate New York. Though he later watched his once-successful father lose his knack for business, the plucky young man developed self-confidence, physical toughness, and intellectual curiosity. His family were abolitionists, and he also grew in sympathy for oppressed African Americans, even joining on one occasion a wild melee that erupted when U.S. marshals in Syracuse captured a hapless, longtime black resident under the Fugitive Slave Law—a scene that would be comical were it not so harrowing.[4] Stoddard recalls his youth in wonderful detail—but then, such powers of observation and recollection are what separate those who merely live their lives from gifted writers who can evocatively record them.

In time, his interest in politics expands, too, and young Stoddard actually enjoys the opportunity to hear and see such fabled orators as abolitionist Wendell Phillips and golden-voiced Senator Daniel Webster. After losing his beloved mother to consumption, Stoddard goes off to the brand-new university at Rochester. But deep in debt, he abandons his academic career before his senior year[5] to try his chances on the western frontier, landing in the sparsely settled, heavily wooded farmlands of Tolono in Central Illinois. There, Stoddard encounters a cast of characters worthy of an Erskine Caldwell novel—animal as well as human. He brings them to life on these pages with both scathing humor and genuine affection for his neighbors. This picaresque section brings the young adventurer to adulthood, into the roiling world of newspapers, and his first face-to-face encounter with Abraham Lincoln.

Here Stoddard introduces us to another larger-than-life character—"one in a million," he calls him—the unforgettable Dr. John W. Scroggs (1817–74), the rough, easily distracted, plain-talking, incorrigible owner of the Champaign *Illinois State Gazette*. Readers will not soon forget the frontier sawbones, as he happily hands the reins of his newspaper to the untested Stoddard, gives him complete freedom to editorialize early for Lincoln's presidential candidacy, and then shows up in Washington among the crush of patronage-seekers after the inaugural to hilariously demand political jobs for which he is totally unqualified. This is Stoddard's version of their relationship, anyway. Years later, the publisher was elected to the Illinois state legislature and became a trustee of the University of Illinois. Not surprisingly, in an 1866 letter to Lincoln's law partner, William H. Herndon, Scroggs himself took credit for his newspaper's early support for the future president: "On the *17th of April 1859*, Mr. Lincoln was in the '*Central Illinois Gazette*' office, where a conversation occurred upon the subject of the probable candidates for the Presidency in 1860. I suggested his name, but he—with characteristic modesty—declined. However his name was brought forward in the next issue, *May 4th 1859*. In the 'Gazette' of *Dec. 7th 1859* another article appeared setting forth Mr[.] Lincoln's claims. On the *21st of Dec. 1859* his name was placed at the head of the editorial columns where it remained until after his election. In the 'Gazette' of *January 18th 1860* an editorial appeared setting forth the claims and fitness of Mr. Lincoln and arguing at some length the absolute policy of nominating a western man, and especially Mr. Lincoln."[6]

Actually, the newspaper report of Lincoln's visit was likely penned by Stoddard a few mornings after the day when Lincoln, who assiduously courted newspapers, comes calling at the *Gazette*. "We had the pleasure of introducing to the hospitalities of our sanctum a few days since the Hon. Abraham Lincoln. Few men can make an hour pass away more agreeably. We do not pretend to know whether Mr. Lincoln will ever condescend to occupy the White House or not, but if he should, it is a comfort to know that he has established for himself a character and reputation of sufficient strength and purity to withstand the disreputable and corrupting influence of even that locality."[7]

To his own credit, Stoddard never claims to have fixed on Lincoln early as a future leader; in fact, he candidly admits in his book that he does not mark Lincoln for greatness the first time he lays eyes on him (although he occasionally told twentieth-century interviewers that "there was something about the man that commanded instant attention").[8] Soon enough, Stoddard does find himself strongly drawn to the tall, sad-looking lawyer, awed by his powers of concentration, his encyclopedic knowledge of local politics, and, later, his ability to enthrall friends and colleagues with an endless supply of stories. He later told a magazine that "every time you saw or heard him your respect increased."[9] Though judging from his manuscript, Stoddard remains inexplicably unaware of (or no longer recalls) the 1858 Lincoln-Douglas senate campaign that by all accounts set the prairies "on fire,"[10] he eventually (with or without Scroggs's help) becomes one of the first editors (not the very first, as he will claim) to back Lincoln for the presidency. In later years, he reported of his editorial, "I had two hundred and fifty proofs pulled, one of which I sent to each of the papers in Illinois. Many of them printed it when I did, and thus we started the presidential boom of Mr. Lincoln."[11]

At this point the author's memoir begins to diverge a bit from recorded history. In the pages that relate the story of Lincoln's election, Stoddard professes indifference about his own future chances for political reward. In his old age, he even suggested that it was Lincoln who asked Stoddard to work for him, not the other way around. "How would you like to go to Washington?" Lincoln asked him after the election—at least according to the autobiography. "I am pretty well satisfied where I am, Mr. Lincoln," Stoddard remembered replying, adding, "the only thing that would tempt me [would be] a place on your personal staff," to which Lincoln asked him to write a proposal to that effect. According to the memoir, Stoddard received a letter in December asking him to proceed to Washington and wait—though this would have been two months before Lincoln himself departed for his inaugural. In a later interview, Stoddard romanticized the story a bit, recalling that Lincoln offered him an official position "a day or two" after their initial interview, adding, "In this offhand way, he reshaped my life."[12]

Surviving correspondence, which he fails to mention, shows that, "a little nervous" about his future prospects, he worked hard behind the scenes to secure a place on Lincoln's staff—a reward he believed he deserved. He got two New York friends—"men of high character and position"—to write to Lincoln "in my behalf," and admitted to Lincoln's Springfield law partner that the president-elect "knew little of me." Making his hopes for a White House assignment "bold, even to presumption," he even offered "to begin" the job "'on trial,' as the Dutchman took his wife."[13] So much avarice and ambition manifested itself in post-election Springfield, and post-inauguration Washington, that Stoddard was probably reluctant to portray himself later among the patronage-greedy applicants who descended on Lincoln after his elevation, determined to share in the political loaves and fishes. But Stoddard was certainly among those seeking office. At first unrewarded, then with little to do, he commences an eye-opening, if bloodless, three-month tour of duty in a Washington volunteer army unit known as the National Rifles.

He finally gets his job from Lincoln in July 1861—not as an official member of the White House executive office, but as a clerk assigned to sign Lincoln's name on land patents in the Department of the Interior, on what might today be called "permanent loan to the president's staff." Stoddard leaves no doubt in his memoir that he becomes only the "third secretary" in Lincoln's clerical triumvirate—later expanded (though Stoddard only briefly so acknowledges) to include additional clerks. From the beginning, he knows his place. John G. Nicolay and John M. Hay are his superiors, and Stoddard's access to Lincoln, though frequent, is limited. Still, Stoddard manages to memorably relate each of their encounters with an ear for colorful dialogue and an eye for scene setting. Touchingly, he portrays a chief executive worn down to exhaustion by military failures and an avalanche of administrative duties, yet somehow able to dominate every situation, every room, in which he finds himself.

Armed with an antique but still functional front-door latchkey that gives him twenty-four-hour-a-day access to the White House to attend to his duties, Stoddard meets and greets many of the great men of the age—and more than a few crackpots—who relentlessly beat a path to the President's office. The workaholic aide often finds himself in the right place at just the right time to watch the chief executive make history. At one point, Lincoln gives him a sneak preview of his great "Conkling Letter," a masterful defense of administration policy on black freedom, written to be read aloud to a Union rally in his Springfield, Illinois, hometown—for which

Stoddard cautiously, but self-confidently, proposes an editorial change that Lincoln rejects.[14] On another occasion, the President calmly asks his clerk to copy a seemingly innocuous document—which midway through his task, Stoddard suddenly realizes is no routine order, but rather the long-awaited Emancipation Proclamation that will change history forever.

Novice though he is, Stoddard learns to intuit Lincoln's changing moods—from the anguished leader who endlessly paces the White House floor, to the joke-teller who chuckles at his own stories (and Stoddard's) with a strange, soundless laugh. Like his fellow aides, he knows when to interrupt Lincoln, when to retreat from his presence, and when to leave him totally alone. Nicolay is but twenty-nine at the beginning of Lincoln's presidency, Stoddard twenty-six, and Hay only twenty-three, "young if you count by the almanac," Stoddard concedes, pointedly adding, "that was a time when a day could be a year, and we grew gray internally."[15]

By 1862, with a brother and sister now living with him in Washington and depending on his support, Stoddard's day-to-day work proves less fulfilling, not to mention less remunerative, and it is outside the White House where he begins to find challenge and adventure. Unashamedly, he pursues a host of unusual activities that Lincoln's two senior secretaries have neither the time nor inclination to pursue—some of which might today ensnare a modern presidential aide in the web of a special prosecutor. Bitten with the money-making bug—a disease that will come back to haunt him years later—Stoddard openly speculates in stocks and gold (contending that both Mr. and Mrs. Lincoln knew in advance and saw no conflict, a claim for which there is no corroboration). Later, he asserts, he helps found and claims to lead the pro-Lincoln Union League movement, and attempts to corner the turpentine market for the North Carolina–based navy (again with Lincoln's blessing, he insists). He takes up arms to help put down the bloody 1863 New York City draft riots, writes anonymous pro-Lincoln columns for a New York newspaper, and speaks at a Thanksgiving rally for freedmen, claiming to urge that African Americans fight in the ranks for their own liberty even before Lincoln publicly endorses the idea of black enlistment.

All the while, getting, and apparently needing, little sleep, he tirelessly keeps up with the drudgery of his principal, "official" assignment, signing Lincoln's name to land patents while serving the President in Nicolay and Hay's absence, and to their enormous relief, handling the whims of the mercurial first lady, with whom Stoddard gets along so famously, he relates, that observers dub him "Mrs. Lincoln's secretary."

With Nicolay ferociously guarding the President's perpetually thronged door, and Hay tending to important correspondence and political matters, Stoddard eventually becomes the principal sorter of Lincoln's unsolicited daily mail from ordinary Americans, a "very curious department of American literature," as he jokingly describes it. He swiftly learns to slice much of it to ribbons with his trusty paper cutter and dispose of it "in bales" in a ceramic wastebasket he keeps close to his desk.[16] Stoddard tells the memorable story of one furious visitor who, observing his routine, concludes angrily that the young man is censoring the President's important mail. In response, the secretary coolly lets him examine one of the vicious diatribes with which he deals daily. Mortified, the onlooker congratulates Stoddard for his efficiency and tact. It must have been a highlight of Stoddard's White House career—a vindication of his loyal effort to spare Lincoln from the harangues of his enemies—because he tells the story twice in the manuscript (and again in his published Lincoln books).

Stoddard has always been considered a prime source about life behind the scenes at the Civil War White House. Historians may wonder, however, whether he can be relied upon for some of the book's more startling revelations, especially his claim that President Lincoln personally asked him to engineer the dumping of Vice President Hannibal Hamlin, and his replacement by Tennessee's Andrew Johnson, at the 1864 Republican (Union Party) national convention. If true, the story significantly alters the prevailing belief that the President sat by benignly while the party acted without his knowledge or influence. Defending himself in a letter to John Hay eleven years later, recalling that there was "no tidal wave of personal enthusiasm for Johnson wandering around the streets in those days," Stoddard insisted that "the impression got around that the proposed renomination of Hamlin with Mr. Lincoln was distasteful to the President. . . . I fully believed that Lincoln did not like Hamlin. . . . Right or wrong, I went in on it like a beaver."[17] Hay's reply is lost, but presumably he remembered a different version of the circumstances, prompting Stoddard's spirited defense.

His office colleagues—both of whom, it must be noted, hoped to dominate the postwar "Lincoln recollection" trade with books of their own—tended to dismiss Stoddard's reliability. John G. Nicolay charged him with a "tendency to exaggeration . . . useful to him as a writer of fiction," and John Hay complained that Stoddard was "worthless" and "stuffy."[18] The other secretaries, stuck for years in their own low-paying government jobs—though at salaries, it might be noted, higher than Stoddard's[19]—may well have resented their colleague's financial schemes, too. "Received a more than usually Asinine letter from Stoddard," Hay angrily confided in his diary on October 30, 1863, "who is in New York stock jobbing & writes to me pretending he is working for the election."[20]

In the end, the grinding burdens of office—in this case the busy outer office next to the President's—wear down Stoddard far more than the amazingly resilient Lincoln. The President faces a brief bout of smallpox in late 1863, but otherwise remains healthy. As for his secretary, when "the typhoid fever and a relapse compelled me to give up my very arduous office work and take a post that promised only open air occupation,"[21] he looks westward. Following a summer 1864 trip to inspect federal armies in the West and South, where he is well received as the President's emissary, Stoddard obtains a new assignment. Though the presidential election is only weeks away—an odd time indeed for a presidential aide to depart the White House staff—he takes leave of Washington permanently after securing a presidential appointment that September as Marshal of the Eastern District of Arkansas.[22]

Stoddard departs, it might be noted, over the strenuous objections of his sister Kate, who thought "it seemed like throwing William's life away as he was not calculated to contend with the rough times and men that awaited him in the southwest." Kate even convinces Senator Ira Harris of New York—a longtime family friend—to go to the White House and urge the President "not to send my brother to border life," arguing that "he was unfitted & not in the temperament to contend with the . . . difficulties that must arise at the close of such a war." Added Kate: "But Will went. It was a bubble soon to burst and left him a sick man, a very broken man, and I think his full strength never came back."[23]

Neither did Stoddard. Arriving in Arkansas before his Senate confirmation, he spends the last Christmas of the Civil War at an officers' party in Little Rock. His Washington life is over—though for a time he harbors unrealistic thoughts of returning to the capital as a United States senator. A few months later, when he hears the terrible news of his former chief's assassination in the distant capital, William O. Stoddard is no longer at his familiar, paper-filled office in the northeast wing of the White House, but at his new post in the remote outpost of Little Rock.

"The terrible news was some time in reaching us," he reported a week later of Lincoln's death. But when it did, "men who had never seen him wept. . . . How shall *we* say our sorrow, who knew him well?" he writes to John Hay in evident anguish. "To others, the *President* is dead. I can only remember my benefactor." Far away from the hurly-burly action he once craved, Stoddard can do little more than silently don a black mourning suit to show his undying respect for the martyred "benefactor" he had served, "loved and venerated."[24]

In 1955, Stoddard's energetic eighty-two-year-old son, William O. Stoddard Jr., published a severely edited version of this volume, under the title *Lincoln's Third Secretary.* A spare distillation of his father's weighty manuscript, abridged to satisfy the constraints of commercial publishing, the book, though intended to introduce this relatively unknown figure to the public, included only a fraction of the elder Stoddard's thick manuscript—yet offered enough material to kill off future interest in producing another, more comprehensive adaptation.

And while the book was offered as a much-abridged version of his father's original tome, it also added material from other Stoddard writings—including a chapter on the tragic death of Willie Lincoln that does not appear at all in the massive autobiographical manuscript. Few people have seen the typewritten original. Stoddard's family deposited the two volumes at the Detroit Public Library, where they remain available for scholarly inquiry, yet all but unknown to the general public. The Stoddard family made and retained two faithful copies for themselves—from one of which this book has been adapted.

Fortunately, one of the old secretary's descendants refused to settle for this state of affairs: an out-of-print abridgement and an out-of-sight original. Eleanor Stoddard, the still-thriving granddaughter of William O. Stoddard, for more than ten years patiently encouraged my suggestion to edit a fuller version of his autobiography. She entrusted me with her copy of the typescript, along with her own index of citations and considerable background material. For years, she has kept after me to bring out the kind of reliable edition the work deserves. She has been a genuine partner in this enterprise, and deserves far more credit than a mere acknowledgment can repay for her vital role in shepherding the real book into print.

In part out of respect for both of the Stoddards, William and Eleanor, both of whom I feel I have come to know with great respect and affection (though Eleanor was not at all adverse about making changes), I have done as little editing as necessary on the manuscript in order to preserve the tone and character of the author's narrative. The truth is, the recollections were so arresting and original that substantial editorial intervention would have been presumptuous, and unfair to future generations of readers.

In deference to the sensibilities of modern readers, I have brought the author's occasionally archaic spellings up to date, and eliminated some of his quaint asides, like "more about that later," and "as you are all aware"— meant perhaps as personal quips to his children. Stoddard also tended to compose in long, long paragraphs, and I have revised his indentation system to make the book easier to read, and of course added extensive footnotes to identify the people and places to which he made fascinating but often oblique reference throughout. I have transposed a few words here and there, and on one occasion borrowed some descriptive paragraphs from a postwar chapter and inserted it within the context of a childhood memory. I can only hope that these changes do no violence to Stoddard's original concept for his memoirs.

Eleanor Stoddard invited me to use my discretion to "cut, cut, cut," but I found the author's account of his early life, education, and adventures so arresting that for the most part I left all the opening chapters, and all the incidents they described, intact and unabridged, drawing on certain footnote material supplied by his granddaughter, whose own research has corrected many of her grandfather's faulty recollections of family genealogy and helped make sense out of scattered references and unclear chronology. As for style, I have left the manuscript much as I found it, deleting only the most glaringly repetitive phrases, and the occasional transitional paragraph that telegraphed, Dickens-like, the tales to come in the following chapter.

As the long manuscript progressed chronologically, however, particularly once Stoddard began what evolved into a second volume commencing partway through his White House years, the repetitions and digressions began coming more frequently, and it became increasingly necessary for judicious cuts to be made. Much as I wish even my generous and patient university press could have accommodated the full recollections of Stoddard's old age—he lived long, so there was much of it—I felt it prudent to eliminate altogether most of his postwar reminiscences so that the final book could appear in manageable length. I have done so without the least injury, I hope, to the historical importance of Stoddard's manuscript.

For the record, after enduring his exciting, sometimes frightening "guerilla days" in malarial, and still bitterly divided postwar Arkansas, a deathly ill Stoddard left his post there in 1866 and headed to New York to recover his health. There, living in "very plain" circumstances,[25] he renewed his career as a journalist for the *New York Examiner,* and began writing reminiscences and novels as well, some published under his own name and others under the nom de plume Chris Forrest. (In later years he would also produce a shelf of boys' books with titles like *Chris the Model Maker* and *Lost Gold of the Montezumas.*)[26] He also renewed his interest in church activities and, in 1870, married a schoolteacher ten years his junior named Susan Eagleson Cooper. They began a family that by 1887 grew to include five children (two sons had died in infancy).[27]

Throughout the 1870s and 1880s he continued his prolific output of writing, and, always drawn to money-making opportunities, however improbable, dabbled in "railway, telegraphic and manufacturing enterprises." He came to know artists like Albert Bierstadt and Emanuel Gottlieb Leutze, obtained a patent for a "printer's chase"—a frame to lock letterpress type in place—and worked with the entrepreneurs who laid the second Atlantic Cable. But like his father, Stoddard was no businessman, forever amassing small fortunes—and then losing them. The economic downturn of 1873 ultimately forced him to take a job as chief clerk of the Bureau of Engineering in the city's Dock Department. He was back where he started—in government.[28]

And he was still not entirely free of controversy. In 1878, he was horrified to find his wartime speculating schemes making unexpected news when his name was mentioned—along with those of a number of Lincoln-era congressmen—in the so-called McGarrahan-New Idria case, a corruption inquiry involving the murky title claims to a California quicksilver mine.[29] Announcing the discovery of a trove of damning 1861 letters, a New York newspaper dropped the bombshell charge that the evidence purportedly showed "that W. O. Stoddard, President Lincoln's secretary to sign land patents, used his position to sell Cabinet and other government secrets for effect in Wall Street and for other purposes."[30] Another journal suggested that Lincoln himself had signed the Interior Department document that granted final title in the land-claim tug-of-war, after which Stoddard had obligingly carried the parchment to the General Land Office—and, his critics implied, promptly invested in the mining scheme.[31]

Stoddard, then residing in near anonymity in Brooklyn, was not about to be libeled. "I deny this flatly," he replied. "No Cabinet or other government secrets available on Wall Street were in my keeping, nor were my means of obtaining information half so good as those of the agents of the Associated Press. The letters showed that I speculated in stocks and gold, but all who knew me at the time were already well aware of that fact. Stock and gold gambling was the mania of the day, and for a time I had it very badly, but I made no concealment of it, for I thought no evil." For once, Stoddard emphasized his *lack* of wartime access to Lincoln. "I attended no Cabinet meetings, received no government despatches, had no access to hidden matters of state," he wrote. "I did not consider, nor did others, that there was anything in the nature of the clerical duties from time to time assigned me which made Wall Street operations morally worse for me than for another."[32]

To his old colleague John Hay, he confided, "I believe God will not let me be harmed by these people." In a more playful and self-confident vein, he added: "Your suggestion about killing the newspapermen is hardly a good one. It might bring me great popularity, but I think of the time and the expense. Did you pause to consider how many there are of them and how much killing long practice enables them, to bear?" Stoddard confessed, "I hope never again to be mixed up with the evidence in a 'great case' . . . indeed, I become more of a pachyderm."[33] Fortunately for Stoddard, following a Senate investigation the sensational McGarrahan-New Idria dispute was soon enough forgotten.[34]

Six years later, in 1884, Stoddard earned far more positive headlines when he published his major biography, *Abraham Lincoln: The True Story of a Great Life*. But as a result, he found himself embroiled in a dust-up with both Hay and Nicolay, who were still busy working on a long-awaited Lincoln biography of their own. After Stoddard wrote Hay on Lincoln's birthday, 1885, to boast that his "first edition went sooner than I expected" because "the press-critics . . . have been very kindly indeed," Hay testily complained that Stoddard's book would "take away market value" from his own. Insisting, "I have certainly not stolen a march on anybody," Stoddard held firm, his sharp wit intact: "Long ago," he replied to Hay, "I wrote you and Nicolay that I had a book in my mind and it was my idea, year after year, that yours would come out first. Is it too much to say that that idea died of old age?" Still, Stoddard hoped that Nicolay and Hay would "make as full and valuable a work as I have thought of your making and that it will succeed *enormously* Mine seems to find its place. So will yours."[35] Undaunted, the "third secretary" began making revisions for a second edition. The senior secretaries' work only began appearing in serialized version the following year. Their ten-volume set of books did not come out in book form until 1890. The Hay-Stoddard exchange suggests how competitive the Lincoln biography market remained twenty years after the President's death—and how determined Stoddard was to compete in that milieu.

The year of the kerfuffle with Hay, 1885, Stoddard moved to Hempstead, Long Island and commenced an ambitious series of eleven books on the lives of American presidents from Washington to Cleveland. In 1894, he relocated again to the healthy suburb of Madison, New Jersey, where he became something of a local icon.[36] Tragically, his daughter Sarah died of tuberculosis two years afterwards, in January 1896, and later that month, so did his "saintly" wife, as "the sun of her face passed from me into Heaven," staggering him with sadness.[37] Yet the author still had nearly thirty more years to live.

Not until 1907 did he finish his autobiography. It had been nearly forty years since the publication of his first notable book, *Scandaroon*. By one count, he produced more than one hundred books altogether,[38] some of which became favorites of "all the boys in my special constituency,"[39] others as standard references for future historians, while a few, as he joked in his autobiographical typescript, "vanished between the waters of oblivion." But not their author—not as long as he could so vividly recall the president he had known in the Civil War White House. And this he could do for sixty years. In part he attributed his longevity to a dietary supplement that did not come into vogue until the late twentieth century. "I have been vastly benefited by the free use of olive oil in place of other foods or medical agents," he boasted. "A table-spoonful after each meal, with a drop of red wine."[40]

But the memory of Lincoln sustained him, too. "Very few men ever actually knew him or understood him," the old man wrote emotionally to his grandson in 1923, clearly facing his own mortality, "but it is my belief that in God's Garden, he is still growing, expanding, elevating in continuance of his wonderful growth on the earth."[41]

February 12, 1925—his final Lincoln's Birthday—found the old gentleman in "feeble" condition and "confined to his room at the home of his son, Ralph." But he was still alert enough to regale reporters with stories of "seeing the great emancipator pacing the floor in intense concentration," and remembering "the battles Lincoln had with some of his cabinet members."[42]

Six months later, on August 29, in the age not of Abraham Lincoln but of Calvin Coolidge, William O. Stoddard died quietly, a few weeks shy of ninety, at his son's home in Madison, New Jersey—long-since deaf, but no doubt still hearing the great voices he had heard early in his eventful life, still seeing the epochal scenes he had observed and recorded in his bulging manuscript.

"I shall meet Mr. Lincoln again, not many days hence," he had written plaintively in the throes of what he called "extreme old age" just a few months before his death. "I can only look back through memory to my old time association with him."[43] He was sure he could still see the great man standing before him. As the last-surviving private secretary to Abraham Lincoln recalled, in verse:

> The sad face lit with a smile,
> I think I can see it yet,
> As if he were back in the old peace time,
> With the Sangamon courthouse set.[44]

1

The Stoddard Family Tree

In the year 1635, Governor John Winthrop founded the Connecticut Colony by building a fort at the mouth of the Thames River and landing a number of adventurous settlers who had sailed with him from the port of Yarmouth in England[1]. He was himself a Suffolk man and his recruits were of course largely drawn from Suffolk and the neighboring county of Devon. One of the ancient families of the latter county bore the name of Stoddard. The name is a derivation of Stod- or Stud- or Stodherd, and the crest on the family coat of arms is a horse's head surrounded by a ducal coronet for the Stoddards were Dukes of Devon during many generations. One of the colonists who landed at the mouth of the Thames with Governor Winthrop was a gentleman from this family by the name of Ralph Stoddard. He was a man of substance and position and he brought with him some property that was hardly in place in a log cabin. One specimen of it, with other silver, was a large silver punch bowl bearing the family arms. Only two or three generations later, this priceless relic of old English life was melted up by the then head of the Stoddard family to provide wedding outfit spoons for his marrying daughters.

Ralph Stoddard obtained [in 1696] a grant or purchase of three thousand acres of land on the left bank of the Thames, opposite the present city of New London and somewhat above it. His grant included the ferry right. He at once built a comfortable log house and the logs of it were tremendous. Long years afterwards, when a larger mansion was erected upon the same spot, the original cabin was carefully preserved and became part of the new kitchen. I have seen it and wondered at its black logs when I was a boy. The farm which then remained of the old estate was still large, part of it being owned by my granduncle Guy Stoddard and part by his son Ralph.

Other members of the Winthrop colony were Smiths, Averys, Tabers, Morgans, Knowltons, Hales, and so forth, and there was much intermarrying. More than that is said to be true, for one of the earlier Averys married the daughter of a Pequot chief and my own father bore very distinctly the indications of that remarkable addition to the roots of the family tree.

The early Stoddards were all fighting men, from the days when they had the great privilege of shooting stray Indians in their front yard. I well remember how vividly my grandmother, Mrs. Smith-Stoddard, related to me the family military traditions. The last time was during the Civil War and although she was then nearly ninety-odd, and she died at ninety-seven, her memory had not at all failed her. She told me how, in the old French War, when she was a child, every able bodied member of the Stoddard family was, as she expressed it, "out." Again, in the Revolutionary War, they were "all out." Once more, in the War of 1812, the breed was well represented but I can only recall that my granduncle Guy was in the Connecticut contingent. In the Civil War, however, she said, every one of her Stoddard grandchildren of military age was in the Union army. That included the Morgans.

She had long before told me, and she then repeated the story, how when Benedict Arnold burned New London [in 1781], she was a girl of thirteen or fourteen and fled with her family to the hills above the town. There she stood, with her neighbors, and saw her home and theirs burned to ashes. At the same time, she told me, several of my ancestral kindred, of more than one name, were in Fort Griswold, and no less than four of them were slain in the pitiless massacre which followed the taking of the fort. Their names are on the monument. The Revolutionary Stoddard who was my immediate ancestor was a Continental soldier under Putnam,[2] from the days of Bunker Hill, and was severely wounded at the battle of White Plains.

He had five sons, Vine, Guy, Isaac, Ralph, and Frank. The latter became a successful physician but died of the cholera at somewhat over fifty. Ralph was a druggist in New London and lived to nearly eighty. Isaac became a Methodist minister and was during many years Presiding Elder of the Nantucket and Martha's Vineyard circuit. Guy received for his portion the old family farm and was a prominent citizen, long in the State Senate. The older brother, Vine, received a farm which included the head of Noank

Cove, hear New London; and there I visited him in my boyhood. Guy lived to be ninety-three but Vine dropped off at ninety-two. His first wife was Sabria Avery, of New London and my stepmother, a great genealogist in her way, told me that Sabria's family were the very best of the Averys, for some of whom she appeared to have less admiration. Sabria's children were Harriet and Samuel Prentice. The former became Mrs. Morgan, in due season, once more adding that old Welsh name to the family tree. Not long after Sabria's death, which occurred as a consequence of the birth of Samuel, Vine Stoddard married a widow Smith, whom I have always known as my grandmother. She already had four sons, Erastus F., Amos, and James Y. Smith, who settled in Providence, one of them becoming governor of Rhode Island, and Gilbert A. Smith, who became a merchant and manufacturer and ship owner at New Haven.

One other "root" was all this while preparing. Among the earlier colonists of Massachusetts Bay were the Osborns. One of their members removed to Connecticut and then passed on into New York settling in the Mohawk Valley. He resided for a long time in Albany and then joined with the Whites and others in founding the town of Whitesboro, near Utica. Still another "root" was planted when the Rev. John Cotton landed upon Plymouth Rock, if he really did so. Some of his descendants passed on westward and one of them settled in the Mohawk Valley.

My father, Samuel Prentice [the son of Vine Stoddard Jr.] received his middle name from an ancestor, but I have no knowledge of the Prentice family. At an early age he so strongly objected to the nickname of "Sam" that he changed his titles to Prentice Samuel and so it continued to be. He received a good common school education, which was about all there was to be had, but during all his life he was fond of books and became a well-informed man for those days. After serving a few years as a clerk with his New Haven stepbrother, Gilbert A. Smith, he was taken by the spirit of adventure and removed to what was then the "Far West." Buffalo was then a mere muddy village but the village of Rochester in Monroe County already contained his stepbrother Erastus T. Smith and a cousin, H. F. Smith, whose wife was also a cousin, having been a Miss Barbour. All this had much to do with the fact that the young adventurer selected Rochester. He was a fine penman and a good bookkeeper and before long he was Deputy Postmaster of the village with what was then the enormous salary of nine hundred dollars. He was enterprising, moreover, and he laid up some capital as well as a high character and good business credit. Something more had been preparing for him, however, in the Mohawk Valley and elsewhere.

Many years before, John Osborn had been born, in Albany, and had grown to manhood before his family removed to Whitesboro. He had served his apprenticeship as a silversmith and jeweler, and been successful in business and had accumulated or inherited property. In later years, he was fond of telling me stories of his life in Albany and one of his amusements was to scold me furiously in Mohawk Dutch. He had also met and married Amelia Cotton, a direct descendant of the witch-burning Rev. John Cotton. During their entire married life they had nine children, of whom all but three died in infancy or childhood. The oldest, Amelia, reached the age of twenty-one and died of heart disease. Two remained, Sarah [Ann] and Adeline. There came a time when the western part of the state of New York was securely pacified of the Iroquois Indians and the new country that was opened appeared to offer inducements to settlers. Several families from Whitesboro and its vicinity decided to migrate to the new county of Cortland in company. Among them were branches of the Whites, Tubbs, Dickson, and other well-known Mohawk Valley families. My grandfather, John Osborn, sold out all his Albany and Whitesboro interests and made good investments in and about what was to be called the village of Homer. When, however, the time for moving came, there were no stage coaches over the intended route and the trip must be made in wagons or the saddle. Sarah [Ann] Osborn, Clara Tubbs, and Miss Dickson declared in favor of a journey on horseback. Just before leaving Whitesboro, each cut a riding switch. That of Miss Tubbs was a long slip of willow and that of Miss Osborn was a fine cutting from her favorite "balm of Gilead" tree. They had a merry time on the road and, on reaching their destination, each of the girls carefully planted her riding whip. Both sprouts grew and when I was a boy the "Tubbs Willow," at the forks of the Truxton road, was a mighty affair, while the balm of Gilead tree in our own yard was taller than the house.

On reaching what was to be Homer, John Osborn built the first brick house in all that region. It was said to have been the first of its kind in central or western New York. Not a great while afterwards, his friend Mr. White built a brick store and dwelling upon the neighboring corner. It was in this house that my schoolmate and to this day my friend, Andrew

Dickson White, was born, two years before I was born in the Osborn house. The Dicksons had settled in Truxton and to this place the Whites afterwards removed, for Miss Dickson was then Mrs. Horace White. The Tubbs family also had at the first selected Truxton.

Young as was the village of Rochester, it at that time boasted of the best seminary for young women in the state, above New York City. This was the Phipps Union Seminary and at its head was a learned lady whose maiden name had been Phipps but who had married an equally learned Greek by the name of Achilles. To this school, therefore, it was necessary to send the best girls of Cortland County. Miss Dickson, Miss Tubbs, and Miss Osborn went, as a matter of course, and they were "chums" off and on at the institution. There were consequences, but not all of a pattern. Miss Dickson was already spoken for by young Mr. Horace White, who was to be the father of Andrew, and Miss Tubbs was to wait a while,

Miss Osborn was a singularly handsome young woman, with blue eyes and beautiful, waving, light brown hair. Young Mr. Stoddard, whom she was so likely to meet when she went to the post office, was said to be the handsomest young man in Rochester. Before she finished her collegiate course they were engaged and, before long, he came to Homer and there was a grand wedding. The officiating minister was Rev. Alfred Bennett, one of the noted characters in the frontier history of New York.

After the wedding, the newly married couple returned to Rochester and I have heard from several of their old friends that they were considered the handsomest pair in the village. They now had sufficient means to go into business for themselves and my father, in company with a young friend named Heaton, purchased a business property in a thriving and central village called Richmond, some distance south of Rochester. The firm name was Stoddard and Heaton, and the enterprise rapidly assumed large pro-portions. Long years afterwards, Mr. Heaton became a prominent and successful storage and forwarding merchant in Brooklyn.

I of course know nothing of Richmond by memory, but it appears to have been a pleasant village and our house was a pretty one, opposite the store across the road. My father had extensive connections in Rochester and in New York, after a while, and these were his ruin, for they involved the pernicious custom of endorsing friendly paper and taking the risk of it. All went on swimmingly, however, until the terrible money crisis and panic of 1835 and 1836.[3] Much money was made and my father bought largely of wild western lands, as a probably good investment for the future. The great pressure came, at last, and found Stoddard and Heaton heavily involved in accommodation endorsements. They did not go into bankruptcy, but their concern was hopelessly wrecked and they had to close up the business.

I was born in 1835, while my mother was on a visit to her father and mother in Homer [New York]. Twenty-one years afterwards I was planning my first adventure in the West and my father desired me to go through Michigan and stop at Kalamazoo, long enough to examine that city. He gave as a reason that when he shut up his Richmond concern he had several odds and ends of property remaining upon his hands. One was the village of Richmond, or an uncomfortably large part of it, and one of the others consisted of a tract of nine hundred acres of unimproved western land. His wise friends counseled him that Monroe County property was "sure" and would in time increase in value, while there was no market for western lands and never would be, there was so much of it. So he sold the Michigan tract and upon it much of Kalamazoo was afterwards built. It cornered in the very middle of the city and when I did examine it, for I went to see, I concluded that it would have been a good thing to hold.

On the other hand, De Witt Clinton dug his ditch, and the Erie Canal was the making of Rochester and the utter ruin of Richmond. My father's property there went back to farm land prices and he sold his buildings for less than it had cost to construct them. I remember many fragmentary stories of the family life in the little business village but they are of no importance now, except that I gathered an impression that all the Monroe county people swallowed enormous quantities of Malaga wine, brought all the way from Albany and the Hudson River in vast forty-horsepower wagons.

Upon giving up his produce and grocery and commission business, my father established the first regular bookstore of Rochester, on the corner of Buffalo and State Streets, which is, to this day, the very center of that municipality. The firm name was Henry Stanwood and Co., but my father was really the concern, for I never saw Mr. Stanwood and suppose him to have been a mere money partner who rarely made his appearance at the store.

Meantime, to go back to Homer, Miss Tubbs had married young Mr. Ira Harris,[4] a special protégé of John Osborn's, and he was beginning to make his mark as a rising young lawyer. He removed to Albany and in due time became celebrated as a jurist. He was sent to the U.S. Senate and his son William was my college chum. I shall have more to tell of the Harrises on some later page of these reminiscences. Prior to that, however, I will try to recall points of my childhood in Rochester; for it was an odd sort of childhood—for so very young a fellow as I was then.

2

Childhood in Rochester

*I*can imagine that not many people have clear recollections of their first and second years. I do not know just where my memory begins its mysterious record. I do know, however, that at a very early age I went to an infant school, kept by a grim old woman whom I did not admire. She must have been an expert teacher, nevertheless, for I learned to read wonderfully soon. It was a small school, with only one really large boy in it, for Johnny Stitt was almost ten. Next to him was Johnny Philpot, whose father lived in a dreadfully large and gloomy brick house with a gigantic iron railing in front of it to keep out the boys.

We were then living on Fitzhugh Street [in Rochester], in a frame house which had a wide stoop that reached to the sidewalk. One of the boys lost a splendid alley marble under that stoop and father refused to have the whole thing taken away to find the missing treasure. We burned wood in the parlor fireplace and I carried for many years the scars on my hands caused by a dive into that awful mess of red coals when I was one day running away from my sister Julia. She was three years older than myself and I believed her to be absolute perfection. As she grew older, and until the day of her death, at twenty-four, she was my boy idol. She was of medium height, graceful, intellectual, and if my children wish to know just how she looked, they have only to think of their own sister Sadie, of whom she was a fine likeness.

I can remember going with my mother and others to see the Upper Genesee Falls in midwinter, when all was white with ice. I can remember, also, a grand ride in a barouche with a green body, to Mount Hope cemetery. It was when my father was entertaining Mr. Jared Babcock, of Homer, and I believed that he was a great man. He was an organ builder and he was in Rochester to sell organs, but he may have had them in his pocket for all I knew.

It was the custom, in those days, for clerks to board with their employers, and among the young men from our store was a Mr. Rollo, who afterwards became the managing partner of A. S. Barnes & Co. of New York. Another was Samuel Sheather, who went to New York and founded the great fur house which bore his name. One other of my memories of the Fitzhugh Street house relates to the front stairway, down which I rolled repeatedly—it was such a fine playground. Even now, as I turn and examine my left hand, I can find the ridged scar left by a piece of window glass upon which I fell one day and which went clean through. I am afraid that I was not what is called a quiet boy, although very good.

My goodness took a queer form, at one time, for I was seized with the fever for travel and adventure. That is, I ran away and was found by a gentleman who knew me, already out into the great world and trudging somewhat tearfully along the towpath of the Erie Canal. At all events, I knew my part of Rochester pretty well and was often entrusted with errands. One of these came to me when there was a new baby in the house and the nurse, a tall woman whom I knew as Miss Spence, wished to send a note to my father at the store. She was impressive and she said to me, repeatedly: "Tell him that it is very important!" That was where the ignorant woman lost all my respect for her, for I was strongly of the opinion that she should have said "portant," the superfluous "im" changing the whole word into a negative. In like manner I severely criticized the first persons who erroneously spoke in my presence of "turnips." They should have said "poturnips" and I had learned that "taters" were entitled to be called "potatoes."

It was in my fifth year that we removed to a frame house of moderate size but quite respectable on Clinton Street, away across the Genesee, on the eastern side of the town. There was a Methodist church on the corner and right across Buffalo Street, on another corner, was the Second Baptist Church, to which I and my growing family belonged. It had a large and enterprising Sunday school and not long after I entered that school there were prizes offered for varied proficiencies. For the largest number of Scripture texts recited, and for excellence in reading other quotations I won a prize of a really elegant polyglot Bible, gilt edged and bound in English calf. It was a bad piece of fortune for me, for it convinced some friends of my father, including that great man Professor Dewey, that I was a rare boy and that I could not begin my classical education too early. The professor himself was the principal of the Rochester Collegiate Institute, which had a big stone building all to itself and was a grand affair.

Therefore, before long, I found myself perched upon a high stool before a long desk in the second story of the Institute, and digging away at Andrew's *Introduction to the Latin Language*. Of course, I was also in other branches, but my own favorite was arithmetic, it was so queer to see how the figures and sums would come out if you worked them rightly. It may have had something to do with Latin, or a desire to visit Rome, that I again determined to run away and made considerable progress southward, down the Clover Street road, before I was caught, brought back, and severely dealt with.

I have many pleasant remembrances of our Clinton Street home. One of them relates to little Miss Julia Barton, for Deacon Barton's pew in church was just in front of ours and Julia, aged three, was prone to get up on the seat and disturb the services by a vigorous romp with me, to the great discomfort of so good a boy. I was cuffed for her sins, nevertheless. On the Methodist Church corner occurred a direful accident, one day, for my sister Julia and I had been to the grocery after a two-gallon jug of molasses. It was not then the custom for shop people to send home purchases and so we took the willow wicker baby wagon. We obtained our cargo and all went well until in my zeal I tried to make too sharp a turn into Clinton Street at that corner. Julia was pushing, I was pulling, and over went the chariot. Crash went the jug and the brick sidewalk was darkly sweetened for a wide area. It was a childish grief to both of us, but in after years I learned that much older people may now and then turn their corners too rashly and upset their wagons.

Halfway down Buffalo Street, toward the store, they had placed the swift Genesee, on its roaring way to the upper falls. There was a long bridge over it and I acquired much faith in that bridge, after several experiments at walking over it. After that, it was awfully fine to hunt for knotholes and cracks and peer down at the rushing, glancing water.

Back of our house was a garden patch and beyond that was a barn that opened upon an alley. I had a strong prejudice against that barn. Somehow or other, I had seen a bear or heard of one, for one night I had an awful dream of a procession of bears that marched up to the back door of our house from that mysterious barn. They were dreadful and it was more than I could bear, for I can see them to this day, with their noses close to the ground and growling.

I can remember pretty well the exterior of the bookstore but not much of its contents. A stronger impression was left by a remarkable sign upon the front of a large stone building across the way. It was under the windows of an upper story and it read in big, black letters, "Job Printing." Now it happened that I had heard a great deal about Job, at Sunday school and elsewhere, but I had not known that he did any printing until I saw that sign. Many years afterwards, revisiting Rochester, I went to see if Job were still there and was agreeably surprised to find that his sign, though old and in need of repainting, was still in the old place.

So the years went by until I was on the edge of seven. It was in the trying financial year of 1842 that my father had been again extending his business operations, with successes but with consequent endorsements. As a still further consequence, he was compelled to sell out his bookstore to his friend William N. Sage and quit his other undertakings. As late as when I left college, Mr. Sage was still in charge of the old bookstore. The only thing to be done, while my father was engaged in unraveling his affairs from the effects of the panic, was for the family to take refuge in my grandfather's house in Homer. Most of the furniture was put away in a storehouse but a splendid haircloth sofa of which I was proud and some other articles went to ornament the Homer parlors.

I was now a well-grown little chap with a strong liking for travel and adventure, to whom the prospect of a long journey was the best thing that could have been proposed to him. As for the business disasters, I had not yet attained any eminence as a financier. In fact, my knowledge of money was narrowed down to a few facts. One of these was that the amount of copper coin in circulation was large and varied. I wondered at the hugeness of the Canadian copper pennies, which were often taken in trade but were hard to pass again. So were the numerous "halfpenny tokens" and the bits of copper stamped with "Not One Cent for tribute. Millions for defence," which had been coined along of the War of 1812. Then there were Log Cabin cents, but these came later. I began my political career with Harrison and Tyler's hard cider campaign[1] for my father was a Whig and I had not only a brass Log Cabin medal, bright as gold, but a Tippecanoe handkerchief printed with campaign songs, some of which I learned by heart and believed that I could sing them. In other matters I took a deep interest but in none more than the Greek rebellion, the massacre at Scio, and the wonderful career of Bozzaris the hero.[2]

I do not know how much of my pro-Greek enthusiasm came out of the fact that Mr. Achilles, formerly of Homer, was for a long time superintendent of the Sunday school to which I belonged. At all events, in due season there came to Rochester a celebrated Greek patriot and he gave an eloquent lecture in the largest hall in town. Of course, my father and mother were there and I talked Greek enough to make them take me along. Little did they guess what they were doing! Among the attractions of the lecture were many articles of Greek dress and equipage, warlike and otherwise, but chief among them all, to my enthusiastic eyes, was a long, curved sabre, declared to have been the sword of Bozzaris the brave. The lecturer drew it from the sheath and was flourishing it gracefully to show how brave it was, when a small boy who had neatly escaped from his preoccupied parents came up the sidestairs and upon the platform with a shrill demand to be allowed to handle and swing that sword. The Greek hero was a wise man, for, amid the cheers and laughter of the packed audience, the small boy was permitted to do what he would with that keen and glittering saber which had cut up so very many Turks. Then, because there were no Turks present for me to cut up, the sabre was taken from me and I was forcefully removed from the platform. I still believe it was an interesting feature of that broken English lecture.

Speaking of money, I must tell one more financial incident. My mother's sister Adeline had married Rev. Edward Bright, a rising young Baptist minister, and at one time he and his wife came to pay us a visit. I took to him kindly at once for at our introduction he gave me the first silver coin I had ever owned, although my mother had always been liberal in coppers and so had some other people whom I admired. This was a "sixpence," for we had then very few American five cent pieces, or any other form of American silver and were compelled to use Spanish and Mexican coins as a substitute. Gold was not in circulation. I took stock in "Uncle Edward," of course, and the next day I brought him a large pine shingle with a modest request that he would make me a bow. Instead of that, he made fun.

3

Boyhood in Homer

The days of the railroad had not yet come. From an early period of the civilized era in the history of the state, there had been a stage route through the center of it, from Albany westward. It was still in existence, but it was supported by such passenger traffic as did not belong to the line of the canal, or that was desirous of traveling faster than six miles an hour, the limit of the new waterway passenger or "liner" boats.

These carried freight as well as passengers and were not as aristocratic. Both depended upon horsepower in its original form, sometimes going as high as three horsepower to the boat. Places were secured upon a craft of the best kind for the [eastward] migration of the Stoddard family, and the voyage was begun, for one member of it at least, in a high condition of mental exhilaration and with some curious questions in his mind as to whether or not such a vessel were at all liable to shipwreck. There were wonders all the way, including the bridges in passing under which all the grown-up people had to bob their heads, while a short boy might safely stand erect and stare up at the bridge. Then there were the locks, by means of which the boat was to be let down to eastern and lower levels, through vast, cavernous clefts in the surface of the earth, while the boat staggered back and forth as if she were frightened. I can well remember how, before dinner time, the entire boat would be pervaded by the rich aroma of boiling corn, sweet corn, of which I was fond when hungry.

I do not now recall any remarkable incidents of that voyage, but at night it was wonderful to be out away upon a shelf at the side of the cabin and to be darkly curtained in. I saw two luckless power horses slide from the towpath into the dreadful water at Syracuse and that is all there was to interest me in that then very young village. It may have contained six thousand people but it contained us only long enough for us to be transferred to the "extra" which was to convey us to Homer. This vehicle received its name from the fact that there was a regular stage line running, with the regulation pitch and roll coaches, and that whenever the rush of passengers overflowed it was needful to put on some other kind of wagon instead of building another coach.

The vehicle provided for us was a long two-horse carryall with a closable hood and curtains. It was warranted to do the required thirty miles in one day, with several stoppages. It will be seen that if a day [trip] contains six hours, that stage speed had to be worked up to the high pressure point of five miles an hour. I saw them do it, myself, in spite of the long, long hills and the danger we were in from the Indians. This peril belonged to the fact that a part of the road from Syracuse southward runs through the Reservation of the once-proud and merciless tribe of the Onondagas. At the date of this my first long journey, the dangerous nation numbered, I was informed, about three hundred souls, chiefs, warriors, squaws, and papooses. There was nothing terribly warlike in the aspect of the one-story wooden Council House, which was pointed out to me on the left as we went by, but my acquaintance with the red men and my interest in them may be said to have begun then and there, although I believe I must have heard a great deal about them at even an earlier day. It stuck in my mind that the Council House stood upon the spot where in former ages had burned the Sacred Fire of the Iroquois, the Six Nations, who had killed and scalped so many white men. I think that it was in pleasant September weather that our trip was made; it was warm and sunny and we reached our destination in first-rate order, in the evening.

My uncle Edward Bright was at the time and during several years which followed the pastor of the Homer Baptist Church, and he and his family had been visiting at my grandfather's house until their own could be made ready for them. They were hardly out when we came in and my cousin Osborn, four years older than myself, took me around the premises next morning on a tour of explanation, exhibiting with pride his father's horse, Jerry, and our grandfather's horse Nig. In after years there was a long succession of horses under the ownership of Uncle Bright, but they all fell heirs to the same name. As late as after the Civil War, I visited their home in Yonkers and took more than one ride upon a Jerry who much resembled the old sorrel-bay I had admired in Homer.

I was now seven years old and I was mentally prepared to make a thorough exploration of the new town and home to which my fate had brought me. I did not know, then, that my grandfather had suffered business reverses, from endorsements and the like, and that his property had dwindled to what seemed to me a very large one. It consisted, mainly, of his residence, a shop on Main Street, some land between Homer and Cortland village, and a farm of about twenty acres on the hill east of Homer.

The residence lot was a wide one, with a fine side yard and possibly an acre and half of garden and orchard behind it. In front was a line of fine maple trees and the sidewalk was of stone. So was the inner walk, away back beyond the house. This was a well-built, two-story affair. It had no wings. The main part contained on the ground floor two large parlors and a bedroom and above were chambers to correspond. Behind this was a brick addition, on the ground floor of which was an ample dining room. Over this was a large chamber lighted by a delightful dormer window, which at the first had had two windows in the rear. These were now closed, for, after the first building, of brick, a large frame kitchen addition had been put on.

This addition also contained a large pantry and milk room but its chief importance to me was soon to become the fact that all its upper part was one immense, mysterious, wonderfully occupied garret, in which I was to have free play room. Opposite the kitchen door was an excellent well, housed over, and cold water might be bucketed up from that well and the depths of the earth in the hottest of Summer weather. Just back of the well began what was called "the granary," a long, two-story frame building, painted red. All the brick houses in the village were painted yellow and if any barn was colored at all it was like a new brick. More than half of the lower story of the granary was a woodshed, large enough to contain a full Winter's supply of fuel. Next to this was an apartment given up to bins for grain and to an awful shower-bath arrangement which I abhorred. I would any day have taken a moderate switching, rather than to be rained upon from above with cold water while tubbing it under that direful machine. The upper story of the granary was little more than another wonderful garret, swarming with ancient machinery and the wrecks of all manner of domestic and mechanical undertakings. I have sometimes thought that these two garrets had much to do with some parts of my education. So far as they were concerned, I had more play room than any other boy in the village but I was not allowed to bring the other boys into my places of wonders.

Away back, on the granary side of the lot and to be reached by a long lane, was the barn, containing stables for horses and cows, and much hay room. Behind this was a cow-lot and a comfortable pig pen. All the lower part of the lot was orchard and some of the fruit was very good. About twenty paces behind the house, however, was its star fruit tree. It was a large old pear tree, bearing really splendid Winter pears all over it except upon one mysterious branch which had been taught how to carry yellow-backed Summer pears. How it could do so was always a puzzle to me, but a more important branch than that was the strong one which carried the swing.

There were many plum and cherry trees on the place when we went there but the curculios were already in the land and three or four years later all these had passed away. In the side yard were dark and sweet smelling cedar trees and my mother's "balm of Gilead." All along the rear of the house were ranged hives of bees, but for some reason unknown to me, the keeping of them was given up a couple of years afterwards. They were there, however, long enough for me to get well acquainted with them and to know that they considered me a special friend of theirs. I loved to go and watch them at their work, an hour at a time, and it was a grand treat to be with them at swarming time and to see how Mr. Smith, the miraculous "bee man," would fearlessly gather them into their new hives without one of them saying a word to him against it. At all events, I learned a great deal about bees and I knew why the wicked kingbirds were so fond of visiting the trees around our house. Of course, there were plenty of hens and their husbands and families at the barn and one of my first experiences of country life was that I was entrusted not only with the important business of feeding chickens, but also with the exciting sport of hunting for eggs all over the barn, even up and into the shadowy recesses of the haymow.

The topography of Homer was mainly governed by two immovable circumstances. The first of these was the old north and south highway which naturally became the Main Street from which all other thoroughfares went off as branches, although not one of them crossed it to make a "four corners." The other compulsory was the Tioughneauga River, running along somewhat to the eastward of the middle of the valley. It was a considerable stream until the forests which covered the hills on either side of it were cut down and then it gradually lost both size and beauty. There were many reaches of fine woodland in my childhood and I prefer to remember the river at its best. Above the village and below were two large millponds, with grist mills and sawmills, fishing in Summer and skating in Winter. The lower mill was owned and carried on by a man named Riggs, honored by all Homer boys for the liberality with which he provided them with a first-rate spring-diving board at the swimming hole, near the mill. The upper mill owner was a man by the name of Smith, I believe, but he was invariably spoken of as Nore R. Smith and I finally gathered the idea that he was supposed to be descended from Noah.

The side street upon which our house stood went out eastward from the Main Street in the lower or southerly part of the town. At the left corner was the two-story brick house in which Andrew D. White was born, and its lower story was still occupied for mercantile purposes, the rest of it being occupied as a residence by its owner, a Mr. Chittenden. The opposite corner was adorned by the Temperance House hotel, a pretty large country tavern with a dining room well suited to occasional festive or theatrical entertainments, as I may relate hereafter. Its leading attractions, to me, were its very fat and jolly landlord and his pet rooster, trained to crow whenever duly called upon to do so. Between this and our own was a small, frame dwelling.

On the Main Street, the next house above Mr. Chittenden's was my grandfather's shop. It had been one of the first buildings erected in all that valley, for John Osborn's business had been well established there before he brought on his family. One large part of his trade had been with the Indians, as I understood it had previously been in the Mohawk valley, from Albany days onward. A consequence of this had been that the first name of his new settlement, before the white men who laid out the county into townships had gratified their classic tastes by remembering the old Greek poet, was a string of Iroquois-sounding syllables and a grunt which were to be interpreted "The Place where the man lives who sells the silver ornaments." That is, it was "Silverville" until it became Homer. He still plied the trade, of a silversmith and jeweler, although he had retired from a part of it and had leased the small front shop to a close friend of his named Ormsby. All the rear part, in which were the forge and anvils and endless other tools, was still his own and therefore became an important addition to my already remarkable playhouse. Next above the shop were the Universalist Church, its wide yard and sheds.

My own memories in connection with that house of worship are mainly concentrated upon a great battle which I fought in its side yard. What had taken me in there I do not know unless it was a stray ball, but I was attacked furiously by an ugly-tempered dog. I had in my hand a hickory stick, as thick as your finger, and this was broken to pieces in a desperate attempt to make him let go. I would surely have lost the battle but for an old foot-and-a-half-long fragment of a wagon trace which lay near on the ground ready for use. It had been provided that the tongue of the buckle at the end of it had been rusted stiff at right angles and had kept its point. When, therefore, I gathered the strap and began to pelt the dog with it, the buckle tongue went through his hide at every clip. In a moment more he was racing away down Main Street, singing loudly. I carried the marks of that fight for many a year after my ninth, in which it occurred. He was not so very large a dog and I cannot be sure about his breed but believe him to have been a thoroughbred cur.

Across Main Street from the end of ours, which had no name, were the residences, handsome ones, of the Schermerhorn and Williams families, close friends as well as neighbors, which at once provided my sister Julia and myself with first-rate playmates. With the Williams family began my political education. Mr. Williams was the owner of a woolen factory in the upper part of the village, in which the wool crop of the neighboring farmers found a ready market and in which very good cloth was manufactured. Two years after my first acquaintance with little "Eb" Williams, I was greatly grieved to hear that his father had failed in business, the factory was to be shut up and the Williams family was to move away. When I asked what they did it for, I was informed by my Whig "Protectionist" father and grandfather that the failure was caused by a new, Democratic, Locofoco, Free Trade Tariff,[1] and that it would not thenceforth pay the Cortland County farmers to raise sheep. It became fixed in my mind that the sheep were to be killed and the factory shut up for the benefit of some Englishmen across the ocean, and I never got out of my mind how desolate the Williams factory looked when I went to pay it a visit and see if it were really done for.

As to other political items, my father was a strong "Seward Whig"[2] and my grandfather was one of the first subscribers for a small weekly journal which had been set going in New York City by a queer character by the name of Horace Greeley.[3] I will note at this point that John Osborn had all his life been an active politician until his deeper interest in religious matters destroyed his interest in other things. He had represented the county in the State Legislature as long as he would consent to go to Albany, and among his best personal friends were a number of prominent politicians, with whom, as I afterwards discovered from old letters in the garret, he long kept up a vigorous advisory correspondence. I was informed that, owing to his great personal popularity, he had twice been elected county judge, but had refused to take the oath of office, from some unexplained religious scruples. He was an intensely religious man, having even become almost a Quaker in the matter of non-resistance, and suffering himself to be plundered, rather than go to law. On the other hand, he consented to be elected Justice of the Peace, perennially, and was a general peacemaker for much more than the township of Homer.

I think I will now let go of all these things that happened afterwards and try to get myself into better relation with my seventh year and particularly with my enthusiastic explorations of my grandfather's house and farm and our end of the village.

Right here it may be well to add to my family tree memoranda the fact that through my grandmother, Sabria Avery, I am directly descended from the celebrated Elder Brewster of the Pilgrim Fathers of Massachusetts Bay.[4] So my children are of what somebody has called the "Brahmin blood" of the old New England stock and ought to be aware of their inheritance.

In earlier years, I had paid more than one visit to Homer but had been too young to take any kind of possession of the place. I had traveled on the canal and in stage coaches, of course, with my mother and the other children, as I was to do afterwards, but now, in looking back, all of those journeyings appear to melt into one and I cannot separate them, if I had any good reason for doing so. Now, however, that I understood that we had come to stay and not to visit, the case was altogether different and I made myself at home.

Perhaps my first important discoveries were my grandparents themselves. I had from birth been a special favorite of my grandfather. He had made for me with his own hands, from melted-down Mexican dollars, a tall silver cup, bearing my initials, now in the possession of my beloved cousin Mrs. Mary Bright Bruce, and a silver porringer in my own keeping. My name, at first, was William John, after a son of his who died in boyhood and after himself. It was not until I was nearly sixteen years of age that I substituted, with my father's assent, the name Osborn for "John." It was an idea of my own, entirely, and I remember telling my father that "John was anybody's name" and that if I were to be named after my grandfather I would take his own.

I soon learned that all who knew him spoke of him only as the "the Squire," or "Squire Osborn," except that a large number of them pronounced it "Square." He now made a great pet of me and liked to have me with him in the shop, where I soon began to obtain clear ideas of how silver spoons and many other metallic affairs were manufactured. It was slow work, compared to the machine rapidity of our modern shops. He also soon began to take me with him to church prayer meetings, in which he was a leader, even when I was so short that I had to reach up to take one of his fingers as we slowly walked along. I found, also, that he had a great deal of fun in him and that it was simply impossible for him to give me a whipping, however much I might be in need of correction.

That was about the case with my grandmother, for whom my affection grew tremendously. She was not in very robust health although still a busy, active woman, with a strong will of her own and a great deal of character. She was not tall, was slightly made, and she had singularly graceful manners, including the "drop curt'sey" greeting of the old school of gentility. When I grew old enough to make such a criticism, I was more than a little proud of my grandmother's dignified way of receiving company. One of my first alliances with her and with good behavior grew out of the fact that she could, and continually did, manufacture wonderfully good sweet "cookies," and that she retained the custody of them in a large stoneware pot that was kept in the dark, deep closet which opened into her bedroom from its cave under the front stairs. In this closet also would at times be stores of maple sugar and the like and her influence over her grandchildren was all that could be asked for. We had the house to ourselves at first, with the exception of a long line of varied "help," obtained with some difficulty and for brief terms of service from among the families of the neighboring farmers. During the Winter, however, several boarders were admitted, most of them sons of old friends of Squire Osborn and all of them students in the village Academy. He had been one of the founders of the institution and it now had a high and wide reputation. My own impression was, and it was afterwards confirmed, that quite a number of promising young men had from time to time "boarded" with John Osborn and been otherwise provided for, when they had no means for paying board anywhere. He was very proud of the subsequent successes of some for whom he had in this manner lifted over a tight place in their educational careers.

Now, for the first time, I discovered my splendid aunt, Mrs. Adeline O. Bright, and her children, my cousins. She, like my mother, was a woman of strong intellect and unusual culture. Instead of being blue eyed, for my mother resembled her father, Adeline was a Cotton and had dark eyes and hair like her mother. The same type was afterwards wonderfully reproduced in my sister Julia, my daughter Sarah, and my cousin Mary Bruce, who is almost a likeness of her grandmother. I think she was as handsome, too, and that is saying a good deal. The children were Osborn, nearly fourteen and no playmate for me; Matilda, about ten and a constant companion for my sister Julia; Amelia, about six and just the mate for my younger sister Kate; and Mary, perhaps three and disposed to look on while the others did the noise and the romping. My aunt Adeline and I soon became great friends and I remember her to this day with the tenderest affection. As for my uncle, I heard some of the good people say that he was "too bossy," but I knew that he and I were all right and that I could make him laugh almost anywhere but in meeting.

The street upon which our house stood ran down a gentle slope to the bridge over the Tioughneauga, and beyond that it was but an eighth of a mile to the forks of the roads at the foot of the East Hill. Here one road turned away at right angles toward Truxton. One inclined somewhat to the right as it went upward steeply and was called "the brewery hill road." The third highway slanted northerly and was not so steep and I was glad of it for, at about five minutes quick walking, on the right, was my grandfather's land, extending away up and over to a cross road far beyond my immediate explorations.

Just at the forks of the roads stood the oldest brewery in those parts and I was yet to learn more about that and its conductors. At right angles to the left ran yet another road, almost parallel with the river, and on the lower corner of this was a frame homestead painted red and occupied by a family by the name of Ford. They were excellent people and before long I learned that they had both boys and dogs. It was a matter of course that I made a thorough search of the house but I had a shy feeling about the front parlor, into which I rarely ventured, for fear, perhaps, of unexpectedly meeting "company," for which kind of being and for their impertinent questions

I had a strong aversion. It was well furnished and among its ornaments were remarkable specimens of ancient art needlework and painting from the hands of my lost aunt Amelia and my grandmother. Besides the outer blinds there were hanging calash blinds or wooden green curtains within. So it was in the back parlor but that could never, to my mind, be made quite so chilly and gloomy as the company parlor.

Over the front door was a latticed porch which was covered with honeysuckle vines in Summer, and around the door were queer little narrow-paned windows, the bits of glass being set in leaden sashes. All around the house were rose bushes, of red and white flowers, and the walks were myrtle bordered. It was a very pretty, tastefully ordered home and I loved it at once immensely. The front hallway extended only a little beyond the door into the back parlor. It left here only just room enough to accommodate the tall eight-day clock which is now in Mrs. Bruce's care at Rockledge, Yonkers. It is fairly hers, but she was too young then to have the treat that I did, every Saturday evening, when I regularly went with my grandfather to see him wind it up. It is still a tall and wonderful clock but it does not seem to me to tick as loudly as it did then. I noticed, however, that the pendulum never appeared to be in any kind of hurry and there was never any change in the expression of its face.

In the parlors were fireplaces, with brilliant brass andirons and woven wire fenders, and I thought there could be nothing finer than a wood fire on a Winter evening and all the family gathered in front of the blaze. When I think of it, I am of the same opinion still. The door into Grandmother's bedroom opened from the back parlor and it was a remarkable room. At the right, as one entered, stood a large mahogany "secretary," which was a cupboard below in which were shelves for papers. All the upper front could be rolled back and made to disclose many small drawers, while a green cloth-covered writing table shot out ready for use. In one of those drawers were usually kept the small pair of rifled derringer pistols that were made for me, but I was allowed to take them out and practice with them frequently, after I reached the high age of eight, on condition of molding my own bullets. That secretary was for a long time an object of respect which was almost awe to me.

Over the front parlor was a well-furnished "guest chamber," into which I probably never ventured more than a half dozen times, it was so unnecessary to me and was so secluded. Over the back parlor was another chamber as large and this was my mother's. It was a pleasant room, for she made it so, and I was in it a great deal. It was the room in which I had been born. Over the bedroom below may have been another of the same size, but into that room I never once looked, so far as I can remember. It is one of the unexplained mysteries of my boyhood.

The dining room part of the house was all my own and it was grand. It fronted on the long, wide piazza, and it extended all the way across the building. It had a flight of boxed and steep stairs which went up to what was now the children's bedroom, with the dormer window. Near the foot of the stairway was a square little window into Grandmother's bedroom. Opposite this was an ample buttery, with an opening into the kitchen. Next to this was an enormous chimney in the bosom of which was the old fashioned "bake-oven," which after a while always made me think of Mr. Nebuchadnezzar's furnace for burning pious Jews. Next to the oven, to the left, were crypts, the upper of which contained the liberal sporting tackle which John Osborn's earlier tastes had accumulated. His fishing rods and so forth were equal in quality to any I saw during many an afteryear.

And now I think I will make a new chapter for the rest of that dining room and the garret, as this one appears to be long enough and there must be stopping places upon every well-ordered highway. Besides, I am remembering too much and some of the curtains which are lifting disclose bright places over which hang clouds which threaten rain.

4

The Old Garret and Other Wonders

In the middle of the village, on the westerly side of Main Street, was the village green, containing many acres. Upon this green, beginning at the north, all of them well back from the street, were the public edifices of Homer. First came the Episcopal Church, in which John Osborn owned two pews, by reason of his contributions to its erection, for he was a liberal-minded man and not at all sectarian. He had been born and brought up in the Presbyterian fold, which he had left for the Baptist when little more than twenty-one, publishing a considerable pamphlet account of his reasons for so doing, which was a remarkable thing for a young Albany jeweler to do, or for other people to expect.

Next to this building, at a distance of perhaps thirty feet, was the "cannon house," calculated to contain with comfort one of the glories of the village patriotism. It was a six-pounder brass fieldpiece which had been captured from General Burgoyne at the battle of Saratoga. I mention it here, because it was always associated in my mind with some of my findings in the garret. They also had probably fought at Saratoga, but I learned that Squire Osborn himself had not been there and had not captured Burgoyne.

South of the cannon house was the really large and respectable Academy building, built in the style usual for church edifices, steeple, bell, and all. The next affair on the green was the small frame structure which we called the "Presbyterian Conference Room." Then came the Presbyterian Church itself. It was separated by a good width of grass from the Methodist meetinghouse and beyond that was a street which ran westward and on which was my uncle Bright's first residence, a neat brick dwelling, the side yard of which bordered upon the wide and well peopled graveyard, behind the green and separated from it by a long line of sheds for the accommodation of the teams of worshippers from the country side. South of this street was a large bit of pasture land, cut off from the green that upon it might be built the Baptist Church, with a "prayer and conference meetinghouse" of its own just behind it.

As I have said, the military idea was one of the first to take hold of me when I began to explore the garret. It came by way of a sheathed cavalry sabre which hung from one of the central wooden uprights. It was a weapon worth looking at, when one dared to draw it out of its sheath and to swing it as if it had once belonged to some trooper as brave as Bozzaris the Greek. On its edge were deep notches, such as your sabre is sure to get when you are fencing with a British trooper who has another sword very much like it, and there were several dark blotches which may have been rust but which I preferred to consider the stains of the blood which had poured in battle from the many victims who had been mowed down by that tremendously curved scythe of war. The brass hilt had a guard and ended in an eagle's head and I felt sure that it was an American eagle of the best kind. Not long after unsheathing the sabre, I found in an old chest a long bright dirk, without any haft, which I was informed had once been the weapon of a British midshipman, but I am now not clear in my mind as to how he came to part with it. My next find, in the chest, was a terrible, three-cornered, sharp-pointed, long-bladed man-sticker, which I learned to glory in as the distinctive weapon of a British sergeant of artillery who had been compelled to give it up at Saratoga. All these went along with the cannon to make me feel a growing sense of patriotism and to entertain a belief that my Osborn ancestry, like the Stoddards, had been "out" in the old fighting days and had served their country in battle, at Saratoga and elsewhere.

Hardly less interesting than the weapons, after ideas of peace had a chance to return, were the remnants of an ancient loom, upon which the girls of the Cotton or Osborn families had woven much wool before there were factories to do it for them. Before a great while, however, I was to witness the cutting up and twisting of huge quantities of gathered cloth fragments, linen and woolen, for the manufacture of "rag carpets," and I was to have the inestimable privilege of going to a house in the upper part of the village, where dwelt a woman whose loom was still in running order. With my own eyes I saw the woman develop those long rag twists into the most beautiful carpeting that you ever saw. It was for the dining room and it exhibited all the colors of the rainbow, with some which I never yet saw on any cloud anywhere. There were spinning wheels as well as a loom, and these were in a good state of preservation. So was the reel which went with them and I in due time acquired a strong aversion to that reel.

The way of it was this. Mother and Grandmother were good spinners and every now and then there would be carded wool in the house and the largest wheel would be taken down into the dining room. I did not mind that, for I loved to watch my mother at her spinning. I believe she enjoyed it and she certainly never showed how very graceful she was more perfectly than when she was stepping back and forth at the side of that tall wheel and feeding the spindle of it with snowy wool. My trouble came always afterwards, when my grandmother and the reel required me to hold out my small hands and help them in transferring endless "hanks" of yarn into balls, ready for the knitter of stockings and the like. I had to play assistant reel, sometimes, when I would much rather have been somewhere else, or anywhere else.

Under one of the now blind windows between the garret and the dormer-window room lay an enormous horsehide-covered trunk, the lock of which was broken, probably for my benefit. It was in this trunk that I found the dirk but there were other treasures almost as brilliant. Here were numbers of old dies, for stamping silver work; scales for fine weighing, with the cases of weights belonging to them; bits of colored glass jewels of many varieties; queer tools and a general mess of inestimable uselessness.

Near the trunk stood a large red chest of my father's, of which and its hidden availabilities I was to learn more at a later date. There were hosts of other things in the garret and in the entry at the foot of the steep back stairs which led up to it there was one thing which caught my wondering eyes immediately, but which was for the present withheld from my handling. High up on the wall were wooden hooks and upon these rested the first gun I ever became acquainted with. When I did come to the happy hour of being permitted to lift and level it, I discovered that it was really a first-class piece, for those days. It was a single-barreled shotgun, not very heavy but of the best make. It was, of course, a flintlock, for the percussion cap had not yet arrived upon the earth. Beside it hung a leather shot pouch, double, to carry two sizes of pellets, and a beautiful powder horn. Through the thinly scraped horn I could distinguish the dark and dangerous powder, such as hunters and soldiers did their killing with. I knew at once that it was to be my gun, but did not dream how long and how much I was yet to carry it.

My next trips took me from the top of the house to the bottom, for the cellar was a vast cave requiring an explorer. It extended the entire length of the building and was quite deep, so much so that all mince, pumpkin, and other pies upon the swing shelf that hung in the center of it were entirely safe from rats or other marauders. So was the closed store room and its closet where the main lots of maple sugar were kept but I did sometimes overcome some difficulties. At the right side of the cellar and at the far end were bins for apples, pears, and potatoes. Grandfather had another orchard up on the hill and his fondness for fine apples had descended to me. Also for pears, as soon as their flinty hardness at gathering time had ripened into their midwinter mellowness. On the opposite side were barrels and I soon knew that one of these contained good cider vinegar, made on the place. I was to learn how vinegar received its peculiar character, for cider came in exchange for apples and was treated to perfection in our side yard. The next barrels, two of them, contained sweet cider, which bye and bye would acquire a hardness of its own and strongly resemble vinegar. The only preventive was to drink it expeditiously and I soon acquired the science of long straws. One barrel there was of bitter beer, and I did not at all admire hops in a liquid form. A smaller barrel contained the oldest of currant wine, but I was debarred from that.

Our garden was bordered, and so were its paths, by luxuriant currant bushes, and these were for the benefit of the neighbors, as soon as our own requirements were filled for abundant jelly and as much wine as Grandmother cared to make. At the rear of the cellar was a crypt under the chimney, down into which all ashes from the family fires were sent through a shoot. The ashes were possessed of qualities which I began to learn that very Autumn. A first and highly interesting ash experiment began with a barrel perched upon a frame. Into this, when filled with ashes, water was poured which came out below colored deeply a brownish red and this was strong, pungent lye. With it and much boiling, all sorts of garnered fats were transformed into soaps, soft and hard, and the quantity of them was not small. Second to the soap in the opinion of the unwise was the manufacture of "hulled corn," sweet corn carefully selected, and this was also prepared in quantities. I watched it all, from day to day, as I did in seasons following, but before long I was to be an eye witness of a different and to me a much more thrilling operation.

I may suppose that throughout the civilized world, including Paris, London, and the City of Washington, the chilly month of November is "pig killing time." Not that all the pigs are then disposed of, but only those for whom this present world has come to an end. I had at once taken peculiar interest in the hog pen, and had paid it a number of visits of inspection. Its occupants were remarkable animals and appeared to be quite intelligent but I had heard them squealing tremendously in a gale of wind and could not imagine any good reason why they should invariably do so. I was now about to hear them squeal yet more loudly, one after another, upon being "stuck," although I was assured that the sticking did not cause them any pain. Their squealing, the men told me, was merely an expression of anger and astonishment. Nevertheless, they bled a great deal and then lay down and the men cut them all to pieces. I saw it done and I saw how the hams and shoulders were put aside for the smokehouse, with some bits for bacon, and how the remainder, barring tenderloins and the like for immediate cooking, were consigned to the salt-pork barrel. Also, I observed the subtle processes of manufacturing sausage meat and headcheese, and I knew that some of our pork had been traded for much beef for the "corned beef barrel." So much more there was, therefore, to go down into that dark and capacious cellar.

Fully equal to the pigs in interesting characteristics, from the very beginning, had been our cows. One of these was a large, red, matronly looking animal, of a higher order of cowhood, but she was not by any means so handsome as was her brindle-yellow mate, with sharp and tapering black horns and a very uncertain temper. I was to be much better acquainted with that brindled heifer thereafter, but I saw her kick over the milk pail soon after my arrival. My grandfather sat down upon the grass at the same moment but he kept his temper and spoke to her about it quite kindly. Milk I had always been fond of and I could recall an occasion, in Rochester, when a young woman fresh from the rural districts came to our house to borrow some. She was liberal in her ideas concerning milk, for she brought with her a wooden water pail and I knew that our milkman employed only tin and that our own milk came in by the quart. Now, however, by frequent attendances in the barnyard at milking times and also in the milkroom off the kitchen, I was to learn the nature and, the gathering of cream. Alas for me! Ere long I acquired the most complete and experimental knowledge of butter-making, for many was the weary half hour that I was to spend at the churn, as soon as I grew tall and strong enough to ply the dasher up and down. Equally unpopular with me was at a later day a new, patent churn whereof I was made to turn the dismal crank until the butter and the buttermilk should be divorced the one from the other.

In November and afterwards came the storms and snows of the long Cortland County Winter. The average level of that hill region is several hundred feet above the level of the sea and the Winters come three weeks earlier and stay three weeks later in the Spring than they do at Syracuse, thirty miles northward. Nevertheless, the snow time was at first house time, for a seven year old, and I had an abundance of leisure. All was well with me except that the cold shut me out of the garret and that a journey as far as the barn was sometimes difficult. It was even easier to reach the shop, because of better paths, and I patronized the shop. It was during this semi-imprisonment of arctic weather that another step in my curious education came to me. My good grandmother may not have fully agreed with Professor Dewey of Rochester as to boys and Latin, but Mrs. Amelia Osborn was of Pilgrim stock and believed that I could not too soon begin my studies of the Bible. Had I not already won a Bible prize in a Sunday school and might I not grow up to be a preacher or a missionary?

I was not, however, to be confined to the small print of my own polyglot, for the great quarto family Bible was at my service and I was commanded to read it through. Beyond a doubt I did so and in after days there came an era when I deemed it my duty to read it from cover to cover, once in each calendar year. At the beginning I think I was somewhat more discursive. The special time for Bible was upon Sundays, of course, and the big book was regularly laid down for me upon the dining room floor. Here also I lay down and it must be said that I took an astonishing interest in much that I went through. The quarto was of the only kind then printed, so far as I know, of that size, for it contained the books of the Apocrypha and my grandmother had by no means lost the old notion that these were only a somewhat less sacred kind of Bible. At all events, it was not wrong to read them on Sunday. Were they not bound up with the rest? She probably never took the trouble to consider that precisely that authority, that of the printer and binder, is about all the warrant there is for the general belief in the "inspiration" of sundry other books of the inestimable collection which we all reverence and love. I became quite fond of the Maccabees and of all the other Bible men who did any traveling, like Jacob, or any fighting, like David and Saul and Paul the Apostle, of whom, the latter, there was a splendid picture of his tumble from his horse among mounted soldiers, under the influence of a great glare of blinding light. I have a feeling of personal fondness for Paul, to this day.

This regular Bible reading continued during all my boyhood in Homer, but there were several other books which I was permitted to delve in on the Lord's Day. First among these, of course, was the *Pilgrim's Progress* and I soon all but knew it by heart, both parts of it, giants and all. Next to this was Bunyan's *Holy War,* but it was hard reading although there was much good fighting in it. My mother also permitted me to take up, on Sundays, the works of Hannah More and the altogether harmless poems of Miss Amanda M. Edmonds. I think that Good's *Book of Nature* was not entirely forbidden me, but some of my prime favorites were. Among these were Shakespeare's *Tempest, Midsummer Night's Dream*, and two or three of his fighting plays, but these came when I was nearly ten and I could go no further. Earlier was Scott's *Lady of the Lake,* and I believe I could almost have repeated it, from end to end. With that came *Rob Roy* [and] *Ivanhoe,* and I read them over and over. So I did Cooper's *Leatherstocking* [*Tales*]. There was an illustrated *History of the World* which gave me much occupation, but it was nothing at all in comparison with the wonderful volumes of the *Works of Josephus*, all of which I finished before ten and at the same time I took a long and thrilling course in Fox's *Book of Martyrs*. There were other books, of course, including the *United States Speaker,* but these are all I can remember just now and I believe they were quite enough for a beginner. Of periodicals, the only visitor I cared for was *Peter Parley's Magazine for Young People*, but it came only once a month when it ought to have come at least every week.

During that first Winter and afterwards there was more than one Apple-paring Bee and Sewing Society at our house, and there was a constant stream of day and evening callers. It was not difficult for me to gather the information that numbers of men were in the habit of coming to consult with John Osborn concerning their affairs of all kinds and that his decisions were generally regarded as final. I afterwards heard that he was considered almost as an enemy of law practice, he killed off so many promising suits in their infancy. At the same time I saw that my mother was the life and soul of the Grand Ligne Mission Society and could talk better about missions than could any of the other women. She was better looking, too, and I had an idea that Homer contained some very ugly pieties.

Right in the middle of that first Winter came the cold beginning of yet one more educational experience, for my entrance into the Academy was just after New Year's, when I had been intending to devote myself entirely to my new and beautiful sled. It was an affliction, but I had to endure it. My next affliction was that my proficiency in arithmetic, reading, and so forth, put me into classes where all the others were much older than myself. None of them liked my being among them and the other small boys keenly resented what to them appeared favoritism. From the beginning of my academical course, therefore, I was placed in a position calling for all the gentleness, forbearance, and love of peace for which I became distinguished.

5

In the Village

Beginning at the upper end of what was now regarded, in central New York, as a pretty ancient kind of village, the first object of interest to an exploring boy was the Upper Pond. It was long and irregular, with both deep and shallow places, and here and there still stuck up above the surface or were visible under the clear water, the stumps of the trees that were cut down when the valley was invaded by the destroying white men. It was no larger, perhaps, than was the Lower Pond, but it undoubtedly contained more snapping turtles and not so many pickerel. With the mills, grist, and saw, I had little to do, but not far away were the smokehouse and the tannery, for both of which I was one day to have repeated important errands.

As for Nore R. Smith, I was inclined to shy him, for some unexplained reason, and was more deeply interested in his neighbor, Don Brown, by all odds the blackest and, some said the most peculiar character in Homer. He was not only black but dreadfully lame of one leg and also in his reputation, for his not very large corporeal was full to the skin with all sorts of mischief. He was said to be fond of fat chickens and I myself have seen him shoot "doves" as the pigeons were called, to which he had no other ownership than that of a dark sportsman who innocently mistook them for wild game. He also was a sawer of wood and it was well to pay him by the cord rather than by the day. Not far from Don Brown and the mill was the other dark man of the village. He was the mulatto barber and his distinguishing characteristics were vast personal dignity and a conscientious opposition to the payment of small debts. Once, when he owed my grandfather a quarter, the claim was presented to me on fish-hook account, if I would manage to collect it. I think

I must have overcome the [in]dignity, more or less, for I did get some of the cash and the fish hooks, by installments, with more than one expression of disgust and more than one quizzical laugh from John Osborn.

Only a little further down the Main Street from Don Brown and the pond and the mill, was old Uncle Jed Barber's really great country store, the largest in those parts, in which all that the country needed was offered for sale. It was a frame building, a cellar, three tall stories and a garret. I was told that Uncle Jed's first store, on the same spot, was but little larger than a drygoods box. Over its front had been a small, gilt sign, "J. Barber." That sign, dingy with age and weather, was now visible to the naked eye, away up over the third tier of windows. Under the same tier was his second sign, larger and brighter, painted when prosperity and the new building arrived, "J. Barber & Son." Over the lower windows, at the time when I first saw the store, was the culmination of the sign matter, for a long, wide, glittering plank carried in brilliant gold letters, "Jedidiah Barber, Son & Co."

My great interest in this store arose from the fact that my father was now the bookkeeper and chief clerk of the establishment. He continued to be so during an entire year, while he was collecting the pecuniary remnants of his old Rochester business and preparing to strike out again on his own account. Of course, Uncle Jed and John Osborn were strong friends and the big brick house of the latter was painted in the same shade of dark yellow with our own. One of his daughters had married a Mr. Schermerhorn, our near neighbor; her children were our playmates, and I at once took kindly to their grandfather. He was a short man who knew everybody and he had a large, clear voice. He also appeared to have an idea that the people who came to trade with him were mostly deaf and it was worthwhile to see him stand in front of a tall man and shout at his head as if it had been on a housetop. He also shouted down at me but I was not afraid of him. On the upper corner at the right, very near Don Brown and the mill, was a comfortable tavern, from the barroom of which it might have been well for Don to have kept away more than he did. There was another tavern in the middle of the village, opposite the green, looking all the churches impudently in the face, although all of their members were supposed to be against the sale of liquors, except as occasional medicinal agents susceptible of complete and convincing explanations. I heard some of them and was convinced. There was nothing else of very great interest, after leaving Don Brown's part of the village, until one came to the green.

In after time, it was ruined by the requirements of a railway and all the graves were transferred to a new cemetery on the West Hill, at the expense of the railway company. As, however, my Uncle Bright's house was on the cross street beyond, my shortest cut to it, when coming southward from the store, was through the place of tombs. I explored it, thoroughly reading all the inscriptions, some of which were literary gems. I became accustomed to that kind of company and before long I astonished some of the Homer people, older as well as younger, by the perfect nerve with which I was ready to pass through that graveyard after dark, in the night! When ghosts and ghostesses might possibly be cutting up—or down. Then I obtained the admiration of the small boys by the extreme recklessness with which I was willing to go, at night, and knock on the door of the Presbyterian Church and stand still and wait to see if anybody would come. The fact was that my mother had so instructed me that I had not an atom of the fear of spooks in my growing mind. It never got in afterwards and I was able to assure the superstitious that if I were ever to meet a ghost I would kindly bid him good day.

Of the Baptist Church across that narrow street at the end of the green, I have few memories, other than such as belong to the routine of church going. From this broad and sweeping assertion, however, I must except one of the upper windows in the back of the building. As time went on, I became an acknowledged expert in the casting of stones at any kind of mark. One ill-starred day, when coming down that street, I was seized with the subtle temptation of an ambition to throw a stone over the church, for I vaingloriously believed that I could do it. Perhaps I could, but I did not. The fragment of gray limestone I selected from the gutter, as young David McJesse once picked his slingstones from the brook, was a smooth, oval pebble which was just the thing for a throw. I threw it and it went well but my aim, like that of many other ambitions, had not been high enough. Up went the pebble, in a great and graceful curve but it did not go over the meetinghouse. It ended its curved career against an upper pane of glass in that rear window. The result, to me, was consternation, but to the brittle oblong up yonder it was no great disaster. There was no general crash, no panic in the glass market, for the hole made was hardly larger than was necessary to let the pebble into the church. I have sometimes thought that the admission of others who get in must be through similarly close-fitting entryways. I wisely kept my dreadful secret, then, but when, thirty years afterwards, on a visit to Homer, I passed along that street and looked up at that window, there was the hole in the pane in a state of perfect preservation. I am inclined to believe, consequently, that hardly anything will wear longer than will a hole in a pane of glass, if it is high enough from other things to escape the eyes of impertinent glaziers in search of a job.

Next to the church was the long, frame "big building," a window of which was said to have once been broken by the concussion of the discharge of the Burgoyne cannon on the green. I did not see that done, but in the Main Street entrance of the building was Deacon Short's harness shop and I knew what happened to a greenhorn, once, when he was sent to that shop to borrow "a quart of strap oil." McNeill's house, in which Miss Molly McNeill kept the "infant school," was a little below, on the right and old McNeill raised a kind of beans out of which he made what he declared to be the best of coffee, but he preached his doctrines in vain to the people of Homer and a new coffee sect was not formed. Away along on the left, half way to the lower mill, was Sanders's furnace, wherein I became convinced, almost against reason, that hard iron might be melted and poured into a mold, like candle fat.

Before long, also, I learned that old Sanders would pay two cents a pound for old iron scraps, if they were good scraps. I am informed that the present price of the metal is somewhat lower, but then his furnace was far away from any mine and transportation was costly. So were other factors in the price of iron. The furnace man himself was a noted character. He was of a literary turn and when his furnace went out of existence he did not do so but turned author. He wrote and composed *Sanders's Spellingbook* and my father was one of his publishers. It was said that more copies of that work were printed and sold, per annum, in its day, than of any other current work in American literature. I had one, myself, and became deeply interested in it.

Across the way from our house was the home of my immediate playmate Hank Babcock, almost precisely of my own age. There also lived his mother, who at once became an aunt of mine, God bless her kindly face, and so did his father, Deacon Jared Babcock of the Baptist Church, who had visited with us in Rochester. They had a pretty place with much garden, but down beyond that garden and toward the river was the wonderful organ factory. I spent many a happy half hour in that factory, watching the workmen shaping pipes of wood or lead to carry music in. The melting of the metal and casting it into sheets and then the processes of shaving smooth the sheets and cutting them to fit the measures of the required music was a depth of mysterious inquiry. So was the boy-process of obtaining enough of the leaden shavings for the subsequent re-melting processes demanded for the production of sinkers for fishlines and of small cannon which were sure to burst, but you might hammer up the bursted place and try them again with less powder and see them go all to pieces. I have a fairly distinct remembrance of an occasion when Hank Babcock might have associated a small organ pipe, which he mistook for attainable lead shavings, with what appears to me in retrospect to have been at least a half-quart of "strap oil," applied by his musical father. Hank also was musical, for at least that occasion, and they were training him as a music teacher in defiance of the fact that he had little music in him, other than such as might better be elicited by a strap than otherwise.

6

The River

*D*own sloped the road from our house to the Tioughneauga, and it led into a new world in which a large part of my small boyhood was to be passed. The bridge itself was strongly built, of rough stones, and had several low arches, under which one might row a boat at ordinary times and against which the water would dash and foam and roar gloriously at floodtime, often hurling at them masses of ice in a manner which was grand to see.

Above the bridge, the water was shallow as well as wide and most of the teams passing that way were driven in fearlessly and halted that the horses might drink while they scared off the fish for which, and their never coming bites, the village boys strung along upon the low, much whittled parapet, were waiting. Below the bridge, not far, was the "baptizing hole," in which I was yet to see numbers of converts immersed and to obtain a distinct, ineffaceable idea that just so did Jesus of Nazareth receive immersion in the Jordan. Still, I did not quite understand Uncle Bright, Elder Bennett, and other good men when they spoke of that hollow place in the Tioughneauga as "our Jordan." And then all the country people pronounced it "Jerdan" and I heard them talk and sing of its "stormy banks" when I knew better.

On the right of the bridge and opposite the place of baptism was the blacksmith shop. It was under the management of Frank Smith's father. Both of them were awfully redheaded, the old man to such an extent that I did not go into that place to see them shoe horses unless he had the hoof already in his leather apron and his back was turned. I knew I could get out in a jiffy and he never went for me unless I had a troop of other boys with me. Opposite the blacksmith shop, at the heel of the bridge, was the pottery. It was owned, when it first passed under my inspection, by a Mr. Letts, and he could make almost anything out of the really fine mud of which the bank of the river was at that point constructed. It was a study to see him at his wheel, itself a relic of the most ancient days, and to note how a pot or a jug would grow into shape and ugly beauty under his skillful thumb and a small stick, as the platen spun around with his foot upon the treddle. The roasting furnace was a huge and rude affair of brickwork, but I looked into it once when it was all a-going. I was able to tell the other boys "he didn't pay a cent for all that wood. It's nothing but floodwood that he gathered when it was floating down the river." A year or so later, the making of pots at that place was given up and I saw a vast brick kiln take its place, for the purpose of teaching me how to make bricks. They all went into it of a muddy gray or brown and the fire reddened them.

One narrow but deep and swiftly running arm of the river separated the claybank from Spice Island, which I preempted for a Summer playground. It may have contained a long, straggling acre of grass and bushes, grass in the middle and spice and alder bushes around its edges, but it has now disappeared. It might be more nearly correct to say that it has vanished only as an island, by reason of the filling up of the old channel between its former wildness and the main shore. Above that island there was nothing to interfere with navigation until an explorer should come to the dam of the upper millpond and I one day at nearly ten, persuaded Hank Babcock to aid me in overcoming even that apparently impassable barrier. We had a small, flat-bottomed boat of our own and I proposed that we should imitate Columbus and sail upon a voyage of discovery to reach the source of the river. It would be a great thing to do and we went. We managed, with much toil and some small disasters, to get our ship over the dam. Then we sailed gallantly on over the rude waves of the Upper Pond and followed the further windings of the dashing Tioughneauga.

It was all delight and success and heroism and excitement until the water itself gave out. That is, we went on up to a place where the billows became so shallow that even our craft, however little it might draw, could float no further. As commander of the expedition, I was obliged to imitate our Arctic explorers and decide that we were near enough to the head of the river for this time. If we were to try again it would be needful to have less boat or more water. We poled our boat homeward, both of us getting a ducking in once more beating the milldam and both of us receiving rewards of merit on arriving at our destinations. My reward was a good deal of fun and quizzical questioning from John Osborn, but Hank's, I am sorry to say, consisted of a music-making warning against letting Willie Stoddard get him into any more wild escapades. Nevertheless, he did require and obtain another, one of those days. *Peter Parley's Magazine* and other instructive volumes in my library had taught me how folks at the seashore made and sailed their ships and I determined to improve our own. All we would really need would be a mast, a boom, a bowsprit, another sprit to spread our canvas, and a mainsail. Anything like a keel, ballast, or rudder, was not in my head nor upon my boat. Grandmother Osborn gave me half of an old sheet for my mainsail and I somehow obtained cordage for the rigging.

Such a ship as that might well be steered with a paddle but it was just as well that her crew had already been taught to swim. One splendid Summer day, Hank and I set out upon our trial trip and we got our gallant bark past the bridge by taking down the mast so she could go under. The wind was fair, the way was clear, and we glided on and out upon the glittering waters of the Lower Pond in complete security. Thus far, with the wind astern, we had needed no keel nor any other addition to our outfit, but now I saw before me an opportunity. I had learned from my books that all ships tacked, at times, and sailed right across the edge of the wind. That was what I now would do and I fearlessly made my first tack. The ship obeyed her helm but, as she did so, the wild wind smote her rippling mainsail sidewise, so to speak, and in one moment our voyage was ended. The boat was on her beam ends and was filling fast while Hank and I were paddling for the shore. I think that he gave it up entirely and sat upon the shore to drip and to guess what his folks would say about it, while I went out again and pulled the boat in to bail her out. We went upstream without help from sail or wind and we were admonished not to try that thing again. My admonition came from one of the apple trees down in the garden. In fact, it was at an early stage of my Homer experiences that I discovered why apple trees so meanly sent out sprouts or "suckers" near their roots, and why even a sweet-smelling "balm of Gilead" tree would follow their pernicious example. It may or may not have been true that the sprouts grew larger as I grew older, but since then I have met men of whom I feared that in their earlier days their educators either did not own any apple trees or did not understand the moral and intellectual bearings of pliable sprouts.

The Lower Pond had a few distinguishing characteristics. One of these was said to be that owing to the reception of much refuse from the slaughter house, below the bridge, its eels were more numerous and fatter than elsewhere, but I vainly tried to catch one of them. They may have been too well fed but all of us boys complained of the unbiting habits of the fish in that river. It may be that they had too many hooks offered them and became educated in the art of self denial in that shape. After a while a wide area was added to the pond, and it was mostly quite shallow. Here, indeed, I had a new experience, for the pickerel would lie and bask in the shoals and I could drift along toward them silently until near enough to shoot them, after learning how much below the apparent fish the refraction of sunshine in the water required me to aim. I actually brought home a reasonable number of them and some were not shot at all but only stunned long enough for me to scoop them in. On the easterly bank of the pond was a long meadow and near it were wheat fields. Both were a choice feeding ground for meadow larks and blackbirds. The larks were hardly fair game and I did not care for blackbirds except at one season. When, however, at the end of a season, they were gathering for migration and were fat and fine, they were sure to gather among the acres of low bushes of the flaggy swamp on the opposite side of the pond and were worthwhile. I remember one morning's shooting when Hank Babcock and I took home fat birds enough for potpies for both our houses and some to spare.

In the Winter time, both ponds would often afford good skating and so would the overflowed swamp land on the western hillside, not far from Paris Barber's black barn and the big butternut trees. I used up two or three pairs of skates and bumped the back of my head severely while I was a resident of Homer and investigated those sheets of ice.

Spice Island became a rare resource, after I had dipped into *Robinson Crusoe,* a work which I believe to be not yet out of print. I shortly undertook to be cast away upon Spice Island, as he was upon his. Aided by Hank Babcock and Hank Short, the son of our neighbor the harness-maker, I constructed a palace of broken boards on the upper part of the island. We were short of cannibals but we found and took there an old furnace pot which was just the thing to cook in. We even had a length of old stove-pipe and a skillet and part of an iron kettle. In these appliances we boiled potatoes, gathered in the fields on the mainland, when we did not prefer to roast them.

We also cooked fish, when we could catch any, but I had bad luck in one of our many daring expeditions after eggs. Old Mr. Babcock had a fine, large hennery, up near his house, but Hank had not sufficient enterprise to visit it on a collecting tour. The duty, therefore, fell upon me. It was a warm, Summer afternoon when I ventured there for a supply of fresh eggs. I was barefooted, as was usual with me in warm weather, and had on a "shilling straw" hat. Anything more expensive would have been wild extravagance, for a boy who had more than once been known to come home bareheaded. Well! I reached the hennery all right and was superfluously successful in finding eggs. I had my straw hat in my hands when I came hurrying away, down the garden path. I was a complete success until I heard somebody laugh and looked up to see Mr. Myron Babcock, Hank's grown-up brother, standing in the path before me. It was a moment of defeat, perplexity, and exasperation, and in my haste I stubbed one of my toes. That is, I tripped and fell forward, coming down full weight upon my hatful of fresh eggs. Not one of them but followed the example of stampeded soldiers upon a lost battlefield, they all broke and ran. It was too late for me to run and our entire force was shortly compelled to surrender ignominiously. The other boys obtained prison rations of strap oil and I of apple tree luxuriances. We did not give up our island fort, however, and just as the autumnal floods were arriving to sweep it away, we all three and one more boy with us had a thrilling adventure there in the early darkness of a gloomy evening.

We went over in our boat, of course, and we hitched it well before we went into the cabin to play Crusoe. It was grandly romantic fun until we were startled by the whang of a stone upon the wooden walls of our citadel. Another and another came and one of the boards was knocked off. Then we heard yells and shouts of derision from the mainland and the nature of our dilemma was explained to us. A lot of the uptown boys, with whom all the downtown boys were at feud, had ruthlessly undertaken to bombard us. The other boys crouched down as if they were frightened but I became wrathful. Out I dashed to get to the boat and they crept over the grass after me. Alas, for us! The wicked marauders had stolen our pretty scow and had hauled her upon the land on the other side of what was now really pretty swift and deep water. Then they had gone further and were hidden by the increasing darkness. Here we were, apparently helpless and "marooned," while still the flying pebbles were rattling upon the island, occasionally hitting our doomed shanty. It seemed as if the boys had now something worth crying for but I took a different view of the situation. It was necessary to regain that boat and into the uncommonly cold water I went, without hesitation. That was not what our assailants were expecting and before they suspected such a military or naval maneuver, I had crossed the raging flood, swimming and wading, and was quietly paddling my boat back after my crew. In they came and all of us were shortly and in silence landed downstream near the bridge, without pursuers. We were safe, but I believe that was the end of Mr. Crusoe's adventures upon Spice Island. The Winter floods carried away his palace and he did not care to build another.

Many another memory lingers along the crooked lines of the Tiough-neauga and one which I will not omit belongs to the wonderfully beautiful nests of the fishes. I never tired of watching those beds of gathered gravel and the finny folk who came and went around and over them. It was such an unanswerable conundrum, how did the fish manage to pick up all those little stones and carry them and arrange them in the nests? I had watched birds at their nest making and knew how they did it, but never did I actually see a fish with a pebble in his or her mouth. Probably, they knew I was watching them and were determined that I should not discover the secret of all that transportation. I was curious, indeed, as to all manner of stones and I knew the names of all the kinds in that vicinity. The habit of studying the rocks stuck to me for many a long year. Among my earlier and later mineral trophies, moreover, were Indian arrowheads, spearheads, hatchet heads, and I wish I had been able to retain the collection that I made. It passed from me, in the end, leaving behind it little more than some knowledge of the ways of the red men and a strong conviction that what some wise anthropologists call "the stone age" is not so very far from ours in point of time. It might be of more instructive value if among their gathered bits of shapely flint they had found an ancient oyster or tomato can, such as those by the vast heaps of which future ages may yet study our own tinsel civilization. It may not be out of place to add that with Grandmother Osborn's assistance, I also garnered a knowledge of the names and qualities of every tree, flower, grass, root, and plant of which I had a chance to inquire during all those questioning years. On that account, I might be entrusted with the collection of wild herbs for her uses and of sarsaparilla, checkerberry, and other ingredients for the manufacture of "root beer."

7

The Hill and the Woods

My acquaintance with the regions east of the river did not fairly begin until the following Spring. Just at the end of the cold weather, there was a brace of fine calves in the barnyard and one of them was assigned to me as my own peculiar property. The title to that calf may have been somewhat defective but I valued it all the same. It did not altogether cease, indeed, after the greater part of the pretty animal was turned into veal. The hide was still declared to be mine and I conveyed it, in the baby wagon, all the way to the tannery. Thence, in due season, it returned in the shape of leather and was devoted to the manufacture of my own shoes for the Winter next to come.

During all the remainder of my stay in Homer, such was the history of my pet calves and such was the origin of my footgear. That first Spring, while yet the calves were on the earth, so to speak, the grass greened in the broad and sloping pasture on the hill. At once began my career as cowboy and the critters of some of our neighbors were brought to climb the hill with them. It was serious business and promotive of early rising, for it was needful for me to be at home from my cow driving in time to reach the Academy before its bell ceased ringing. It was a study in punctuality but I was to have other studies on the way. One of these grew out of the tendency of all the hill dogs to bark at any cow from the village. I had many stones to throw and runs to make but a particularly troublesome point was at the forks of the roads at the foot of the hill. An alarmed or exasperated cow was as likely as not to set off at speed up or down one of those other highways.

The worst of the situation grew out of the boisterous character and muti-nous conduct of a cur owned by the Ford boys, who lived in the red house at the forks. My own dog, Watch, who disappears from my memory at about that time, was not worth two cents for protection and I was unsupported. Stoning a dog is a small incident to anybody but a small cowboy, but I was to meet the Ford family again. Long afterwards, as I will tell in its place, John Osborn died in the house of his friend, old Mr. Ford. Long, long years after that, when I was a deacon in Alexander Avenue Baptist Church, in New York City, I discovered that one of my most highly esteemed brother deacons was the elder of the Ford boys whose dog had troubled my cows at the forks of the hill road. Moreover, he had two sons, and both of them were already frequent visitors in my family. In fact, neither of them ever got out of it, for the younger, Charles Bigelow Ford, married my daughter Mabel—God bless them both and their children!—while the older, E. Lewis Ford, married my sister-in-law, Harriet Louise Cooper, and obtained one of the best of women. I do not quite determine whether he is a brother-in-law or a nephew and am willing to call him both.

There were several houses on the road before getting to the bars of our pasture but the way was peaceful and the return easy. It was at night that the occasional waywardness of animal mental organizations now and then made trouble for me. If the cows were at the bars, waiting for me, all was well, but if they were wandering far and wide I had to do the same until they might be gathered and brought to a sense of duty and to the gap in the fence.

There was a ploughed field at the roadside beyond our pasture, but above that, spreading over all that part of the hill, were the gloom and the green-ness and the beauty of Shearer's woods. Among them were sugar maple trees, at the feet of which I bye and bye learned the art of sugar making. Chipmunks were numerous along the fences and among the branches were squirrels, red and black and gray. I was to spend days and days among those woods and others, after I became master of the gun then hanging upon its hooks at the foot of the garret stairway. There was not one solitary oak or pine among them and it was long before I was to know anything about them. Maples, beeches, butternuts, hemlocks, birches, ironwood, basswood, and some others, were to be found, but I was told that all the chestnut trees had been cut down for fence timber because their trunks would split so easily and straightly. Far down to the southward were the Hemlock Woods, back of the precipitous cliffs of the old stone quarry. They were the right place to go to for sassafras and sarsaparilla but were vastly more precious on account of their abundance of wild raspberries, red and black. But then I only knew them as "rawsberries," like other Homer boys, and resented the rasp when told of it.

The woods, of course, bring me to my gun. I think it was in my eighth or ninth year that my grandfather began to teach me how to use it. I was carefully taught the mystery of its flint lock and soon was able to take the entire piece to pieces, clean it, and put it together again. It after a while became a frequent companion, with which I went out and wandered unquestioned. I can remember, once, when my father, on a visit from Syracuse, remonstrated at the idea of making a hunter of so young a boy. "Oh," responded my grandfather, "Willie is a pretty good shot. He is trustworthy. He only has the gun on condition of always going alone. He is not allowed to take any other boys with him." That condition of care may account for the strong liking I acquired for my solitary wanderings among the woods. I brought home game, too, furred or feathered, and was all the while gathering physical endurance as well as a high degree of confidence in my ability to find my own way anywhere. Not once did I get lost or feel any doubt as to the right way home from wherever I might be. Perhaps my longest jaunt was one which took me on from forest to forest, one beautiful autumnal day, until I came out upon a bold headland with a broad valley below me. I was struck, child as I was, with the exceeding fairness of the scene which I had discovered. It was a vision of enchantment and I can see it now. No one was there to tell me at what I was gazing, but I knew that the bright strip of winding water at my right must be the Tioughneauga. Then the larger stream at the left must be the upper, west fork of the Chemung and I could see where they mingled into one.

Far on to the southward must then be the place where Anthony Wayne's[1] men fought the Iroquois and forever broke the power of the Six Nations confederacy. I sat and looked at it all for a long time and I must have needed a rest, tough as I was. I needed another and a long one after getting home. It is strange to me, even now, that I was allowed, when not yet ten, to spend day after day in the forests, alone with my gun. At the same time, too, I was practicing with the short barreled rifle-bore pistols and was becoming quite an expert. I believe I can do better, to this day, with a derringer pistol than with a long barrel. One of my most annoying disadvantages as a sportsman arose from the costly nature of both powder and shot and out of that financial consideration grew about my first acquaintance with the great and perplexing currency question. The circulating medium of rural New York, in those days, was in need of a sweeping reform. Its copper was to the last degree miscellaneous, like that of Rochester, as I had seen. The silver was almost entirely Spanish or Mexican and all trading was transacted in shillings and sixpences. The name had its origin, for the Spanish dollar was a "piece of eight," as is known to all readers of *Robinson Crusoe,* and each of its eight "reals" is of nearly the cash value of the colonial "pinetree shilling," sometimes called a York shilling. Of course, these shillings were worth twelve and a half cents each. Of gold there was absolutely none in circulation and I think I never saw an American gold coin until I was in my teens.

The all but universal medium, therefore, was bank notes, and these, like the copper, were miscellaneous. I remember hearing that the only sure way to detect a counterfeit was to compare it with a bill known to be good. If the new bill proved to be better made it was probably spurious, for the counterfeiters were splendid workmen. Much bad money was said to be afloat and the expert detectives were rare in all that region. Added to these were the innumerable remnants of the unredeemed promises of broken banks. Now it happened that among my treasures in the garret was that old red chest of my father's. In it were stacks of canceled checks, with which, as my arithmetic prospered, I was allowed to play "store." All the contents of the chest were fully and formally presented to me and I had clear, definite ideas upon the subject of property. All went well until one day when, delving at the bottom of the coffer, I uncovered a time-worn wallet. Open it came and in it were the treasures of Crusoe's island. There they lay, that heap of one dollar bills, and with me was no one to advise me that these were counterfeit and broken bank relics of the deceptions practiced upon my father's clerks and salesmen. Whatever they might be, they were indisputably my own and I proceeded to use them as such. I think I am not in error in believing that my part ownership in my boat dates from that discovery. Very sure am I that my powder horn and shotbag were shortly full to overflowing with a surplus for future consumption. Fishing lines and hooks came with the other ammunition but so, ere many days, came a crash in the currency, for one of the bills returned in disgrace and had to be redeemed by John Osborn. Then out was hunted the secret of my liberal expenditures and my wealth disappeared as does all fictitious capital in a "panic" for I had one of them. It may be a practical commentary upon the existing disorder of things to note that only that one bill ever showed its head again to trouble me or mine.

Having a gun of my own and being a sportsman, it was a matter of course that I took a lively interest in the village gun shop and particularly in the manufacture of rifles. I saw the long bars of soft iron bored out, day after day, and wished I had one of them. I was yet to own precisely such a soft-iron rifle and I am in doubt whether the inefficiency of my right ear dates in any manner from the bursting of it. I heard well enough afterwards, but when the breech of that rifle skipped past my ear so closely, I felt a jarring twinge all through my head. None would have been felt probably, if it had varied two inches in either direction. If that did any harm, more may have been done by the flying heel of our horse "Nig." He was sold about a year after I reached Homer, for he was only a four year old and not quiet enough for a family horse. He and I, however, had been good friends and I liked nothing better than to be allowed to get him out of the barn and lead him down to the river to water him. Leading was not all, for I delighted in making him play and prance around and he was always ready for a romp.

So it happened that on one of these trips he was no sooner out of the yard gateway than he began his fun. He jerked the halter from me in a twinkling and up went his heels. He had intended no harm but one of his hoofs hit me a little behind my right ear and I fell to the ground insensible. Nig ran to the river and out into the middle of it as if aware that he had made a mistake of some sort. I was carried into the house and it was a full half hour before consciousness returned. The surgeon in charge informed my mother that it was well the hoof glanced for if it had not done so I would not have known what hurt me. He may have meant that there would have been an end of me but his language was defective for, as it was, I knew nothing at all about it, except that it was three weeks before I was permitted to leave the house.

Any effect of either hit must, I think, have been hidden until later days, for in all my boyhood I had the keen hearing of an Indian hunter and could catch the chipper of a squirrel in the tallest tree.

8

The Academy and the Shop

L ong ago did the old Homer Academy building disappear in fire and smoke, but it was a great credit to the liberal-minded first settlers who planned and built it. I hope that when it was burned, the fire spared the cannon house so near it. There must have been time to take out the cannon, if anybody could find the key of the door. The Homer boys managed to do that, once. It was in an early Summer when the village trustees had inspected the honeycombed relic of the Revolution and had wisely decided that it was not in condition for the firing of Fourth of July salutes. It might burst and do harm to its artillerymen. Vast was the indignation aroused by that prudent decision. Did not the Homer boys know their own cannon, which they or their forefathers had captured from Burgoyne? At all events there came a dark night and a silent procession of young patriots across the green and when, shortly afterwards, the trustees peered in to take a look at the precious gun, it was not there.

An excited spirit of inquiry ran all over the village and so did the trustees. Barns and outhouses were searched and so were the woods. All was in vain and something like a mystery brooded silently over the whole affair until the night before the Fourth. Then there was another youthful procession and precisely at midnight the villagers were startled from their slumbers by the loud beginning of the customary cannonade. There was the ancient gun and it was roaring its very best as if to express its indignation at its hard luck in having been imprisoned so long at the bottom of the Lower Pond, for that was where the patriotic boys had hidden it.

Of the Academy itself, as an institution of learning, I have few memories, except such as belong to the ordinary routine of a boy at school. There were elocutionary exercises in public, every Saturday forenoon, but these were the special province of the very largest students until one day when the ambitious youngster who had somehow won the nickname of "Old Put" or "Put Stoddard" managed to obtain the permission of the principal, Professor Woolworth, and marched out upon the high platform to recite "Hohenlinden" with variations of his own. He was a proud boy, for his elocutionary effort was well received and he was not called upon to repeat it.

In one of the reception rooms of the building were preserved the oil-painted portraits of the founders and among them was that of John Osborn. It is my information that the painting of those portraits was one of the earlier commissions of my friend Frank Carpenter,[1] the well-known artist of *The Signing of the Emancipation Proclamation*, for he was a Homer boy and was the first artist I ever heard of.

Not long after the signing of the Emancipation Proclamation, Frank conceived the idea of painting the scene of its presentation by President Lincoln to the Cabinet. In due season he came on to Washington on that errand and I introduced him to the president. Lincoln was pleased with the notion and its first fruits may be found detailed in Carpenter's book, *Six Months at the White House*.[2] Here he made his studies from the several originals, most of whom he hit off well—all except poor Mr. Caleb B. Smith, secretary of the interior, who to this day looks on the canvas as if he were made of wood, in spite of all I could [do] while his face was in process of putting into oil. [Smith died before Carpenter completed his canvas—ed.]

Long time went by and the picture was completed without being finished. Frank never finished anything in his life and no power could induce him to stop building a fence after the top rail was on. In his feverish imagination, there always ought to be some more rails. He came to me in something like despair, one day [years later—ed.]. A bill for the adoption of his picture for permanent lodgings in the Capitol had been prepared and presented but it had gone to sleep somewhere and he wanted me to go on and wake it up. I consented to go, if he would pay my expenses, for I was deeply interested in his undertaking, being aware that it had been Lincoln's desire that this memorial of the greatest event of his career should be made national property. Six times I went to Washington for Frank and often success was close upon us. It would surely have come, but for the habit of the House, or Senate, as the case might be, of putting all such bills off, to pass them in a confused lump at the close of the session. That is the way the bills to which I object get through and many of the measures of which I approve are drowned before they get ashore by the way in which the time of Congress is shamefully wasted in the antiquated grotesquerie of counting the yeas and nays and in the other antiquated humbug of allowing the most gaseous exhalations of long-corked senators or congressmen to use up for their own glory the precious time of the United States for which the said orators have been already fairly paid, so that it does not belong to them and they have no right to steal it from the people generally. Certainly not from any enthusiastic artist who has a national picture about to be adopted for the perpetual ornamentation of the Capitol.

[Back at the Academy,] the very large room at the southeast corner of the main story was the gathering place for over forty boys and girls, of all sizes. I believe that I was about the smallest member of that assembly and there came a time when I wearied of being told so and of being treated accordingly. There was no mischief in me, no spirit of revenge, but I was inventive and was fond of trying experiments. I tried one. A square pasteboard box was procured that shut into itself with a deep cover. An oblong cut in that cover developed a door which would open and shut. A small tin matchbox also had a cover which would go on and off. It was at a time when the old kind of exasperators were giving way before a new sort of sulphurheads, almost every other one of which would actually ignite by scratching instead of by being rubbed against a red hot coal, unless they put out the coal. It was early in a hot Summer day that I drove my cows to pasture and lingered among the thistles and other efflorescences all the way, coming and going. Bee after bee, honey and bumble, with wasp and hornet, many as might be found among the flowers, were captured deftly and transferred to the pasteboard box. I was not afraid of bumblebees for I had robbed many a nest of them with much battling and I also knew the nature and armament of a wasp. The box was densely populated therefore, with an entirely new class of Summer boarders and they buzzed outrageously, so that I was half afraid lest some enemy of their peace might discover them prematurely. The point with me was that all those ignorant insects were about to go to school.

My own seat and desk were in a corner near a window and within reach from that window was a lightning rod and I could climb. Before a great while, after the beginning of the day's educational toil, the big room was silent except for the buzz of whispered study and the voices of varied recitation, for the buzz in the box was as yet inaudible. Now, however, that imitation of Pandora's case was deftly pushed along at the end of a stick, until it was under an unoccupied desk not far from my own. Then a slight blow of the stick knocked off the cover and the new candidates for admission to the academy were free to present their credentials. Every bug of them was angry enough to do so and they all arose into the Summer air in a humming throng. That was at the very moment when I myself was getting out of the window and reaching for the lightning rod. Upon that I clung for only long enough to discover that the schoolroom had suddenly become a scene of heterogeneous and exclamatory confusion.

During days which followed, the wise men of Homer struggled with the problem of how so many different kinds of stinging insects could have broken out of the same nest and how and why they had made their nest in the schoolroom. Very similar problems are at this day floating around among the latest works of the greatest scientists. As for me, I held my peace, as became a small and unassuming scholar, but thirty years afterwards, I heard my cousin Matilda Bright, now Mrs. Hughes of London, relating to a circle of friends the story of that sudden breaking up of the morning session of the Homer Academy. She had been in the room at the time. I was glad to be able to solve for her the mystery but if it had been divulged at an earlier day I fear that my own part in the matter would have been looked upon with strong disapprobation. As for anything else that happened in the Academy, I was only half sure who it was that climbed into the belfry in midwinter and so packed the bell with snow that it would not ring at all, next morning. Neither did I know, for sure, who it was that drove Judge Keep's red cow into the chapel and all the way up stairs and left her with her horned head projecting from one of the upper windows. If I was learning some things at the Academy, I was also finding out a great deal at the shop and I really liked that school the better of the two.

In much that interested me, the forge and its accompaniments, for instance, there is little worth telling. One specialty which fascinated me was the melting of chopped-up Mexican dollars and the molding of long bars to be rolled out thin for the manufacture of silver ornaments for the Indians. I was willing to be my grandfather's assistant in any amount of silver work, including the stamping out of small articles, in which I actually acquired some skill. Deeper and sometimes almost breathless was my interest in the red men themselves and in their squaws and papooses. When they came to see John Osborn, they were sure to be arrayed in their best for they had great respect for him and he was their counselor in many affairs as well as their silversmith. He had been of service to them during his long legislative experience at Albany. The warriors, as a rule were dressing much like white men, but the squaws adhered to their picturesque natural apparel, beadwork, porcupine quill work, and all, and they invariably wore moccasins. Of these, I myself wore out several pairs and found them a comfortable kind of footing. More than that, my first bow, and it was a good one, was made for me by an Onondaga warrior. It may appear that my acquaintance with Indian affairs began early and my after liking them is accounted for.

My best and most important school, all the while, was my own home. In it was the quiet and gentlemanly wisdom of Squire Osborn, the gentle and watchful care of my grandmother, and, most of all the overruling presence of my exceedingly lovely mother. I think of her, now, as an embodiment of unvarying patience, dignity, cultivation, and intelligence, with the addition of graceful manners and a keen sense of humor. It is upon my mind that not any other boy in the village found his mother's copy of Bacon's *Essays* fairly interlined with critical and analytical comments, and it was so with some of her other books.

Our family circle was now full. My sister Julia was in her teens and was developing at her piano a good talent for music. My sister Kate was a fat and merry little girl and my brothers, Henry, Charles and John, were aged down as regularly as the steps of a ladder. I must say that I regarded them all as small boys, too young to be entrusted with any kind of sportsmanship. As for that, had I not fished all over the several "Little York Lakes," a dozen miles away, with my grandfather? Had I not been with him as far away as Skaneateles Lake, for the capture of big pickerel and lake trout? Had I not even driven cows as far as Preble, seven long miles, and found my own way home on foot with three earned shillings in my pocket? I felt ready, after that, to take a whole drove of cattle to Syracuse or Albany. In the Autumn of the year in which I passed my ninth birthday, however, there was prepared for me a journey of extent and importance, for it let me out of Homer again and gave me a glimpse of a larger world, several times larger and full of all manner of things that were new and strange.

9

Syracuse: The Young City

ot a city at all but still possessing only a village organization, was Syracuse when the stagecoach which bore me rolled into it, in the latter part of September [1844]. I was received by my father at his boarding place, the American House, on the site of which the First Presbyterian Church was afterwards erected. It was a grand experience to eat supper in so big a hotel, but a larger one came next morning when I went down with him to the bookstore of Stoddard and Babcock. The latter was a Cortland County man, from Truxton, the home of the Dixons and Whites, and I at once took a liking to him. Just how much of railway track had at that date been constructed, I do not know, but a vast, hollow, smoky railway depot stood in the middle of the village. It reached all the way through from Salina Street to Warren Street.

Next to it, on Salina Street, the longest and most important thoroughfare owned by the corporation, was William Winton's Hotel and next to that was our store. At the upper side of that square was Canal Street and the canal itself, spanned by bridges, there and elsewhere. Of the store, I need as yet say nothing, nor of the depot, for I was at once turned over to the care of friends with whom I was to visit. The first of these were Horace White's family and Andrew White in particular. Then began the treasured friendship which has lasted to the present day. Of his father, then the cashier of the Onondaga County Bank, I saw but little, except at meal times, but I took to him, for he was full of fun and tried hard to make me like Congress water, of which he was using freely. I drank some of it and then broke off, much preferring what was called "Teall water," from Mr. Oliver Teall, the originator of the village water works.

One of my first explorations of the municipality led me, in company with Andrew, his younger brother Horace, and some of our friends, to see a walking match at Winton's Hotel. Two planks had been set upon barrels in the long front room of the tavern and upon these a pair of pedestrian rivals were pacing back and forth. It looked to me like boy's play and I promptly offered to walk against any boy in Syracuse but the challenge was not taken up.

Only a few evenings afterwards, however, I might have suspected, if I had been wiser, that Andrew and his crowd, including Jeff Hall and Carroll Smith and some older fellows, were inclined to let me follow my own lead, if it would but lead me into fun for the people. There was to be a great temperance meeting in a public hall and they went with me in a swarm. They gathered near a small table, well forward. An eloquent orator had spoken and subsided and hardly had he seated himself before there came an unexpected addition to the program. His successor may not have been quick enough in arising to fill the vacancy and it was filled for him. I had avowed a conviction that I could beat that speaker and in an instant I was standing upon the table. The crowd may not have recognized me correctly but they cheered enthusiastically and I spoke right along. When afterwards I became a young citizen of Syracuse, man after man shook hands with me as the youngest temperance orator he had ever heard and favored me with choice quotations from my address. I have made more than one speech since then that was not so well received by the audience.

After spending a few pleasant days with the Whites, I was transferred to Judge Johnson Hall's, on Warren Street, for the Hall family also were almost as if they had been kindred. Where else I went and what I saw or what I saw or did is a kind of far-off mist now. What I was really doing, nevertheless, was of importance, for I was making the acquaintance of a town into which my entire family was soon to find its way. Only one year more was left of my Homer life, for when the leaves began to wither in the following Autumn, our household goods were in wagons, our family was in a coach, and the valley of the Tioughneauga was behind us. At the end of that trip was a great change in my life. I was ten years of age, with a curious suggestion always in my mind that I was much older. Among other things which I had left behind me was my old nickname of "Put" and as yet I was unable to guess when, how, or why I was to obtain another.

Long before there had been any considerable settlement at Syracuse, a prosperous village had formed upon the shore of Onondaga Lake, a mile or so northward. The Indian name of that water had been Genantaha and was said to have something to do with the fact that the deer came to that neighborhood to enjoy the "salt licks." At all events, the salt springs had attracted the white men and a profitable salt-making interest began its growth soon after the red men lost control of Onondaga Valley. The little river of that name which runs through Syracuse into the lake had also an Indian appellation of its own and it was said to mean "Crooked Creek." I never tried to find the source of it, but I was soon acquainted with all there was of it for several miles from its mouth. It made a millpond on the east side of the village, of land which is now occupied by houses.

The canal, on a due east and west line, and Salina Street, running due north and south, determined the topography of the entire town, except where it was interfered with by old roads and the windings of the creek. The line of the railroad was only one long block south of the canal and of course its presence gave the name to Railroad Street. There was then no such corporation as the New York Central. As I now remember, there was an Albany and Schenectady Railroad; a Schenectady and Utica; a Utica and Syracuse; an Auburn and Syracuse; an Auburn and Rochester; a Syracuse and Rochester Direct, and a Rochester and Buffalo, all built at different dates as separate enterprises. It would be worth any young man's while, today, to go as I did and make a study of that railway as it then was in Syracuse.

The rails were thick straps of wrought iron, spiked down upon logs. When the head of one of those rails worked loose, by the breaking of its spike or the rotting of its log, it would sometimes fly up at the arriving car wheel and penetrate the car itself, dangerously. There were sad stories told of the work of those "snake heads," as they were called. The engines were unlike anything that is to be seen nowadays, but they were said to carry express trains at the dangerous speed of twelve miles an hour. Think of a passenger car letting go of its iron strap at a gait like that! Passenger boats were still running on the canal and it may be that many people distrusted the steam wagons.

Years afterwards, I went to inspect the first T rails, before one of them was put down. Their use was still a matter for discussion, and I was confidently assured by an eminent citizen that they would never be adopted. They were not only unwieldy but were much too expensive. No railway would ever have business enough to carry such extravagance as that. Then there came a time when the venturesome railway company caused the construction of the wonderful locomotive "Lightning." It was believed to be capable of going a mile a minute. It actually did so, with one passenger car and one freight car. I worked hard to get a ticket for that first trip of the Lightning between Syracuse and Rochester and expected to find the passenger car jammed with fellows eager to have the credit of riding that race against time. It was hardly so, for my fingers and toes would have done for the counting of our human freight. Did they all miss the train, or were there secret doubts as to the fate of that engine?

I suppose I must leave the road, now, and come back to our first house and its neighborhood. It was on Fayette Street, two doors above the Park, and it was a two-story red brick house. Of course, it was detached and had front, side, and back yards. Except [for] the hotels and stores, there was not then a three-story house in the village, nor was there a connected "block" until two years later, when a gentleman named Farmer ventured upon the very doubtful experiment of building one. It was a permanent success! Fayette Street and the Park were but one square south of Railroad Street and our house was only a few minutes walk from the middle of the village. So was everybody else's house unless they lived out of town or up in Salina. The other name for that was "Salt Point," only that some of the wicked boys gave it a worse one yet, by way of translation. It is now the First Ward of the Central City.

The Park was an oblong of about the size of a city square. It had a neat wooden fence around it and much grass and shrubbery in it but its glory was its fountain in the middle. I saw that fountain play, once, squirting real water to prove that it could do so. I am not sure that it ever did it again. Around the Park were the residences of some of our most substantial citizens. At the upper-right-hand corner was Hamilton White's house. He never spoke to small boys but his wife did and she was a special friend of my mother.

When we came, a large house on the Fayette Street side was occupied by the Wyman family and I was there a good deal with the Wyman boys, but it was afterwards purchased by Horace White and that made Andrew again my near neighbor. Just above that place was the Butler house and the two Butler children, John and Mary, were soon prime favorites with us while their mother won my highest admiration and esteem. Then came a large open yard in the middle of which was Bill Teall's law office with a swinging squirt of water in front of it. That was a lesson in hydraulics, for the water itself spun the squirt, which was remarkable. On the upper corner, toward our house, was the Fitch place and that too became one of my abiding places. Across, on our corner, was the Forbes house, but Burnet Forbes was too much my junior. Opposite that, next to Hamilton White's was the Outwater house and in it were jewels. Mrs. Outwater was one of them, and her daughter Mary, afterwards Mrs. Andrew D. White, was the other.

On the other side of the Park were fine residences and lovely families but I will not catalog them now. It is enough to say that never elsewhere, within the same space, have I known such a settlement of excellent people. I already had acquaintances among "the Park Boys," as all who lived near it were called, and I soon knew all the rest. The Wyman boys went to the Parochial School of St. Paul's Church but all the rest went to the "Academy" kept by Messrs. Allen and Stebbins in the upper floor of the big wagon shop just below the Park on the right. I must not forget to mention that the Congregational meetinghouse faced the lower end of the Park, for that brick building was to have a great deal to do with me. As for the school, there had once been a genuine academy in Syracuse. Its founders, however, had been ahead of their time and had built their large, expensive brick edifice away out of town on a hill. It looked well, at a distance, but it was too long a walk to reach it for any but its few near neighbors. Its finances also kept away from it and it was at last voted a failure. As an academy it ceased to be, but, to the great credit of our citizens, it survived as a well-filled and well-sustained orphan asylum. My mother was almost immediately elected one of the trustees of that institution and I have heard from Mrs. Hamilton White that when any subject of importance was before the board it was sure to be tabled if she were not present, for several of them would refuse to decide until they "had heard what Sarah Osborn had to say about it," for they had known her in her girlhood. She was a good majority, at any time, with all who really knew her.

I was a busy boy during that first Winter in my new country. Then, as afterwards, I was the factotum and errand boy of the family, besides having the school to attend and the bookstore to investigate. Spring came and the Summer and all sorts of fun with the Park Boys and I think it was on that Fourth of July that I discovered what might be done by inventive genius for a young city which did not have any Burgoyne cannon. The big wagon shop near the corner of the Park possessed a tremendous anvil and the foreman of the shop was a true patriot. So, perhaps, was the anvil, for in it was a deep, square hole, large enough to admit the shank of the cold chisel used in severing iron bars for wheel tires. When that anvil was hauled out into the wide open space near the shop, it cheerfully assumed the attitude of a piece of ordnance. Much powder might be poured down the throat of that chisel socket and a hard wood plug hammered in on top with a small aperture on one side for priming. If then a paper slow match were lighted in due relation to the priming, all that we boys had to do was to stand still and see it burn, for a truly national bang was sure to reward us in a few seconds. We fired salutes for all the states and territories and for the flag itself, the night before the Fourth, until all our ammunition was used up and it was time to go home and see what our several families might have to say about it.

Autumn came again and with it were important changes. One of these was in the school, for it disappeared. Perhaps it was because the wagon shop had changed owners and perhaps it was because Professor Allen had gone into the music business and had opened a new store on Salina Street, opposite our own. He had also undertaken classes in singing and where Mr. Stebbins went I never knew. The place of that academy was shortly filled by another kept by a Mr. Weld in the conference-meeting building of the old, and about to be abandoned, Congregational Church, near the middle of the village. I attended it, of course, but my memories of its instructive power are vague. One of them is the frequent assurance of Mr. Weld that if we did our duty by our books we might in time become even presidents of colleges, and that such a prospect was perpetually responded to in my mind by a blind self assurance that I did not wish to become any such thing. I would vastly rather be something else, and if the other boys were of my mind, all but one of them had his own way.

The other change carried me away from the Park for a short distance, as my father had secured a more commodious residence on Onondaga Street, between Salina and Warren Streets. My father's business was now flourishing, his family was growing, and all the future appeared to look reasonably bright. I was not by any means separated from my former playfellows and I immediately began to make new ones and at the same time to reach out into the surrounding country for [in 1846] I had attained the ripe age of eleven.

10

The Onondaga Street House

Our new house was somewhat larger than the other, [with] a high stoop basement, two stories, and a most attractive garret. There was also a considerable frame addition in the rear, a woodshed with finished rooms over it. The garret was promptly preempted in memory of the grand one in Homer and became a new realm of work for me. There was a general likeness between this and the Fayette Street house, externally, and another in the fact that both were infested with large Norway rats upon which I might now and then practice with my gun, which my grandfather had permitted me to bring with me. Here, however the yards, fore, side, and aft, were larger and more susceptible of improvement, if hencoops are to be regarded as entitled to that ascription.

Hardly were we settled before there came one more reminder of my earlier experiences. Warren Street, at the left, was only the continuation of the old stage road down the valley to the Indian Reservation and the red men and their families were frequent visitors in Syracuse. It offered them their best market for berries, moccasins, bows, small game, and other products of their otherwise not very well tilled acres. Before long they became frequent visitors at our house and my old interest in and studies of them were renewed. Added to this was the fact that only one square beyond Salina Street on the right was Onondaga Creek, with the pond just below, as near to me as had been the Tioughneauga, and about as hopeless a stream to fish in. I was never to own a boat on it although I once did build one, with immense toil, and it positively refused to float after I dragged it to the creek and launched it. I had not acquired the art of shipbuilding at that time and many of the ships which I afterwards built and sent to sea did not come back again.

I shall not attempt any tedious and useless accuracy concerning precise dates, but if I were to attempt to correct my cloudy chronology at this point, I should place our entry into our new home on the first of May, in the middle of my eleventh year, leaving behind me a year and a half in the Fayette Street house. That may have been the reason why so soon afterwards I seem to have had a long Summer vacation for purposes of exploration in the neighborhood and elsewhere.

Be that as it may, I was well supplied with powder and shot and my head was filled with the legends which I had heard concerning the many attractions of Onondaga Lake and the forests around its western shore. The eastern shore was occupied by villages, farms, saltworks, and I took no manner of interest in its somewhat shabby civilization. Only the village of Salina had attractions, for in the edge of it boats were to be obtained and in it were the residences of several families whom I knew and liked.

The lake may be somewhat over six miles long and at its widest place about two miles wide. In Summer it contains any amount of undisturbed fishing and in Winter it often affords good skating. In very cold Winters it sometimes also furnishes a fine temporary horserace track. In Spring and Fall, the wild ducks and geese gather here to discuss the propriety of a southern trip and numbers of them go to the Syracuse markets instead.

Their interruptions, for the greater part, are occasioned by what some sportsmen deride as "pothunters" and the favorite ducking method of these gentlemen requires a small flock of wooden decoy ducks. When these deceptions are anchored at point-blank range from the shore, the real birds, in search of companionship, will come and alight among them. The man with a gun, hidden behind a breastwork of bushes, then has them almost at his mercy, but I saw one eager shooter fall into a kind of trap, once.

I was tramping along the lakeshore and caught a glimpse of a fine flock of decoys, bobbing up and down upon the water at some distance beyond me. At the same moment I espied an excited young man in pretty good clothes who was stooping, creeping, and dodging from tree to tree in his eager haste to reach that point upon the shore. He succeeded in doing so and then there was a careful taking of aim. Bang! Bang! went both barrels of his gun but his game did not so much as try to fly away and time was given him to reload. I was all the while drawing nearer, enjoying the sport, and had just reached the usual bush cover when both barrels went off again. So did an all but lunatic yell of laughter from a pothunter who was rolling upon the sand and trying to hold his sides in while he shouted to me that "That blessed lubber yonder is killing my decoys!" He discovered, himself, the sportsman did, that it was not worth his while to swim out after his well-peppered game and I think he at once traveled onward. On the whole, I found pretty good shooting around the lake and brought home many a creditable string of snipe and plover in their season. Away up the creek, above the village, was another range of lowland where I often went after snipe.

It was two or three years later before I accomplished much with ducks and the like. I then became better armed for long-range shooting. One day, in an old gun shop, I discovered a genuine, old-fashioned, bell-muzzled fowling piece, of the pattern with which our Pilgrim fathers killed deer and red men and their descendants blazed away at the British from behind the breastwork on Breed's Hill. It was heavier than any rifle I was acquainted with and its muzzle stood on a level with my cap front. Not yet had I obtained any reverence for relics of antiquity. In the most barbarous and ignorant manner, I purchased the priceless antique, had its bell muzzle sawed off and a sight put on, and had the great old flint lock exchanged for a modern percussion. It proved to be the best kind of "boat gun," but I honored the stalwart forefathers who were able and willing to tote such a weapon around all day. The amount of powder that was required to charge it fully accounted, in my opinion, for the historical fact that Putnam's men ran out of ammunition when the British came up the slope the third time. I believe I killed a diver with it at fourteen rods.

The other addition to my armament came from my friend Andrew White. He made me come home with him, one day, and showed me a really beautiful rifle which had been presented to him by a friend of his father. It had telescope sights and was a treasure of a gun, but he said to me: "Now, Will, the fact is that I never go hunting. I haven't any use for a rifle. You take it and use it as long as you want to, just as if it were your own. Take it home with, you, flask, pouch, and all." I was delighted to do so and if I afterwards became a pretty good rifleman, it was because I began practice so early with Andy White's beautiful gun. I kept it through several seasons, for he persistently refused to become a hunter.

My nearest boy neighbor was William Corning, in the frame dwelling on the southerly corner of Salina Street. He was a nephew of Mr. Corning of Albany,[1] the well-known iron merchant and politician, in whose business concern he afterwards became a partner. His father was a man of wealth and had been a minister of the Episcopal Church but had left the pulpit to devote himself to business pursuits and to scholarship. He was said to be a very learned man and he had at that time about the best library in the county. Before long that library was a favorite place of visitation with me. Its owner was a silent, gloomy faced, unbending sort of man, and was not popular on that account, but I shall always remember his unvarying kindness to myself.

I may have been something of a favorite, for he appeared to like to have me come and spend as much time as I pleased among his books. He was an antiquarian, an Oriental scholar, and his collection was rich in rare old copies, vellum-bound folios and the like, which were objects of deep interest to a boy who was beginning to believe that the world was made for books. Will Corning and I became partners and we soon discovered that we were much alike in one particular. Neither of us had enough pocket money for the continual drains of our small exchequers. We held more than one solemn council upon that subject and one day a brilliant financial idea came to me. It was chickens.

I had no coop but there was a small corncrib on one corner of the Corning place and we easily obtained lease of it, rent free. I had found out that fowl of all sorts might be purchased in the rural districts at lower prices than such as we could sell them for to hotels and dealers in the village. The next requirement was capital and Will Corning not only had none but was uncertain as to his father's confidence in his business ability. I had more impudence, if that was what I had, for I went right down to the store and laid my plans before my father, with a schedule of possible profits. He was standing at his counting-room desk and there were others listening. At the end of my program he smiled audibly and so, I think, did his friends, but he opened the cash drawer and handed me out five dollars. That was on a Saturday morning and Will and I were ready with our baskets for a chicken trip. It was in a vacation time and we omitted Sunday only from a week of unintermitting commercial enterprise. At the end of the week, I was able to go down to the store and pay back the borrowed five and report that I had as much more in my pocket, besides what I had paid to my industrious and vigorous partner. As I remember, we paid twelve, fifteen, and twenty cents a head, as the case might be, and sold readily at an average of twenty-five. It was only a question of how many we could find and carry, for the distances often made it hard work.

At the next Thanksgiving time, we had our old corncrib all but packed with garnered fowls, including turkeys, but there the season began to be against us and we wound up the business. Will went out of it entirely, but I had begun upon my own account in another direction. I had made enough to pay for the erection of some pretty good coops in our backyard and to buy selected stock to start them with.

There must have been purchases and sales to advantage during the Winter, as well as eggs and chickens, for in the Spring I was in funds. A neighbor named Hudson was a fowl fancier and had obtained some of the first Chinese fowls ever brought into this country. They were huge, they were new, and they were hard to get. Therefore they commanded high prices and Hudson made money out of his investment. So did I, for I paid him two dollars for a dozen of eggs, instead of ten for a pair of fowls, and I am sure that I obtained five dollars a pair for some of my chickens. Some of them I kept and remember well one rooster whose crow would have put to shame a trombone in the middle of the German band. At about this time, too, I became the happy owner of a pair of genuine Maryland gamefowls, of the ancient ante-revolutionary breed. They were indeed rarities, both for fight and for beauty, and I reared some of them with care, keeping them separate. As long afterwards as when my brother Charles joined me in Arkansas, he told me of a great cocking main between Onondaga and Cortland counties which he went to see. To his astonishment, it was won by a gang of "the Stoddard gamefowls," so long had the fame of my birds been kept up. In my own time, however, the net result was occasional trouble with neighbors whose roosters had wandered within reach of mine and did not return to their homes, and more than one unpleasant episode with the "sporting" fraternity and the birds which they brought unduly to be killed by mine.

More than that and in the way of fame, I won my new nickname, for it was not long before I saw "Game Stoddard" scrawled upon the fences of all that part of Syracuse, including the Park.

I must not forget that among my treasures, brought from Homer, was a small pickheaded tomahawk. It had formed part of the regalia of a company of pale-faced Albany Mohawks to which my grandfather had belonged when he was a young man and I learned to throw it into a tree, at short range, in the precise manner in which the red men never threw their own hatchets if they could do anything better with them. Somehow or other, it is always associated in my memory with a family legend often told me by my father. He said that he had been informed, when a boy, that one of his ancestors on the Avery side married a daughter of an Indian chief, Pequot or Narragansett, he thought the former, and that so we were descended from the oldest families in the country. At all events, his face and bearing and his very black, straight hair, would put any man in mind of an Indian of the best kind. He also had Indian traits of character, one of which was a disposition to take his own part. My own notably unpugilistic nature must have omitted most of the Pequot, but I was proud of the line of descent.

I had also kept my stone arrowheads and now added several more to my collection. Moreover, my interest in rocks increased, spurred a little, if I remember correctly, by my learned friend Mr. Corning, and I began to gather specimens. Among these, in the course of time, were a number of rare fossils from the famous Onondaga limestone formation. A geologist told me once that I had the only perfect trilobite he had ever seen, whatever that unusual bird of chaos may happen to be. To these were added, by way of ornament, a quantity of the lime crystals which are often formed to perfection in the process of the solar evaporation of salt water.

There was one feature of my collection which was a kind of testimonial to my mother's zeal and ability in sustaining foreign mission work. One of her early friends had become a somewhat noted missionary in India and he came home on a visit while we were in Homer. He brought with him a number of Oriental prizes in which I took an especial interest. In acknowledgment of her zeal, rather than mine, I may suppose, he made me the happy owner of a genuine "Hindoo" idol. It was a statue of Godama, sitting down crosslegged, carved elegantly in sandalwood and richly gilded. With it came a curious specimen of a Hindoo "shastra," or sacred book. It was a manuscript on heavy, dark-blue paper, about fourteen inches wide and unfolding to a length of eight or nine feet. The handwriting was white, large, and beautifully uniform. These were things which I was proud to show to my friend Mr. Corning, to convince him that I also was beginning to be an Oriental scholar. What became of them when at last our household broke up, I do not know. On the whole, my little front bedroom, over the front door, was beginning to be a curious kind of an affair and I was all the while on the lookout for further works of art and ornament.

1-1

Hoyt's School

I think it was at about the end of my twelfth year [in 1847] that the school enterprise of Mr. Weld ended. He may have had a call to some church or other, but at all events, Syracuse was once more without an "academy."

Several gentlemen who were encumbered with boys took the matter up and decided to have a first-class select school—very select—of their own. The number of students was at first limited to sixteen, but afterwards three or four additional fortunates were grudgingly admitted.

The basement of the Congregational Church, opposite the Park, was obtained for the schoolroom and was neatly fitted up with desks and benches. They were exceedingly fortunate in their selection of a teacher. He was a tall, handsome, pleasant-mannered young man, named Hoyt, and a more skillful instructor for such boys as we were it would be hard to find. From the very beginning, he enforced upon us the idea that we were distinctively "young gentlemen" and that we must never say or do or think anything ungentlemanly. Any boy who could not or would not live up to that hard rule had only one thing before him. He might expect to gather up his books and walk out of the schoolroom as a fellow who was unfit to be in it.

At the same time, Mr. Hoyt possessed a rare talent for getting young brains at work to the best advantage. He did his whole duty by us and made his mark upon every one of us. It is my opinion that the remarkable record of the boys of that school, selected material as they were, was largely due to the stimulus and direction which they received while under his care. I can sit at my desk now, and look around that schoolroom and I cannot find one failure in it. Yonder, in front, is our star boy, Andrew D. White, foreign minister and educator.[1] Just behind him are sitting three successful leading editors. There is a notably skillful surgeon. Across from him is a United States District Court judge. There are two army colonels. There is a prime good preacher. The rest are businessmen, lawyers, authors, and so forth, and among them all is but one hard case. He began brightly but he did not end well. I must sadly correct my assertion, for he, with fine abilities, was a failure, because he rejected the wise counsels of Mr. Hoyt and forgot to be a gentleman, for the Golden Rule and the Ten Commandments were made to us the fundamental thing in the idea we were to form of what might become a gentleman.

One of our lines of instruction, from the first, was in journalism, and our Saturday elocutionary exercises were varied by "compositions" and weekly journals, prepared, edited, and read by ourselves, each periodical having but one editor. The name of my own was *The Frolic Manual*, wherever I found such a name, and I obtained printed heads for it at a newspaper office. Immediately my invention was stolen, for the other editors went to the printers also. What made my own enterprise peculiar and somewhat celebrated as well as made fun of, was the fact that I was beginning to manufacture verses and each week found one or more strictly original poems in the columns of the *Manual,* to be read before the school by the unabashed author. By the way, our select school was considered to be a "Park Boys" affair, no matter what part of the village any member might come from, and it was a rival, somewhat at war, of the Parochial School of St. Paul's Church, of which we formed a poor opinion for it did not have any periodical press.

Our Saturday exercises were a great affair and were attended by our mothers and our sisters and our cousins and our aunts to an extent which turned them into a kind of social gathering and made us think very well of ourselves. Our games, ball and races, and wrestlings and so forth, were much the same as those of all other schoolboys everywhere, and I discovered that my somewhat peculiar physical education, as cowboy, boatman, and sportsman, had developed in me an unusual degree of toughness.

No boy of my own size in the school could throw me and my running jump was as good as any other fellow's but, to my great chagrin, a slender, handsome chap named Jacob Arnold, who was with us only for a few months, could run right away from me. All the while, my chicken business went along with good success and my "game" reputation grew until it was uncomfortable. At the beginning of the next Summer vacation, Mr. Hoyt invited the whole school to a grand fishing excursion and sail on Oneida Lake. We went in two hacks and an omnibus and we caught many fish. The really large and good-looking sloop that carried us on the lake gave me my first ideas of the rolling ocean and of the wide, wide sea.

Another year went by, and it was to me one of an exceedingly useful character. I was doing well at school and my early beginning in Latin, under Professor Dewey at Rochester, came to my help remarkably. So did my early arithmetic and mathematics. All the while, too, I was fairly devouring books at home, in all the intervals between the demands of my other miscellaneous avocations. It was in that vacation that I founded the Rambler's Club, for general pedestrian expeditions into the surrounding country. Its membership was somewhat variable and its trips were of all sorts, including hunting and small fishing. It was not uncommon for us to make from fifteen to twenty miles a day, before the end of the following Autumn. With me, alone or in company, a favorite jaunt was to Fayetteville, eight miles out, and this was the village in which Grover Cleveland had his early experiences.

My knowledge of its topography aided me afterwards in writing my *Crowded Out o' Crowfield*, which is the other name for Fayetteville. A year went by and we knew that Andrew White was to leave us and go to Geneva College, afterwards Hobart Free College, to prepare for Yale. None of the rest of us were yet old enough to think of college at once, but a strong determination grew in my mind that I would go, some day or other. It was not until just as the term was ending that we were informed by Mr. Hoyt, to our great grief, that he must say goodbye to us. Our banner school had come to an end and we were to see him no more. We had grown to regard him as our personal friend, to each of us individually, and there were some of the boys who actually cried at their desks.

As for me, I went back to the Rambler's Club, fowls, Onondaga Lake, and my books, with frequent visits to the bookstore, with all the appointments of which I had become thoroughly familiar. I do not mean that "our crowd" went to pieces. By no means, and one of our favorite ball grounds was the wide, gravelly open in front of the City Hall. Here we could play match games with even the boys of the Parochial School and chance comers from the village. Among these, however were the usual allowance of roughs and toughs, who were disposed to regard us with more or less contempt on account of our disposition to wear good clothes and all that sort of thing.

I must confess that we, on our part, had generally imbibed an impression that such fellows were the bodily superiors of our sort. They soon began to invade us, in various ways, and we understood that there might be trouble coming. Especially were we bidden to stand in awe of a certain marvelous young boxer who had earned the proud name of "Buffalo Jack" and was said to be a ferociously merciless fighter. So he may have been and he should not have interfered with a peaceable fellow like me. He did so, however, one day when we were playing baseball.

I was at the bat when a number of unbeautiful fellows came around the nearest corner and rushed in upon the ballground, with a yell. They were headed by the dreaded prizefighter and he made a set upon me, attempting to take away the bat. I am afraid that my mild temper gave way, for I threw the bat behind me and went for him. I knew that he must be the better boxer, and after a few swift exchanges I managed to close with him, for we were of about the same size. Almost to my astonishment, I quickly discovered that however good a boxer he might be, he was not a champion wrestler. I, on the other hand, had been in constant practice and had acquired some fine lessons at the expense of heavy falls.

All the other boys had suspended operations to watch the result, and I do not believe one of the Park Boys really expected for me anything but defeat, although they knew that I had thrown every one of them. It was a test of strength, for a minute's grapple, but then I was under his weight and up he came, over my right hip and down upon the gravel, so heavily that all the fight was banged out of him. It was a surprise and I was glad that he was not badly hurt, but I was ready for the next when they all, with one accord, walked away from the ballground, for their confidence had been in their leader and he was out of the muss. I do not remember that we ever were interfered with again. It is also my impression that I must amend my chronology and explain why we were all down there at the City Hall, for that is an important part of my story.

On the corner west of the City Hall Square was a large, four-story brick building, known as the Frazee block. The upper story of this building had been arranged for the meetings of the Odd Fellows and Free Masons and was therefore, with its main hall and anterooms, just the thing for educational purposes. The gentlemen who had presided as the originators of the Hoyt School had consulted with themselves and others and had determined upon another academical experiment. They had organized, to a certain extent, and had selected a Board of Trustees, of which my father was a member. They had also secured the services of a learned gentleman named Caruth, a Presbyterian clergyman, and the number of pupils was no longer limited. It included, however, nearly all of the boys of the old concern. There may have been forty, in all, at the outset, and the gravelly desert in front of the Hall was our natural playground. Before going on into the brief, peculiar history of Mr. Caruth's enterprise, I must say something more about that Summer.

More of my time than ever before had been spent in the bookstore, for which I had imbibed a strong liking. It was really as large and miscellaneous a library as any young bookworm need have asked for. It was also a place where all the odd characters of several kinds had formed a habit of drifting in and a fellow might see them to advantage if he took the interest in them that I did. It was during that vacation that I first became aware of the presence and very strong personality of a gentleman by the name of Wells, an old particular friend of my father, who was making frequent visits at the store and was able to tell stories to any crew he found there. He had great confidence in my father and a son of his shortly afterwards came into his care as a kind of guardian, for Mr. Wells himself had become a perpetual traveler. He had formed a wild idea of his own that, now the railroads were becoming hitched together at their ends, with Hudson River connections, there might be formed a system of small-package deliveries in all the towns along the lines. He called it an "Express," whatever that might be, and my father agreed with him as to the practicability of the notion, although cautious and critical men of business shook their heads and said that it could never be made to work, not to any paying extent.

Now, our store was a deep one, with an irregular jog at the rear, caused by the ins and outs of the hotel alongside. The width of the store at that end was diminished to nine feet and the length of that narrowness about twenty feet. When a coop at the far end was cut off by a high desk, that was just the place for an Express office. There, therefore, did Mr. Wells begin his crackbrained experiment, so far as Syracuse was concerned.

Before he had any office at all, I had seen him come striding in, carrying a heavy satchel, containing packages of value which he delivered in person. He was an industrious and cheerful man, with much fun in him and a tendency toward practical jokes. As soon as the packages began to come in any quantity, somebody had to take them to their destinations and I was that somebody, for I could charge from two to five cents for lugging the small merchandise and I was always in need of pocket money. It was in this way that I became the very first Express Messenger of Syracuse. It was not long before Mr. Wells took in a partner by the name of Fargo and there were endless puns upon that nomen and his, but I have since heard that the enterprise succeeded fairly well in spite of the prophets who averred that it would neither go far nor well.

After the opening of the Caruth School, I was, for a few weeks only cut down to morning and evening carrier work. I did take hold of my school books again with energy, but it quickly became evident that our new teacher was not by any means a good copy of Mr. Hoyt. He may have been both learned and experienced, but he knew very little about boys. He devoutly believed in the old and pernicious idea that all boys required more or less flogging. None of us felt any suspicions when he put into his desk what seemed an unnecessary allowance of flat rulers, but there was an inaudible buzz all over the room on the morning when he somewhat ostentatiously added to these a three feet cowhide. My own blood rose to the danger line at once and I was ready for mischief. I did not say anything at first except to some of our Park fellows, but I had my eye on "old Caruth."

It was in the third week of the existence of that institution of learning that Joe May, son of Rev. Dr. Samuel J. May, by all odds one of the very best behaved and studious boys in the school, was unjustly and severely punished with a ruler. That was shortly followed by a few strokes of the cowhide upon another chap, a newcomer, who may have been somewhat out of order.

The next day, I came to school with a burning in my face but all went quietly until the class in algebra was on the long recitation bench. Mr. Caruth had adopted the unwise precaution of carrying his cowhide with him, under his left arm, as a kind of intimidation or doleful warning. He was pacing dignifiedly up and down in front of the class and I was watching him. Suddenly he paused in his march and began to administer terrible cuts over the head and shoulders of a boy in the middle of the bench. It was Matthew Myers, son of another Presbyterian clergyman and an old boy of Hoyt's school.

I heard Matt call out "O! Moses!"—something or other—and I sprang forward, for the blows were again falling. Some of them actually drew blood and there were red marks upon his neck. It was afterwards stated by

Mr. Caruth that Matt "looked at him disrespectfully." I must have done at least that, for I was now standing in front of him, storming at the top of my lungs and forbidding him to strike another blow at any boy in that school. Strangely enough, he did not hit me, but turned and spoke to the whole crowd. Exactly what followed, I cannot now remember, but the school was in an uproar and several fellows whom he did go for were escaping across the desks and benches. It was a complete rebellion and all that the poor man could do was to lock us all in, take the keys with him, and go out upon a tour among the trustees to secure reinforcements.

As soon as he was gone, the boys who were already marked out for punishment were put into one of the anterooms, so that as soon as he returned and opened the large outside door they could slip by him and get out. I myself did not cut out in that way for there was a stove in the room and the cowhide and the rulers had been left behind by their owner. They were all in the stove in a twinkling and they burned well. The trustees did come, but they had seen the gouts upon the neck of Matt Myers and I believe they were mainly in sympathy with the rebellion. At all events, school was dismissed and it was never opened again. Whether or not it was at all as a consequence of my outrageous behavior on the flogging question, I do not know, but it was shortly decided that the proper place for me was in the bookstore as general clerk, salesman, messenger, and all-the-books reader.

This was a sudden change, but it was not one to which I had any disinclination. I had been under Mr. Hoyt a year and a half, but when he went away I had already mastered all the Latin and mathematics usually required in a freshman class at college, besides being well up in several other branches, but I had not touched Greek. I had reached the mature age of fourteen that September [of 1849] and it was now well on into the fall of the leaf. Tough as whipcord, full of fun and energy and ignorance, I was ready to march on into the future with little thought of what it might be.

12

The Bookstore

Speaking of corporal punishment, I had an earlier experience than that under Mr. Caruth. I think it was at the beginning of my ninth year that my grandfather showed his good will to the common school system by starting me in the District School at our end of Homer instead of at the Academy. It may be that a change would be for my good and I never thought of rebelling, although I went sorely against my will.

The presiding genius at the time was a stalwart young woman by the name of Hathaway, of a family whose house was half way up the hill on the road to our pasture. The school was pretty well crowded with all sorts and sizes and the whip was there as one of the educational instrumentalities, according to the received ideas of the time. All went well enough for a few weeks, more or less, but one morning I was bending over my book at my desk when down over my shoulders came several sharp cuts of a heavy switch. What it was for was not at once told me but I afterwards learned that another boy, name undiscovered, had been throwing "paper-balls," and it was necessary that somebody should suffer for it. That is the idea which lies at the bottom of most of the national declarations of war and the people who suffer are rarely the ones who were to blame. I never whimpered, but I quietly gathered up my books and went home. Nothing in the world could have made me go into that schoolroom again, but I forgave Miss Hathaway and afterwards went to a maple-sugar pull at her house in the most friendly manner. I was fond of peace and maple sugar and I went back to my old place at the Academy.

During the years following our removal to Syracuse, I made several visits to Homer, generally in the company of my mother, but do not remember any occurrence worthy of especial record. There had also been a quiet process of political education going on. It was of several kinds. First, my family were all Whigs and were opposed to the annexation of Texas and to the war with Mexico.[1]

So was I, but when the war did come there was one Syracuse schoolboy who read all the newspaper reports and participated in all the battles. I was familiar with the names and achievements of all the heroes. Of our own family connection, I remember but one actual representative in the invading army. It was my cousin, Erastus W. Smith, a captain of Regulars, who served through the war with credit but died at New Orleans on his way home.

The second line of instruction related to the tariff and its effects upon the prices of all sorts of things. Over and above all these, however, was the growing slavery question, and I had a number of acquaintances among the colored people and the more prominent abolitionists. It was my custom to attend the political conventions when they were held in Syracuse, as they generally were, on account of its central position. It was called Central City and Conventionville. Many a big speech had I already heard and such colored orators as Fred[erick] Douglass,[2] an escaped slave from Maryland, were my especial favorites. I also had a strong personal liking for Rev. Samuel J. May,[3] who was a leading abolitionist. There were to be consequences of that early training.

Counting in the Express jog at the end, when it became so, the store was said to be a hundred feet deep and the cellar under it had no jog. It was therefore a pretty large cellar. The stock in trade upstairs consisted of all manner of books and stationery and the business was large, for it was a wholesale as well as retail affair and we supplied a number of small dealers in the towns around, away from the railroads, even as far as Oswego and Cazenovia. There was publishing business enough to put us in connection with a prosperous bookbindery and among my first acquisitions was a knowledge of the way in which books are put together.

I did not rest until I had actually bound a book. Of course, there were gilt edges to be put on and I saw how that mysterious thing was done. In another direction was the engraving of cards and the like, and we had a really skillful copperplate engraver. He was also a good wood engraver and already I had spent many an hour in his place, watching the movements of his "burin."

In the front part of the store were show windows and long glass cases for the exhibition of fine stationery and fancy goods, but the days of plate glass had not come and the panes were not enormously large. The lighting at evening was accomplished by means of large camphene lamps which were my detestation, for one of my many small duties was to clean, fill, and light them. I also had to wash the windows and sweep the sidewalk to the middle of the street. As for camphene, it was a villainously dangerous and explosive compound of alcohol and peril and was liable to flash at any moment. My special hate of it, however, grew out of the sad fact that my pretty friend and neighbor, Miss Sarah Corning, was burned to death by the explosion of one of those camphene lamps. They were the cause of half the great fires of that day. It was the fashion to speak of the stuff as "spirit gas," but it was a general blessing when coal gas came to take its place. The heating apparatus consisted of a huge coal stove in the rear which was also in my program and sometimes it would warm the store and sometimes its effects were more comfortably perceptible when one was near enough to touch it.

I must not let go of my friend Mr. Caruth without one more record which did him credit. It showed that he was a Christian and had no malice. Not long after the break-up of the school, so far as I was concerned, I was out in Onondaga Hollow, hunting, and encountered a remarkable milk snake. They are constrictors and not venomous and are a really handsome reptile. I carefully killed the snake and carried him home with me. What to do with him I did not know but was going down Warren Street, intending to take him to our store for exhibition, when whom should I meet but Mr. Caruth.

He was enthusiastic over my prize, for his fad was natural history and amateur taxidermy. He offered at once to stuff that boa for me, so that I might preserve him for future reference. He did so, and when we came to measure him—the snake, not Mr. Caruth—he was four-feet six-inches long. He made a grand addition to the other attractions of my bedroom collection and I can remember now the customary yell with which each successive cadet in our long list of Irish or German help would make her first entry into that charming chamber. The first thing she would see was a dragon, coiled on the bureau and ready to go for her. That may have had something to do with Draco's final disappearance from the scene of inaction.

There were two gold pen factories in Syracuse and we were agents for both of them, much to our profit, but at the time my service began, our most noteworthy specialty was not pens, but ink. All the rear part of the cellar, from the foundation of the concern, had been devoted to the manufacture of "Smith's Gold Pen Ink," a blackness of much excellence. A queer customer was Smith, the inventor thereof, and it was his delight to tell me how good was his ink and how he made it.

I never perfectly learned how and before long he removed to other parts of the earth. With him departed the ink factory and its place was filled in a most disagreeable manner. All the forward part of the cellar was assigned to our increasing business in paper hangings and these after a while became my own unpleasant specialty, compelling me to spend many toilsome hours below when I would rather have been above. The very back den of the cave, after Smith vanished, was given over to the collection of rags for the paper makers and these unsavory relics, gathered from all the region round about by the dirtiest of human beings, fell to my share of the book business. Oh, how I hated the entire economy of rag picking, storage, bagging, weighing, and sending off. We were also agents for wrapping-paper mills and I learned much about all manner of wrappers. My father had a good knowledge of fire insurance and had obtained the agency of one or two good companies, to add to his income the dollars which it much needed, for he was not an economical man and had ideas of his own as to what it became him to do, in his position. One consequence, increasing as time went on, was the necessity I was under of making insurance surveys, knowing rates, delivering policies, collecting and the like, and of professionally attending all fires, by day or night.

Of course, I was a salesman and one of my first results here was a renewal of my old inquisitiveness concerning copper coins, whereof our money drawer was sure to have an unwieldy surplus, at all times. I found many curiosities, but one day there drifted in a queer, cent-sized wanderer, which puzzled me entirely. The characters upon it were such as I had never seen before and I carried it at once to my old friend Mr. Corning, the antiquarian scholar. I was entirely astonished at the interest which he took in my discovery. He pronounced it a Hebrew coin, of rare antiquity and of much value to him. In exchange for it, he gave me a vellum-bound copy of the book of Job, in Latin, to stimulate me in bibliology, and I had another splendid feature for my curiosity shop. No other boy in Syracuse had anything like that. I do not believe that a boy among them had a snake four and a half feet long.

One long counter was given up to paper-covered novels and periodicals. Into the novels I was wading, with all enthusiasm, but with a growing taste for the best among them. I was becoming well acquainted with the current literature of the day, by swallowing loads of it, and knew what was the opinion of the received judges. As to the periodicals, among my earlier friends was the *Knickerbocker Magazine*, much written-for by a tip-top contributor by the name of Irving—Washington Irving. He had also written several entire books in which I greatly delighted. So had a Frenchman named Dumas, another named Victor Hugo, and a pair of Englishmen, [Edward George] Bulwer[-Lytton] and [Henry] Kingsley, who wrote better novels than G. P. R. James himself.

All of these writers, I am informed, obtained popularity, and I was already familiar with the works of J. Fenimore Cooper and Sir Walter Scott. I think that the next periodical to make its appearance was a handsome thing, as big as a novel, called *Harper's New Monthly Magazine*.[4] I knew it afterwards when it was no longer new. Then came *Putnam's* and the *Atlantic Monthly*, and in the latter I read whatever was written by a Boston physician named Oliver Wendell Holmes. He was a funny sort of fellow and he also became widely known after a while. There were several smaller monthlies, but I did not seem to take to them. Perhaps the others were enough. As to that counter, I can well remember the day when it and the floor in front of it were heaped with the rapidly disappearing piles of Mrs. Stowe's *Uncle Tom's Cabin*, the most daringly, incendiarily antislavery novel that anybody had ventured to write and print.[5] At the first of my political teaching, however, there was a strong tide of conservatism sweeping over the country and it was almost like incipient treason to utter what one felt or thought upon the slavery question.

Under that tide was a yet stronger counter current which was bearing the country forward, for in it, unknown to themselves, were many thousands of peaceful young fellows like myself, who were studying, thinking, receiving impressions, and preparing for the days which were to come.

There were false prophets who now and then lifted their croaking voices, even in conventions, to tell us that the nation was marching on into a bloody revolution, but they were always promptly silenced, for there could be no real trouble as long as the abolitionists were kept under and nothing done or said to irritate the slaveholders or to interfere with their sacred right to own black men and women, half-black, quarter-black, and sixteenth-black, or white which might be called black.

There was almost no military feeling among the masses, but the county had what it called a regiment and the village had the Syracuse Citizen's Corps, commanded by Captain Walrath, the gold pen maker. On the other hand, there was a fair amount of interest in athletics and a really extensive public gymnasium was set up and maintained. Its teacher was a fine swordsman

I joined the gymnasium as soon as it was opened and soon knew something about boxing and fencing which has since been of value to me. I never learned the proper management of the sabre, but I was still practicing, now and then, with Andrew White's rifle. The fact was that I was getting curious notions of the value of mere bodily strength and was all the while training myself with heavy boxes of merchandise, in the lifting of them, and was also boxing with reams of wrapping paper, downstairs, to see how far I could knock one. I was developing a pretty hard pair of fists for any emergency.

13

The New Garret

There had been a garret over our Fayette Street house, but I had made no manner of use of it. Our Onondaga Street garret was for a while neglected but its day of usefulness came to it very soon. I was beginning, while at Hoyt's school, to take a deep interest in chemistry and that soon led on into a series of practical experiments in acids, gasses, combinations, and electricities, in which I took more delight than I can tell. While I was in Homer, my cousin, Osborn Bright, had constructed a pretty good electric machine which would give shocks and even charge a Leyden jar, to torment the ignorant with. I did not now go as far as that but I made loads of hydrogen gas to create explosions and lift paper balloons.

It was somewhere about this time that a man by the name of Morse accomplished a kind of miracle. He actually invented a machine by means of which a fellow might write a letter in the town to which he sent it instead of putting it upon paper in his own place in the old way. I had no idea how much of my future life was to be related to telegraphic enterprises, but I went to see the first Morse telegraphic instrument that was set up in Syracuse and thought it a wonderful affair. Everybody said that Mr. Morse would make millions out of it; and perhaps he did, but, many a long year afterwards, sitting with him in his study, he intimated with a sufficient clearness, that he had made much less than the public gave him credit for and that he had subsequently lost much of what he did make in unprofitable enterprises. I was sorry to hear it and told him so.[1] If in this manner I was learning something about chemistry, in another I was obtaining ideas concerning journalism. I determined to print a periodical of my own. The first requisite, in my opinion, was a printing press, and I made one, taking the copperplate press in the engraving shop as my model, because it appeared to be easiest of construction. With a great deal of toil and with a rolling pin for a roller, I set up my press. Then I went for type and obtained a lot of second-hand stuff at the *Standard* office, where the foreman was jocularly disposed to encourage me. It was a long, hard job to set up the first and only number of *The Gem*, but I succeeded in doing so and acquired my first knowledge of the noble art of typesetting. A number of copies were laboriously struck off and there the matter rested for I had learned my lesson and had no more time or enthusiasm to waste in that direction. It was better to allow the other journals to go on without competition. Possibly the next occupants of the garret may have wondered what on earth that queer machine was made for.

They did not find many relics of my laboratory, for I used Florence flasks for retorts and they would break. As to glass in any shape, however, I already knew something. Among the odd character citizens of Syracuse at the time of my arrival had been an old Englishman who made thermometers. He and his fat wife took a fancy to me because of my intense interest in his continual experiments with glassblowing. He could spin glass into fine down and do a great many other wonderful things and I liked to come and watch him doing it and carry home specimens for my collection of rarities. The garret was less frequently a workshop after I became settled in the book-ink-rags-paper hangings-insurance-stationery and Express business.

There were still occasional games with the Park boys and now and then the Rambler's Club would make an adventurous excursion, but my strongest alliance with my old friends grew out of music and social rivalries. On the demise of the Allen and Stebbins Academy, as I have said, Professor Allen went altogether into music. One of his grandest musical ideas was the formation of a perpetual class in vocal music and it became a success. I attended those classes, somewhat irregularly, although I had but little genuine musical genius. I preferred to hear it rather than to make it, but there was one feature in Professor Allen's program in which I took the deepest interest. This was the annual May Day Festival performance and the election and crowning of the May Queen. The elections were held in the basement of the Congregational Church, on the Park, and all the recognized musical scholars were entitled to vote.

I was an attentive scholar for some time prior to the election and so was my friend Carroll E. Smith, one of the Hoyt School boys and afterwards a well-known editor and politician. His father was at that time editor and part proprietor of the *Daily Journal* and was also superintendent of the salt springs. Carroll and I considered the matter and decided that the right Park girl for queen was my beautiful friend Mary Butler, whose mother was so good a woman and whose brother John, afterwards a colonel in the army, was about our nearest friend. What the professor's views were we did not inquire, but when the election came off, every small voter that we could reach had a ticket already provided, under a solemn promise not to vote any other.[2] Of course, our candidate was elected, but I noticed that it was with some difficulty that I obtained a post of honor as one of the flowery "Heralds" at the great exhibition and that the professor looked sidewise at me as if I had meddled with some of his plans.

Another of my remaining school adventures grew out of the fact that I had been considered the best speller in the Hoyt School. Up at the left of Onondaga Lake was a small old village called Geddes, after its founder, or he may have been the man who found it. Here was a large and exceedingly ambitious public school, larger than any in Syracuse and ready to consider itself famous. Its faculty laid great stress upon the proficiency which their pupils had obtained in spelling, and they issued a challenge to all the world, including Syracuse, for a grand Spelling Match, to take place in the large hall of their big institution upon a certain Winter evening. Syracuse and other villages took up the challenge, but when the time for the fight arrived, a carriage came to the store after me and I was conveyed to Geddes as one of the schoolboys of the Central City. It was really a grand affair and the hall was crowded. My claims to entry were not disputed and the match began. Down went boy after boy and girl after girl, until of the two long lines which had stood in the middle of the hall at first only two remained, one on each side. Opposite me was a bright-looking, red-headed girl, of about my own age, and she stood up finely to the reputation she had won as the best speller in all Geddes. The school faculty were manifestly disturbed in their minds but they should have fought it out fairly. They did not do so, however, for I was turned down upon an asserted error which I did not make. I said so and I think the audience agreed with me. So did all the Syracuse boys, while the country fellows bitterly resented the insinuation. The consequence was that we had to almost fight our way to the hacks which had brought us and I had opportunities for showing how much I had learned from the boxing teacher at the Syracuse gymnasium. The next day, the entire population of our village was ready to aver that their champion could not possibly have spelled "beryl" with two "r"s.

Yet another important change was coming to me and it was a sort of consequence of my father's church relations and his ambition. He was the managing deacon of the First Baptist Church, in which also my mother was by all odds the most influential woman. Both of them paid very dearly for their usefulness and zeal in the course of time but their church troubles had not yet come.

At the time of our arrival, the Baptist meetinghouse, centrally located on West Genesee Street, west of the middle of the village, was an old, unhandsome, frame building, not by any means a credit to the denomination or an ornament to the municipality. Its meetings were well attended, although the larger part of its membership lived out of town. It did not contain any bankers, merchants, or lawyers, and its finances were left largely in my father's hands, to his great detriment. At an early day, he determined that a new and elegant structure ought to take the place of the old, and it was there that the worry began. Some of the old stagers, after a unanimous vote had declared for the new building, declared that the old lot itself was in a manner consecrated ground and must be used over again, although it was not large enough for the building plan adopted and although a much better lot was to be had a number of rods eastward. My father carried his point and the old concern was sold to pecuniary advantage. That might possibly have been forgiven if a vast profanity had not been deftly hidden behind the deed of sale. It was but a few weeks before the faithful were informed that their former house of worship, in which they had been so extraordinarily religious, was in process of being transformed into that prime instrumentality of Satan, a Theater! Words cannot describe the shock to all the Baptist sensibilities and I believe that in the minds of some of the sisters and brethren my father was looked upon as in a manner the founder of the first theater which had ever been known in the highly moral village of Syracuse. He really had nothing to do with it and he was as much opposed to theaters as anybody needed to be.

The building of the new church began and was vigorously prosecuted to its completion. At the same time, the Presbyterians, with much larger financial resources, were erecting a fine new edifice on Salina Street, on the site of the old American House, in which I had eaten my nine-years-old first dinner. If I remember correctly, its stone spire was to be 187 feet in height, while our more ambitious steeple, of wood, was to tower up to 193, including the lightning rod. Ours was done first, while yet its stone rival lacked about forty feet of its intended grandeur, but there were envious tongues that unkindly asserted the insecurity of our tapering woodwork. They had seen it weave back and forth in a gale of wind. Some day or other, the whole structure would come tumbling down to kill people. Wild was my indignation at such an aspersion upon my own meetinghouse. Had I not watched the digging of the cellar for it and every brick of its subsequent progress toward completion? Had I not been a Sunday school scholar in the old concern and did I not intend to be one of the most active fellows in this? It was at all events as strong as was the Presbyterian spire, besides being higher. Well, there came a tremendous gale and there were men in the street, watching my steeple. Some said it swung back and forth and some said that it did not do so and had no intention of doing so. As for myself, I at once declared that I could settle that matter.

I somehow obtained possession of the key and went in, then it was nothing but steep stair climbing, as far up as the belfry, in which had been placed a bell which was my pride for its tone and ring. In the belfry, however, I was a little set back, for, on looking up, I discovered that there were no more stairs. Only the wooden cleats nailed across from timber to timber on the sides. They did not even form a good ladder. I believed that I could use them, at all events, and I did so. Up I went, at a serious risk to my neck, until I came to a sort of landing, at the base of the upper, slender needle, which arose perhaps thirty feet above me. There was no means whatever of creeping up into that needle, but I could look out at the small, unglazed apertures on the sides and shout down to the men in the street. I did so, at the top of my voice but I was all the while holding on hard for here I had indeed settled the problem. The steeple did weave, back and forth, and I may have had exaggerated conceptions of the number of feet to which it swung, this way and that way. It was a pokerish place to be in and I remained only long enough to show that I was not in the least afraid—that I would let go of those cross pieces. Then I made the best of my way down, to be severely scolded, even by my father, who was glad to know the truth, that the steeple needed further fastening.

The fame of the reckless feat of climbing went the rounds, of course, and it at once stirred to emulation a Parochial schoolboy who had been a kind of rival of mine. Time had been when he had thrown me five times running, at a wrestling match, and if I afterwards threw him as many, it left him with a sense of jealousy which now came to the front. He was of my own age and size and if he was not my equal in main strength, he was in agility and pluck. He tried on his own experiment, next day, by getting into the Presbyterian building at noon, when the workmen were at their dinners. There were still the wooden stairs here that were required by the workmen, and they carried him up to the opening at the top of the uncompleted stone spire. Here there was a derrick, reaching out over the street, and out went Jim Lawrence upon that derrick, to the great terror of all who saw him. He went back and came down in safety and I was beaten for he had undoubtedly done a more foolhardy thing than I had—with no use whatever.

All this preliminary talk about the church only brings me back to the subject I began to begin with. My father was now doing well in a business way, and he was ready to purchase the old Slocum residence, only one lot west of the new church, and be nearer to his pet project and its duties. He shortly afterwards purchased also what was called the Montgomery house, a smaller residence just west of his own. Beyond that was an alley and then came what the wicked people were vexatiously in the habit of describing as "the Baptist theater."

For my own part, I had very little sentimental regret at leaving the Onondaga Street home. The millpond had long since disappeared. Will Corning was all the while away at boarding school and there were other personal changes in the neighborhood. Besides, our new house was nearer to both the church and the store, had much more land around it, and was in some respects more comfortable. Over and above all that was a boyish excitement at the idea of a change into a new country, half a mile nearer to the saltworks and the lake.

This was a time when politics were once more beginning to run high. The Mexican War was a thing of the past. Texas had been annexed, rightly or wrongly, and it was said that many vexed questions had been forever settled. They may have been, the questions, but a great many vexed people had not by any means been settled. In the General Taylor campaign of 1848, my only interest had been that of a young Whig who wished to see the victor of Buena Vista made President, and some hundreds of thousands of votes may have been cast for him on war account.[3] At all events, they and I elected him and in a few weeks he was succeeded by that exceedingly excellent gentleman, patriot, and statesman, Millard Fillmore, for whom my esteem grew stronger in after years, when I knew more about him.[4] Nevertheless, before long, his name became combined with that of Daniel Webster and other leaders as being responsible for what were called, in a curious lump phrase, "the Compromise Measures," and offensively foremost among these was the obnoxious Fugitive Slave Law, concerning which and its workings we Syracuse people were before long to know a deal more than we did at the time of its passage.[5]

The new home was a frame building, large, well built, roomy, with a good rear addition, woodshed, and so forth. The lot was four or five rods wide by about ten or eleven rods depth. There was a fence at the middle of it and behind that was a garden the soil of which was none the worse because it had formerly been a barnyard for two generations of cattle and horses. I was truly delighted with my house and my room in it, and I had transferred every stick of my hencoops to a good place in the rear. Every fowl had also been transferred and they did not seem discontented. Perhaps I was less so because of the fact that my old friend the Onondaga Creek, after several windings, was now even nearer than formerly. It also had a slower current and was wider, deeper, as it went on towards the lake which was its destination. Our lot ran through to Church Street and that thoroughfare came to a sharp end at the point where it joined West Genesee Street, a few doors beyond the Baptist Theater. It was to me a striking characteristic of our house that it had no garret to speak of and it may have been equally remarkable that I no longer cared to have one. My garret days were over and I was becoming an exceedingly active young churchman and businessman, with sporting tendencies.

14

The Church

Between our house and the church was but one dwelling, a large frame building, then, for awhile, occupied by the Slocum family. Behind it was another dwelling that fronted on Church Street. Our lot had a back gate, so that my brothers and sisters might go through by that way to the public schoolhouse at a little distance. By the way, the Syracuse public institutions were now attaining a degree of excellence of which our citizens were justly proud and which rendered private educational enterprises of less account.

My older sister, Julia, had now become a young woman [of] whose loveliness of character I could not say too much. She was of a gentle, affectionate nature, with a bright intellect which was expanding well under the direction of my mother. She was away at her boarding school much of her time and her vacations at home were special treats to us all.

The meetinghouse was as yet unfinished and only the ample "conference meetingroom," in the rear, was available. It was really a well-finished and handsome room and the church was in a prosperous condition. The pastor who had ruled in the old affair, a Rev. Mr. Taggart, had left us and we had succeeded in replacing him with Rev. Robert R. Raymond, a gentleman of exceptional ability and culture. He was an eloquent preacher, a fine elocutionist, and his social qualities were of a high order. It was our good fortune that he was not at first prepared to bring on his family, no proper residence having been secured for them, and during nearly six months he was an inmate of our own family. Among his accomplishments was vocal music, for which he possessed a rich tenor voice, and it was our delight, and his, to get him seated at the piano. His repertoire included all of *Moore's Melodies*, a long list of old English songs, Jacobite and other, and

I then heard a great many grand old songs which have somehow been left behind, nowadays. There was much music in them. Of course, the church had a Sunday school and it had a library and I was installed as librarian. Was I not a clerk in a bookstore and did I not know just what to do with books? At all events, I discovered that a certain line of fiction, including *Edwards on the Mill*, and *Baxter's Saint's Rest*, appeared to be as fresh and new as when, years before, they had first made their interesting way into that library, while another kind of literature was sufficiently thumbed to call for new copies at an early day.

The cost of completing the church edifice appeared to grow from day to day and my father's responsibilities were increasing upon his hands, for there were church promissory notes out upon which his name appeared as an endorser and it was hurting his credit at the banks. He was a good manager of such things, however, and all seemed to be going along pretty well.

It may be that one of the early difficulties of that meetinghouse was pigeons. I had undertaken to add them to my stock of feathered curiosities and had taken a little back loft over the woodhouse as my dovecote. It should have been enough to satisfy any reasonable birds, but the perverse creatures had religious tendencies. Moreover, they had explored the steeple and had found the small, unglazed apertures at the foot of the upper needle. In they had gone and all the upper part of our proud spire, before long, all the steeple above the belfry, was little better than a pigeon roost. So was the roof of the building, and so were the roofs of other houses nearby and I was commanded to make an end of my enterprise. I did so with regret, but I shot forty-four of my own birds as they flew over our yard, every one of them falling within our fence. More help than mine was required to finish the work of finally obliterating them from the steeple but the task was fully accomplished and I gave up the pigeon business.

The garden, from the outset, was a special field of enterprise. There had been a good one behind the old house in Homer, and this was to be made the equal of that. It soon became, for its size, greatly superior, with a better soil and a more favorable climate. My father added to the vines on the trellises, but one enormous, unbearing vine, which covered half the side of the house, had to come down. He set out a number of pear and cherry trees which prospered amazingly. In the back corner of the front yard, we had found an ancient, tangled Damascus plum tree, and it also was to have been cut down, but I begged for its life and for an opportunity of testing the virtues of pruning. Consent was given, although I was assured that there had been no fruit upon that tree for years. At it I went, with saw and knife, and it was soon only a skeleton of what it had been. Nevertheless, in the next season, its outreaching branches required strong propping, so very abundant was its yield, and it was permitted to continue its existence.

I must not forget to record, while it is in my mind, one pleasant incident at the end of my first Summer in that house. My old friend Andrew White went to Geneva College on leaving the care of Mr. Hoyt. There he remained for a year before going to Yale. At the end of his freshman year he spent his whole Summer in Europe, making quite an extensive pilgrimage. On his return and just before once more setting out for New Haven, he made his appearance in the store one afternoon, and I was glad enough to see him. He had a special errand, however. After giving me a sketch of his wanderings in the Old World, he told me of what quantities of odd things he had collected. He was well aware of my own weakness in that direction and he said: "Now, Will, they are all arrived at the house and I haven't opened them. You are the only fellow I know that can appreciate them. Come up and spend the evening with me and we'll have a real good time of it."

I was ready to jump at the offer of such a treat as that and I went. I think it was a pretty late evening before we gave up opening and admiring the decidedly miscellaneous gathering of all sorts which was the fruit of Andrew's travels in Europe. In after years, his tendency to make collections remained with him, strengthening as he went onward, and more than one college library is the richer for the taste, good judgment, and liberality with which he has gathered and given away. From that day forward I was to see less and less of him, but the boyhood friendship remains unbroken and I am as proud as ever of the star boy of the Hoyt school, my earliest friend in Syracuse. We are old now, but once in a while I get from him a reminder that all his cares and troubles and great public uses have not chilled in him the warm heart which made us all so much attached to him. He has had trouble enough, poor fellow!

The church enterprise struggled on until we were actually in the main body of the edifice, and shortly after we did so a disagreeable experience came to me. Mr. Raymond was still our pastor but he had purchased a residence away up on Foot Street, now renamed James Street. There had been little squabbles in the church and our old sexton had left us. I cared less for that during pleasant weather, for I could sweep any church of that size and I was angrily proud to do so. The bell was a trial, at first, for it had a perverse tendency to swing my small weight up with it, as it rolled around in ringing. When that difficulty was mastered, and the art of tolling, there were unkind critics to say that I did not ring it loudly enough, not one of them being aware that the ringer did not make the bell.

After ringing the bell, I was needed in the small choir, for I could sing, to a certain extent. Then came my duties in the Sunday school, but yet another sadness was before me. Cold weather came and I had mastered the mysteries of the huge furnace in the cellar. If I was to be regarded as volunteer sexton, that also was within my province and I went at it bravely. Much heavy-sized coal was required to even start it and the fire had to be well going at daylight, if the audience room was to be warmed in time for morning worshippers, coming in half frozen, for it was an exceptionally severe Winter. It was the hardest kind of work and it brought me no praise whatever, for all the shortcomings of the furnace or the thermometer were charged upon the bungling of the young sexton. In fact, there was a rebellion and before the Winter was over the church hired a grown-up fellow from its own membership to take my place. To be sure, he succeeded, for, as the weather grew warmer the furnace did better. Still, as time went on, I had my revenge upon him for being an Old Hunker Pro-Slavery Democrat[1] as the critics went for him in his turn. At the first, moreover, I was oh, so glad to see him at that bell.

I think it was in that Spring that the second of Professor Allen's May Festivals came off. He had formed a numerous class, largely composed of small boys and even smaller girls, and the Congregational Church was again the scene of action. Among his best singers, of course, were Carroll E. Smith and myself, although we were well aware that neither of us was a favorite performer. As the day for the election drew near, we were once more in consultation as a pair of gloomy conspirators. Carroll came to the store one day with a bit of secret information and a beautiful electioneering plan of his own invention. Professor Allen had announced with smiling emphasis that the election was to be entirely at the disposal of his pupils, by a majority vote, and that there would be no interference with their selection of a May Queen.

Now, Carroll was a printer's son and he had surreptitiously discovered that the professor had already made his own selection. He had even had an abundance of tickets printed, with her name upon them, for distribution at the election. His choice was a very pretty, stylish young lady, living on Salina Street, whose father was a prominent lawyer. He was also a Democrat and we were Whig abolitionists. Carroll had one of the tickets to show me and it looked as if the professor was sure to succeed. It must have been understood that my action was of some importance, for even Will Hamilton, our chief clerk, came to me and urged me to support the regular ticket. But then he too was an Old Hunker Democrat. There was more than that to be considered. It might not do to select one of the Park girls as a candidate, for fear of exciting local feeling. The only way was to have a candidate ready without announcing her to anybody and so we did.

Living a little above the Park was a bright and pretty girl named Amelia Bassett. I was but slightly acquainted with her and Carroll was only on speaking terms with her, but we decided that she would do. The next thing was the tickets and he said he could get them printed at the *Journal* office. There was where my part came in for I called attention to the small, neat white ticket he showed me and said that we must beat that. We went to the card drawer in our store but it contained nothing which caught our conspiring eyes. Away we went, therefore, to Redfield's small bookstore on Canal Street, and there we were in luck for we found and purchased a quantity of highly embossed, brightly colored cards, half as large as your hand. They were gorgeous and they became more so when they were printed with Miss Bassett's name in glowing bronze which was as good as gold. Not a word did we let out except to the foreman of the printing office, who went right in with us as soon as he understood that we were packing a primary. When the evening set down for the election arrived, there were we and there were all the Park boys, ready to distribute tickets with phenomenal celerity. The plan was a good one.

The small people were the vast majority of the voters. Each of them was to receive two tickets, one to be voted and one to be kept as a lovely souvenir of the occasion. They all had the professor's small, pretty white tickets, also, and these they were instructed to retain with ours and so have double keepsakes. They kept them and when the votes were counted our candidate, to her great surprise, was chosen by an overwhelming majority, from which there was no appeal. The festival went off with complete success, but I believe it was about the last of its kind in Syracuse.

Perhaps that was because soon afterwards Professor Allen sold out his music store to a very pleasant gentleman by the name of Timothy Hough, who was not disposed to take up the May Queen business. He prospered well otherwise, however, and a daughter of his is now a niece of mine, having married my nephew, Henry Gibson. I do not know that Carroll Smith and I had anything to do with the sale of the music store, but there was a great deal of astonishment expressed publicly and privately, at the unexpected result of that election. It was the pretty tickets that did it, and all political parties have since tried their best to steal our invention and provide their voting machinery with something attractive, the names on the tickets being as little known to the voters, sometimes, as was that of the fair maiden who lived just above the Park and was just the girl to win with against Professor Allen.

Speaking of politics, I must not forget the General Winfield Scott campaign. He was defeated, as all men know, and the main cause of his defeat was that he was suspected of being somewhat unsound upon the slavery question.[2] That aroused all the timid conservatism of the North against him.

During the campaign, he passed through Syracuse and made a brief speech from the rear platform of a railway car. There was a large crowd gathered to hear, but I managed to squeeze in and get a good place, pretty near that old hero. I had never seen him before and was not to look him in the face again until a far different occasion which I will talk of when I come to it. For that matter, I had long since developed a strong curiosity concerning public or prominent men, and never missed an opportunity for seeing and studying one. It may have been this which made me an outside member of so many political conventions, and the time came when it was to exercise an important influence upon my course in life. The results of that presidential election left behind them a strengthening feeling among the antislavery men, and the debates of Congress that Winter, upon the Compromise Measures, were read as few debates had ever been before.

The administration of President Franklin Pierce began, with all apparent guarantees provided for the continued peace of the country and for the all but absolute supremacy of the Slave Power. There was all the while a rumbling and grumbling, however, and such statesmen as Daniel Webster were well aware of it. So had been Millard Fillmore and he had earnestly pointed out the perils into which the nation was surely drifting while he had no power to stay the tide. It was reserved for Mr. Webster himself to imprudently set and light a slow match and to prepare for a destructive explosion.

15

The Jerry Rescue Riot

There came a day when the citizens of Syracuse were startled by the announcement that the great statesman, Daniel Webster, was coming to address them upon the questions of the day.[1] He had selected the Convention City as the proper place for the delivery of one of his most important public utterances.

Due preparations were made for his reception and the open space in front of the City Hall was made ready for the speech which was to come. An ample platform was provided for the speaker and the local great men who were to sit behind him and start the rounds of applause. Just in front of the platform was a wooden arrangement for the necessary brass band, for he was to have music as well as applause. I read all that the newspapers had to say and they said enough to set me on fire, let alone my determination to have a close look at the Great Expounder and to hear his eloquence.

When the day came [in May 1851—ed.], it brought bright sunshine for the occasion and the town was astir early. Mr. Webster was to be escorted to his platform by the Syracuse Citizens Corps and these warriors, as a guard of honor, were to stand at parade rest in front of the speaker's stand. My selected, but with difficulty obtained, position, was just in front of the foremost line of soldiers. I did it by going early and waiting and then by keeping step with a soldier so closely that I jostled him. The preliminaries were tediously over and then Mr. Webster arose and came forward, amid all the cheering any man need have asked for. He was indeed a noble presence, all that his pictures had taught me to expect,[2] and when he slowly turned and looked around upon the crowd he appeared to be a very impersonation of political dignity, if not of national authority. He wiped his forehead with a handkerchief, and then his deep, mellow, sonorous voice rolled out, as it may have done when in the United States Senate he replied to Hayne of South Carolina.[3]

"Fel-low Cit-i-zens of Syr-a-cuse and On-on-daga County," he began, with impressive deliberation, and the stillness became breathless. Shortly he said things concerning patriotism and the Constitution and the great country in which we live, and its future prosperity, which were cheered with sufficient heartiness but at last he came to his dangerous ground and he walked on into it with only too much courageous statesmanship.

"Fellow citizens, the Fugitive Slave Law will be enforced! It will be enforced everywhere and at all hazards. It will be enforced even in Syracuse and even if the Abolitionist Convention shall be here in session at the time."

He said it slowly, solemnly, with tremendous emphasis, but his words were greeted by silence only, for something like an electric shock went through the crowd. On he went, after a brief pause, and he had no idea that he had been making a proclamation of war which hundreds of his hearers were mentally accepting. The speech ended, the brass band played patriotic music, the crowd dispersed and so did Mr. Webster, but an untellable amount of out-and-out mischief had been unnecessarily done.[4]

The average American is an unhandy man to threaten and we all felt that the great orator had left a threat behind him which it might be well for us to remember. Never, to that day, had any black fugitive been troubled in our city or county, although many were there and I knew some of them. Among them was a large, brawny, not ill-looking and entirely peaceable mulatto who worked in the furniture store of Ashley & Williston, opposite our own store. I had seen him often. He had a weakness for whiskey which now and then brought him before the police court and a mere arrest was to him no occasion for resistance or ill feeling.

When the time came for the assembling of the Abolition Convention [in October 1851—ed.] Webster's words were called to mind and men spoke about them, but there was really no general expectation that there would be any attempt to carry out the unpleasant threat. The too-eager servants of "Conservatism," however, were taking a different view of the matter and their plans were all laid beforehand. Jerry, whose rightful owner was said to be a Marylander, was selected for the victim and he was to be seized and carried away before the elements of rebellion and sedition could have any opportunity for rallying. "The best laid plans o' mice and men gang aft aglee," as has been remarked by a Scotch fellow by the name of Burns. It was easy enough to arrest poor Jerry, leaving him under the impression that this was only one of his accustomed affairs, whereof he declared, as usual, that he was entirely guiltless. But when men saw deputy United States Marshals leading him to the office of the United States Commissioner, there were yells and shouts all up and down the street.

For a perfect rendering of the affair, the topography must be given. Going up Salina Street, from our store toward the bridge over the canal, on the right or eastern corner was the old Syracuse House, and I knew a man whose bars to his cow pasture had once let down where was now the main entrance of that celebrated tavern. Around that corner down Water Street, three long blocks, was the City Hall in which the convention was at that hour debating. Across the street to the left, on the corner, was a large, dingy, brick building, the hardware concern of Horace and Charles A. Wheaton.

Around that corner, to the left, on Water Street, was the stone-faced Townsend Block, reaching on to Clinton Street, which had another bridge over the canal. Beyond the bridge was a long row of brick warehouses and in the front of the one of these at the bridge was a room large enough for a country store but which was now used as the police courtroom and temporary station house. Ten feet in the rear of it had been planked off by strong partition to make a jail or calaboose of it. In front of the building was a broad platform, about level with the bridgeway.

In the middle of the Townsend Block was an ample entrance and stairway, leading up to a suite of offices on the next floor, occupied by his honor, Judge Sabine, the United States Commissioner, upon whom fell the duty of returning fugitive slaves to their asserted owners. Up this flight of stairs and into Sabine's office had Jerry been conducted, but he was now powerless to resist, for he was handcuffed. He was not yet manacled.

Behind him and his captors, as they went up, followed a growing pressure of excited men, of both political parties, and among the foremost of them was a boy who had heard Daniel Webster and had come to see about it. There stood Jerry, in his handcuffs, and just this side of him stood a stalwart policeman, grinning defiantly at the crowd. Even while the judge was reading something aloud—it may have been a warrant—that guardian of the public peace said taunting words to those in front of him but he had not taken due note of a tall, country-looking chap who had suddenly slipped past him. I saw a long arm flash out, and a set of hard knuckles smote the unwise officer on the side of his head. Down he went and over his prostrate form, and that, it may be of the Fugitive Slave Law, sprang Jerry. All made way for him and down the stairs he went, for he had no enemies at that point.

Of course, I experienced some delay in being squeezed out of the court-room, but I gained the street at last, only to see a huge crowd surging along back from some distance down Canal Street, for Jerry had been retaken. He had been instructed to run for the City Hall and he might have reached it but for some Hunker who ran in front of him and tripped him up. Before he could regain his feet, his pursuers were upon him and his last chance for liberty seemed to have departed. I needed no one to tell me that they would take him to the police office and I started for it at once. When I reached it, there were policemen already busy in strengthening its defenses. They were spiking heavy wooden bars across the windows, in view of a possible storming party.

Nearer came the yelling crowd, the captors and the captive. A cart had been impressed into the service of its country and prone upon that lay Jerry. He had struggled furiously and several men seemed to be kneeling upon him to keep him down, while others were beating off the crowd with the cart stakes. Eager to see all, I clambered up the wooden bars in front of one of the windows. I had but a moment for my observations, however—I looked down and saw the mulatto, now half naked, bruised, bloody. I saw the men who were swinging the clubs, and then I was seized by a super-serviceable policeman and thrown out upon the heads and shoulders of the dense throng which now packed the wide platform. It was not easy to get to my feet, but I did so, other fellows being too excited to even hit me. Something else had hit me, for the whole devilishness of human slavery went through my mind like a red hot flash and I had been taught all I needed to know of it by that grim object lesson.

Jerry had been guilty of no crime but that of being a colored man, but on that account he must be seized as a criminal, convicted of his color and sentenced to lose his freedom. Mere burglars had to go for a term of years, but the black man's sentence was invariably for life. I did not care ten cents for Daniel Webster and the Compromises and there were others like me.

The colored culprit was safely landed inside of the police office and then locked up in the inner prison. It appeared to be all day with him, for there was no known power to come to his assistance and the evidence against him was overwhelming. Nevertheless, the whole town was in an uproar. Stores and hotels were crowded with angry disputants and the supporters of Webster and Conservatism and the Constitution seemed to be in the majority. There were fierce orators at work at the convention, both male and female, and the news of the affair was going out into the country, far and wide. This was in the afternoon, and before long all our ears were startled by the sound of bells. Bell after bell took it up, as if they were answering one another, until every steeple in Syracuse was sending out a tocsin of warning.

It was not a ring but a toll. The bell would toll slowly, as for a funeral, a minute or so, and then pause as long to think the matter over before he began again. It was what was long known in Syracuse as "the Jerry bell." Perhaps one of the maddest men to be found was the Hunker Democratic sexton of the Baptist Church, for his bell was tolling like the rest and he could not get in to stop it. The fact was that the church key was kept at our house and I cannot swear positively that Rev. Robert R. Raymond went and obtained it of my mother. If he did and got in, he left a more muscular man than he was to do the tolling and went off to the convention. I had to be on duty at the store, even after supper, but I had an idea that all the bells in the surrounding villages must be tolling also, for the country people were pouring in, in streams, afoot and on horseback and in wagons.

Hardly did the darkness fall before there were bonfires blazing in many places and there was a demand for tar-barrels as if it had been Fourth of July. Of course it was the duty of the county sheriff to call out the military, for the first time in the history of the county, and the police authorities were busily swearing in extra constables and deputy sheriffs and deputy marshals.

Just here was a break in the Conservative calculations, for Colonel Origen Vandenburg, of the Fifty-First [Regiment], was not in sympathy with the Fugitive Slave Law. He was a very popular fellow and a strong friend of my father. He afterwards, for years, had his lawyer desk in my father's office. On this occasion, it was said that after some of the captains of companies had gathered their men, by command of the sheriff, he followed up that mere civilian and stormed at his subordinates for receiving orders, irregularly, from anybody but their commander. He ordered them to disperse their men and wait for orders from him. Then he went and shut himself up in the Syracuse House, with proper provisions for a siege, and threatened to shoot any man who should be unwise enough to discover his hiding place.

The United States Commissioner, however, appeared to have done enough when he had gathered in a hundred or so of the roughest fighting men of Salt Point, professional pugilists and all. They were gathered at the police office, inside and outside, and threatened to smash entirely any blessed abolition mob which might dare to come foolishing around their wooden-barred fort. I do not now remember how my own warning came, but at about nine o'clock I suddenly darted out of the store and ran for the Syracuse House corner. Looking down Water Street toward the City Hall, I saw a torrent of men coming. Looking across Salina Street, I saw a pile of crowbars, axes, axe-helves, and other agricultural implements piled upon the sidewalk, and Charles A. Wheaton's men were bringing out more from the hardware store. I saw what was up and wheeled away with the tide toward the police office. It was easier to keep ahead, for the foremost of those men stopped to pick up the axes and things, which may have been put there for them.

On we went, and I have heard that crowd estimated at three thousand men. It may have been so, for it contained both parties, to a certain extent, and the friends of Law were rallying fast. They were too late.

As we surged onward, I saw several hack carriages, standing just beyond the Clinton Street crossing, at the curbstone, and among them was Charley Wheaton's team of fast trotters, and a top buggy. What it was there for, I did not know. Then followed a few minutes of the most utter confusion you ever saw or heard of. I was lost in the rush but was close enough to see the axes and crowbars go up and down upon those wooden window bars. In poured the mob, for that is what we were called, and there was only a brief struggle against such overpowering numbers. The whole concern was cleaned out so perfectly that when I visited it again, next morning, it reminded me of a fire without any fire. There was neither furniture, partition, desk, or window sash left.

Just then, however, I was hearing crashes and being swept almost off my feet by the returning tide of angry men. Nobody had been killed, although quite a number had been severely bruised. One black man had a pistol bullet in his thigh, and the chief Deputy Marshal had been lifted bodily and dropped over upon the heel path of the canal, the fall breaking an arm for him. The next thing, I saw the several hacks set out in different directions, but I saw no more of Charley Wheaton's sorrel team. Some of the supposable Fugitive Slave Law men pursued those hacks, but cunning was at work and at several places in the crowd might distinctly be heard the clanking of chains, as if to invite all sorts to follow that racket and seize or rescue Jerry.

I was among the largest of these half-crazy congregations and cannot tell how on earth it wandered down Water to Warren Street and how it got in front of St. Paul's Church. There had been all sorts of fighting in that crowd. Now the good Episcopal people had been repairing their house of worship and a great heap of plaster, lime, fragments of lumber, and old bricks lay in the road. It was just at that heap that I was hitting out at somebody unknown when something or other unknown, but strongly resembling a set of knuckles, hit me on the shoulder. Down I went, into the plaster, and I and my hat were badly stepped upon before I could regain my feet. I had had enough, and a little more, and I set out for the store. The blinds were up but the store was open and I went in triumphantly. Not until that moment did I know what a mobbish figure I was cutting, for Will Hamilton from the rear, sang out:

"There, Willie! I'm glad of it! Served you right!"

It may have done so for I was a sight to see, but I cheerfully responded:

"Well! I don't care! We got the nigger!"

So we had, for he was on his way to Oswego behind Wheaton's trotters and there a schooner took him over to Canada. I brushed myself as well as I could and then Jim Lawrence and I went the rounds of the hotels to see and hear a great many things.

The next day, the exciting news was going out all over the United States and elsewhere and nobody then had as clear an idea as might now be formed that the storming of that police station was, after a fashion, the first skirmish of the Civil War. John Brown's raid into Virginia[5] was the next [in October 1859—ed.], and then came a number of others which are forgotten now, but which were really the beginning of violence and of an appeal to arms for the settlement of the Slavery Question. At all events, it was days and days before Syracuse settled down to its customary quiet, and it contained one boy who was rather proud than otherwise of any bruises which he had sustained in rescuing Jerry.

16

Miscellaneous

At the time of the riot, we had emerged from the Sunday school room into the body of the church, and Mr. Raymond was preaching with great acceptance, so far as the greater part of his congregation was concerned. But his politics and some of his liberal ideas had made him enemies among an old and somewhat influential clique.

The fact was that the church was out of date a little. It contained few men of brains or cultivation. Among these I must mention our family physician, Dr. Richardson, one of the best of men, for whom I formed a strong liking. But then, after losing his first partner, a good Presbyterian named Clary, he had taken in a fine-looking, scientific gentleman, who was looked at with horror by the good as being a, "Swedenborgian," whatever that monster might be, and not one of them could have told, except that it was a kind of Parsee and Mahometan and Infidel who believed in ghosts.

As a consequence, perhaps, of the shortage of men, the prayer meetings were largely dependent upon the women, and of these we were not by any means destitute. They were the strength of the church and, in spite of the misrenderings of St. Paul, I was confident that not one man in the meetings was at all the superior, if he was at all the equal, of my own mother. She never appeared more graceful, dignified, and altogether in her right place, than when she was addressing a crowded assemblage of men and women.

The drift of events went on, after a troublesome fashion to my father and some other people, and the day came when Mr. Raymond gave it up and left the pulpit to take charge of the *Daily Chronicle*, a journal with pronounced antislavery tendencies, which was only a few years too far in advance of the times for pecuniary success. It was, at least, an out and out good paper and had a good circulation to begin with, but it had no party behind it, for the Republican Party was as yet unborn.[1]

At the close of the next Summer, I had been in the bookstore a year and a half. Aided by my other enterprises, as to pocket money, I had been able to lay up nearly two thirds of my vast salary, of seventy-five dollars per annum. It was the year of the first World's Fair in America [1853], and the wonderful Crystal Palace had been built for it in the city of New York.[2]

My father promptly consented when I proposed to him to go and see that palace and to travel elsewhere, as far as my money would take me, especially to see our relatives in Connecticut and the old family places. My wardrobe was in good condition and filled a small, old, hair trunk, while my plans and expectations would have filled several larger caskets than that. I went as far as Albany by rail and the baggage management of the Albany and Schenectady road was emphasized by the fact that I did not see my trunk delivered as its check required. I found it in a corner of the depot at Albany, where it had been forgotten by the careful baggage master. I had heard that similar forgetfulness had been even chronic and that a number of trunks theretofore missing had never been found at all.

My trip down the river was performed by boat for two good reasons. One was that I wished to see the Hudson River, and the other was that rival steamboats were running a fierce competition, so that the fare was only one York shilling. They may have been losing less money from the fact that both boats were floating restaurants and did not give away their provisions.

On arriving at the city, I went over to Brooklyn, to visit with the two boys of my father's old-time Richmond partner, Mr. Heaton. They were prime good fellows and we went and caught a mountain of crabs in what was then Gowanus Bay and is now covered by blocks of buildings. I also went to see Mr. Rollo, at A. S. Barnes & Co.'s, and as I entered the store he came forward to meet me, saying, "How are you, Willie!" He had not seen me since I was seven, but explained that it was one of his peculiarities to never forget a face he had once seen.

Most of my time, after that, was for several days passed at the Crystal Palace, and a grand affair it was. With the aid of a guide-book, to get the spellings right, I wrote a long account of what I saw and sent it to the *Syracuse Chronicle*. As my young eyes had been caught, of course, by the more striking objects, my story was a good one and it was printed in full.

That was my first considerable venture in journalism and it brought me much feathers among my old schoolfellows. After that was done, I diligently explored the city, going as far up out of town as the recently erected Bible House. There were residences all the way up Broadway, and Bond Street was the fashion. Downtown, I had the great good luck to fall in with an old citizen, a handsome, stylishly dressed man, who caught me spying around his village. After laughing at my country-boy enthusiasm, he told me all sorts of things, showed me the Bowling Green and told me of the melting down of the leaden statue of George III, which once stood there.[3] He explained to me the Battery and the Washington's Headquarters, and Wall Street and any amount of colonial and Revolutionary history, so that my education as a New Yorker was fairly begun.

My stay in the city ended by a calculation of my cash resources, for I had carefully husbanded them and I went on to New London [Connecticut], by boat. There I was splendidly received by my uncle Enoch V. Stoddard and his family and struck up a strong friendship with the young people. It seemed to me that all New London was full of cousins of mine, of several names, and I took them all in. We went over to see the forts, Trumbull and Griswold, and the monument of the Arnold massacre, on which were four names of my Revolutionary kindred. When I had finished New London, including a tremendous bluefishing expedition, as far out as Point Judith, in my uncle's own sailboat, I went over to Noank to see my grandparents.

Enoch and I stayed there several days and had a grand time. We went out fishing and caught no end of porgies, blackfish, and other fish which were as new to me as the bluefish which had so tired my arms in the sailboat. Of them I had hauled in a round dozen and was proud of it. In all the intervals of other excitements, Grandmother Stoddard told me stories of ancient days, which were enough to set me on fire. For instance, when she was a girl just entering her teens, she and all her family were driven from home one day, and had to stand on the hill and look on while Benedict Arnold's marauders burned New London, her house included, while her kindred and mine were being slaughtered in the fort. I formed a bad opinion of Arnold but I was glad to know that all my forefather people had been fighting men. I was especially proud to know that my grandfather's father had been an Old Continental, one of Israel Putnam's men, and that he had been shot down at the battle of White Plains, in New York. He got well again but I could learn very little of his further exploits. I had been an admirer of Nathan

Hale and it was wonderful to know that Captain Hale's own company had been recruited from my own kith and kin and their neighbors. I feel as if he also were a kind of cousin of mine—and he may have been.

From New London I went over to Providence, to visit with my cousins the Smiths, the great mercantile house of Amos & James Y. Smith. One of them was governor of Rhode Island. I had a fine time there and went on to Boston in a steamer that sailed through a storm which was exceedingly interesting for I had had an ambition to be in a real storm at sea, the salt sea.

My visit in Boston was with my Uncle Bright's family, and they did me up in the most splendid manner. Osborn went with me to see all sorts of places and I saw more alone. Among them were the Bunker Hill monument and where my ancestors under Putnam fought the British under Howe. I went all over the Common and remembered all the stories I had ever heard of it. I had another family of relatives, the Buttons, of the great clothing concern of Button, Call & Co. Mrs. Button was a sister of Mrs. Sarah Allen Stoddard, Enoch's wife, and she took to me. She had a "one hoss shay" and as I could drive she took me everywhere in that shay. One day we drove out to Mount Auburn Cemetery, and I found it a beautiful place but did not know until afterwards that her especial errand that day was to arrange for the funeral of a Rev. Mr. Bolles, who had married a cousin of hers and mine by the name of Smith. Neither did I dream that the widow Bolles, for whose husband's funeral Aunt Button and I were arranging, was in time to become my own stepmother.

From Boston, after a bewildering time of it, I went to New Haven, to see my stepuncle, Gilbert A. Smith, and his family. He was a paper manufacturer but I cared less for his factory than I did for the pleasure of climbing Mount Holyoke and Mount Tom and seeing the Connecticut River.

After this it was time for me to go home and it hardly need be said that I reached Syracuse without a cent in my pocket. In return for my expended savings, however, I had been to a great school for a boy of my age and came back with a vast number of new things in my head.

I was still writing poetry in those days, and my success as a newspaper correspondent stimulated me to attempt another appearance in print. It was a small item of some kind and then it was a poem. Carroll Smith got them into the *Journal* for me, but the roguish typos beat him on the poem. They set it up without remorse and printed it without correcting the proof. Such a hash as they made of it, you never saw, and I did not tempt them again.

I had another string to my bow, however, for I believed that I could deliver an oration. There was organized what is called a Debating Society. It contained all the young lawyers and several politicians and I cannot say just why they elected me Secretary. So I was, however and my oratorical ambition burned high within me. At each meeting some special subject, generally political, was up to be torn in pieces, and I studiously prepared myself for one after another of those forensic contests. Each time, nevertheless, my courage failed me and the audience lost me, until an evening came when I daringly arose in the middle of a long pause. I was greeted with moderate applause and I managed to say "Mr. Speaker." There, however, all my ideas took wing and my head was empty. After some delay, I made out to say once more, "Mr. Speaker," but there I broke down and the audience cheered uproariously. I sat down for that evening, but not long afterwards I tried it again and succeeded in making my speech. During years which followed, the experience of my first effort hampered me and it was only with the greatest exertion of will and courage that I could get upon my feet, even in a church meeting.

There were sad changes coming for me at that time and although their coming was slow it was only too sure. During two whole years, my idolized mother was slowly fading away with consumption. She withstood it bravely and never complained, but her strength went away from month to month. It seemed to me, and I am glad to remember it now, that all the while she appeared to draw nearer to me and to lean upon me. I was more and more her companion in drives and visits, and at home she loved to have me near her, for I was her oldest son and my father was more and more confined by the harassing cares of his business.

My mother, as a last resort, was under the care of a specialist whose office was at a distance, on the hill by the orphan asylum. I went there in the morning to obtain a supply of the medicine he was administering. On leaving the house, my mother was in her room on the ground floor, appearing much as usual, and I had no idea that she was in immediate danger. I have sometimes thought that she sent me away purposely, for she was as calm and smiling as ever and yet must have known. All the way as I went and came, however, my mind was in a remarkable inner process which I have never been able to understand. I saw without seeing. I saw myself returning and being met at the gate by Mr. Palmer [the new minister—ed.] with the announcement of my mother's departure. Then followed a panorama of the next few days, as distinctly as if I were looking at visible objects on the earth. I did reach home and was met at the gate by Mr. Palmer.

"Willie!" he exclaimed, "Your mother is gone!"

"I know it!" I replied and from that moment onward I was as one in a dream.

Whatever occurred, I seemed to myself to have seen it all and heard it all before. My Aunt Adeline Bright came on to attend the funeral. I had allowed nobody but myself to watch by the coffin at night, as was then the custom, but the last night before the funeral Aunt Adeline watched with me. It was an old custom, and for some reason or other I had often before been a watcher. Perhaps it was because I was considered a good nurse and was continually in demand to watch by the sick and the dying. It was a strange reputation to have been won by so young a boy. All went on until we were gathered in the parlor for the funeral, but I had not so much as shed one tear. I could not weep and hardly was conscious of a feeling of grief. Right there, however, relief came, for a torrent of blood burst out at my nose and mouth and I had to leave the room. A blood vessel had broken under the pressure upon my brain and this was the escape from the awful weight I was enduring. This was my first great sorrow and it was also the first and greatest possible change for our entire family. From that time forward the strong will, clear brain, [and] unselfish love [that] had been the jewels of our house, were lost to us and there were to be sad consequences, as the years went on.

I may as well set forth a few of them here, to clear the record. My grandfather was in Homer at the time of my mother's death. She had been his favorite daughter and her loss was a severe blow to him. He began to run down and lose his hold on life. His own house was rented, as he no longer cared to be burdened with it, and he went to board with his old friend Mr. Ford, then occupying one of the dwellings in the "big building." Here, a few months later, he met with an accident, a fall on the stairs, and in a day or so he passed away. I was not able to attend the funeral, but was told that such another had never been seen in Cortland County. It seemed, men said, as if all the old people had come out of their graves to say how grieved they were at the death of their honored and trusted friend. He left behind him no money but instead a memory which all his descendants might thank God for.

My grandmother came to live with us in Syracuse, but she did not long survive her husband. She was taken to Homer for burial. So the old-time associations passed away and new ones were rapidly forming.

During all these years, our social position had been all we could have asked for. Owing to my sister Julia's need of company, perhaps, I was in the habit of attending sociables and parties where the rest of the company were older, as well as all the gatherings of my own age and set. I was therefore somewhat older, on that account, and hardly regarded myself as a boy. With reference to one party that I remember, there was a decidedly unexpected incident. It was to be at the Outwater place, on the Park, and was given by Miss Mary Outwater, afterwards Mrs. Andrew D. White.

It was in the last week of March and the ice had but just floated out of the lake. Now, there had been a theory that the fish were under the ice all Winter but cleared out into the Oswego River and Lake Ontario in the Spring, to escape the too numerous fishermen of Salt Point. Ed Wheaton and I discussed the matter and determined to try it on. We went, early in that day, to Salina, and secured a small, rather insecure, sailboat. It was a sunny day and the water was ice water.

Out we sailed, toward the western shore, and anchored our boat for a trial of the fishing all the sooner because of a dead calm which forbade us to sail any farther. We did not intend to remain there and lazily left the sail up. I was stretched out in the stern, watching my useless line, when I saw Ed get up in the prow. He wished to go to the other side of the boat and the sail was in his way. I saw him try to step around in front of the mast, rather than crawl under the boom. In an instant the boat began to tip, as his weight and his grip on the mast carried it over. There was but one thing for me to do, if I would not be carried under in the probable capsize, and I sprang out into the water.

Ed was in it when I came to the surface and he called out to me as to what we were to do, under these chilling circumstances. I told him to cut the anchor rope and he did so, putting his knife back into his pocket with the coolness of a veteran. Then we tried to right the boat, but the sail was still up and it did but swing over and come down upon us, driving us under water. "Cut the halliards!" I shouted, and he did so and then we were able to bring our wreck to a level, [but] with the water an inch over her gunwale, so that bailing was out of the question.

We determined, nevertheless, to take her ashore, for we were both good swimmers and the land was only a half mile away. One would swim in front and tug at the painter [a line used for securing or towing a boat—ed.] and the other would push behind and we divided the work fairly. Our mishap had been noted on shore, as far away as Salina, and the news of it was spreading fast. Right near us was a party of sportsmen and they tried the water but decided that it was too long a swim for them in fluid of that temperature. All that they could do was to wait for us and see us come to them. We did so, but we were so chilled through that they had to pull us out of the lake, nearly insensible. Like good fellows as they were, they took off our clothes and rubbed us in the regular way prescribed for the resuscitation of the drowned.

We both were dreadfully sick before we came to life again and could stand up. Then along came a rowboat and into it we went while our rescuers, or rubbers, followed with the sailboat. The exercise of rowing to Salina was good for us and there a carriage was waiting to take our corpses home. We went to my house first, and found and drank all there was left in my father's bottle of old Madeira wine. Then Ed went to his own house and I took another rub, of my own making.

That evening, at the Outwater party, for some reason, the gathered crowd was still in ignorance of our escape. Many had but just heard the sad news of our unfortunate drowning and all were ready to greet us enthusiastically when we came marching in to tell them that we, like John Quincy Adams, "still lived."[4]

One change that came a few months after my mother's departure was not so much a change as the formal doing of a known duty. I had not yet been baptized into church membership and it was so mainly because of a confused idea in my mind as to what was called "conversion." I had been led to believe that it was a sudden change of mind or soul, to be accompanied by much pain of conscience, remorse, and what was vaguely described as "repentance."

I was serious enough in the inquiries I made of a number of older church members, but not one of them, minister or other, could give me any satisfactory information on the points in my troubled understanding. At last, my own mind was made up and I came before the church, at a regular meeting, to say: "I believe and I wish to be baptized." Some of the older members put me through a severe cross examination as to my experiences and emotions. Of the latter, I frankly told them that I had none at all.

On consultation, they consented to admit me, although it appeared to be an unusual case, where a young man merely wished to obey the divine command to "believe and be baptized." At all events, most of them had known me a long time and knew I had been in the Sunday school and had rung the bell and kindled the church fires. It had been many a long day since there had been a baptism. I was the first candidate in the new edifice and in the elegant new font, under the pulpit.

The Sunday came and the weather was bitterly cold. The ice in the font was half an inch thick and had to be broken. Pieces of it were floating around my head when I went under, but I did not feel the chill of that water, for all over me was a strange glow and I astonished good Mr. Palmer by smiling in his face when we went out into the anteroom to dress. It was too solemn a time for smiling, in his evident opinion, but I was glad that I had done what I believed to be my duty. It is my belief, now, that I was led of God and that He whom I was so determinedly obeying took note of it for me. There had been a more than usually large attendance and I found that my position had changed in the opinion of many men.

Among these was my father's partner, Mr. Edward Babcock, and he at once took me in as a teacher in a mission school which he had established in the First Ward, formerly Salina, for Syracuse had now become a city and had annexed its old neighbor. Also, I was made a teacher in the church Sunday school and was expected to take an active part in the meetings—and there, at least, one more worker was much needed.

17

Going to College

Something or other has made me think, just now, of army affairs. There was always a kind of military colony in Syracuse. On the Park corner was the house of old Major Burnet, a retired army officer for whom I had vast respect. One of my first friends and playfellows was Win Sumner, whose father was a colonel. Win became Colonel E. V. Sumner, the distinguished cavalry commander, in due time, while his father was a corps commander in the Army of the Potomac.[1] So, for awhile, was our neighbor Major J. J. Peck, of the regulars. An equally notable example was Major General H. W. Slocum,[2] who afterwards commanded the left wing of General Sherman's army in the West. When I first knew him, he was our county clerk, having graduated at West Point without any immediate army service of importance.

Another one of our bright district schoolboys who worked his own way up to the rank of schoolteacher, before the war, was Major General Henry Barnum,[3] who obtained his double stars by leading the assault at the battle of Lookout Mountain. It was said that no other village of our size sent into the Civil War as many as four major generals, three of them corps commanders. Besides them were many minor officers, from the rank of colonel and under. At the same time, we were apparently short of statesmen and I had to watch for my great men and orators at the conventions. Just how many really great ones I found, I do not know, for the world knows nothing of its greatest men, but I certainly did manage to turn up a large number of remarkable-looking men and women and wish, now, that I had their Kodaks to show.

Among the changes which had already arrived was one in my father's affairs. By the end of my second year in the store, the burden of the church debt had proved too much for him. It did not bankrupt him, but it compelled him to sell out his business to Mr. Babcock and try something else. The new firm included William T. Hamilton and the style was E. H. Babcock & Co. The Express office had removed to larger quarters and young Mr. Wells had gone away. I believe the next title of that concern was Livingstone & Wells, afterwards Wells & Fargo.

My father was a man of resources and he turned to his insurance business, which was already pretty good. He readily obtained other companies, rapidly, until, I think he had as many as fifteen: Fire, Life, and Marine. He even invented a "Health Insurance Company" on the mutual plan, but it did not work well. It seemed that as soon as any man became insured he "took sick" and became a pensioner, while the other subscribers were slow in making payments. With great energy, however, my father went ahead, until he had the largest insurance business in central New York and an income of three or four thousand dollars a year. His office was in the Malcolm block, across the street from our store. He was guardian for Young Malcolm, one of the heirs of that property. He made it one of the handsomest offices in Syracuse and my duties at fires were increased considerably.

In that connection, I must mention two other members of our family. Charles and John were still at school but, before long, Henry went into the Onondaga County Bank, under Mr. Horace White, Andrew's father. With him went our very remarkable dog, "Dash," one of the best-known characters in the city. I raised him from a pup, beginning on Onondaga Street, and he had been my companion in many a hunt and ramble. He also insisted upon attending me at fires and answered every alarm bell, whether I did or not. Nothing could keep him in the house after he heard the fire signal, and the moment he was let out he would run to a particular engine house and bark up the energies of that fire company. When the men set out, his place was at their head, barking furiously at every delay, and he never left them until their duties were over. They formally elected him a member of the company for it, like all the rest, was a "volunteer" organization. There were endless stories told of his sagacity, and when Henry went into the bank he went along, deciding that his services were needed as guardian of the institution.

I will only mention one point, for the study of the curious. He would lie in the president's office, eyes open, and would permit bank clerks and others whom he knew or approved of to pass the little half-door between the bank office itself and the outer entry, until the clock on the mantel struck "three." After that no man or boy might come in until he did so by command of a bank officer. Now, how did Dash know that the bank closed business at three o'clock and how did he distinguish human character? It was the same with other features of the office management: he obtained a knowledge of them and insisted upon their due observance.

Well, during all these years I had been an omnivorous reader. During part of the time, I had been required to sleep in a bunk under a back counter, as night watchman, sweep, and general regulator. My duties were miscellaneous and very exacting but I will not dwell upon them. Suffice it to say that they began at six in the morning and did not end at all. Two other boys who, at different times, were put in to try it, broke down pretty soon. At the same time, my own strength appeared to increase with hard work and my training lift at the gymnasium rose to 460 pounds, or more than that of any other fellow of my weight. That, too, kept steadily at 144 and afterwards, in Rochester, rose to 157.

I tried to vary my educational exercises. One effort related to anatomy, but when my father discovered that I was attending evening lectures and actual dissections at the Medical College, as it was called, he put a stop to it, declaring all that new-fangled stuff needless. So he did an attempt at a Commercial School, with bookkeeping and a vain reaching out after the Law, whereof he seemed to have an especial dislike. Of one thing, however, I had made up my own mind. That bookstore was no place for me. I wanted to go to a New York house, Sheather's or Rollo's, for instance, but that was also voted down.

At last I settled upon my old idea of college, long ago almost given up as impossible. It was strongly opposed by my stepuncle Gilbert and others, but it was supported by some of my father's Syracuse friends, including, I believe, the Whites and Mr. Fitch, of the Mechanic's Bank. At all events, my father began to think well of it and to discuss the comparative advantages of Providence and Brown College, and the entirely new University at Rochester. At both places we had friends and relatives, but I think the nearness of Rochester carried the day, with other considerations. If at that time I had gone to Brown, I might sooner have made the acquaintance of one John Hay,[4] for he would have been a classmate.

I must not forget to record that during my last Winter in the book business I returned to authorship and invention. I made what I supposed was an improvement in watches, until Andrew White came to see me in his Winter holidays. He pooh-poohed it and I was convinced that the regular dealers were ahead of me. I had all the more pride in him because he had won the hundred-dollar Sophomore Prize declamation medal at Yale and was a model college boy. As to the other matter, I wrote a long novel. It was during the time when the other candidates were occupying my old bunk under the counter at the store and I was sleeping in the little parlor bedroom at home, over the front door. It had no arrangements for heating and I remember writing at night until the ink froze in the inkstand and I had to quit until I could thaw it out in the morning. It was a work, I should say, of over one hundred thousand words and was in many ways remarkable, but I never finished it to suit me and it was not sent to any publisher.

When the Spring months had fairly begun, I was informed that I might begin my preparations for college and I did so. My Latin began under a remarkable German ex-professor who had left his native country for distinguished conduct in the revolution of 1848. He was a fine scholar but we disagreed, for he insisted that I employ what he called a "bridge" in my translations of Virgil. I rebelled against that, and also against my very irregular chances of finding him in properly unlagered condition to read anything. My next tutor was a Professor Maltby, and I also brushed up my mathematics, etc., but I made a note of it that on the Fourth of July I had not yet touched the Greek alphabet. I was aware, however, that the professor in that ancient tongue at Rochester was Professor Asahel Kendrick, the distinguished author of *Kendrick's Introduction*, and several other schoolbooks of the kind. So I obtained a copy of the *Introduction* and committed it to memory, examples for translation and all. It was quite an undertaking, in hot weather, but I wish that I now retained the retentive memory I then was blessed with. It would retain anything and it sometimes seemed to me that I remembered all the books I had ever read. I did not do so, for among them were all the octavo copies of the English poets which were in the store, and there were large desert places, even in Byron himself, which I had voted not worth stacking away in my brain. As to all the minor branches set down on the schedule for examination, I felt no anxiety whatever and I went to Rochester in full confidence that I was sure to pass.

Some way or other, I have forgotten how, I was provided with a boarding house at the start and took my small baggage into it. The next morning I set out for the university. I had settled on the extreme east of the town and the Institution was at the western end. I had, therefore, to patrol the entire length of the central avenue, Buffalo Street, and about half way was the Genesee River and the bridge. Every foot of the distance appealed to my memory of my earlier childhood, for there, just off on Clinton Street, was one of our residences. There was the Second Baptist Church, the first I had ever entered. There was the corner on which Julia and I had upset the baby wagon and spilled the molasses. There was the bridge itself and Deacon Barton's axe factory and then I came to the corner of State Street, to see my father's store with the sign of Mr. Sage on it instead of his, while across the way and away up was the sign of my childhood's puzzle, Mr. Job Printing.

On I went, block after block, until I reached my destination. The new Institution had not yet been able to erect a building of its own and it had secured for educational purposes what had once been a considerable hotel. It stood near the bridge over the canal and it was no longer of any use in that regard, for the railway had ruthlessly killed the canal passenger business. It was a rainy, gloomy morning and I had been cultivating what was almost a fit of the blues, but anything like low spirits vanished the moment I made my way into the big hotel dining room which was now employed as the university chapel. The hour for opening exercises had not yet arrived but a large number of young candidates for examination had done so and they were standing all around, in various attitudes of discontent and apparent apprehension. Not a boy among them looked as if he expected to pass, and some of them were even poring over textbooks, as if they were freshening their minds before facing their inquisitors. It struck the vein of fun that is in me, somewhere, and I was all right in a moment. It was my obvious duty to quiz and otherwise encourage that damp mob of homesick, trouble-minded candidates for admission and I did so. Before long, a tall, handsome, curly-headed fellow came lounging in, with a look of disgust on his face and I made for him viciously.

"Hullo!" I said. "'Who are you? You're the first decent lookin' fellow I've seen. What's your name?"

"Hop Strong," he said, in a somewhat astonished manner, and a few other inquiries gave me the facts that not only was he a Rochester boy, but that his father and mother had been early friends of mine.

"Come on!" I said. "Let's hunt up some other good fellows!"

The very next man we boned gave his name as Harris, Will Harris, whose father, Judge Ira Harris of Albany, was Chancellor of the University. He was also a Homer boy who owed much to John Osborn, and he had married Miss Tubbs, my mother's intimate friend, boarding school chum, etc., so that Will was a sort of cousin of mine at once. The next man we cornered was Will Abbott, son of the esteemed missionary of that name, and we went on until we made up a squad of more than half a dozen and felt much better.

As soon as the chapel exercises were over, the examinations began and I had first-rate luck. My other branches were all right, of course, and when I came to my Greek I was in front of Professor Kendrick, answering his questions by quotations from *Kendrick's Introduction*. Even the passages he gave me for translation were from a thin little book in his hand, and I could translate them without looking at them, quoting them from my *Kendrick* in my memory. He was delighted with my proficiency and I started in his class with a fine reputation as one of the best-prepared of the sixty-odd candidates. Some of them were very odd, but fifty-seven of them managed to squeeze through and the "Class of '58" was to begin its career as the most numerous that had as yet blessed the records of the Institution. It was afterwards to have a great reputation of its own.

I was exceedingly gratified by the evidences which I quickly received of the high esteem in which my father and mother had been held by their friends in Rochester. I was at once taken hold of and invited here and there in the most cordial manner. My father's stepbrother, Erastus T. Smith, one of the handsomest men I ever saw and a great figurehead as the dignified chairman of public meetings, was ranked as my uncle. His daughter was Mrs. Dr. Dean, wife of a prominent physician, and their house became one of my Sunday dinner places. So did that of Mr. E. F. Smith, only a cousin, but his wife was also a cousin and we were the best of friends. Her maiden name was Barbour and I do not know how the relationship came in. Hop Strong's house was as the rest, and so was that of his uncle Alvah Strong, editor and publisher of the *Democrat*. Hop's cousin Augustus was one of my first acquisitions. He afterwards became president of the Rochester Theological Seminary, after a career at Yale and in the ministry.

I need not make a catalog of the many new friends who rapidly turned up. My boarding house was selected for reasons of economy, which I well knew I must exercise, and part of my agreement was that I was to provide and saw my own wood and attend to my own fires. My landlady was a good woman who was struggling hard to get along, but her husband was a queer character. He was an enthusiastic local politician, of whom it was related that when Henry Clay was defeated for President, this admirer went and sat down by the Upper Genesee Falls and wept aloud. He shortly did me the honor to assure me that he "had read dixinaries 'fore you were born sir!" but he failed to tell me how many of them he had perused.

18

College Days

If there is one occupation more than another to which I never took kindly, it is the sawing of wood. Chopping, on the other hand, I have really enjoyed and I have had plenty of it. I had more than plenty of wood sawing, that first Winter in Rochester. My first roommate, for a short time only, was a young law student named Brand, and after him came another, a rough country fellow named Titus B. Eldredge. Of Brand's after career I never knew much, but Eldredge went to New York, attained success, and I saw a great deal of him in later days.

Of the ordinary incidents of student life, there is very little to be said. They are of a well-known pattern. The university was fairly well equipped, for a young one, and it had the foundations of a fine library in which were many books that were new to me. Among these were works on architecture and they opened a field of especial interest in which I dug pretty deeply. The faculty were all first-class men in their way, or ways. The president, Dr. Martin B. Anderson, was just the man for the extremely arduous task which he had undertaken, that of building up a brand-new concern. My own studies never brought me under his personal care to any extent, except in History, of which he was the professor. He taught me how to read history, how to use a library, and put into me a good deal of enthusiasm concerning the old days of the world. By some accident or other, perhaps, my seat was just opposite his in the classroom, when I at last got up to it, and he formed a habit, at the beginning of each of his admirable lectures, of half closing his eyes and calling upon me for a digest of the day's field of operation. The other boys voted that I was the most useful man in the class, for I delivered them all from the necessity of looking at their text-books before they came in. It may be that he believed that I was more in sympathy with his fad than that indicated.

Professor Dewey, Chemistry, was no other than my old childhood ven-eration, the principal of the now departed "Institute," in which I had begun my Latin, at six, perched upon a high stool to reach the level of my desk. The Latin professor, Richardson, was full of that ancient tongue and any fellow might readily get it out of him. In Greek, the country was believed to contain few scholars who were at all the equals of Professor Kendrick, and he did his teacher work faithfully. Our mathematical professor, Mr. Quimby, had been professor of mathematics at West Point, and was all that could be asked for. He was afterwards a Major General in the army, during the Civil War.[1]

In modern languages, we had Tutor Mixer, said to be entirely competent, but I was under him but a short time in French. During the vacations of that year and at the end of it, I was at home, aiding my father in his office, especially as a collector, in which line he was himself not any too good. The whole year passed in a continual effort to keep my expenditures within the limits of my limited and sadly irregular remittances, for my father was spending all he was making and was still carrying a heavy church load.

One of the first of my college experiences was the customary search by the upper class men for members of their secret societies. I carried all of our crowd into the Alpha Delta Phi and thereby earned much disapprobation from those who were left out and from the rival societies. In any merely electoral contest, I might thereafter count upon adverse votes enough to defeat me, but was consoled by the consideration that I could even more surely defeat anybody else.

That society contest, however, brought me two lifelong friends, at least. One was John R. Howard, afterwards of the firm of Fords, Howard & Hulbert, who published my Lincoln.[2] The other was Manton Marble, who became the editor and manager of the *New York World*. He was the somewhat too distinguished manager of Hon. Samuel J. Tilden's political campaign in the great historic contest for the presidency between him and Rutherford B. Hayes.[3]

Another member of my class very soon began to win peculiar distinction. It was a young fellow named Harkness, who could write the finest hand you ever saw. He could put the Lord's Prayer inside of a five-cent piece.

What was more, he was a stenographer. One day he came into the Rhetoric room, all prepared to read his thesis. The professor, Dr. S. S. Cutting, was a sharp-eyed, capable man, who had been an editor and whom I liked very much. We were warm friends to the day of his death. Well! He called upon Harkness and the youngster arose, with the most solemn of faces and began to read something from a card which he held in his hand. Of course, that "Exercise" was bound to be a short one. So we all thought and there was even a cloud on the face of Professor Cutting, but the reading went on until half the recitation hour was consumed.

"Harkness!" exclaimed the professor. "Let me see that thing!"

"I'm almost half through, sir," replied the reader, but he delivered his remarkable manuscript and first another cloud and then a grin went over Dr. Cutting's countenance.

The essay, whatever it was, had been reduced to stenographic type and to the finest of penwork. It called for a microscope and an interpreter and Harkness was allowed to take his seat without finishing the reading. He is now Professor Harkness, the star finder, at the National Observatory at Washington.[4]

Our special crowd started a serenade and glee club, of course, and were soon known all over the university and the city itself as "The Quails." Among them, although a sophomore, was Charles De W. Bridgeman, who at last, to our surprise, attained eminence as a clergyman. I cannot mention all the good fellows who afterwards did well, for their names would have no value for the few eyes which will ever peruse these fragmentary records.

My sophomore year [1855] began under about the same circumstances as at first except that I had by that time obtained a pretty firm place in my class rating. Perhaps it was partly due to incidents. In the Hoyt School my drill had been thorough and it stood me in good stead now. I remember when I was first called up in mathematics. The arrangement was alphabetical and the letter "S" was not reached until the third or fourth day. When I was called, I stepped to the blackboard, drew my diagram, and went through the required demonstration precisely as if this had been the Hoyt School instead of the university. As I turned away toward my seat, Professor Quimby threw away a cud of tobacco, took a fresh one and remarked:

"Young gentlemen, that is the first recitation I have had!"

It was about the same in Greek, while in Latin we were reading books with which I was already entirely familiar. This gave me more time for the library and for many other things, and I was beginning to enter into all social affairs with a great deal of zest.

With the new year came in a new freshman class and there was another war between the rival societies. The Alpha Delta Phi won again, and among our winnings were two fellows who at once became also enrolled as "Quails." One of these was Francis Macomber, my lifelong friend and a man of sterling worth. He was for many years a United States District judge. The other, the drollest and dryest of prime good fellows, was Oscar, or "Ort" Folsom. He also became a success as a lawyer but was killed by an accident while district attorney of Erie County [in upstate New York, embracing Buffalo—ed.]. He left a daughter who in due time became Mrs. Grover Cleveland and the lady of the White House at Washington.[5] It was during my sophomore year that I really began my work as a constant contributor to many periodicals. What I wrote did not amount to much but I was in good lines of training for the career which I was to follow and was actually acquiring some reputation. It was this that afterwards gave me my first start in life.

During all of my college days, I was a regular attendant at church, but we boys were in the habit of distributing our presence around among various houses of worship, according to circumstances. Perhaps some of the influential circumstances wore bonnets, etc., and needed company to and from the meetinghouses—at least, all the way home. It was a part of our duties, calling it so, that we did not at all neglect.

The most important change that came to me at the beginning of my second college year was a change of boarding house. At the far west end of the city where the winds from Lake Ontario could get at it without any interruption, was a large house known as Halsted Hall. It had been put there by a medical genius of that name and had been used by him during many profitable years as a "water-cure" sanitarium. Its front part was of brick and comfortable. Its long rear extension was of one-story wood and was not comfortable except in moderate weather. Any of those rear rooms could freeze a thermometer in a lake wind of the kind that frequently came that Winter.

My chum at Halsted Hall was Will Harris, and in the concern as a whole, was an exceedingly pleasant company. We had two professors, to begin with. One was our Rhetorical professor, Dr. John H. Raymond. Dr. Raymond was a brother of my old friend, Rev. R. R. Raymond of Syracuse, and an uncle of Jack Howard, who also was with us. So were two or three other good fellows of the sophomore and upper classes, with variations. Dr. J. H. Raymond afterwards became president of Vassar College, retaining that place until his death. He was a fine elocutionist, and one of our enjoyments, that Winter, was to gather in the parlor and hear him read Shakespeare, etc. Dr. Kendrick was also with us, but his favorite reading was Byronic.

The house was kept by the Misses Porter, three very cultivated and intelligent old maids, of the highest personal character. With them was their brother, Judge Porter, an eminent lawyer, and his family, and their sister, Mrs. Farley, and her husband and children. So the house was full. There was a fair bowling alley and there was a walk of a measured mile to the university which we turned into a running exercise pretty regularly, in order to improve our legs and get to chapel in time. The Misses Porter were arrant abolitionists and Halsted Hall was one of the stations of what was then known as "the underground railroad" for the benefit of runaway slaves. I saw more than one dark face come flitting by. They were also in favor of "woman's rights" and I obtained some ideas from them on that head. Professor Raymond, by the way, encouraged my fad for studying successful men in a way of his own. For instance, when Wendel[l] Philips was to lecture at Corinthian Hall, he advised us all to go and get a lesson in oratory.[6] We went in a body but the Quail part of the body had young ladies who also needed lessons in elocution.

The Spring vacation of that year was spent by Will Harris and me in a visit to an aunt of his, Mrs. Guernsey, down on the west shore of Cayuga Lake. It was a pleasant farmhouse and she was an exceedingly kindly woman. Her son Cyrus was a good fellow, too, but our announced object was catching fish and shooting wild fowl. I think we did more rowing around along the edges of the Cayuga marshes than anything else, but we had a prime vacation. When Summer came, I was invited to spend a few weeks of my vacation with the Harris family at Albany. I do not know that I ever had a more entirely agreeable time. The family, in the absence of Judge Harris and his (second) wife at the seashore, consisted of his son, stepson, and daughters. The stepson, whom I liked very well, was Henry Rathbone and he afterwards married the older of the daughters, Miss Clara Harris.[7] I shall have more to say of them bye and bye.

Will's aunt Clara Harris, his father's sister, lived at the farm, a few miles up the Hudson, with her widowed mother. I was out at the farm a great deal, for I formed a strong friendship for Aunt Clara. Among the pleasant incidents of my visit was a whole day that we spent at the old Schuyler mansion. It was then in the possession of Mrs. Mackintosh, who afterwards married ex-President Millard Fillmore.[8] She deserved anything good for she entered with all her soul into my revolutionary enthusiasm. She took me all over the house and grounds and filled me full of old-time legends concerning General Philip Schuyler,[9] the Tories, the Indians, and all that sort of history, but I was never able to accept her kind invitation to come again.

This may be the right place to record that Will Harris and I, in our next vacation, took a hunting jaunt into the Adirondack woods, by way of Gloversville, where I had previously visited with my cousins the Thomas family. I then became acquainted with my cousin Sara Thomas, now Mrs. Sara Randall, Harry's mother. Her father was an excellent man. I learned a great deal about the making of gloves and I went to the Sir William Johnson mansion, away back in the woods. It was in good preservation, particularly the marks of the tomahawk of the angry Mohawk chief Brant, Tha-yen-da-ne-ga,[10] on the massive rail and balusters of the great stairway.

In Gloversville I then saw, for the first and only time, my grandmother Osborn's two maiden sisters, the Misses Cotton, both quite old and neither of them as handsome as she was. The next year, Sara Randall came to visit us at Syracuse and was with us at the time of my grandmother's death.

To return to Rochester, the university had two "literary societies," the Delphic and Pithonian, and the debates and other exercises of these in their weekly gatherings were thought much of by the students. Toward the end of the sophomore year, there were competitive debates in each society and the winner of each was the "Prize Debater" for his Society in the grand contest before the University. In the Pithonian, that year, there were eleven contestants and I was calmly informed by good authority that I had no chance whatever. That aroused my temper somewhat, and so did an attempt to hiss me down when I began speaking, for I had made jealousies as well as friends.

That temper was the making of me and I carried the prize unanimously. Then followed the more important contest in the chapel, before a densely packed audience of all sorts. My opponent was Lemuel Moss, in later days Rev. Dr. Moss, of *The National Baptist*. It was a tough pull, for he was several years my senior, but the faculty, sitting as judges, refused to decide between us, so that we both won it, just as Frank Stockton and I once both won a Harper prize, with the difference that Lem Moss and I received nothing but honor while Stockton and I received a hundred dollars apiece, which was more to the point.

At the end of the sophomore year came the grand declamation contest in Corinthian Hall, and there were to be three prizes. Again I was confidently assured that I was no speaker and that while my class standing compelled the faculty to put me on the list of competitors they did not expect me to win anything. If this was the opinion of even my friends, including Mant Marble, what a small show I must have had! The hall was crowded to suffocation and it was said to hold two thousand people. My temper was up again and when the debate was over the first prize fell to El Otis and me. The committee decided between us by flipping a copper. The cent turned up heads for Otis and he got it as Number One. He went on winning until he is now known in history as Major General Elwell S. Otis of the regular army, our first commander in the Philippines.[11]

There were trips to Lake Ontario. There were studies of the upper and lower falls of the Genesee, and once I failed entirely in a hairbrained attempt to swim that river at the rapids above the city. I discovered that a seemingly smooth current may be a dreadful hypocrite, running like mad and ready to sweep a reckless college boy over the upper fall. That failure cost me oysters for six.

There were drives in Winter and Summer, whenever I could get a horse and buggy or cutter and there were many social affairs. There were serenades and that sort of thing but I must not forget my first experience with the Spiritists [Spiritualists]. The Fox Girls had begun their experiments upon popular credulity and all the country was talking about the "Rochester Rappings."[12] A congregation of "Spiritists" had formed and were holding regular meetings in a small hall over Sage's bookstore. One Sunday, Hop Strong and his cousin Henry, Will Abbott, Will Harris, and I went to see and hear the performances.

With the termination of that Summer vacation came a most important event. My father told us children of his determination to marry again and it was really no news to me. Mrs. Frances M. Bolles, to whom he introduced us, was a woman of much intelligence and we all hoped that she would be a good companion for him, although I do not believe that any lot of grown-up children ever took kindly to the idea of having a stepmother.

It was, I think, easier for the boys, who were less at home, than it was for the girls. It may have been easiest of all for a fellow away at college, but I did what I could to keep peace in the family. That I did not succeed and that many troubles came is all that need be said in that connection, for we must let the dead past bury its own dead and that history may as well be forgotten.

The wedding took place at Pomfret, Connecticut, on September 18, 1856, and the bride and groom came to Syracuse without an extended wedding tour. Mrs. Stoddard was a fervent Episcopalian and it was not long before she led my father to join her in the communion of St. Paul's Church. It was natural that both of them should wish the children to go with them, but at that point the lines of separation began to be drawn. It was a matter of continual discussion that produced disorder. With my stepmother came her very engaging and agreeable little daughter Fannie, for whom I readily formed a genuine brotherly affection. She in due time became the wife of Rev. Herbert Patterson, but she has long since passed away, as has her mother. With the latter, I retained pleasant personal relations to the end of her life. She was a most remarkable preserver of all manner of odds and ends of biographical lore, relating to the several families with which she was in any wise connected. She kept up a tremendous correspondence with kith and kin at all the ends of the earth and could tell, off hand, what had become of twigs and branches which other people had lost sight of.

My father's affairs now appeared to be in fair condition. The new Mrs. Stoddard was said to be a woman of some property, but that feature of the case turned out to be somewhat mythical, for it was little Fannie to whom the moderate estate belonged and in keeping it up, still another burden soon fell upon my father. One way and another, therefore, my own affairs were becoming unpleasantly restricted and the worry and fret of poverty, in an unpleasant form, began to tell upon me pretty severely.

On returning to Rochester, I did not again board with the Misses Porter. At first, for a while, I was an inmate of the Strong family, parents of my old friend Hop. Then a new idea, related to economy, took possession of me. I would take a room and board myself.

Away down on State Street, half way to the railroad depot, had been put up a new brick building, somewhat ahead of the current demands. There were stores below, but almost all the upper part was empty and I secured a large back room at a merely nominal rental. Hop Strong joined me in the enterprise and was able to bring part of the furniture out of quantities which his family were not using. Nevertheless, my share was far the larger and put me sadly in debt. The room was well-lighted and exceedingly cheerful, and the heating was done by a wide mouthed "Franklin" stove, burning bituminous coal. I slept upon a sofa bedstead which became mere sofa in the daytime. Over a round table in the middle was a gaslight chandelier, with a drop, and from the chandelier also hung a wide-winged black hawk of whom I remember writing, "How like a ghost he swings, / With the dust upon his wings. / Like the phantom forms he seems, / That float over us in dreams." That may have been so, after the gas was turned off, and a sort of remedy was to be obtained by brushing off the dust.

Hop was musical and a friend of his loaned him a piano. There was also a guitar, big horse pistol, "used by Andrew Jackson at New Orleans," according to an inscription card tied to its neck, and there were many other oddities and semi-elegances. It was a room worth visiting, and before long everybody who could find an excuse did so, including whole parties of our young lady friends. It was so soon called "Quail's Nest" that we had a silver plate made for the door carrying that title. Not long was it before yet another idea came, and in many a periodical, east and west, were printed the poems and stories of "The Quail o' Quail's Nest."

19

Junior Year

The political situation of the country had been steadily growing more and more cloudy, year after year.[1] There were increasing evidences that both of the old parties, Whig and Democratic, were disintegrating, but it did not yet appear what was to take the place of them. In the year 1856, however, the discontented elements had gone far enough to organize what was known as the People's Party and of course I belonged to it. So did my father, and I went home at election day to cast my first vote for Frémont and Dayton.[2] I was challenged at the polls and compelled to swear my vote in by an Irish Pro-Slavery "Old Hunker" Democrat who proved to have been in this country only about six weeks.[3] From that time onward I paid more attention than ever to political affairs and was really beginning to know something about them—but not a great deal, for the situation was a puzzle to older heads than mine.

I went back to Rochester with an assurance that now my finances would be regularly cared for, but only to find myself plunging deeper and deeper into difficulties which harassed me dreadfully. Something worse than that was in store, however, for when I went home for the Winter holidays I found my beloved sister Julia apparently recovered from a severe attack of typhoid fever but really drifting into the pitiless grip of bronchial consumption. She lingered until February and I came home to be with her at the last. She died in my arms, with her head upon my shoulder, for I hardly had left her for a minute, day or night, and she appeared to depend on me more than upon anybody else. She was at rest, and poor Kate was left alone with many troubles before her. I returned to my studies almost broken-hearted and it was some time before I recovered from the blow.

There were changes among my associates at the university. Mant Marble had gone to New York, into journalism. My friend Norman Fox, of the same class, had gone into the Theological Seminary. Will Harris had gone to West Point on his way to future distinguished army service. How those picked boys did turn out!

During most of all this time, I was doing more or less in the Rochester Gymnasium, presided over by a short, cast-iron genius by the name of Shadders from whom I did not learn a great deal, but then I was keeping up my muscles and activities pretty well and preparing for the hard service which was before me. On the whole, I was keeping up my reputation and my place in my class and winning the good opinion of the faculty, as their after action was to show. The Quails of Quail's Nest were all the while a noted feature in the university life and I was more and more widely known as "The Quail," perhaps somewhat to my detriment in the eyes of the best of good people. Well, the end of the year came, at last, and I went home burdened with debt, discouraged and determined not to go back into that kind of torment again. I had nominally borrowed two hundred dollars from my stepmother, but it turned out to be from the "Bolles estate" and while I gave my note for the whole and afterwards paid it, with interest, I only received actually one-hundred-and-sixty for my college debts, so pressing were the requirements of home affairs.

I do not think my father was then any longer the good businessman that he had been, and his wife was anything but a good businesswoman. I looked over his affairs and decided that although his income was good and business flourishing, it was time for me to get out from under. That meant that I could not consent to stay in Syracuse, as he would have preferred. Indeed, he strongly urged me to go back to college, but a condition precedent to that had to be the liquidation of my debts. As that was not to be, I would go west to seek my fortune as best I might.

Slowly and painfully the junior year dragged on to its close and I was at home in a state of mind that was anything but comfortable. I had been proud of my class standing and my college career and had hoped to go on to a completion which would aid me in a professional career. That would have been the law, beyond a doubt, although my father was unaccountably opposed to my adopting that profession—or any other, for he had no substitute to propose. I say thus much to justify the independent and somewhat rebellious course which I actually took.

Before leaving Rochester I had sold out Quail's Nest, my books, etc., and had paid some of my most pressing debts, but there was a pile of them left, accumulated under continuously illusive promises of cash from home. I still had a few dollars remaining but not enough to carry me to the Far West—that is, not very far.

There were many sadnesses connected with the giving up of Syracuse and my college courses at the same time. There were the graves of my mother and sister, who had been to me as angels of God, and I went to see them. There were our old residences, and the Park and the Lake and the bookstore. I took a last look at them all, but I was not at all sorry about the bookstore, for it was connected in my mind and memory with an enormous amount of overwork. I said goodbye to many people, and almost every man or woman among them appeared to know why I was going west and to be ready to send me off loaded with good wishes. As for my father, he gave no hearty consent, although he did not positively forbid. He told me, however, that if I did go, I must "go upon my own responsibility." I had a dim idea that he expected that shortly I would be writing to him for help. He did not know that I would have digged cellars first.

One of my old bookstore acquaintances was not only a schoolteacher but an arithmetical crank and he had invented and printed a considerable volume of "countinghouse tables." The thing was too big and clumsy and was not selling well and he proposed that I should make an effort to introduce it in the West. I knew too much about bookselling to see a gold mine in it but believed I might work off a few [volumes] and took a dozen or so on commission. My brother Henry, still a clerk in the bank, lent me twelve dollars and off I went, stopping at Rochester to pick up Hop Strong, who was going at the same time. He had long since left the university, as uncongenial, and had entered upon a commercial career as traveling salesman for his father, who was a manufacturer of and dealer in all sorts of trunks, whips, canes, and the like, and whose trade in the West needed stimulation, for the times were cloudy.

They were so, but few men seemed to be properly aware of it. The whole country, if not the rest of the world also, had gone mad upon speculation. The West, in particular, was crazy with wild expansion, beyond all immediate possibility of realization. A hundred times as much real estate, mostly unimproved, was for sale, as there was any demand for. Cities and towns were everywhere springing up—on paper. Railways without traffic were going out in all directions and trying to market their bonded indebtedness upon a clogged market. There were twice too many banks, such as they were, on a balloon basis, and twice too much currency, such as it was, with the notes of different states selling across the state borders at two and three per cent discount and endless counterfeits of a high grade of execution. It was what some people called "flush times," and the end was not far away.[4]

Hop and I went on to Buffalo, to take a lake steamer for Detroit. I may have sold some books in Buffalo, but do not remember. The great thing was to be actually on that steamboat, a fine one, and on my way west. I seemed to myself to be already another man and my depressions all fled from me. I went into the spirit of the hour with tremendous zest and had no doubt whatever of my entire success. Why should I have had such an overflowing sense of suppressed but ready energy? Some books may have been sold on the boat and others at Detroit, for here I parted company with Hop. My next stop was at Kalamazoo, that I might see the house-covered land which my father had once sold for almost nothing. I saw it and took courage determining to also buy much western land and keep it until it should be built upon.

From Detroit I went to Chicago and to a hotel kept by old-time Rochester acquaintances named Blossom, who had once been proprietors there of the Eagle Hotel. I made my footing good at once, for I took Mrs. Blossom and her daughter Nellie to the theater the first night. The next morning, without telling them what I was up to, I went out with my books, but a day's hard work dissuaded me from sending back for any more. Then I fell in with a queer genius who had invented a complicated mathematical instrument for measuring lumber. I walked many a mile through the great lumber district before I would be fully instructed that the Chicago dealers were able to do without it and were not just then selling as much lumber as would make them ready to buy extravagances.

The city itself was in a peculiar condition. It had been started and built up at the level of the lake, large areas having been actually swampy. It had been determined to "raise the grade" to a height which would admit of cellars and sewers, and the work was going on. Whole brick or framed blocks were being hoisted in a marvelous way and it was in contracts for this engineering that Pullman of the Palace Car marvel made the beginning of his colossal successes.[5]

Each of the business streets, however, was a mountain country, one house on the old grade and the next on the new. A day's walk was a fatiguing, if not perilous, climb. All the city was drinking hard, speculating madly, and tumbling up and down stairs.

It was just at the end of my lumber measurers that I again fell in with Hop Strong, and he was in difficulties as to his business. For some firm or family reason, he had been unexpectedly ordered home. He had closed out all the goods sent on with him except a lot of cheap sword canes, and loaded "plug-ugly" canes, which he did not care to carry back with him. Liberal terms were offered me if I would sell them and I took up the offer. He went home and I went out into the streets of Chicago as a peddler. I did pretty well, too, in my new vocation, but left the hotel for a cheaper boarding house, away down on the "west side," not at first knowing that it was to be my side of the young city. My stock in trade had been small, however, and it was needful for me to seek some other means for making a fortune.

Now it had happened that, at the request of some Rochester friend or other, I had contributed reviews, letters, etc., to a recently started afternoon journal called *The Chicago Daily Ledger*, and my work had met with approval. So my mind went from peddling all the way back to literature, and I determined to call at the *Ledger* office. The editor and proprietor was one of the most curious of unusual characters and believed himself to be a great man. So he was. He was the leading "Spiritualist" of the Northwest and had even carried on a bank under spiritual direction until the ghosts ran it under water. He had lectured all over the country and was prone to anything but steady hard work.

One of my good points was that I had proposed to be jauntily well dressed and my long collegiate hair was not closely cropped. So it was in fine uniform that I entered the editorial sanctum of the Hon. Seth Paine and dignifiedly introduced myself as his well-beloved eastern correspondent. He was glad to see me and I informed him that I had already been several days in the city, looking around. My conclusion was, I told him, that any man of sense would be likely to look around a good while before making a settlement in business at the present time. I was in no hurry and might prefer to go somewhere else.

He fully agreed with me and added that a position on the editorial staff of a rising journal, like the *Ledger*, would be the right place for any man in search of information. All the channels would be open before his eyes and he might wait for favorable chances. I replied that I saw it as he did but doubted if he could offer me sufficient wages to cover my expenses. As to that, he could give me twenty dollars a week and I could be economical. So I yielded and found, off hand, that I was to be "Literary Editor," because my predecessor had gone off on a strike. Somewhat later, I learned that my excellent and spiritually minded chief had gone to the hotel and had received glowing accounts of me from my old Rochester sporting friend, Bill Blossom. That fellow could have written a short novel, with one hand, any day.

We had first-rate accommodations in the upper story of a large brick building, occupied otherwise as a foundry and scale factory, and our job-printing office was as good as any in the city, with a fine run of trade. That part of the business was presided over by a fat genius who informed me that a mere editor was nothing in comparison with a full-fledged printer. He added, with just pride, that in the City of Washington itself, printers were admitted into the best society because of the well-established fact that one Benjamin Franklin had himself been a printer.

I was glad to know it and determined that I also would be like Benjamin. I obtained a printer's guide and learned how to correct proof and as much more as the small volume could teach me. On the whole, I was quite contented and rapidly acquired a great deal of general information concerning Chicago and the great West.

It was not until afterwards, down on the prairie, that I learned from Old Man Howe that the original name of the locality had been shortened a little. All that the term we now have means, in the tongue of the Miami Indians—"The place of"—but the word for Skunk in the same tongue is "Nugh!" The whole name was "Chi-ga-go-nugh," the place of Skunks.

There were enough of them there, on two feet each, in the Summer of 1857. My boarding house was pleasant, had it not been for the enormous activity of innumerable mosquitoes, the sole produce of the lakeshore marshes. Among the boarders, however, was an English lady and her daughter, who pronounced it "Chicaygo" and pretended to teach music. The idea of learning something of music and of helping them took possession of me and I went to the piano with the old lady. I made a good beginning but had to give it up, for no sooner would the good woman get me to the keyboard than she would invariably go to sleep, and I suspected that it was not altogether on account of fatigue. The days were getting wonderfully full, moreover, for the news editor also struck and I had to take up his dropped burden. He had quarreled with Seth over money. It was a tough problem, but I solved it. Ours being an afternoon journal, all the newsboys came for us as soon as they had closed out the morning prints. I went for them and promised them a tip for each really good item they might find and bring me. Sometimes a dead horse or a knockdown had to be divided among several reporters, but nothing could occur in Chicago without my getting hold of it in first-rate order and full life size.

I made short work of my reviews. It has been a lesson to me ever since, for I know very well how the review business is worked by tired editors. So far, so good, but Seth had been seized by a sharp attack of politics, lecturing, and spirits of all sizes, and I found myself Leading Editor also, to an uncomfortable extent. I knew whom to abuse, including "Long John" Wentworth,[6] then Mayor, and it was safe to talk any kind of radicalism, so that I did fairly well, only I had to write like lightning and care nothing for small slips of the pen.

When I found time for sleep I do not know, for it was needful to keep up with the theaters and give reports of performances. That I did, going from one to another every night, and getting the run of theatrical business in a way that led me to try my hand as a playwright. In the course of the Summer, I had written a local comedy which was duly accepted at Ford's Theatre. It was all ready for presentation in the Autumn, when that theater burned down, my comedy perishing with the flies and footlights.

As to Spiritism, I must not forget to say that I tried to make a study of it. I talked with our printers who were in it and gathered an idea that the best "mediums" among them were using too much of either opium or whiskey, or were nervously out of order in some way. They were not healthy or sound-minded men. One night, there was to be a grand exhibition, by several noted Spiritists from the East, in the largest hall in Chicago, and I went to see. A committee of well-known citizens was called for to act as judges, and they were ceremoniously elected.

One of the newsboys shouted for me, however, and in an instant all the peanut-eaters in the crowded hall were yelling "Stoddard!" The general public followed their lead and I was sent to the stand as "one of the best-known and most trusted of our fellow citizens." Such is an election by a unanimous vote of a free and enlightened people.

The performance was really of intense interest and my own experiments brought me some things which I could not then understand but think I can now. There were no ghosts present but there was a high order of animal magnetic telegraphy. Not one name or fact or thought came back to me in any manner which I could not readily find in my own mind or memory. To these facts or names something or other might readily be hitched. Not to elaborate that business, I saw that its best hold, just then, was to make great men like Seth Paine and wrecks like some in my office.

The *Ledger* might have done well in the hands of competent businessmen, but its finances were in Seth's hands and my salary began to run behind. So I put in as much time as I had left in getting cash-down advertisements and waited for the next thing in my queer enterprise. It was of course that I should inquire into the real estate business, for we were advertising lots of it, and the fever of real estate speculation began to burn in me. I had even begun to make my selections. Perhaps it was with a view to examining the rural districts that I also availed myself of my editorial privilege of obtaining railway passes of any kind that I could get. They were issued freely in those days, for competent railway managers were glad to have somebody upon some of their trains.

It was a hot and feverish time, and there appeared to me to be a sort of desperate struggle for existence all around me. The air seemed dusty, and it was not difficult to detect a growing feeling of uneasiness. Into this state of things there suddenly came sweeping a kind of financial cyclone. Its course began in Europe but it crossed the Atlantic with a rush and a whirl and struck the eastern states. It did not pause there for a day but came furiously westward. It struck Chicago and in one day every bank and banking house and almost every commercial or manufacturing concern had closed its doors. The *Ledger* had to shut up shop, for the bank in which Seth Paine had trusted was one of the first to close. I was no longer a leading citizen or a prominent editor. I was an adventurer out of employment, and so were thousands of others. The streets were swarming with young men of all sorts who had nothing on earth to do. A great palsy had fallen upon all manner of ambitions and enterprises and the entire United States appeared to be standing still.

A day or so only was needed to convince me that I must get out of Chicago if I really expected to get anything to eat that Fall and Winter. It may seem too much to say, but I was hardly dispirited. I did not lose heart for a moment, but promptly decided to push right out into the country and try my hand at agriculture, at least until the storm should blow over. I had a little money and a pretty good outfit of clothing, and besides that, I had my railway passes and could get more of the same sort.

20

Grand Prairie

Beginning, at the east, somewhere in Indiana; at the north on the shore of Lake Erie and Lake Michigan; at the south in the woods of southern Illinois; at the Wabash and the Ohio; [and] bordered at the west by the Mississippi River, there is an immense, irregular, undulating plain of alluvial country to which the early French explorers gave the name of "Grand Prairie." They were entirely justified in so doing.

For further geographical particulars, please consult the maps. These will give all outlines and some of the watercourses, but will not give any idea whatever of what so large a prairie really is. In the first place, it is a deceptive humbug, giving to the eye of the innocent observer the impression of a vast level, when the fact is that the waves of land which became solid to make the prairie are some of them very high. No such thing as might truthfully be called a "table land" actually exists.

Anyhow, it was down into the heart of this plain that I was going, at the end of my remarkable residence in Chicago. I was not to go alone, for I had picked out as my companion and partner a stalwart young fellow named Ezra Kendall. He was from Chautauqua County, New York, and had been raised on a farm. He had been a drygoods clerk in Chicago. Just at this time, all real estate was a drug on the market and sales thereof, except by the sheriffs, had almost ceased. Perhaps it would be the more easy for me to obtain a partly cultivated patch of prairie, of about four hundred acres, with a provisional contract for another section. A section is a square mile and would contain 640 acres if the surveys were accurate and the earth not so round. The curve continually lets in more land and I knew one section which stretched itself out over 700 acres and more.

The Chicago branch of the Illinois Central Railroad runs nearly due south, and if your eye follows it on the map about 170 miles you will see a point where it is crossed by the Toledo, Wabash and Western road, on its way to the Mississippi River. That road takes you to the capital, where Lincoln lived and the day came when I had passes on it and used them.

At this railway junction were a hotel, a stationhouse, a corncrib, a real estate office, two dwellings, and a barn, the whole constituting the town of Tolono. Ten miles north was the old town of Urbana and at its right elbow was the new railway station town of West Urbana, now the thriving city of Champaign, standing in the middle of the large prairie county of that name.

It was to the southern edge of this county, on the border of what was then Coles County, that my land title was to take me, with the help of the road.[1] Ten miles due east from Tolono is the village of Homer, and a plumb line dropped from it to the county line would hit my farm but I did not get to it that way. Ezra Kendall and I left Chicago in the night and I had to buy a ticket for him as my pass would not carry double. We left the cars at what we had been told was the town of Pesotum, ten miles south of Tolono, and we did so in the dark which comes before the dawn. It was a lovely morning in early October, and there we sat on our trunks, on the station platform, waiting for the sun to rise.

When at last it rose, we saw the town. It was about a hundred yards from the station, and appeared to be full of corn in the ear. That was the south half of Pesotum. The north half was further off and resembled a farmhouse but not in any direction did we see any fences.

Far away southward, on a roll of prairie high enough to be called a hill, was a bit of forest. We were informed that it was "Lost Grove," but could not learn where it had wandered from. There was no hotel in Pesotum, but we heard of a good-hearted young farmer at three miles or so southerly, and we left our baggage in the lockup and went for him. I will call him Kirby until I can be sure whether or not that is his name. He was from Kentucky and had put a whole section under wheat the previous year. It had yielded him thirty bushels per acre, at a dollar a bushel, and had paid for his land and house. With the money that was left, he was putting in that section again and another with it, and felt rich. I regret to say that the next crop was a complete failure.

That morning, he gave Ezra and me a tiptop breakfast and was almost offended when I offered to pay for it, asserting with much dignity that he "did not keep a hotel" and that his neighbors were always welcome, and strangers too. I afterwards found that this was only customary prairie hospitality and that any lonely dweller would be ready to overfeed a fellow who would bring him any news from the world.

From Kirby's we footed it on till we could feel sure that we were looking at our own palace. It was a small, one-story frame concern and almost new. It was also much occupied. Our tenant was a curious Yankee who had received permission from the previous owner to live there long enough to raise a crop of corn. The corn was raised, twenty acres of it, and "old man Southwick" refused to budge until Spring. His wife, a fair pattern of a cross between an Italian and a Maumee Indian, came to the fore with a liberal offer to let us have one of the two bedrooms and to board us at three dollars per week.

There was still enough of daylight for us to take a look at our domain and we did so, aided by Southwick. I do not now remember how many children he had, but my first hard look was at him. Positively, as a student of great men, I decided that he was the ugliest looking man I had seen yet. Short, broad, long armed, heavy jawed, large headed, pug-nosed, red-mud haired and stubby bearded, his eyes were his strong point, for each of them seemed larger than the other and to be set in a blotch of red paint, a little below his shaggy eyebrows. His forehead was an oblong square and he conveyed an impression that he was aware of the scarcity of water on that prairie in the Fall of the year. His apparel looked as if he had found every piece of it while wandering around a poor country upon the peddling expeditions which he soon began to tell about. For some good reason he was not now in that business but it could hardly have been the fault of the panic which had "shut up" so many other concerns. Perhaps the banks had distrusted his securities.

The approach to the house was through a long, narrow lane, between the bare prairie and a fenced-in field of corn, northerly. At the end of this ten-acre corn patch was a small, frame house which we were told was occupied by a family named Shoemaker, of whom our handsome tenant appeared to have a poor opinion. He described them as being not only "ornary" but also as "torn down poor." There certainly were no visible signs of prosperity about the Shoemaker ranch, but Southwick gave us the impression that he was disposed to be critical.

Half a mile southward was another fence, a lane, and a small house beyond it and we soon learned that it was the place where all the preachers put up when they came to ministrate in the schoolhouse meeting house, which was hidden from view by the hazel bushes at this side of the line of timber along the Little Upper East Fork of the West Ambraw Slough. Not far from the schoolhouse and the hazel bushes was the double establishment of Old Man Jim Williams. It consisted of the log house which he had built when he first settled, buying two hundred acres of land at $1.25 per acre, and the frame structure of about the same size which now witnessed to his increased prosperity. He and his blooming wife "Liz-Bet" were each over thirty, but I soon learned that as soon as a prairie boy and girl were married they became "old folks." Nearer, but across the slough, on a rising ground, was the pleasant home of Old Man Lemon. To the north, a half mile or so, was a considerable neck of woods upon another branch of the many-branched Ambraw. It obtained its name, the entire river did, from the manner in which the French explorers had been embarrassed by that tangle of water courses. So they called it the "Embarrass," and the new settlers who could not spell the word managed their own pronunciation of it and got their teams stuck in the sloughs for all the world like so many wandering Frenchmen.

The next morning Ezra and I continued our explorations, but the first weight upon our minds was the condition of our cash resources. We went out for work and discovered that there was little or no money on that prairie, owing to the frost-bitten failure of the corn crop and a partial failure of the wheat crop. There were, however, large standing crops of frost-bitten corn and there was really a great scarcity of labor, so that many farmers were at their wits' ends as to what they were to do.

Ezra and I obtained temporary employment at fifty cents a day, but saw that something better must be done. We therefore took the ungathered fields on contract. We intended to husk, or as the neighbors called it, "shuck," as much as we could, and cut and stack the rest for sale to the cattlemen. We made tiptop bargains and were getting at once into a paying business, wondering why so many fellows preferred to let us make the money while they went visiting or put in their valuable time "in town" at Urbana, Homer, or Upper Embarrass.

In due time, we learned that this tendency was only too general and accounted for some of the lost crops. And now followed a season of few interesting incidents, because of the style in which we were pitching into our profitable contracts. We were also trading for hogs and had secured the use of a fine team of horses and three yoke of oxen "for their keep," as their several owners were temporarily non-residents and had no other means of caring for their quadrupeds. The horses were a large bay team, well matched and in fine condition. The wheel yoke of oxen were large, long horned, and powerful. The next yoke were lighter and handsomer, a tawny brindle pair, with sharp tapering horns and bad tempers. The fore yoke were short, active reds.

I found a strange, wonderful fascination in my entirely new manner of life. It was a page from a frontier romance and I began to understand the born borderers who are unable to live in anything but a new country but must pull up their stakes and move westward as soon as the clearings of other men come too near and crowd them. I found Ezra an energetic, hardworking fellow, but the business part of our enterprise had to be left altogether in my own hands. I may as well say that before cold weather came I lost him. His father, the owner of a large farm in Cattaraugus [County in upstate New York], died suddenly and Ezra went home as one of the heirs of about five hundred acres of New York land, cleared up, paid for, and under cultivation. That is the last I ever heard of him, but hope that he did well.

Cutting and husking corn was hard work, but the autumnal weather was magnificent. So were occasional glimpses of deer, the scurry away of rabbits, the whir of many flocks of prairie hens, the gangs of cranes, the honk of wild geese overhead, and the flight of ducks, when they began to go southward. My letters were to reach me by way of our nearest post-office, Upper Embarrass, seven miles away in Coles County. I soon began to receive many and they were a variety. Those of my sister and brothers and the college boys were full of admiration and encouragement, but my father appeared to be taken aback by the idea of my becoming a prairie farmer. He even asked how much it would take to get me out of my scrape for "all his friends disapproved of it." It was then and is now my belief that he was altogether too ready to be advised and that the opinions of his "friends" had been the ruin of him. I did not want any advice just then, and I knew that the Syracuse coterie did not really intend to put in any money. As

for him, poor man, it was drawing down upon him and his wife in a very
unpleasant manner. It was an idea of hers that was shortly to get me into
a curious predicament.

We were still boarding at Southwick's when an enterprising stranger who
purchased a neighboring section of land began to build upon it the finest
mansion ever yet seen on that prairie. It was asserted that it would cost
him two thousand dollars, exclusive of his exceedingly extravagant barn.
Workmen came and had to be boarded around while that vast structure was
going up, and among them were odd characters that I was to meet again.
I will call one of them Hiram, having forgotten the right handle, who had
with him a wife who always spoke of her baby as "it." Poor thing! She was
not fit for baby handling and he was a loose fish. There was a strong vein
of humor in him, nevertheless. As I have said, down at the county line was
the house of pious hospitality and Hiram was not pious. One morning
he came to his work laughing spasmodically at frequent intervals. When
inquired of as to the cause, he had a story of his own which I cannot tell
worth a cent.

"Wal, boys, you see as how it was this way. Old Woman Jones used to
have loads o' hens and chickens, and she's out an' out good an' whenever one
o' them thar parsons kem along she was bound to kill a chicken. Nothin'
else was good enough, ye know. So they kep a comin' an' the chickens kep
goin' till thar wasn't ary one left 'cept that thar old Shanghai rooster. He's
as tall as a barr'l and when he crows the folks in Injianny kin hear him.
Now I was a comin' along to work an' I looked back along the timber an'
I seed another o' the preachers a ridin' on toward Old Man Jones's house
and I knowed that the Shanghai rooster's time had come. But I was in the
lane an' I heerd a yell behind me an' thar was Old Woman Jones a leggin'
her level best this way. She was runnin' well, but away ahead of her, comin'
along ten feet at a jump, was the old Shanghai an' it was his yell I heerd
for he was a screechin' Good God! Good God! Good God! at every jump,
and he got away into the corn, somewhere. He knew what was the matter
with him, as soon as he saw the preacher comin.'"

Hiram had another adventure, a few days later, for he was not on good
terms with the sheriff of Champaign County and was all the more willing
to find employment so near the county line, beyond which no constable
or deputy sheriff was likely to pursue him. The men found it out and they
put up a job on Hiram. It was at about the close of a day when by looking

north he and they might see a pair of men coming briskly along on horseback. In an instant these wayfarers were recognized by Hiram's friends and fellow workmen as the sheriff and a deputy and beyond a doubt they had a warrant and were armed.

"It's only a half mile to the line, Hi! You can beat 'em if you run well. Cut it!"

Hiram was a long-legged fellow and away he went while the entirely innocent horsemen plodded down the lane, somewhat in the same direction. Over the county line fence he went with the spring of a somewhat clumsy and out o' breath deer, but the instant he was in a foreign land he turned courageously and leaned against that very fence to hurl at the county authorities a series of bitterly sarcastic remarks of many varieties. He had escaped, indeed, but the boys had their fun with him the next day.

Right here, while the gang was at the new house, with noonday additions from the neighboring cornfields, one of which was keeping me there, occurred as funny a thing as was ever too much for a painter. It contained a pair of entirely unique characters. It was said of Old Man Southwick that he had never been known to buy a horse, but that he always owned four, getting successors as fast as any of them frequently died. At this date he was in full supply and his team was well known in those parts.

One of his critters had been named by the neighbors the Elephant; another was the Setter, from an asserted habit of his to sit down if he felt a load behind him; another was Jim, but the cream of them all was a dark, mud-colored beauty who took on the title of "Old Lije." He was a large hide, drawn loosely over a huge skeleton, and his head was one that you might put into a barrel. As to his tail, it was no longer encumbered with useless hair and stuck out behind him as if it might have been a kind of equine rudder.

Now, on the farm of Old Man Lemon there was employed a youthful cousin of his by the name of Romeo Smith. He was full grown, but wore an exceedingly youngish face and an expression of contentment with himself. He was fond of spending his evenings in the society of the prairie girls, far and near, and he was believed to have many ideas. Perhaps some of them were ambitions also, but at all events it now occurred to him that he would rest from cutting corn and become a mighty hunter. He would not stoop to grouse and rabbits but would go after deer and he would go on horseback. He could not persuade Lemon in that way but Old Man Southwick cheerfully let him have Old Lije on consideration of a division of the game.

Somebody lent Romeo a rifle, although the deer gun for horseback hunting is a double-barrel and buckshot. Early one beautiful hunting morning, Romeo set out, mounted and equipped, and Lije carried him well. Just how far he wandered or how many deer he did not see, does not appear from any known record, but at last he drew near unto a gang of sandhill cranes and he determined to consider them even as deer. He took aim, blazed away, and all but one of the cranes took wing. That one did not do so because Romeo had taken him on one of his wings. The gallant bird was only wounded, however, and stood upright upon his pins.

At once, an entirely new idea entered the busy brain of Romeo Smith. Young cranes were said to be good eating, as good as turkeys, but no one had ever had sufficient enterprise to coop and raise them for market or for the table. He would do that very thing and here was to be a beginning of his long-legged flock, if he could capture that first crane. He therefore did not shoot him but followed upon Lije while the bird walked rapidly away from him, and it was not difficult to drive him in the right direction. That is, he did so for some distance until the bird rebelled, refusing to be driven any further. He walked out in to the middle of a wide, shallow pond, such as the rains leave in prairie hollows, and there he stood defiantly at bay.

Now was Romeo's chance! He would follow in and capture his game. Old Lije had no objection to wetting his feet and allowed himself to be driven in until near enough to put out his great head for a smell of the winged brute whose own head and neck were poised and ready, in the attitude of a crane taking aim at a horse. The long, sharp bill flashed forward and the point of it struck Lije upon his nose.

It was unexpected, it was severe, and Lije backed out of that pond. No amount of beating or coaxing could make him go in again. The captivity idea had to be sadly given up. Romeo re-loaded his rifle, took a careful sight across the saddle and dropped the crane where he stood. So far, all was reasonably triumphant, but Lije was still obdurate and Romeo had to wade in himself to complete his triumph. He did get the crane and he waded ashore but now there came to pass a new difficulty. Not on any account would Lije allow his borrower to come near him with that peaked nose bird and it seemed as if it were a question between horse and game as to which of them must be given up. Genius has its resources, however, and Romeo's trouser pockets were perennially bunched with string.

From one of them he now extricated a long, strong piece of twine. One end of this hawser he tied behind the head of the crane and the other to the hairless tail of Old Lije. That done, the willing steed was mounted and the invention appeared to be a success. Pretty soon Lije was aware of some obstruction upon his rudder. He halted, turned his barrelhead, and lo, that awful thing was pursuing him. It may have been many a day since he had raced after deer at any faster gait than a good walk, but he began to run, now. In vain did he do so, if escape was in his mind, for the air got in under the wings of the crane and made a kite of him. Up he arose at the end of the twine and the next glance of Old Lije showed him his enemy as if coming to pounce upon him.

Romeo could hold on and that was all, while his affrighted beast plunged wildly across prairie toward the kindly shelter of his home. It was not so far to go but that his doubtful wind held out and we were at noonday luncheon in the lane when he came powdering along into it with that wide-winged wonder soaring behind him and Romeo shouting to us to stop him. We had no such thing to do, for Lije halted of his own accord among a gang of settlers, some of whom were rolling over and over upon the grass and others were standing up to hold their sides and laugh. We never knew whether or not Romeo and Southwick divided the game.

While we were living in our own shanty, which was Southwick's house, after Ezra's departure, a queer incident occurred in connection with our neighbors the Shoemakers. There were three of the men, father and two sons, long, lank, ugly-looking fellows, of the "poor white" class of Southerners.

We had heard that they were soon to migrate, and it was a saying that some kinds of settlers did not remain in any locality longer than to run in debt, raise some corn and sell it, and then "light out between two days." That was just what the Shoemakers did, a week or so later, but before going they were inclined to settle their old feud with Old Man Southwick. If there was any mean thing which one foul-tongued man could say of another and which the parties to that internecine war had omitted, the dictionaries are *enfants perdus*. I knew what was going on, but did not yet understand the pernicious process by which brutes of that sort work themselves up to the homicide point. It was a lesson I needed to learn. I was, as ever, the most peaceable of human beings and only with reference to grouse, deer, etc., had I provided myself with a double-barreled shotgun, large bore, a hair-trigger rifle, small bore but good range, and a pair, of wide-mouthed, short-barreled derringer pistols. The latter carried ounce balls and were ugly looking customers in the hands of a fellow who had been weaned on derringers and could hit a card with one at ten paces. Fellows appeared to like to have an admiring look at those toys and to see a spot hit with one.

Well! I was coming home, at the close of a Saturday, and had reached the head of the lane by Shoemaker's, when I was halted by a scene out of a western theater. There stood Southwick, in front of the Shoemaker shebang, and in front of him stood the three "poor whites," who had their shotguns but were not quite ready to use them.

Southwick was unarmed, but the stubborn old brute was not flinching one hair. As soon as I came up, he told me that they had threatened to kill him. I laughed at him, and at them, and told him to go home. That was what they did not intend him to do, but I handed him the long, cutlass-like cornknife in my hand and told him to take care of himself. He at once begged for one of my derringers but I refused, telling him that he would not know what to do with it. Part of what I meant was that he was crazy enough to shoot instantly and was pretty sure to miss and be replied to with buckshot from those guns. That, at such short range, would very likely have been bad for him.

"Go home," I told him, and he slowly backed off, down the lane, while I stood guard and scolded the Shoemakers. It was the old man who made the replies to me and all that he said was bitter with his bad opinion of Old Man Southwick. At the same time he was even kindly in his references to myself, for he could see that a broad-mouthed bit of iron lay in the palm of my hand, ready for prompt elevation. Several times did he assure me, "I wish you how well you may do, but I'm gwine to get even with Southwick, the ——!"

There I laughed at him and left him and went on homeward with an eye over one shoulder, and scolded Southwick for his folly in coming down that lane or having any words with such a lot of men. He was as surly and ugly and boastful as might be, and blamed me severely for not allowing him to cut up the Shoemakers. My own idea was that no cutting would have been done and I told him so. The whole affair appeared to me exceedingly ridiculous and I supposed that there would be the end of it, but I was still ignorant of the depths of that kind of stupid iniquity and had something to learn as to the ways of the border and the border men.

Sunday morning came and as usual I was up and out at daylight, a feat never performed by Old Man Southwick. Well for him that he did not attempt it that morning. I left the house by the front door, taking with me a gun for incidental chickens. I did not mean to be wicked and go hunting, but the Southwick dinners would bear any amount of improvement. On I went, along the edge of my own cornfield, until I saw something more interesting than any chicken. There sat Old Man Shoemaker, crouched down under the corn, with his rifle ready to fire and his dull eyes glaring at the back door of my house. He was waiting for Southwick to make his appearance in that doorway and to take a pot-shot at him at about twenty paces.

He arose to his feet on seeing me and said something about chickens but my blood was up, at so meanly murderous an undertaking, and I told him plainly what I thought of it. He replied with much energy and again warmly declared that he and his sons "Wished me how well you may do," but it was of no use. I ordered him home under penalty of all the buckshot I had not put into both barrels of my gun, for they were loaded with double Bs, for prairie hens, but the consequences would have been about the same for him at short range and he gave it up and went home, swearing vengeance upon Southwick. I afterwards imbibed an idea that that morning's adventure had something to do with the fact that we never saw any more of the Shoemakers and that within twenty-four hours the sheriff was down on that prairie making miscellaneous and utterly vain inquiries as to their whereabouts.

As to the rest of my reminiscences of that first residence on the prairie, I only remember an occasion when I went down to a slough to pull out Southwick and his four-horse team and told him I would hitch on behind the wagon and he and his four in hand might do their best the other way. I pulled them all out in no time and he told me something was the matter with his gearing. So it was, if half dead horses are to be described in that heartless manner.

William Osborn Stoddard at age twenty-six as he looked in 1862 as a member of President Lincoln's White House staff. Madison Historical Society.

ABRAHAM LINCOLN.

From the original negative owned by GEORGE B. AYRES, Artist,
Philadelphia.

(Copyright.) Over.

Abraham Lincoln, photographed by Alexander Hesler in Springfield,
Illinois, June 3, 1860. This is Stoddard's own, personal copy of the
famous Hesler pose, which was widely circulated during the 1860
presidential campaign. Stoddard family photograph.

Mary Todd Lincoln, photographed by Mathew Brady in Washington in 1862. Stoddard retained this carte-de-visite photo of the president's wife long after he—and Mrs. Lincoln—left the White House. Stoddard family photograph.

Stoddard's beloved mother, Sarah Osborn Stoddard.
Stoddard family photograph.

Stoddard's upstate New York boyhood friend, M. H. "Hop" Strong.
Stoddard family photograph.

Stoddard's siblings, who often followed him as his career took him far from New York. Brother John (*upper left*) and sister Kate joined him in Illinois. Brother Henry (*upper right*), also known as Harry, shown in his National Rifles uniform, reunited with him in Washington in 1861, as did sister Kate (*left*), who was photographed there by the capital's leading photographer, Mathew Brady.

Stoddard family photographs.

BRADY,   WASHINGTON.

Schuyler Colfax, Speaker of the House of Representatives during the Civil War. Stoddard owned and retained this carte-de-visite even after Colfax, later vice president, was implicated in the Crédit Mobilier scandal and disgraced. Stoddard family photograph.

Susan Eagleson Cooper, age nineteen, future wife
of William O. Stoddard. Stoddard family photograph.

Stoddard's formidable and supportive mother-in-law, Susan Eagleson Cooper, as she looked as an eighty-six-year-old in 1901, photographed in Mount Vernon, New York. Stoddard family photograph.

Three of the children of William and Susan Stoddard: Daughters Margaret Stoddard Buttenheim (*opposite*) and Mabel Stoddard Ford (*above*). Madison Historical Society. Son Ralph Stoddard (*right*). Stoddard family photograph.

Stoddard as he appeared in 1908, a year before the centennial of Abraham Lincoln's birth. Madison Historical Society.

A distinguished, vigorous-looking William Osborn Stoddard, age seventy-six, as he appeared in 1911, fourteen years before his death. Madison Historical Society.

William O. "Bill" Stoddard Jr., who excerpted and published the first version of his father's autobiography, as he looked in 1940. Madison Historical Society.

2-1

Log Cabin Home

From the corner of the cornfield on the four-hundred-acre patch, a man might have walked away, northwest by north, sixteen miles, without being unpleasantly interrupted by a fence until he arrived in the outskirts of Urbana, the county seat of Champaign County.

There, he would find a considerable village, at the upper end of an old farming settlement that extended for some distance down an upper east fork of the Sangamon River. It was a queer notion of the earlier settlers, who were mostly from forest states, to avoid the fertile prairie as if prejudiced against it and to actually make laborious and timber-wasting farms in the riverside woods. Not until a later day were men enterprising enough to go out into the already-cleared-beforehand prairie. The first settlers in this neck of woods were from Ohio, and they had brought with them the name of their nearest town in that state. They were an industrious, intelligent class of people, but along with them or closely following them were immigrants who were occasionally industrious, intelligent only in a few specialties of their own, and almost entirely illiterate. As for that, it was the same down on the Embarrass timber, for very few of my own neighbors could do more with a pen than to write their names or more with a printed page than to light a pipe with it.

In spite of seeming discouragement, there were two weekly journals printed at Urbana, one Whig, one Democratic, and the place carried an air of business prosperity. My visits to town were not many, during that Fall or Winter, and they all carried me straight through to West Urbana, whether I were riding, driving, or walking. The reason was this. Both places contained Baptists, but the greater part of them were in the new town although the old possessed a small semblance of a meetinghouse while the new town had none. It had a good hall, however, and it had organized churches energetically.

Meetinghouses had been provided for the Old School Presbyterians, the Congregationalists, and New School Presbyterians acting together, for the Methodists and for the Episcopalians. The small population was therefore somewhat cut up, theologically, and threatened to become yet more so. The double-towned Baptist churches, moreover, had succeeded in obtaining the services of an old and warm college friend of mine.

Bright and genial indeed and ever to be remembered well by me was Rev. Archibald LaMont Farr, who had married Jenny Strong, sister of my old chum Hop, so that I seemed to myself to have had kindred sent to me in my Illinois loneliness. It was to their house, therefore, that my town visits were made and I soon began to have a pretty clear idea of what might be done with a municipality which was only two years old from the bare prairie and the arrival of the railway hotel in the middle of it. My physical condition in those days was such that if a saddle horse was not handy, I rather enjoyed a morning walk to the county seat and through it to Farr's, and then a bit of a stroll homeward in the evening. It did not appear to fatigue me unpleasantly.

The fact was that the work of each day began before daylight with the cattle and horses. At sunrise we were in the field, and cutting or shucking did not cease until it was too dark to work. Even after Ezra left me, I remember cutting corn in the open field until the snow was a foot deep. That came in January, for the season, after the corn-destroying September frosts, had been unusually warm and I had found new bluegrass growing in the sloughs as late as the twelfth of that month. In these long walks across prairie as well as in my hunting excursions, I began to learn something of the nature of the prairie. I learned its natural grasses, once the abundant food of the bison whose deeply worn trails were still there as hard-beaten as hickory wood and sticking together in big, adobe chunks when broken by the plow. There were the rosin weeds, with beads of resinous gum as large, sometimes, as buckshot, exuding from their stems and leaves. There were the rolling weeds, growing in balls of stiff twigs nearly four feet high to rot off at the ground and be carried across prairie by the winds until landed against some fence or in the deer-sheltering depths of some ravine. There were the redroot weeds, the enemies of the plowman and, most interesting to me, there were the snakeroot flowers, something like the "everlastings" that I had been familiar with in the East. The root was said to be a sure antidote for any kind of snakebite, especially that of the rattlesnake. Of this reptile, we had two varieties. The "timber rattlesnake," never found except in the woods, is the same as his kind anywhere and he was scarce on account of the searches made for him, as a dainty, by our not-at-all dainty hogs. The other kind was the massauga or "prairie rattlesnake," as deadly as his woodland cousin but shorter. He also seems to me, in memory, to have been thicker than other snakes of his length.

My first sight of one was a startler. Ezra and I were walking along a buffalo path one day, shortly after our arrival. He had on low shoes while I was provided with boots. He was ahead when my ears caught a loud whirring sound and I sprang forward to catch Ezra by the collar and hurl him back into the grass, just in time to keep him from kicking a large and angry massauga that had been coiled for a spring in the middle of the path. The spring was made but it missed and the snake hurried away through the grass while I explained to Ezra that a rattlesnake was considered unsafe kicking. He turned pale enough and both of us made calculations as to the armoring qualities of the cowhide boots which appeared to be the prevailing fashion.

In fact, all the soft leather, calfskin affairs which we brought with us were soon used up by the cutting edges of the prairie grasses. Neither were low shoes the right thing for dewy weeds, mud, slough wading, or kicking oxen. I heard something, then, of a fellow, down the timber, who would let himself be bitten at any time by a rattlesnake, for five dollars. He would chew and swallow some snakeroot, let the reptile bite, use plenty more of the root and come off apparently unharmed. In the next Spring, however, he forgot the time o' year. All venomous creatures are worst in the Spring. The truster in snake root allowed himself to be bitten in April at Urbana. All the root he could chew and all the whiskey he could drink could not save him. He died in less than two days.

Ezra was gone and Old Man Southwick and I did not get on well together. This may have been, in part, on account of a peculiarity of mine which was discovered at an early day by the keenly observant eyes, as black and glittering as those of an Indian—Old Woman Southwick's. We were all at the dinner table and the company included two or three workmen, day-boarders. I had an idea that I was watched but did not know what for until Mrs. Southwick loudly exclaimed:

"Pop! I know! Mr. Stoddard's a gentleman! He eats with his fork!"

It was a rare phenomenon in that settlement, truly, and I was the only feeder at that table who was not employing his broad-bladed iron knife as a food shovel.

There were other points of difference and I decided to move. Somewhat less than a mile westerly there was a large and quite comfortable log house at the unfenced roadside, with twenty acres of corn and half as many more of "sod-corn," or corn planted on the backs of first turnings, just behind it. The occupant was a character known far and wide throughout that region as Old Man Howe. Of him and his there will be more to say, and just here it is enough that I secured Winter quarters with him and his interesting family. Never did a wiser thing in all my life and would not miss the memory of him for anything. The last of my doings at the Southwick farm, which was mine altogether, now Ezra was gone, was of particularly vivid interest to me.

The grass was now dry and the year had been a good one for tall weeds of every name and nature. Perhaps it was in consequence of this that the prairie fires were beginning with more than usual enterprise. We could see the sky at night, in the west, reddening with the light of the coming danger. In other directions, that neighborhood was protected by wet sloughs, watercourses, and wide reaches of plowed land upon which there was as yet no stubble to carry fire. It was a matter of accustomed prudence to begin measures of protection and all other work was suspended for that purpose.

The received method was simple but generally effective. A breaking team and wide-nosed plow were sent out thirty feet or so from the edge of the land to be guarded. Twelve feet wide of sod were then turned over, and the back of a sod is incombustible. That was not all and the next process was laborious. All the strip of dry grass inside of the newly plowed barrier had to be carefully burned over. It was then to be supposed that no ordinary fire would jump so far and it was safer in our case because the cattle had shortened the grass for some distance outside of our lines. At this distance I cannot well remember what it was that then carried my impertinent curiosity a long reach beyond and into the region at which the sweeping volume of the advancing fire was coming. It might have been all well, but for a sudden tornado of wind that blew straight at me, instead of nearly the other way, as it had been doing.

Behind me was a dry slough in which the bluegrass and rosin weeds were terribly high and luxuriant. A fire among them would be a furnace in which a man would wither like a moth. In front was fairly level ground and beyond was a high roll on which the grass would surely be shorter. On those rolls the washed-off black soil is often hardly a foot deep while it may be four or five times as much in the adjacent hollows. Higher, higher, higher, sprang the tall columns of smoke and flame and I saw but one hope for escape from cremation. I pulled my hat over my eyes, tucked my trousers well down into my boots, pulled up my coat collar, stuck my hands into my pockets, drew a long breath and charged that fire, the middle of it, at the best pace I could make.

It was a dark, choking, doubtful, hot, but exceedingly interesting race for life. Probably it was not so long as it seemed before I was out on the high ground. It had been burned over and had now no fire on it but behind me was a great, angry roar and a wall of awful flame. My hat was ruined. My hair was singed badly. So were my eyebrows and coattails, but there was no real harm done, as soon as I could once more learn how to breathe. Then I went around home, much wiser on the prairie fire question and well pleased to find that our barrier had worked well and that the corn was safe.

One of our neighbors, hardly two miles away, had not been so fortunate. He had neglected back firing and that day he and his whole family had gone to Urbana, leaving their house untenanted. It was well that they did so, perhaps. It was a new, neat frame dwelling, and around it were 160 acres of land in full cultivation. He had gathered a good wheat crop and it was in stacks near the house. His corn was mostly in the cribs, his hogs were there or in the timber, and his cattle were free to run away and take care of themselves, except a few in a fenced lot which escaped the fire. It came across the stubble field and in a few minutes all the rest of his farm was bare ground. Not a trace was left of the house and its surroundings except such embers as the fire did not stay to clean up. He had to begin all his establishment over again and so, I was told, did others at greater distances. As for myself, not many days after the fire, I was on my way to Old Man Howe's and I did not even reach the log house without one more reminder of the eccentricities and sad uncertainties of human life on the western frontier.

As nearly as I can remember, it was early in November, a cloudlessly sunny day, when I made ready to convey the last of my effects to Old Man Howe's. My hogs were already there, my clothing and many other matters, but a quantity of farm tools and other light things, like plows and crowbars, were yet to go. I had a light wagon for the purpose and in front of this I had hitched, or yoked, my brindled span of handsome and dubious-tempered oxen.

All went as merry as a marriage bell until perhaps half the distance had been conquered. My clothing was of the lightest and the oxen were stark naked. The sky had been rapidly darkening, however, and now, down out of the clouded heavens, with a rush and a roar and a knife in both its hands, came one of those phenomenal gusts of Polar air known to the dwellers of the Southwest as a "Norther." They are the meanest wind that blows. Others may travel as swiftly or may even be as cold, but the distinguishing characteristic of the Norther is its extreme dryness. It is a desiccating blast of the most perfect kind and men and animals go down helplessly before it. Large numbers of cattle have been known to perish with strange rapidity without one of them being frozen solid.

All hoofed creatures appear to know, by instinct or otherwise, that at the coming of this destroyer their best hold is a shelter in the nearest timber. It would have been wiser for my oxen if they had taken my advice and streaked it for Howe's, but they disregarded my entreaties and turned tail to the blast for only a moment before they began to race that wagonload of tools toward a line of timber to the westward. Not wishing to see the wrecks of my wagon and the whole collection scattered over the prairie on the way, I fought them desperately and they in turn fought with me. The wind was not now as cold as at first—I felt sure of that—and there was no longer any good cause for them to run away. It was getting milder and I could feel a soft kind of languor stealing over me. Then I felt sleepy. I do not know what came next but was afterwards credibly informed.

A team of our neighbor Jim Williams, with him and another Williams in the wagon, had raced it to the shelter of the log house. They and Howe and the women folk came to the door to see me contend with my cattle. They saw me lie down and concluded that the critters had "horned" me. They sprang into the wagon and whipped their horses to where I lay. They picked me up but were unable to find a scratch. Nothing was the matter with me except that I had been frozen to death. They carried me to the house, stripped and rubbed me, and Old Mrs. Howe made for me the hottest bowl of red pepper tea you ever heard of. In half an hour or so of vigorous treatment I was made to open my eyes. Then I knew where I was and inquired for my team but nobody could more than guess that it must be in the timber. I was in bed and was beginning to swallow pepper tea and to know how a fellow feels when he is coming back to this present world after being frozen to death.

If you have ever had a bad case of a limb "going to sleep" and can recall the prickly sensation of its recovery, you may multiply that prickling by a hundred and spread it all over you and you will get the idea. It is a strange kind of unendurable agony which you will not wish to have repeated. At first I could not appreciate the pepper tea, but that inability soon passed away and I could hear good Mrs. Howe say that she thanked God for putting it into her mind to raise those peppers. Good woman. Methodist!

The best way to get at the measurement of that log house may be to consider with a measuring eye the things which it was called upon to contain and was entirely capable of doing so.

In the first place, it had no front yard but in place thereof all the area beyond the wagon track at the doorstep was thickly strewn with chips from the many firewood logs which had there been hacked in pieces. A person contemplating those fragments might be reminded of the romantic tradition concerning colonial New England courtships: that some time always had to elapse before the attentions might go further, on the way home from meeting, than "the chips" [the boards placed between courting–or "bundling"–couples at bedtime—ed.]. The roof had a steep slope and was made of large hand-split shingles. On the ridge of it, pretty regularly, unless he was elsewhere stealing something, was Old Man Howe's pet crow, cursing whoever came in. His prevailing complexion was a shiny black and his prevailing tendency was dishonesty. He was somewhat lame of one leg but he could fly well. He loved to go in and hop around the floor until he could seize an unguarded article not too heavy for him, notably balls of yarn, scissors, thimbles, pieces of paper, and carry them up to a coop he had made on the house ridge. Then he would berate in the fiercest manner anybody coming to rob him of his booty.

The front doorway was not exactly in the middle of the house, and, on entering it, one might see that there was a similar door on the opposite side. Those doors were closed only at night or in bad weather and there was a window at the right of each of them, so that light was let in abundantly. Window sash was hard to get when that house was built and more windows would have called for more severing of the heavy, old-growth logs of which the walls were constructed.

The interstices between the logs were well "chinked" with tempered clay which did not often fall out but would do so occasionally. The floor was of heavy planks which had been put down green and had left cracks in seasoning. Speaking of logs, I never saw any very huge trees on Grand Prairie. The surface formation of that region is not of great antiquity and it may be that the largest of its trunks are those of the "redwood" trees which stop the tools of the borers of artesian wells at the depth of one or more hundreds of feet below the grass. At the right of the door was one large bed, in the corner, and this belonged to Becky Howe and one of her two sisters.

Rebecca had been married once, but her husband had long since disappeared and she had resumed her maiden name. The girls were fourteen and sixteen, and there was a grown-up brother Timothy between them and Becky, as well as a small boy brother Sam, or some other name. All were children of Mrs. Howe the first, for the present head of the house had been a middle-aged widow, of strong and quiet characteristics, when Old Man Howe married her, over on the Brushy Fork of the Wabash River, in Indiana. She sat in a chair on the further side of the room, eight feet out from the wall, toward the fireplace.

Between that corner bedstead and the very large, wide, high one in the middle, there was a space of three or four feet, and there was a similar alleyway between the side of that bed and the double bed in the further corner. The middle bed belonged to Mr. and Mrs. Howe, the trundle-bed under it was for one of the girls and the small boy, while the bed in the corner was mine. Tim, when at home, semi-occasionally, might bunk on the floor like any other transient guest.

I never saw more than sixteen persons of all sorts asleep in that hospitable mansion at once, but I did see precisely that number. In the middle, at the left, was the positively tremendous chimney, made of tempered clay and sticks, most of it outside of the wall. The fireplace may have been five feet wide, three and a half deep and four feet high. The andirons were curiosities for a collector and the cooking machinery was likewise.

All the bread was baked in a big skillet, a foot wide and three inches deep and there was no crane to hang a pot on, but there were big and little pots and skillets. As for bread, I heard Old Man Howe declare that he "didn't see how anybody could eat wheat bread, so long as there was corn to be had." I nearly agreed with him, at least as to the product of his own cooks and their skillet, especially when the result took the form of cannon ball biscuit. In the course of time, it was manifested to me that the only good cook in that neighborhood was Mrs. Liz-Bet Williams, and she was deservedly proud of her unusual accomplishments. Carpet there was none but there were tables and chairs and the one book in the house was a big Bible which I never saw opened but once.

As to religion, all the theology on that prairie was in scattered chunks. Old Man Lemon was a Universalist, I was a Baptist, the Williamses were Methodists, there was a Presbyterian over on the west prairie. Old Man Southwick was an Infidel and proud of the title, the McCarthys were Roman Catholics, and Old Man Howe said that for his part he was an Auctioneer. He really was one, and now and then made fair fees at sheriff's sales, constable's sales, breaking-up sales, and the like, for he had fun in him and could talk off the goods.

22

Prairie Life

Mrs. Howe was elderly and fat and dark and rarely said anything. Miss or Mrs. Becky Howe was plump and dark and could talk, while her younger sisters were lighter or fairer. So was Tim, a broad-shouldered fellow who had a nose like his father's but of a smaller and thinner pattern.

As for the old man himself, he was a figure never to be forgotten: about six feet high if he would stand up straight, which he rarely did, thin, muscular, with a limp on the foot which had been club-crippled by rheumatism. His face was long and the tangled, pointed goatee beard at the end of it, without any side whiskers to speak of, made it seem longer. His moustaches were long, luxuriant, and added much expression to the hawk beak above them. His small, gray eyes were set to twinkle away back under his bushy eyebrows and his deeply wrinkled forehead was covered by a curiously movable hide. All of his face that might be seen was sunburnt to a muddiness and he was said to have combed his hair, once, when he was living over on the Wabash.

He had been a flatboatman on that stream and the Mississippi in his earlier days and he was crammed full of yarns concerning New Orleans, Helena, Natchez under the Hill, and other charming places, as they were seen in those times by the river men. As to other occupations, he had experimented with many and had bursted up at all of them. At the present time, he was occupying this farm for its absent owner, without any rent to pay and with a strong hope that his generous landlord might not soon return. He had a few hogs and a not very exorbitant horse, but no cattle.

How he made a living was a question. No doubt a boarder who paid cash was an acquisition.

I had a large field of corn to cut for Jim Williams and it was while on that job that I formed a strong friendship for him and Liz-Bet. They were genuinely friendly, honest people and the whole timber was full of their kindred. It was on that field that I began to make a reputation, for I was able to measure its irregular form and give them its precise contents. Next came my miraculous ability to give the exact contents, in bushels, of a large and many-sided rail corn pen. I had brought with me, from Rochester and from Chicago, quite a large shelf full of books, more than all that prairie contained, and it was at once entitled Stoddard's Library. People came out of their way to stop at Howe's and get a look at those books.

I myself was making many acquaintances. I had been down the timber several times to Upper Embarrass and was fond of picking up new specimens of frontier humanity. I was also fond of hunting and our trips to our own wood lot, westward a mile or so, were always accompanied with weapons for the slaughter of game; also by Howe's two half-bred pointer dogs, two of the most remarkable canine characters. Bob was all activity and wife Delilah, or Lile, was more than his equal in intelligence. It was worth something to see that pair maneuver a rabbit out of a shock of corn, one tearing in to drive while the other waited outside to catch the escaping jumper. It was better fun after snow came and rabbits might be tracked and one Winter morning three guns of us brought home forty-four at noon. Deer were not so plentiful but grouse or "prairie chickens" were to be had at almost any time. They were a capital variation in the accustomed pork bill of fare. So were rabbits until I got so tired of them that I could hardly eat them. The house of Old Man Lemon was only half a mile away southerly, across the slough and on a rising ground. Lemon had one of the few natural springs in that region, but water was easily to be had by digging.

None of the wells were deep, but I saw one that was abandoned suddenly. A ten feet square hole had been dug and side timbered to a depth of not more than twelve feet when the workmen got out of that place with yells of fear and astonishment. Their escape from an awful death had been narrow indeed. When I went to look at the phenomenon, I saw what appeared to be a swiftly running stream of glistening gray sand. It was sand and water, of course, a "quicksand," and anything dropped into it, as a stick or a stone, disappeared instantly. So would a human being have done and the hole was carefully sealed up with timbers and earth. It was a thing to shudder at, that slimy mystery of the underworld. Where did that river come from and where did it go to? I don't know.

One of the first conclusions to be reached on an inspection of my neighbors and their ways, was that all the poverty to be found was the net result of ignorance, bad management, and waste. No potatoes were raised, the few to be had coming in wagons from Indiana at a dollar a bushel. No other vegetables, not so much as one garden, did I see that Autumn. There were no fruit trees nor vines planting, no chickens to be had nor eggs, and even in such a cattle country, there were few milch cows and hardly any farmer thought of making butter. It was scarce and dear.

My first visit at the Lemon place brought me a brace of interesting acquaintances. There was a wide, uphill lot between the road gate and the house. I went in, one day, and was going leisurely up the slope when down to meet me came a pair of the finest looking dogs I had ever seen. They were of a breed I was not familiar with, too. I think I was told that they were thoroughbred Livonian wolfhounds, as large as an English mastiff but not so heavy and with close, grisly hair and wicked looking heads, fine, sharp, wolfish faces and teeth, and tremendous strength and activity.

I did not at first notice that Old Man Lemon, his wife, girls and boy, and Romeo Smith were out at the door, coming in a hurry, terribly frightened about something. One of the huge creatures sprang up and put his paws on my shoulders and his mate uttered a wolfish howl while I patted number one in undisguised admiration. Then I rubbed the other's ears and talked at them and in a moment they were jumping all around me, as if they had known me from puppyhood—*their* puppyhood. The Lemon family could hardly express their astonishment and gratification, for the hounds were considered exceedingly dangerous as watchdogs to all strangers, but not to known neighbors, and were usually chained up in the daytime unless one of the family could be with them. They took to me remarkably and would shortly follow me anywhere as if I were a kind of outside owner.

I afterwards had a couple of curious adventures with those dogs. The first was along of a prairie wolf or "coyote," that had been howling o' nights in that neighborhood. Somehow or other, I got out after him, accompanied by the two wolfhounds, and I followed him well although I was on foot. I ran him to earth, or the dogs did, and then I went after a spade to dig him out. The den was in the side of a hollow, where the soft, black earth was several feet deep, and the digging was easy. Down I went, deeper and deeper, until the dogs got an idea of what I was going for and dashed in to paw at my side. In a moment more they had obtained a smell of their prey and then my hunt was up. They became crazy with excitement and altogether uncontrollable. They turned upon me in the most savage manner and drove me out of the hole. I had a gun with me and was glad of it, and was also glad that they returned to their digging. There was nothing more for me to do. I had to keep at a distance, unless I was ready to shoot the dogs. I went home, for there was no possibility of their digging out that wolf. The other adventure came at hog-weighing time, in November of that year.

The independent swine of the Embarrass timber, and possibly of all Illinois, were supposed to require little food or care in the earlier stages of their existence. Once born and branded, they might be permitted to roam at their will among the woods and slough, rooting here and wallowing there, until the days of their development for pork. Then, indeed, a hog became an object of human care and the forests were cleared of him. Gathered into hog lots, separated according to brand, much corn was fed to them in exceedingly wasteful ways, not needing description, the object being to bring up each individual porker to the contract weight.

During each season, the Chicago buyers were accustomed to make tours in the country, bargaining for all the hogs at a fixed rate and weight. At a time agreed upon, in each Fall and Spring, they would come again, prepared to weigh and pay and drive their purchases to the nearest railway station. One feature of the timber pork culture was that if any individual pig managed to escape an annual drive and maintain his or her freedom through another year, the wild spirit of the woods would surely grow in him—or her—and with it cunning of the woods, and a second escape was likely.

After a time, such an absentee from the mollifying processes of the hogpen and the porkmakers would return to the wild state, more or less completely, and become a fighting and freedom-loving hog. The breed raised in our timber still retained some of the ancient length of leg, in most cases, although steadily improving. The contract weight fixed for that year was a minimum of two hundred and fifty pounds and it was understood that it would be rigidly adhered to, as the price in Chicago was so low as to threaten the buyers with loss. The weighing scales were permanently at the Bill Williams farm and the number gathered from our timber was not far from four hundred. They were in good apparent condition, some of them a trifle light of weight and likely to be left over until the Spring.

Among the crowd swept in, however, was one high-backed, long-legged, long-headed old lady who had been out in the wildwood for more than three years and was wrathful at now being out of the wilderness. She was as lean as a shark, but large enough to turn the scale at over three hundred pounds. The buyers did not want her, but she was within the contract limit and all the settlement uproariously declared that she must be taken.

The next thing was to take her, for she had decided not to be weighed. The scales were at one side of a small pen in the middle of a five-acre lot. All the gathered swine were in that big lot and small squads of them were driven into the pen, seriatim, to be engineered one by one upon the scales. The process was easy enough with all orderly and mild-minded critters but the wild sow rebelled furiously. Whenever the drivers came too near, she charged them fiercely and her clashing tusks were an unpleasant warning to any man whose legs were not iron-clad. Dogs were sent at her and she used up several of them in short order. One clip was enough to send away any dog howling. She was standing at bay when it occurred to me that I would like to try an experiment.

I told them to go on with the weighing while I went for Lemon's hounds. I obtained them and also procured a white oak stake, five feet long and as large as my wrist. I sharpened it at one end. By this time, the wild sow was alone, all the others having been weighed, and she was holding her own finely. I went for her with my hounds and it was worthwhile to see their intelligence. They did not attack her in front as the unlucky curs had done who had felt her tusks. They started her from her "bay" and followed one on each side of her, so close that they touched her and she could not strike them. I was wise enough to imitate their wisdom and keep a little behind her. In an instant more, the hounds had her by the thick of her ears and they actually threw her flat, after a brief wrestle. I sprang for her head and forced the stake between her jaws, driving it down into the earth. Close behind me was Bill Williams, ready to carry out his part of the game, but while he was sewing up the eyes of that sow, she had twice cut the stake in two with her strong, sharp teeth. The sewing caused no pain, for the needle passed through nothing but the thick cartilage of her eyelids.[1] As soon as this was done, she was subdued and submitted to be weighed. Next day, she traveled all the way to Pesotum with the drove, without any resistance whatever.

There was just one little streak of politics among the occurrences of that November [1857]. In state and national affairs, it was an "off year," although much political feeling was brewing, but it was a great year in the history of Coles County, just south of my farm. It was too large a county and an act of the State Legislature had cut it in two, the lower half retaining the old name and, the northern half becoming "Douglas County," in honor of Stephen A. Douglas,[2] the great leader of the Democratic Party in Illinois, if not in the whole country. His acknowledged opponent in our state was the leader of the Whig Party, a man by the name of Lincoln who had once been in Congress but who had failed of a re-election.[3] Men said that he had ability, but then he was by no means the equal of Douglas, and there were several other men in the state who could make as good a stump speech as he could.

However that might be, there was one question yet to be settled. The new concern would need a county seat and there were only two candidates for the honor. Several hamlets fended it off on the ground that it might increase their local taxes. One of the candidates was a very young railway station village called Arcola, a little south of the middle of Douglas County. The other was a similar infant named Tuscola, a little north of the middle. If it was to become a town, it would be advantageous to all the settlers on the southern line of Champaign County and they began to take a deep interest in that election. It was pretty well understood that the Arcola men were patriotic and would come out strongly, and that they would have the aid of several settlements in the southern part of the county. The entire legal vote was understood to be somewhat over seventeen hundred, loosely calculated, and wise, practical politicians might know exactly what was best for them to do.

All the upper Embarrass River timber country was for Tuscola to such a degree that mere county lines were lost sight of. Especially was this the case with the workmen on the big McCarthy and Sullivant farms. Mac had in about two thousand acres of wheat, that year, besides corn, and Old Man Sullivant was struggling to get under plow a patch that he had there of over thirty thousand acres. He had as much more up in Ford County and more in Ohio and was calling himself "land poor." Just so he was, for it broke him up to handle it.

On election morning the polls were opened early at all the voting places in Douglas County, and the entire population that could get away from home swarmed out to fight. Before noon, one of the southern tier villages, as large as your hat, had polled 780 votes and quit to go and see what other places were doing. All may have been doing well, but the palm appeared to belong to Arcola precinct itself. How many legal voters were in it, nobody seemed to know, but it had cast somewhat more than the entire vote of the county and felt that it ought to consider itself safe. Alas for Arcola! It did not know what may be found in Champaign. Not long after sunrise there were processions of wagons filled with American citizens plodding across the pleasant prairie from the Sullivan and McCarthy patches and there were noble-hearted freemen, on foot or on horseback, traveling southward from the upper timber. All were bound for Tuscola, to show their interest in the election and to encourage the new county seat.

Perhaps a half mile east of the voting place was a large barn. The teams arrived at the polls, the men got out, they were provided with tickets, they were recorded, they cast their ballots, they again got into the wagons, after a brief pause at the counter of a grocery store that was that day doing a lively saloon business. Then the wagons drove away and that lot of Tuscola precinct men had done its duty—once.

Then, however, as if something had been forgotten and left behind, each wagon was driven around that barn and came again to repeat the first operation—both at the polls and at the bar. It could hardly have been said that any man voted twice, for a fellow at the polling table had a copy of the Chicago city directory and the names recorded were selected from that overflowing source. It was said that among the Tuscola voters appeared to be the Hon. Stephen A. Douglas himself, with other prominent citizens of the village at the shore of Lake Michigan.

All sorts of fun was going, and before long even the formality of going around the barn was omitted. Malicious people said that it was because the voters could no longer climb into the wagons and had to be held up to vote. At all events, Arcola was defeated, for not to speak of the work done elsewhere, Tuscola alone sent to the state capital a pollbook which contained nearly 4,700 names, or more than three times the adult male population of the new county. Oddly enough, there was no contest made and the result was formally accepted by the state authorities. Douglas County owes much to Champaign.

23

Prairie Winter

The snow did not come until January, and after that it was what might be called a mild Winter. Still, there were storms, and I had more than one ride to or from the county seat over a spotless carpet of glittering white.

By night it might have been easy to lose my way, but for the stars. As to the ease of wandering from right paths, I had one queer experience, just before the snow came. Old Man Howe and his wife went off on a visit. It may have been to "Brushy," of which she was fond of talking. At all events, they were to be absent for days and Becky and her sisters determined to make the best of it. They arranged for a kind of girl party, without any men, and the girls came. There were not so very many of them, a dozen or so, but to my dismay I discovered that most of them intended to spend the night in that commodious log house. It would be occupied altogether too much to suit my notions and I decided to even go over as far as Southwick's farm, and mine, to obtain a night's lodging.

I ate my supper and escaped from the house and set out along the well-known prairie road. It had no fence but I never dreamed of missing it, by day or night. When I left the house the hour may have been six, and a fine, light rain, of no consequence whatever, was beginning to fall. The next minute, a fine, light wind began to blow and it brought with it a dense mist that was a damp darkness which might be felt. I plodded on, but was soon aware that my feet were on grass instead of on a beaten road. A turn was made to recover the lost track and I pushed rapidly onward. It was not long after this turn that I found myself wading in pretty deep water. "All right,"

I thought. "I know where I am, now. It's that pond back of Southwick's. I'll take a southerly shoot."

So I did, and the pond was waded through but the time was passing and the fog was denser than ever. It is hardly worthwhile to try and remember all the wet places my wanderings led me into, but I crossed both branches of the Upper Embarrass, upper little left forks, east and west, or something of that kind. Late in the evening, or a little after ten, I came whack up against a rail fence and saw a light ahead of me. Over the fence I dragged my wetness and found myself in a cornfield. Near me were tall shocks and out of one of these projected the handle of a corn knife. An idea struck me and I pulled it out to look at it. It was my own knife and I had stuck it there that afternoon after finishing a job of cutting for Old Man Lemon. That is, I was to come and finish it in the morning and so had left my knife. This was Lemon's place, therefore, and I wondered why any of his family should be up and wasting candles at that hour. It was explained when I knocked my way in, for the whole Lemon family was off on a visit and Romeo Smith had but just returned from an unlucky jaunt across the south prairie.

All the girls he had gone to see were not at home because they were even now having a good time at Becky Howe's. He could give me a bed, however, and in the morning I was so much nearer my work, but I had traveled, that night, during over four hours of vigorous walking, as nearly as might be in a complete circle. There is a reason for it, and the difference in the pressure of a man on one foot more than another is well understood. It does not lose him when he can see.

A thaw and much rain came toward the middle of January. All the rivers and sloughs were full and all the roads were rivers of mud. Our patch of prairie became a kind of island, with no possibility of getting to town or even to the stores at Upper Embarrass. We were entirely out of candles, for one of our many privations, and I would have been deprived of my "library" or its uses if it had not been for the good which there is in dry hickory bark. I could lie down in front of the fireplace, all of a long Winter evening and read away, lighting one slip of bark after another and obtaining pretty good results from them.

The special favorite at that time was a couple of second-hand volumes, big ones, of *The Old English Dramatists* and I managed to get fairly well acquainted with a number of old worthies whom I had never known before. Newspapers and letters had to be dispensed with during several weeks. At the end of them, I managed to get my mail again and did make one horse-back visit to Urbana, but I was conscious that I was getting out of order. If I had known anything about hygiene, I might easily have escaped any unpleasant results, but I did not.

There came a morning when I did not feel like going out. I even went and lay down but was aroused by one of the girls coming to tell me that there was a gang of deer, a buck and three does, out in front of the house, within rifle range. I arose and took down my rifle and went to the doorway. My legs felt unsteady and I sat down on the doorstep to draw a bead on that buck, for he was a fine one. The sights of the rifle appeared to be cutting queer diagrams around his head for a moment, and then I fell back on the floor. I had been seized by what people called the "Winter fever," and it is a bilious thing to have.

I think a modern doctor would have had me up in a few days, but the scientist who came all the way from Upper Embarrass at five dollars a visit, to pour poison into me, was of the old kind, "brass mounted." His stock of cure-alls consisted mainly of mercury, iron, quinine, and opium. It was a wonder that I overcame them but I did, and the fever also went away, leaving me a thoroughly doctored-out man.

The Howes took as good care of me as they could, but pig pork and corn donicks are not a temptation to a convalescent. It was therefore genuine Christian kindness on the part of my friends Jim and Liz-bet Williams to insist upon my coming to their place as soon as I could be moved. How I did appreciate the good cookery of that good woman! I was rallying fast when early plowing began and Jim told me that the ducks and geese were coming. Somehow, I had won a marvelous reputation as a rifle-shot among my neighbors and he proposed that I should make a trial for some of those birds. He carried me out in his wagon one morning to a "shock-house" which he had made, and into it I went, to lie down upon some corn fodder and wait for game.

It was not so very long before a gang of wild geese alighted within long rifle range and I took up my shooting iron. It was not easy to handle it but I let drive and lay down. In a minute more, Jim came galloping his team to the shock to see if I had hurt myself and was astonished to find that instead of that I had brought down a fine, fat wild goose, hitting him right through the gizzard. Liz-bet cooked him tiptop and we all enjoyed him, but Jim would not let me go out again. The weather might give me a setback.

I was doing well but was still quite weak when an astonishing piece of news was brought to me by a neighbor who had been to Homer [Illinois], on the Toledo, Wabash and Western Railroad and at about the same time came explanatory letters from home. Much furniture which had belonged to Mrs. Stoddard when she was Mrs. Bolles had been substituted for such as she found in our West Genesee Street house, and the older materials had been "stored" and were even in the way. They were of the most miscellaneous description, and the bright idea came to her that they must be exactly the thing for a young man to make a start with on the prairie. Therefore, without warning or consultation, the whole lot, a carload, had been consigned to me across country.

It had reached Homer while I was sick, the railway officials had been unable to find me and now they sent me word that my goods had been there the prescribed month, unclaimed, and that if I did not at once come and attend to them, the consignment would be sent to Springfield and sold to cover charges. These were pretty heavy and would make a serious inroad upon my already depleted resources. There was no help for that, however, and the next question was, how on earth could I get to Homer and care for those unexpected treasures? I determined to make the effort.

One of our neighbors was a man who always kept more horses than he could use. Among them was a thoroughbred named Turk, a splendid saddle horse who had never been in harness and who had strong prejudices of his own as to who should be permitted to mount him. His owner was one of his favorites and I was another, but it was said that he would promptly "shed" almost any other man. Be that as it may, Turk was sent for and he came in a state of mind which indicated that he had not had an outing for a long time and expected me to take him out hunting, of which he was especially fond.

If there was anything in the wide world suiting his mind better than another, it was a race across prairie after deer. He greeted me kindly when I came out of the house and unhitched him at the fence and he permitted me to get into the saddle. Then off he went, at the long, easy, elastic stride which I delighted in, and it was really far safer for me, just then, than the motion of a rougher horse would have been, even if he were slower. He had hardly gone a mile over the open before a gang of cranes arose from a pond nearby and Turk made a playful rush after them and I was powerless to restrain him. The next thing was a marvel! That horse had discovered that I was sick! He came back into the road of his own accord. Twice, after that, he started off at the appearance of game and each time he returned as meek as a lamb.

Homer was reached, my goods were cared for, and I was conscious that my strength was nearly gone. Out I came to mount Turk, hoping that he would behave himself and he did. He sidled up to a pile of lumber, so that I could get into the saddle easily and then he took the road for home as if he were now in charge of that expedition. The rest of it was told me by Jim and Liz-bet. Late in the day, they saw a horse coming slowly, carefully down the lane toward the house, with apparently something on his back, and they went to inquire as to what it might be. The horse stood still when they came and it was Turk and he had brought me home! I lay with my arms around his neck, insensible, and was lifted off and carried in. The story went the rounds and Turk's owner said that he would not take a farm for him.

I was up again in a day or two, but it was only to discover that all my plans in life had been changed for me. First of all, there seemed no probability that I would be physically capable of hard field labor that season, and management of my farm was out of the question. So was the meeting of my interest and other payments on my land and the procuring of stock, seed, and workmen. The Winter's expenses had about used me up. Ezra had gone, my strength had gone, most of my money had gone, and it was needful that I should look about me for a new opening. My mind went back to literature and journalism as my probable resource and the nearest printing offices were in the Urbanas, east and west. There, too, was the hospitable home of Arch and Jennie Farr and I decided to go and take council with them. My store bills and doctor and board bills were all paid and late one afternoon, a wagon going to town took me as far as Urbana.

I said goodbye to that neck of woods with the most sincere regret, for I had learned to love the prairie and its way of life. Somewhere inside of me must have been preserved some of the wild blood which had led my ancestors across the sea and had made frontiersmen of them. Perhaps, too, I was a little of an Indian. Of one thing I was then and afterwards made very sure of: I had so conducted myself as to win a number of rough but honest-hearted friends and I kept them. To this day, my heart warms toward their memories, although I lived among them only for a few months. On the whole, I may say that I had been in a most useful school and had learned many things which I could not have found out anywhere else. They have been a help to me from that day to this.

24

Frontier Journalism

The broad area of Champaign County was said to contain at that time, the Spring of 1858, not many more than two thousand inhabitants, mostly gathered in small villages and altogether dependent upon the as-yet hardly initiated agriculture.

The specialty was cattle, then wheat, corn, hay, and hardly anything else. The cattle interest was indeed large and the one bank, at West Urbana, was named the Cattle Bank. Such a county had to limit its expenses. It might have a sheriff, with other means of support; a county clerk always on hand and a justice of the peace in each hamlet, not dependent upon his judicial income; but it did not need and did not have a permanently sitting county judge of its own.

It was one of the counties of the Eighth Judicial Circuit and the lawyers of other counties followed the court in its travels from place to place. The circuit judge at that time was Hon. David Davis, afterwards United States senator and Justice of the Supreme Court.[1] It was said that the bar of that circuit, which included Springfield, the state capital, contained a phenomenally large number of capable men, of whom several were of national reputation and left deep marks upon the history of their country. I was soon to come in contact with them, one after another, but I was a fine figure to be introduced to great men that chilly evening in April.

Little had been done for my wardrobe since leaving Chicago and that little had been adapted to prairie uses. My hair, always disposed to luxuriant growth, had last been cut on the shore of Lake Michigan, except a slash from a prairie fire. I was afterwards informed by a fellow citizen that his first admiration of me had been attracted by the remarkable character of my cowhide topboots, into which a pair of coarse trousers was tucked. My shirt was a blue-checked hickory, and under its ample collar was a flowing black silk neck scarf, a remnant of Rochester days. On my head was a broad-brimmed slouch felt hat, black, and my complexion was of the combined tint effects of sun, wind, and Winter fever.

On the whole, there was no other man in Urbana just like me when I got out of the wagon and walked around to shift for myself and to strike for a new field of action. On a corner near the middle of town was the one drug store and it was large, though somewhat dingy and badly lighted. It had been, year after year, the favorite gathering place of the town worthies and especially of the members of the bar whenever court was in session. Here they would come to discuss politics, literature, the news of the day, and to tell stories, crack jokes, and be the admiration of as many of the village loungers as might choose to come in.

It was even said by the malicious that any eminent jurist who might happen to feel the need of special medication could have his accustomed prescription filled for him in a small back room. Illnesses were said to be frequent, and now and then a man would come out of that room with a rye face. Be that as it may, court was in session, and when I entered the drugstore there was a full gathering of illustrious persons around the big egg stove and over them fell a gloomy kind of Rembrandt light, while around them floated clouds of tobacco smoke. The subject up appeared to be the English literature of the Elizabethan age.

I did not know a soul of them but I listened with more than a little surprise and interest. There is no certainty in my mind as to the personality of a very tall man in a stovepipe hat who sat somewhat behind the rest, but "Old Abe" Lincoln was in town and this was his favorite haunt after court hours, unless detained in his hotel room by work. The leader of the Champaign County bar was a middle-aged gentleman who was generally spoken of as "Old Bill Somers."[2] The Somers family was numerous all up and down that timber. One of them was always county clerk, and a township had been named after them. Old Bill was a genius in his way and had a library which was said to contain four thousand volumes of all sorts, including lawbooks. He was by no means a dude in his apparel but he was a gentleman of much more than ordinary intelligence. He was surprised, but not bewildered, that evening. He had but just finished an apt and poetical quotation from "Old Ben Jonson," when a queer-looking crackling near him broke in with, "You are wrong there, Judge. That isn't from Jonson, it's from Sir John Suckling."

Old Bill never so much as turned his head as he responded: "Perfectly correct, my friend. I meant Suckling." I sent another quotation at him however, and roundly disputed his conclusions, while all the other persons present turned their heads and chuckled. They appeared to enjoy hugely the idea of the learned scholar being taken up on his own ground by a raw rough from the prairie. Not one disrespectful word was spoken to me, nevertheless, and that was the beginning of a long friendship between me and the eccentric lawyer, whom I learned to esteem highly. I soon left the drugstore, and walked wearily over to West Urbana to get a night's lodging at Farr's and to make up my mind as to the morrow.

The next morning I was ready for my first attack upon local journalism although the outlook was anything but golden. I had already been aware that a too-sanguine literary adventurer had attempted to set up an "Agricultural" weekly journal in West Urbana. His undertaking had failed and his entire outfit had been bought in for eight hundred dollars at a sheriff's sale by a local medical celebrity named Dr. Walker Scroggs.

He was a man in a million. Of medium height and thin, he was by no means ill looking, and he dressed well, for in Summer or Winter he always had on a black frock suit and a brilliant velvet vest of many colors. He also wore a stovepipe hat and had a pair of sharp, twinkling gray eyes. He was a man of ability, for without any other education he had obtained a good deal of professional skill, medical, surgical, homeopathic, eclectic, and universal. He knew nothing of grammar and nearly nothing of spelling, but he could write, after a fashion. He was courageous, pugnacious, hated all allopathic physicians, was a fanatical temperance and antislavery man and had accumulated a considerable property, part of which was an entire section of land which he was not as yet cultivating. He owned a good house and a remarkably intelligent old mare that could outwalk anything. His wife was a bright and pleasant woman whose maiden name had been Roach.

On the ruins of the lost newspaper enterprise, Dr. Scroggs had determined to establish a journal of his own planning, devoted to his "isms" and to a miscellaneous abuse of the many men whom he did not like. He was one of the best and readiest of haters and had a full vocabulary of free speech, not much of which indicated piety. In fact, he had strong prejudices against the members of the gospel ministry in both of those towns and elsewhere and his feelings were pretty generally reciprocated. That is, it must be said that the doctor was far from being a beloved citizen. The printing office was in the second story of a balloon-frame building on a corner, with a drygoods concern below. The entrance was by a flight of stairs on the outside of the building, in the rear. It let one into the press and composing room, the editorial sanctum being in an ample "cut off" at the front. That building was a tough one, for it could shake and sway in a gale of wind without tumbling down. The press could quiver it and a fever and ague patient might make himself felt.

To this institution, therefore, I made my way that hopeful morning, but I had no letters of introduction, for my friends were not acquainted with the doctor, and Arch Farr had laughed his best when I told him I was going to make a raid upon the *Central Illinois Gazette*. It was already three weeks old and its editor had won a sudden distinction which threatened him with libel suits and personal encounters with angry men. He had written his talk right out, in his wrath, and some of the words that he put in were of the kind mildly described as "archaic." It was, therefore, a dark morning for the *Gazette* and its remarkable conductor and I had climbed into the gloom.

No change had been made in my wardrobe and yet I felt perfectly at home as I entered that printing room. Had I not worked with Seth Paine?

I had never seen the doctor, but there was no mistaking his personality as he sat there, on the other side of the egg stove, hugging his left knee over his right and wearing so sourly discontented a countenance. The printers were at their cases, picking type industriously, and there were no other visitors. I did not give him any card or name, by way of introducing myself, but calmly sat down in another fifty-cent chair and warmed myself by the stove.

"Doctor," I remarked, as if we were old acquaintances, "you are trying to run a newspaper here?"

Only a nod and something between a growl and a grunt was his response, and after a moment of contemplation of the stove I added, kindly:

"You don't know how!" and that brought down his leg as he responded: "The hell you say! I know that better than you do!" and I continued:

"You can't run a newspaper, but I can!"

His hands went behind his head half contemptuously as he replied: "The hell you can! What will you take to try it on?"

"No pay at all, just now," I told him, and he again made a careless allusion to a country where the weather might be warmer than in Urbana.

I went on to make a business proposition, however, for I was well-aware that he was losing money fast and needlessly. I told him that I would get out one edition of the paper to show him what I could do. If all was then satisfactory, I would take no wages. I would run my own risk of making the paper pay its own way. As soon as I should do that, I was to have a full third partnership and control. In the meantime, at the end of the week, he was to buy me a good suit of clothes and some other things and pay my board in a good boardinghouse.

"Done!" he exclaimed. "Take right hold. Take the whole damn thing and run it! I'm going out to see a patient."

As nearly as I can remember, he turned back for a moment to inquire my name and if I knew anybody in the village. Then he disappeared and I did not see him again until later in the day. The printers all growled audibly when they saw me making my inspection, for they had been fairly fleecing the doctor. They had each week been setting up the entire areas of all the four pages of the paper and charging him for it at the Chicago "printer's union" rates, which were not allowable on a country sheet. Even the fine type market reports of New York and Chicago were all re-set or charged for, each week, instead of merely being corrected. The big blazing headlines for many "departments" were all paid for over and over. I at once hunted around the office for some old electrotype advertisement plates which had been in the dead journal, found them and made up a full page with railway, patent medicine, and other dead matter. Then I ordered out all the headlines and had as much permanent "standing matter" set up as I could ornament pages with and not seem to crowd the news. Fully a page-and-a-half being saved in this way, the genuine advertisements filled another half page and the weekly bills for typesetting were reduced more than one half after I had cut down the printers to weekly wages at the ruling country rates to which they were entitled. They swore some and not so many of them were needed. Then I went into the sanctum and rearranged it.

There was room for improvement everywhere and when the doctor came in I told him what I had done. His first objection was that none of those old ads were paying anything but he wilted when I showed him that they were to save him a dollar-and-a-half per column per week in typesetting. He demurred to some other things, for it was his nature to oppose, but he ended by telling me to "go my own gait, this week, if the whole concern went to Chicago." That evening I was at work late in my new office and when I went home and told Arch and Jennie what I had done, it seemed as if they would never stop laughing.

Three days later I sent out the fourth number of the *Gazette* in fine style, looking like entirely an other affair. The contents, too, were of such a character that the doctor was astonished when he read his paper. I had omitted some things that he had written for it and bluntly refused to put in any more personalities. He surrendered only after all the men and women he met had congratulated him upon the improved appearance of the *Gazette*. Although hardly anybody as yet knew how it had happened, folks were curious and it was time for me to put on my new uniform. That was what the doctor had agreed to, and he even seemed in a hurry to keep his word, making energetic remarks about having such a looking customer the editor of the greatest paper in central Illinois. I think it was the cash account that affected him most, and he still kept his own name at the head as editor while he ceased to take any care of the literary business except as a kind of skipping critic, after each consecutive issue came out.

So I had made my re-entry into journalism and really felt at home. My ambition was rising fast and I was rapidly recovering my physical strength after my hair was cut, unlike Samson of old. A good boarding place was provided me and I began a systematic examination of my surroundings. It was well not to seem to seek prominence, but an unexpected notoriety was close at hand. Up to that date, the politics of the village had been in the hands of what Dr. Scroggs eloquently described as the "rummies," who held power by means of imported voters, for the village people were largely against them. The Spring election was at hand and the substantial men of West Urbana held a kind of despairing caucus in the *Gazette* offices one evening, for the purpose, as it appeared to me of sadly assuring one another that there was no use in trying to do anything. The imported voters were generally rough and dangerous men, railway workmen, drinkers, etc., whom no man was ready to face at the polls as a challenger. I heard them all through without saying a word but my temper was rising and at last I said to them:

"Gentlemen, there will be a challenger at the polls on election day and every foreign interloper will be compelled to swear in his ballot." The answer came from three or four at once:

"Who on earth will dare to do the challenging?"

"I will!" I said. "I shall be at the polls all day."

Some doubts were even then expressed, but the caucus broke up and more than one of its members promised me assistance. Among them were the two members of a firm of railway contractors who were ready to put in a quite efficient stroke of work but not to openly make themselves unpopular.

They were wise and able men and they knew just what to do and they did encourage me although they were not to be at the polls. The next morning the funniest kind of rumor went around the village. It was to the effect that the new editor of the *Gazette*, the dangerous desperado who had come from nobody knew where, was to challenge at the polls and be prepared to fight his bloody way through if he had to kill all the bad men.

As for myself, my real idea was that the only difficulty in the way of the respectabilities had been mere pusillanimity, and I had small fear of any gory consequences. Nevertheless, at sunrise next morning, there I was at my chosen post and the first men who came had to "swear in." Great was the current wrath but I was obstinate and I may have looked so. At all events, respectability took courage and before long there was quite a gathering of good men around the polls. It was perhaps as well that "Satan came also." A leader of the opposition, for politics sake, was a handsome, tall, and well-educated young fellow named Daniel Bradley, with whom I was to have a better acquaintance thereafter. He was beginning to cause me some annoyance of a verbal kind when he suddenly found himself face to face with an exceedingly unpleasant character.

This was a carpenter whose esteem I had won when he was at work upon the pine palace and took his meals at Old Man Southwick's house, and mine, down on the south prairie. He was a lean and hungry-looking man and I had noted him then as having an exceedingly black vocabulary. I had done him injustice, however, for I had formed no adequate idea of the foul and abusive things which he could say or how long he could pour them out. Poor Dan was befouled, abused, objurgated, and cursed in the most prolific manner, and anything like a personal encounter was out of the question, for he was distinctively "a gentleman" and an affray with Chadden would have implied loss of caste. He was utterly beaten and had to give it up.

This affair also increased the courage of my supporters, more of whom were now coming in from the prairie. In fact, I had the obvious majority with me all day, but my enemies were like Wellington when he exclaimed

"Oh, that Blucher or night would come," for late in the day they were sure of heavy reinforcements. A construction train, loaded with voters from up the line was to arrive and settle this matter and they felt sure that the impudent challenger would be swept away. So he might have been, but for Clark & Forterfield and the switch at Rantoul, the next station north on the Illinois Central. The train ran off gently into that switch and before it could be on the track again the hour was late. The Blucher party did not make another Waterloo, for sunset came before they did, and the polls were closed promptly. Then in came the belated train and an enormous quantity of bad language. In justice to Chadden, I must record that before the end of the next year he joined the Methodist church and began to make a better use of his free flow of language. He was a born orator. Small as had been my actual personal risk, that day's work set me up and I became one of the acknowledged first citizens of West Urbana, although some who had been there almost two years still spoke of me as a newcomer. They were almost silenced when it became known that I was a prairie farmer, with a large tract of land in the south part of the county.

25

Forward

One of my first duties, after obtaining my regular editorial passes from the railroad company, was to go to Chicago to deed back my now useless farmland. The seller was a just man and dealt well with me in the settlement and he had his reward, for the price of prairie land of that quality was rising. It was already much better than it had been just after the Panic of 1857. I hope he sold it the next time for twice as much.

My newspaper enterprise prospered amazingly and before long I was the editor of two instead of one. That is, our Ford County subscribers were ambitious to have a local journal of their own but were not numerous enough to sustain one. It was better for them that we should make up, each week, a page of Ford County advertisements and local news and then let all the rest of the *Gazette* go in as *The Ford County Journal*. By this means they had a big newspaper to send out as proof of the prosperity of their young and growing concern, and we secured all the Ford County business at a comparatively trifling cost. The *Gazette* was much better-looking than either of its local rivals and our subscription list grew rapidly in all directions. Advertising also came in to an unexpected extent and some of the "dummies" could shortly be dispensed with. The job office was a fairly good one and that part of our business I encouraged in every way that I could think of. In short, it was but a little while before I was able to demand of the doctor the fulfillment of his contract and became a partner in the concern with absolute power of management, to his great relief and disgust.

West Urbana was growing fast, and it had many advantages over its older neighbor. The two towns touched at the edges, however, and there was more than a little jealousy between them. Nevertheless, the Urbana merchants found it to their advantage to advertise in the *Gazette*, and our newspaper brethren turned upon poor Dr. Scroggs the full abuse power of their political and personal wrath. It was easy writing to abuse him and to talk in varied type about "Scroggins" and his pills and his plasters and his eccentricities of all sorts. The fact is that mere blackguardism is the least brain-tiring of any penmanship that a man may turn his hand to. The nominally Whig, and soon to be the nominally Republican, organ was edited by an experienced quill driver named Crandall and his son. They were experts at blackguardism and each week brought out some new evidence of their abilities, as well as of their animosity to the doctor.

So very rough did this thing become that I began to fear results and deemed it needful to "speak to young Crandall." His father being out of the question, I gently informed him that if he should print about me what he did about the doctor he might expect me to come and see him. In fact, I said that one of us two "would get a pretty severe thrashing." He replied that it would probably be me, but both of us had doubts on that head and he never mentioned me afterwards. It was best to treat me with silent scorn. For my own part, from the first, I disgusted the doctor by insisting that the *Gazette* was too dignified a journal to condescend to that sort of thing and that his only proper course was to consider all blackguardism beneath him.

It was a matter of course that the *Gazette* should go at once into politics, which were then in an exceedingly tangled condition all over the country. The aspect of national affairs was cloudy to the last degree, and perhaps the largest party then in existence was composed of both Whigs and Democrats who were scared so badly that their creed was mainly composed of denunciations of all men who had positive opinions and dared to speak them out aloud. I was one of the positive fellows, although I was by no means such an unthinking, uncharitable, venomous abolitionist as was my partner. He considered me almost lukewarm because I could not see my way to indiscriminate cursing of all slaveholders and all pro-slavery men. I could see that there were fairly two sides to the great question and that the right way for dealing with it had not yet been discovered. I went in, however, and soon found that I was going to have enough to do, for in that county we were short of stump speakers and party managers. As time went on, I became more and more familiar with the names and some of the supposed characteristics of the leading men of the state, but was impressed with an idea that those of them whom I had seen were by no means of gigantic intellectual stature.

Parallel with the slowly formative processes of party politics was the growth of our local churches, especially the Baptist Church, which was taking good shape under the wise management of my friend Farr. It was financially the strongest body, if it were yet a body, in West Urbana. One of its members was a bright sort of man named John White, our most successful speculator, who sometimes boasted that he owned "the biggest house, the best overcoat, and the handsomest wife" in the village. He also had, by all odds, the most imperative and largest mother-in-law, and she not only ruled her own household, John included, but the church also, and she persisted in singing in the choir as in her earlier days.

Another leading member was a well-to-do lawyer named Harmon and he and his wife were all the more especial friends of mine because they both were from Monroe County, New York, and had known about me before they came. He had studied law in Rochester and knew many of my old friends. He had a pleasant house, too, but it was a frame concern, not brick, like the lordlier mansion of John White.

The regular services of the church were held in what was called the town hall, although it was private property, and it was really a good auditorium, for so small a place. The congregations were quite respectable in numbers and it was obviously the correct thing to have a Sunday school. Somewhat to my surprise, I was unanimously elected Superintendent and I took hold of my work with all the energy in me. It was a complete success, and before long we had by all odds the largest and best school in Champaign County, greatly to the jealousy of many citizens, both outside of our church and in.

As if I had not enough on my hands, as the Autumn drew near and a need for right methods of spending some of the social evenings, my evil genius suggested the formation of a Young Men's Literary Association, to hold meetings in the hall and to have all sorts of literary and social and musical entertainments. There was much vocal and instrumental ability lying around loose and it was easy to make up a first rate Glee Club. All the fellows were ready to distinguish themselves as orators and essayists and our successes were phenomenally brilliant. Alas, for me, I was unanimously chosen president and for a time it was all glory and congratulation. But every fellow who imagined that it was his next turn to speak or sing or read aloud, and was crowded out by somebody else, visited his wrath and disappointment upon my unlucky head. What between the Sunday school and the Association, I was ignorantly making enemies rapidly. In fact, anybody could see that I was getting ahead too fast, and evil-minded men and women roundly accused me of the dreadful sin of ambition. Dr. Scroggs himself had a bigger stone than that to throw at me.

"Stoddard," he openly declared to me, when his steam was up, "the difficulty with you is that you are an aristocrat!"

I humbly pleaded not guilty of so heinous a crime as that, but he said: "It won't do, Stoddard. It's in you, as big as a horse. Why, any man can see it in you—across the street!"

It must have been bad, to have been visible at a distance, and I could not imagine how he could have formed so insane a notion. At all events, it had not yet appeared to hinder my popularity. Another cause of jealousy was close at hand, however, and it came in the strange shape of friendly finance. The cashier and manager of the Cattle Bank was a handsome, merry-faced fellow named Chalmers M. Sherfy, and of course he was a man of much importance. The large room in the rear of the banking office was his sleeping room as well as the Directors' room and it was fitted up in style. Among its other beauties was a good piano with an Aeolian attachment. It was not a great while before Sherfy and I became close friends and I was invited to become his chum in the bank bedroom.

We got on together capitally well, but there were those who did not like it, and many remarks were made that were indicative of a disturbed state of mind. Among other points, a result was that Chal and I became in a manner society leaders, and no public opinion of any entirely new town will stand that sort of aristocracy. It was not long, too, before my unlucky reputation as a possible blood tub and desperado received another unexpected lift. There came to the village, from Chicago, a pretty and stylish young widow who had business interests thereabouts and her guardian put her under the protection of his friend the bank cashier.

That meant me, for poor Chal was a cripple in one leg and was no sort of fighting man. At about the same time there arrived from the East a young doctor who was drawn there by his brother, the keeper of the one doubtful sporting concern in West Urbana. The doctor was good enough but he had not only that misfortune but also the erroneous idea that the code of honor was still in some kind of dead-alive existence. That is, that a man must be ready to fight. He, of course, went to his brother's place and had a room over the wicked billiard saloon.

Now, it happened that an older physician had two daughters, and their mother was a great friend of mine as well as a strict Methodist, down on gambling and liquor. There was nothing wonderful in the fact that young Dr. Isom began to pay attention to the pretty widow. There was an imprudence, nevertheless, in the act of Chal when he wrote about it to her Chicago guardian and mentioned me as one of the responsible references. He did so because it had happened that good Mrs. Dr. Bearse, at the close of an evening entertainment, had bidden her daughters not to let Dr. Isom see them home and had requested me to do so instead. I had done so, in utter innocence and knew nothing about the warning letter.

The Chicago guardian was another remarkable, for he wrote to his pretty ward, quoting only too liberally and loosely from Chal in advising her that she must discourage her supposed suitor. She was an obedient ward, for she at once told the doctor to stay away and showed him her guardian's letter in justification so that Chal and I were put in the position of declaring him improper company. He was furious and so were his sporting friends, but these told him that it would not do for him to call a known cripple to bodily account. The whole matter came down upon my innocent head and the whole village knew that there was to be what was called "serious trouble" between the injured lover and the editor of the *Gazette*.

I heard of it and paid it no manner of attention although even Dr. Scroggs believed that there was a "difficulty" on hand. Only a day or two passed and at a little after noon I was sitting in my inner office, at my table at one end of it, when in strode the angry doctor, all screwed up to the fighting point. He glared at me ferociously and I do not remember what were his salutations, but I at once arose and went to the door, shut and locked it and went back and sat down. I did so with no other idea in my mind than that if he meant a fight I did not intend to be helped or interfered with by the printers in the outer office. We would fight it out without witnesses. The effect upon him, however, was peculiar, for he at once took the chair to which I invited him and began a fierce statement of his grievances. I of course disclaimed the letter and he sternly demanded:

"But do you mean to say that I am not fit company for any young lady in this village? Do you dare to impugn my character?"

"Well, ye-es, I do," I calmly responded. "Your associations are bad. We don't know anything about you, but some things won't do."

His rejoinder was the reverse of polite or good tempered. In fact, it was what might be called chivalric and threatening, but he kept his eye on me in an interesting manner. It happened that my table drawer was open and that my right arm and hand rested in it. The reason was that he was the larger man and was supposed to be armed while I was not. Just beyond my hand, however, there lay upon the table what the printers call a "shooting stick." It was a bar of steel about ten inches long and having a heavy knob of steel for a head. A terribly effective short club was that same shooting stick, and it was my calculation that if he should draw a pistol or a knife I could crush his skull like a glass bottle before he could do any mischief with either. He now seemed to be growing strangely cooler and even asked me about the Mrs. Bearse business. "Did she do so? I don't believe that she ever did. Do you dare to tell me that what I have heard is true?"

It was true, I told him, and I had seen the girls home to prevent his doing so and should do it again if necessary. His whole manner was changing, but mine was not, for I felt as cool as ice. At last he begged me to go with him to the Bearse place and let him give an explanation. I was willing, the door was unlocked and then a swarm of curious villagers saw the two "dedlie duilysts" walking up the street, side by side. We found Mrs. Bearse at home and in reply to his excited questioning she replied:

"I did that very thing, Dr. Isom, and I think you are not fit company for my daughters. I did speak to Mr. Stoddard."

The doctor burst into tears, exclaiming: "My God! Has it come to this?"

Then he went on to tell of a respectable eastern home, good bringing up, good intentions, and a strongly formed intention to be more careful of his conduct thenceforth. He went his way and I went mine and before night I had the fun of hearing his explanation of the reason why he did not rush in on me and mash me in some terrible way or other.

"It was just this way," he told his friends. "The little Devil got up and locked the door on us, for a close fight. Then he sat down with his hand in the drawer where he keeps his revolver and kept his eye on me, and you know he's a dead shot. If I'd ha' stirred a peg at that distance I was a dead man and I knew it. I had no chance whatever."

He was more than half right but the shooting stick I meant to draw was not the Colt he was thinking of. He would have dropped just the same.

In justice to him, I must record that the to-be-expected consequences followed. He reformed entirely and won a success. The pretty widow hated me like "p'isen" and in due time she married him and they were happy. On the whole, however, the effect upon my unpleasant pugilistic reputation was all that I did not ask for and was not just the thing for a successful Sunday school superintendent.

26

Suppers, Characters, and Incidents

I will finish up the story of the bank bedroom that it may not be entirely forgotten hereafter. It was large and high and when it was thrown in with the bank office in front the two together made plenty of area for reception purposes. Therefore, we utilized it to an extent that it was not originally intended for. The black cook of the Doane House was a fat and dignified party who was exceedingly proud of his ability to do up game and delicacies. Every now and then the village would be honored by the presence of some distinguished visitor or visitors, especially railway officials and their friends, for whom there were but scanty means for social enjoyment in the community.

They always put up at the Doane House and were sure to be willing to meet cashiers and editors and the leading local businessmen. The correct thing, therefore, was to give such a person, if he were at all agreeable, a supper at the bank. Especially when game was in season, we were able to give him a good one, venison, grouse, quails, and the cook's charm was in quails. When game was out, there were chickens which had never known a hungry hour on that prairie and which could be had for a dollar and a half a dozen, the regular price of all feathered game, though I have known a side of fat deer-meat to fetch as much as three and a half.

To the feeding we could add the Glee Club, and our leading clothes merchant was a bright young Jew named Eppstein who was a musical enthusiast and really an expert on the piano or the "cythera," to which latter instrument we generally preferred the piano. I remember one occasion when he was almost disappointed. He had never been allowed to pay any part of the frequent expenses, his music and his pleasant company being all we wanted, but felt in honor bound to put in a food contribution and did so.

One evening he was all smiles of confident expectation for he had brought in a rare and attractive delicacy which he exhibited with pride. It was in little tinfoil rolls, and there was much of it. We did our best and each of us tried a bite, but we were a gang of uneducated, untrained savages and every man was trying hard to relish and smile gratefully over his first mouthful of "genuine, imported Sweitzer kase," as nearly rotten as any such wonderful cheese ever succeeded in getting. It was the tinfoil that had held the stuff together and I had a strong suspicion that I was struggling with a concoction of fat worms and soft soap. We did our best in the way of praise but poor Eppstein saw that we were unable to appreciate his contribution. As to those gatherings, they brought me a number of pleasant acquaintances, but they also gave our enemies a handle for stinging remarks about the orgies of Stoddard and his temperance men in the bank parlor. I got it in various directions and one of my asserted speeches at a supper party was curiously quoted from in Crandall's *Journal*.

The Summer passed away and a new element was added to my perplexities. My dear sister Kate had found it exceedingly difficult to get on with her stepmother, and her father was turned against her to such an extent that she also determined to come west. I had no word in the matter and was altogether at sea as to what to do with her when she appeared in what was soon to be known as the young city of Champaign. I had absolutely no means for supporting her and was at my wit's end. I could have done nothing if the *Gazette* had not now become really prosperous under my management. We had become such a power, politically and in circulation, that we actually obtained the official county printing and advertising, to the boisterous disgust and indignation of our newspaper rivals.

I obtained temporary board for Kate and she went in with an old lady who was trying to keep a select "primary school." I believe Kate's earnings as a teacher during the following year were forty dollars and it was well for her that she brought a good wardrobe with her. She also brought curious social notions that did not diminish the jealousy of some of my plebeian neighbors. On the whole, I was up to my eyes in difficulties of many kinds.

One of my adventures that Autumn was an attendance at the State Fair, agricultural and so forth, away up in the northwest corner of the state.

Abundance of railway passes cut down the expense and the trip had to be a brief one, for Dr. Scroggs insisted upon going with me. All would have gone well if I had not been seized with cholera on the cars of the Central Railroad, forty miles out from Freeport. The doctor did his best but I suffered horribly and came near dying.

When we reached Freeport, however, and I was carried to the nearest hotel, all of its inmates swarmed out of it, remonstrating vigorously against having a deadly plague brought in among them. The proprietor to whom they protested was a sincere Christian, nevertheless, for he told them all to go to "heaven" and said that he would be forever blessed before he would turn a sick man out of his hotel to please such an inhuman, happy, happy set of blessed cowards. He reaped his reward and I was all right in a few hours, for the men and women who ran away had secured their rooms in advance at low rates and the town was swarming with visitors who were unable to obtain quarters and were ready to pay anything. Every room in his house was instantly reoccupied at several times as much per diem cash as he had been receiving before. It was beautiful poetic justice and I shall always remember him with pleasure as a true-hearted man and a good manager of the plague-stricken hotel business.

The year 1858 drew to a close in a mixed kind of success, on the whole much greater than I had any good right to expect.[1] In politics, I could say that I had attended one state convention of the People's Party, now beginning to call itself Republican, and that I had there managed to be so effectively busy as to acquire the lifelong friendship of Hon. Leonard Swett,[2] Lincoln's friend, and other well-known men, as well as to gain the reprobation of another lot, quite as influential, against whom I had figured in the convention.

I had also delivered a number of stump speeches, all over my own county, and was acquiring some facility upon the platform. I was well aware, however, that my oratorical powers were small and that they were in need of much practice before they would amount to anything. One feature of the year, for me, had been that the University of Rochester had given me my degree of Bachelor of Arts, in course, with my class, although I had not taken my senior year of residence. It was kindly declared to be "on account of standing and scholarship." I had kept up my correspondence fairly well with many of my eastern friends, and believe that some of them had exaggerated ideas of what I had accomplished.

Dr. Scroggs was a pretty good financier, and as soon as the *Gazette* was fairly on its feet he decided to dispense with rent paying. With a view to that accomplishment he purchased a gore of land on the corner adjoining the balloon in which we were and proceeded to build upon it. So far as I remember, he put in the first stone foundation ever seen in that village, bringing the stone from a considerable distance.

The new building was to be about sixty feet deep, twenty-five on the street, and perhaps fifteen in the rear. He bought the odd lot for almost nothing and he traded for the stone. The foundation-laying called in the services of the only stone mason to be had, and this was his first job. He was a man of middle height and disproportionately broad-shouldered, with a large head, long curling gray hair in superabundance down his back, a tangled gray beard to his waist, moustaches to match, eyebrows like awnings, and a wardrobe that looked as if he slept in a lime kiln. His boots were of a fine lime red and his hands were as hard as horn. He had two remarkable voices and he knew how to use them in the most effective way. One was in his throat and was somewhat like the voices of other men. The other was away down in his stomach and was as the growl of a hoarse bear, declaring its agreement with whatever, from time to time, might be uttered by voice number one. He was a vast adjunct to our somewhat heated local political discussions and he was always allowed the floor for he was a perfect master of vituperative abuse.

I can almost quote: "Mr. Speaker! I am a man of common sense (voice number one) I am! (voice number two) I have listened to the lies uttered by the last speaker (voice number one) I have (voice number two). He is a complete numbskull—he is! And I believe he is a villain—I do! He does not know enough to go in when it rains—he doesn't. I think all such fellows as he is ought to be in Hell—I do! The fact is, Mr. Speaker, that most of the people of this unlucky village are damn fools—they are. As for that other man over yonder, he ought to be taken out and hung—he ought! And a rope is too good for him—it is!"

The sudden drops from his throat to his stomach were worthy of the most accomplished orator—or ventriloquist—and the multitude was always glad to hear him while it was of no use for one of his victims to lose temper. He could outscold any man and as for hitting him, he was as if he had been made of stone or an old oak stump.

The new building was of pretty solid frame above the foundation. The cellar and the front part of the lower story were rented to a druggist for much more than ten per cent interest on the entire cost, leaving the doctor free. Twelve feet of the narrow rear was cut off for a doctor's office, he had never had one before, and for an editorial sanctum. The entire upper floor was printing office, and as soon as we were in it we had the best outfit in those parts. I was rapidly acquiring a good knowledge of job work and could pick type rapidly, which was often a good thing, owing to the exceedingly uncertain character of the tramping jours [journeymen—ed.] whom we were compelled to employ. I had a row with a gang of them once in the old building, when they came in late from a spree they had been on the night before. I cleaned them out but I carried for many a day the black scar on my left temple where one of them split me with the coal shovel. It bled well and Dr. Scroggs said that it had missed the temporal artery and fatality by only a sixteenth of an inch. I had no more trouble of that kind. Our run of business was good but I had a queer incident on one of the warm days of that Autumn. It was as warm as Summer.

I was upstairs, at a piece of job work which a devil had carelessly pied [misaligned—ed.], and it was on a composing stone near the head of the stairs. I was in a state of mind, my shirt sleeves rolled up to my shoulders, and my hands black with ink. There may have been streaks of darkness on my face. The doctor was below, rolling out some pills and must have been standing with his back to the open street door when a loud voice in the doorway hailed him as "Doc" and inquired into the condition of his health. I did not entirely catch the doctor's responses, but in a moment more he was up at the head of the stairs and at my elbow informing me, in a suppressed tone which might have been heard all over the office:

"Stoddard! Old Abe is here and he wants to see you!"

My reply was in accordance with my state of mind and with the pied type.

"Come right down!" he said. "But do fix up a little. Why, Stoddard, you are looking like the devil."

I could believe that I was not exactly in presentation uniform but I replied that all I would do just then was a kind of compromise. If Mr. Lincoln wished to see me, I would go down and I would wash my hands but I would not roll down my sleeves. The doctor was not at all satisfied but I was aware of an audible chuckle in the room below. Up to that hour I had not met Mr. Lincoln but had heard a great deal of him and did not believe he would care much about a little ink and light clothing. The doctor, on the other hand, considered this visit of so prominent a politician a great affair, and he was a little afraid of big men.

I was not, and I could also perceive that he was unable to comprehend why the visit was not to him but to a mere junior like myself. He may have been under the delusion that the general public did not know who was the editor of the *Gazette*.

Mr. Lincoln greeted me cordially and plunged at once into the causes of his coming. In a minute he had me not only deeply interested but somewhat astonished. I had supposed that I knew the people and politics of that county and he had been told that I did, but so did he. He could ask about the different precincts and their leading men almost as if he had lived among them, and I was glad enough to be able to set him right as to the drift of the voters. They all were drifting, more or less, and out of all that driftwood he was proposing to organize a new political power.

Of course, I could not give him a thorough personal reading at that time but he impressed me strongly, and in after years I was the better able to understand his intimate knowledge of the people he was to govern and upon whom he was to rely. As he was then studying Champaign County, so he was investigating the state of Illinois and other states, and was getting into close relations with the current of thought and feeling, North and South.

The conversation was a long one and Dr. Scroggs soon got weary of it, for he had no part in it, and he went off "to see a patient." Lincoln went out and I went back to my pied job and did not at all suppose that so unimportant an interview was to have any permanent effect upon my life or his. The fact was, however, that I had begun to take a deep interest in the great Whig leader and I soon knew more about him.[3]

Among other things, I had heard marvelous stories of his power over a jury, especially in doubtful criminal cases, and must say that I did not half believe them. I cannot as I write recall the name of the county town west of the Centralia crossing of the Illinois Central Railroad on the St. Louis road, but I believe it was at that place that a man was to be tried for murder. Some things grow singularly dim, at times, after a lapse of nearly half a century.

All I can distinctly recall are the things which at that day impressed me and the railway crossing was not one of them. The murder had been committed in a small country store and the victim had been killed with a spade in the hands, it was charged, of a somewhat loose character living in the neighborhood. The murdered man, a non-resident, perhaps a cattle buyer, was supposed to have money with him and there were three men in the store who saw the deed done and were prepared to testify. In my opinion, it was this precise presentation of the case which drew the attention of Lincoln and convinced him that there was too much evidence and too little motive, as well as too much unreason.

At all events, he had volunteered to defend that seemingly hopeless convict and I availed myself of my abundant passes on those roads to run down and hear him before what was pretty sure to be a prejudiced jury with their minds made up beforehand. The courtroom was jammed full of eager spectators and it was easy to see that the drift of public opinion was mingled with a strong curiosity as to what on earth Lincoln could do in so entirely clear a case. I almost wondered, myself, when I listened to the straightforward and unanimous testimony of the three men who had actually witnessed the murder.

The character of the murderer was badly smashed for him but the truth was that he was nothing worse than an ordinary ne'er do well, of the customary southern Illinois stamp, with no bloodthirsty element in him.

The next singular feature of that case was that Lincoln appeared to be against his own client and doing his best to convict him. Oh, how he did make them reiterate and nail down their evidence, forcing all their several statements to an exact agreement as to all the minute particulars. He had visited the scene of the murder and he now took out a tape line and made measurements to illustrate to the jury the exact facts of the occurrence. At precisely such a spot the victim had been standing and at exactly such a spot by the upright wooden pillar by which he had picked up the sharp-edged spade from a lot of new ones that stood there, the murderer had been standing when he struck the blow.

The measurements between the two spots were carefully made with the tape line and were as carefully verified by the witnesses. That poor convict was doomed! It was wonderfully vivid. Every soul in that courtroom had been transported to the country store and we were standing there, behind the counters or in the back part of the store, looking on with horror as the awful deed was done before our faces. Lincoln now had the spade in his hand and he held it up. He was at that moment, to our eyes, particularly to the eyes of the jury, on the very square foot of flooring occupied by the now trembling convict, his despairing and deserted client, shivering in the prisoner's dock and waiting for a verdict of guilty. At the same time, as Lincoln lifted the spade, we could distinctly see the innocent victim standing on the other spot so accurately proved for him as his place of death. It was awful! Up, up, went the spade at the end of Lincoln's long arm, and down came the fatal blow, but the end of that deadly weapon struck the floor a number of feet short of the pillar. As I remember it, Lincoln had managed to now have his client, a short man, standing so near him that with one step they were side by side and the six feet four of the lawyer's height was in strong contrast with the five feet eight of his client.

"Gentlemen of the jury," shouted Lincoln. "I am a taller man than he is! I could not have done it! He could not have done it! Gentlemen of the jury, he did not do it! Somebody else did it!"

The absolute demonstration of his declaration was apparent to all who heard and saw and the accused man was acquitted. I do not now remember what became of the witnesses but it was pretty plain that they had convicted themselves of that murder and I went home well satisfied with my first look at a trial for murder.[4]

The Winter of 1858–59 passed busily away and the Spring came again in a wet and chilly way. My own affairs were undergoing a few changes. For instance, the Literary Association was played out. My term of office ended and another fellow was elected and he didn't know how and the whole concern lay down and died. As to the Sunday school, there were not only factions and jealousies but also ambitions in that infant Baptist Church. One of these was in the teeming brain of my good friend John White's large and sharp-tongued mother-in-law. She clearly understood that the richest man in the church must be the best and should be its ruler—under her supervision. It was therefore his place to be Superintendent of so very large and fine a Sunday school, instead of a young man who really had no money to speak of.

Therefore, when a day of election came, somewhere after the holidays, I was dropped and the school I had so zealously built up was put into John White's hands. He had not been brought up in anything of the kind and his education for it was of the most original. What was his other education may be seen through the pinhole of his free employment of the term "sect" when what he meant was "sex." To cut that matter short, the scholars did not take to him and began to go off to other schools and before long he came before the church, like the really frank and honest man that he was, and told them he had discovered that he did not know how. It was not at all the easy job he had imagined and he offered his resignation. The question was asked of him "What is to be done?" and he promptly responded, in a businesslike manner, "Put in again the man who built up the school. Mr. Stoddard is our only man for it. I am sorry I ever undertook it."

Mr. Stoddard was at once unanimously elected, Madame being angrily silent, but he positively refused to attempt a restoration of the wreck for there was more stormy weather ahead and he did not care to push himself in among a lot of jarring factions and was well aware that he was not at all liked by the mother-in-law. He was not under her thumb in any manner and she could not brook rebellion. Here may be the place to put in the rest of the church fight, without reference to chronology. The split in the church took form in two religious armies, "The John White party" and "The Harmon party" and the numbers on either side were about equal. My sister and I kept out of the mess as well as we could and my poor friend Farr and his wife did all in their power to reconcile the really ridiculous differences.

All was of no avail and the war grew more and more bitter until a day came when the John White party had a "church meeting" almost to themselves. They proceeded formally to "exclude" every member of the Harmon party, including blindly my sister and myself. In the course of a few days, another "church meeting" was held which was attended only by the Harmonites. It was entirely regular and constitutional and it proceeded to formally "exclude" every member of the John White party. So that entire church had excluded itself and from all its enterprising membership the "right hand of fellowship had been withdrawn." Some of the too severe executioners were somewhat taken aback when I informed them that Kate and I were still members of the Syracuse church and not within their reach at all, not having joined.

My father's elder sister, Harriet, had married a prosperous New London County farmer named Morgan. I think it was in the year 1859 that he and his family, including two nearly grown-up sons, came to our next north county of Ford to settle upon a section of prairie land which he had purchased of the railroad company. It took him only a year or so to discover that his proper home was in Connecticut. I think he then turned his prairie property over to one of his sons and went back, homesick and repentant.

It was not long after his arrival, however, that I managed to squeeze out time enough from my somewhat pressing duties to go up and visit them. Of course I had a good time, but my most vivid remembrance of it is that Uncle Morgan had a good double gun. It was just too early to kill grouse, but the state game law was an old one and did not include any but the older counties. Now Ford County bordered upon Vermillion. Ford was within the law while Vermillion was not and the birds were flying well. Uncle Morgan's farm was on the county line and all I had to do was to walk along the line and shoot at eastward flying chickens. I killed that day more birds than I could well carry home. Every one of them was hit inside of the law and fell outside of it. The legal question involved has often puzzled me.

It was during this year that my old friend Hop Strong came to Champaign to see Arch Farr and his wife and me. He urged me to give up so small and unhopeful a place and come and try my luck in St. Louis, where he and his cousin Henry Strong had opened a fine shoe store. I consented to come over and see them and their village. Having passes, the trip did not cost me anything, but the train I was on came to grief half way. The engineer was killed and some others were hurt and I learned what remarkable figures human beings might cut in pitching out of the upper berths of one of those old-style sleeping cars. I was in a lower berth and did not pitch.

My stay in St. Louis was a short one and I decided that it did not need me just then. Within a year, Hop and his cousin had also decided that theirs was one shoe store more than the place had any need of. On the whole, I believed that Champaign was about the settlement for me and I had no idea of leaving it. My purpose was to grow up with it and if I had done so my western success was really cut out for me. It was not to be so, however, and there was no prophet to tell me how my plans were to be broken up.

27

Lincoln and a New Beginning

Somewhere along in the Winter, I found means to secure a small cottage near the middle of the village and in this Kate and I began small housekeeping. The house contained only two rooms besides the kitchen but it would do. I still retained some remnants of my remarkable shipment of old family household goods from the East and was able to obtain whatever else was needed. At a later day, our old piano had also been sent on, because it was really Kate's property and because the Syracuse family needed something finer. I had with the house a coop of a barn and was provided with stable room for a stout pony which I had accumulated. On the whole, we were pretty well off, for one of our oldest and most faithful family servants, devoted to my mother's memory, had migrated to Champaign and was living near us to take care of rough jobs and washings. Her name had been Helen Linahen and I do not remember her married name, but she was a kind of jewel.

One more burden had been added by Kate's determination to get as much of the family as she might away from Mrs. Stoddard's influence. This had led her to bring on my younger brother, John, and with some difficulty I obtained a place for him in a store kept by a friend of mine, where he obtained board money for his services. I was loaded up to my eyes in the Spring of 1859 and was even feeling somewhat tired of doing so very much.

The new political campaign was opening early and the whole country was getting on fire with excitement. The *Gazette* was also beginning to regard itself as an important journal, for we had a circulation of over two thousand, scattered over several counties, and that was phenomenal.

The doctor watched the cash account closely, as well he might, and believed that in some inscrutable way he was still the editor of the *Gazette*. Nobody else believed with him, and it was not necessary for me to dispute the point.

He was, of course, disposed to launch out into national politics, but with only a dim idea of what these were to be. Other papers, here and there, were taking time by the forelock and were announcing their preferences as to the leadership of the new party which was in process of formation. For an understanding of those processes, a reference is respectfully suggested to the *Life of Lincoln* [a reference to his own biographical work—ed.], for the story of them is too long to be inserted here. He had already taken a position which nobody as yet understood. I am quite positive that he himself did not quite estimate the forces which he was rallying or to what an extent they were gathering in around his own name and character.

His nearest friends were as blind as so many bats. Among all the long list of possible presidential candidates, the name of Lincoln had not been spoken of in any newspaper publication that I knew anything about.[1] Long afterwards, a lot of Chicago editors and other politicians asserted that they had held a hole and corner caucus upon the subject and had ventured to speak of him as a possibility in case Mr. Seward should be shoved aside. Upon this subject Dr. Scroggs had been much exercised and he and I had had several talks which resulted in disagreements. As a New Yorker, a born and bred follower of William H. Seward, I had been disposed to advocate him, but had at the same time a doubt of his ability to secure the western vote.[2] It was my opinion that the situation called for a western man and I was not at all satisfied with any of the doctor's suggested candidates.

There had been changes at the bank, just before I set up housekeeping, and I was temporarily boarding at the Doane House, the square hotel at the railway station. It was a temperance house and had no bar but its office was a large room that had been intended for hospitality. In the middle of this office was an enormous egg stove and near this, in the corner, was the office counter. Just beyond was the door from the dining room.

One chilly morning in March, I came to my breakfast as early as usual and after eating it passed out through that door into the office. Just as I did so, the street door opened and Abraham Lincoln came in. He had been to the post office without any overcoat and he may well have been chilly. At all events he walked toward the stove, drew up one of the much-whittled armchairs which ornamented the office, sat down in it, cocked his feet upon the stove hearth, took off his hat, and settled it between his knees. I think he always wore a very tall hat and one that was respectable for age. This hat, now between his knees, was so full of letters that it might have been wondered how he managed to put it on. That was no wonder, for his law business was large and he was here in attendance upon the court which was in session at Urbana.

I had never before known him to put up at the Doane House. On seeing him come in, I had paused at the counter and there I continued to stand, for there was something in this man's face and manner that attracted me unusually. My old fad for studying remarkable men came back upon me with power and I put away my first impulse to go forward and speak to him. It was much better to watch him, and he appeared to be unaware of any other presence in the room. He and I were alone and he was much more alone than I was.

I stood at the office counter, watching him. His face was not handsome, to be sure, but at any time there was a great deal of expression in it. There are many faces of which so much cannot be said. This morning was evidently a thoughtful one and his expression varied from minute to minute, all the while being cloudy. He read or looked at letter after letter as he opened them, and for some he did not appear to care much.

At last, however, he came to an epistle which I have wished I knew something about. It was written upon a square letter sheet, in a crabbed but regular and very black handwriting, page after page. It seemed to interest him at once and he read on slowly, stopping at intervals as if to ponder ideas which were presented. His face at first grew darker and the deep wrinkles in his forehead grew deeper. I was also getting more and more deeply interested.

Then, if you can imagine how a dark lighthouse looks when its calcium light is suddenly kindled, you may get an idea of the change which came into the face of Abraham Lincoln. All the great soul within him had been kindled to red heat, if not to white, and his eyes shone until he shut them. Before he did that, they seemed to be looking at something or other that was far away and the shutting may have been to more completely keep out of sight all but that far-off object. I had seen enough and I said to myself, emphatically: "My boy, that is the greatest man you have ever seen!"

What else may have been my suppressed mutterings I cannot now recall but I did not disturb Mr. Lincoln or try to speak to him. I turned and made my way out of the hotel through the dining room, and I did not pause until I had reached the *Gazette* office. I opened the door and walked in and there at the table sat Dr. Scroggs, diligently at work upon his accustomed pills. His back was toward me and he did not turn when I came in.

"Doctor," I shouted, "I've made up my mind whom we are going for for president!"

"The Hell you say!" was his mild and appreciative response. "Who is it?"

"Abraham Lincoln of Illinois!" I shouted back.

"Oh, Hell!" he rejoindered. "He'd never do for president. He might do for a nominee for vice president, perhaps, with Seward or some such man."

I was obstinate, and at the end of a sharp controversy he yielded, for I told him that as soon as I could run off the current editions of the *Gazette* and *Ford County Journal* I was going straight to Springfield and to Bloomington, to see William H. Herndon[3] and Leonard Swett and procure materials for a campaign life editorial. That is precisely what I proceeded to do, without telling too many men what were my purposes. On my return, the editorial was written, perhaps two full columns of it, and it was printed but I did not stop there. I sent a letter embodying some of it to *The Century*, a New York weekly journal then recently set up by Horace Greely's old partner McElrath,[4] and it was printed with approval. Meantime I had done something else.

Our regular exchange list was large but for that week I added to it not less than two hundred journals, all over the country, particularly the West. Then I waited to see the result of my experiment and it altogether surprised me. I had marked my editorial in the copies sent out and when the exchange papers came in it appeared to me that hardly one of them had failed to notice it, making extracts, and to give more or less favorable comments. Many of them reprinted it in full, or nearly so, and swung out the name of Lincoln at their column heads.[5]

PERSONAL

Our Next President.—We had the pleasure of introducing to the hospitalities of our Sanctum, a few days ago, the Hon. Abraham Lincoln. Few men can make an hour pass away more agreeably. We do not pretend to know whether Mr. Lincoln will ever condescend to occupy the White House or not, but if he should, it is a comfort to know that he has established for himself a character and reputation, of sufficient strength and purity to withstand the disreputable and corrupting influences of even that locality. No man in the West at the present time occupies a more enviable position before the people or stands a better chance for obtaining a high position among those to whose guidance our ship of state is to be entrusted.

WHO SHALL BE PRESIDENT?

We have no sympathy with those politicians of any party who are giving themselves up to a corrupt and selfish race for the presidential chair, and are rather inclined to believe that the result will be a disappointment to the whole race of demagogues. The vastness of the interests depending on the political campaign now commencing, gives even a more than usual degree of interest to the question: "Who shall be the candidate?" Believing that a proper discussion of this question through the columns of the local papers is the true way to arrive at a wise conclusion, we propose to give our views, so far as formed, and we may add that we are well assured that the same views are entertained by the mass of the Republican party of Central Illinois.

In the first place, we do not consider it possible for the office of President of the United States to become the personal property of any particular politician, how great a man soever he may be esteemed by himself and his partisans. We, therefore, shall discuss the "candidate question" unbiassed [*sic*] by personal prejudices or an undue appreciation of the claims of any political leader. We may add, with honest pride, an expression of our faith in the leading statesmen of our party, that neither Chase nor Seward nor Banks nor any other whose name has been brought prominently before the people, will press individual aspirations at the expense of the great principles whose vindication is inseparably linked with our success. While no circumstances should be allowed to compel even a partial abandonment of principle, and defeat in the cause of right is infinitely better than a corrupt compromise with wrong, nevertheless, the truest wisdom for the Republican party in this campaign will be found in such a conservative and moderate course as shall secure the respect and consideration even of our enemies, and shall not forget National compacts within which we are acting and by which we are bound: and the proper recognition of this feature of the contest should be allowed its due influence in the selection of our standard bearer.

Although local prejudices ought always to be held subordinate to the issues of the contest, it will not be wise to overlook their importance in counting the probabilities of what will surely be a doubtful and bitterly contested battlefield. It is this consideration which has brought into so great prominence the leading Republican statesmen of Pennsylvania and Illinois. If these two states can be added to the number of those in which the party seems to possess an unassailable superiority, the day is ours. The same reasons to a less extent, in exact proportion to its force in the electoral college, affect New Jersey.

From Pennsylvania and Illinois, therefore, the candidates for President and Vice President might, with great propriety, be chosen. It is true that our present Chief Magistrate is from Pennsylvania, and other States justly might urge that a proper apportionment of the National honors would not give her the presidency twice in succession; but, while there are several good precedents for such a course of action, there is one point which outweighs in importance all others: to wit, *We must carry Pennsylvania in 1860*, and if we can best do it with one of our own citizens as standard-bearer, that fact cannot be disregarded with impunity. The delegation from the Keystone State will doubtless present this idea with great urgency in the National convention.

Aside from this, there are other points in favor of the two States mentioned, which cannot fail to carry great weight in the minds of all candid and reasonable men. They have both been distinguished for moderation and patriotism in the character of their statesmen, with as few exceptions as any other States. They are among that great central belt of States which constitute the stronghold of conservatism and Nationality. They are not looked upon as "sectional" in their character, even by the South. They, moreover, are, to a high degree, representative States. Where will our manufacturing, mining, and trading interests find a better representative than Pennsylvania? Or what State is more identified in all its fortunes with the great agricultural interests than is Illinois?

The States themselves, then, being open to no valid objection, we come to the question of individual candidates. Pennsylvania has not yet determined her choice from among her own great men, but as for Illinois it is the firm and fixed belief of our citizens that for one or the other of the offices in question, no man will be so sure to consolidate the party vote of this State, or will carry the great Mississippi Valley with a more irresistible rush of popular enthusiasm, than our distinguished fellow citizen,

ABRAHAM LINCOLN

We, in Illinois, know him well, in the best sense of the word, *a true democrat*, a man of the people, whose strongest friends and supporters are the hard-handed and strong-limbed laboring men, who hail him as a brother and who look upon him as one of their real representative men. A true friend of freedom, having already done important service for the cause, and proved his abundant ability for still greater service; yet a staunch conservative, whose enlarged and liberal mind descends to no narrow view, but sees both sides of every great question, and of whom we need not fear that fanaticism on the one side, or servility on the other, will lead him to the betrayal of any trust. We appeal to our brethren of the Republican press for the correctness of our assertions.

After that, I attended the "railsplitter" convention at Springfield and went into the political canvas head over heels, heels over head, with all the more enthusiasm because I had nearly all the stumping of Champaign County on my own hands.

It may seem odd, but I had not any idea whatever of obtaining any other advantage from my political labors, whether for the party or for any individual, than such as might appertain to my success as an editor. I was proud of the position of the *Gazette* and of the recognition I continually received on that account, and that was all. As for financial advancement, I saw small chance of that.

During the previous year, Dr. Scroggs and I had often discussed the idea of setting up an Agricultural College as an ornament and advantage to our city of Champaign. Precisely what such an affair might be, neither he nor I had any clear perception, but to him it meant a college in which the undergraduates might not be compelled to worry themselves with too much trashy science, philology, and other timewasters. The notion at last took form and it bought up a tract of land between the two Urbanas on credit, easy terms. The land was at once cut up into town lots and I obtained several of them but afterwards gave them up when I went into distant enterprises. I am told, however, that there is now a flourishing educational institution on that spot and if there is, it owes its origin to a sharp talk between Dr. Scroggs and myself in the *Gazette* printing office, long ago. He and I were only at odds upon the "agricultural" idea and the college is not now agricultural, so that my side of the debate won, after all.

Not to dwell upon the minor incidents of the political campaign, it was over at last and Lincoln was duly elected, to my great delight. At an early date after the election, he held a sort of congratulation levee at the State House in Springfield. Hearing that he was to do so, I took a day off and went over to shake hands with him, for I believed that I had a vested right to tell him how I felt about it. I went to the State House and took my place in a long line of people who were there to get a look at the coming president. Some of them, indeed, were from far away and had come to tell him how much they had done to secure his election and how ready they would be to serve him further in one or another of the fat offices at Washington. One of these disinterested patriots was next in line ahead of me and his account of himself may have added point to Mr. Lincoln's question, when he heartily shook hands with me and looked down two feet or more into my face.

"Well, young man," he said. "Now! What can I do for you?"

"Nothing at all, Mr. Lincoln," I responded, "but I'm mighty glad you are elected."

"How would you like to come to Washington?" he asked. "Wouldn't you like to take a clerkship, or something?"

I was just telling him that I was pretty well fixed now and had never thought of going to Washington when a red hot thought came flashing into my mind and I added:

"Mr. Lincoln, the only thing that would tempt me to go to Washington is a place on your personal staff."

"Stoddard," said he, "do you go right back to Champaign and write me a letter to that effect. Then wait till you hear from me."

That was just what I did, but I did not say a word about it to any living soul, unless it may have been Kate. That was early in November, and before the end of the month I had about considered myself forgotten. I did not yet know Lincoln. About the first of December, I received a letter of some length from him, ordering me to close up my affairs, go on to Washington and wait there until his arrival.[6]

It is not now needful to quote from the letter or to try to tell just how I felt about it. It was a hard blow to Scroggs and he got his back up to such an extent that he made pecuniary trouble for me. I made out to sell my effects, however, and had money enough to go East with and to send Kate to some friends. John remained for a while in Champaign and then returned to Syracuse, obtaining a clerkship in the Bank of Syracuse, with our old friends the Whites.

I had all the passes needed to lessen my expenses and selected those which took me by the way of Philadelphia, so that I was not on the Northern Indiana Railroad at the time of an awful accident which murdered scores of people. A telegram of mine, however, had made our Syracuse family believe that I must have been on that very train, and when I reached our house I found all in great excitement. We were gathered in the front parlor, all but Harry, and there were friends with us and I was sitting on a sofa, giving an account of myself. In came Harry and our old dog Dash. They were just from the telegraph office, with a despatch stating that my corpse had not yet been reached but that as soon as it could be found . . .

Harry stood in front of father, talking rapidly and showing the telegram, but Dash came and sat down in front of me and raised his shaggy head and sent out the longest, most doleful howl you ever heard. That was because he knew I had been killed, you know, but then he jumped all over me, barking, before he sprang off after a stick and brought it for a friendly game of fetch and carry.

I had a good but short visit in Syracuse and went to New York. There I saw the Brights and my old Rochester chum, Tite Eldredge, now a somewhat prosperous New York lawyer, but my errand was to the capital and to any orders I might there receive from Mr. Lincoln.

What I really did was to take a ticket for Secessionville by a very miserable route. Instead of going straight through, as the trains do now, there were tedious changes at Philadelphia and Baltimore. On reaching the capital, I put up at a hotel, the United States, and went for a look at the public buildings, one after another. These were all I had expected, but the city itself was little more than a great, straggling village, with only a moderate allowance of good-looking residences. As might be imagined, it did not at that hour contain many fellows who knew less about some things than I did.

It was in the first week of February, and the last days of the Buchanan administration were going out in a tremendous excitement for the whole country. This fever had its hottest corner in Washington and no words can paint the exact state of affairs. The Southerners appeared to be having things almost to suit themselves and there was actual personal danger in being as outspoken a Unionist as I was. I changed from the hotel to a quiet boarding house but I had work before me. I deemed it my duty to attend all the important debates of the dying Congress, in Senate and House, and some of the hotter sessions lasted all night. I sat through them and had an opportunity for hearing many of the foremost men of the day on both sides. I will tell of only one. It was an afternoon session and the galleries were so crowded that my best hold was in or under an empty statue niche of the Senate Gallery. Vice President Breckinridge[7] was in the chair. There were speeches from Stephen A. Douglas, Mason of Virginia,[8] and others, and then Senator Joe Lane of Oregon,[9] the defeated candidate for the Vice Presidency, made a singularly weak-backed pro-slavery, secessionist tirade. Not far from him sat Andrew Johnson of Tennessee and he had utterly lost his not very good temper.[10] At the close of Lane's "effort," Andy was on his feet, with something like a war whoop.

It was time for somebody to make a break and he made it, for of all the torrents of vituperation, denunciation, and genuine red-hot eloquence that I had heard, up to that date, his speech took the prize. He paid his respects to some of the other orators of the day but the worst of his lashes fell upon Joe Lane until that gentleman could bear no more and retreated into one of the cloak rooms. It was just as Andy wound up and before he could sit down that a kind of yell sprang out of the niche in which I was craning forward to hear:

"Three cheers for Andy Johnson!"

The startled audience had begun to give them and Breckinridge was on his feet, hammering with his gavel, while senator Mason was demanding that the galleries should be cleared. I think Breckinridge had so ordered or was threatening to do so, when a portly, elegantly dressed woman, in the lower tier of gallery seats at his left, leaned away out, waving a white handkerchief and shouting, in a wonderfully clear and powerful voice:

"Three cheers for the Union!"

It was thunder and lightning together and the dense throng in the galleries rose to its feet with a swelling roar. It was a moment of intense excitement. The cheers were given, three times three, and the Vice President was shouting to the sergeant at arms to make arrests. The Senate clock was at the gallery rail, opposite the "Chair" and up at the side of it arose a tall, lantern-jawed fellow with a voice like a trombone to respond, tumultuously, to the order: "Arrest Hell!" It was a wicked thing for him to say and it was not by any means the only angrily patriotic remark that was hurled back into that Senate chamber as the audience poured out. No arrests were made for no sergeant at arms could have arrested quite so many half-on-fire men and women. It might have been bad for him.

There was one beautiful thing, to my mind, about those night sessions. Whenever either house was in session, a large American flag was hoisted over that wing of the Capitol. In the daytime it was a good thing to see but at night a strong glare of light was thrown across the flag, to make it visible, and the effect was all that could be asked for at a time when so much treason was being plotted in that very building.

Not all of the Congressional debates were of an interesting character and I had time for other affairs. Evenings could be spent with profit among the excited crowds in the hotel corridors. Here, indeed, the current of talk was not all one way, for people from the North were coming in increasing numbers and by no means all of them were made of putty. It came to pass that any secessionist who repeated the trite saying that "The d———d abolitionist has been elected but he never will be president" was apt to be asked "Why? What makes you think so? You———!"

Another of my enterprises was an effort to get well-acquainted with the other side of the Potomac. I made frequent invasions of Virginia, sometimes going down to Alexandria by boat, but more frequently going across the Long Bridge and making my tours on foot. I had one family of friends, the Godwins, living at a little distance out of Alexandria. They were secessionists but I liked them none the less. On the whole, I was beginning to obtain a clearer idea of the entire South and its people and the near future and was continually surprised to find how few on either side of the controversy agreed with me. At this date it is not easy to believe how many patriotic Americans, including even such men as Horace Greeley, were ready to say of the seceding states, "Let 'em go." Another group of prophets, headed by William H. Seward, steadily asserted that "If a war should come, it won't last thirty days."

My own mind was made up to a long and hard pull of it, and I waited for Lincoln's coming with increasing anxiety. So, I suppose, did the entire list of Democratic office holders and the swelling mob of Republican office seekers. As to these, they were a wonderfully select lot of men, and they had selected quite as many offices as the United States could give them.

Mr. Lincoln arrived, but he was not yet president, and even then there were doubts in the minds of the timid. For my own part, I was well aware that there was danger all around, but I seemed to have no fear of the result. Great preparations were made for the Inauguration. The Address was to be delivered and the oath taken on a temporary platform at the East Front of the Capitol and I went and surveyed the scene beforehand.

I remember how I had managed to hear Daniel Webster and I tried those tactics again. It was at a pretty early hour of the fourth of March that I gave up the procession, the music, the military, and the dense pack of people upon Pennsylvania Avenue. I went and wormed in through the as yet not very suspicious crowd before the East Front until I secured standing room just beyond the line at which the soldiers of the honorary guard were to stand at rest. There I waited and I was well paid for it, for I could look right into Lincoln's face while he was speaking and could hear every word he said.

I can recall a mild feeling of pity for the many great men of all sorts, diplomatic, military, political, whose luckless dignities had wedged them in among the pillars and so forth in the rear of all the show. Among them were Nicolay[11] and Hay, neither of whom I had yet seen.

I did not even try to see the President for several days, but I did go to admire the dense pack of office seekers which had taken possession of the White House. The city fairly swarmed with them and it was a hot time for any Senator or Congressman who was supposed to have influence with the new president. It was pretty well understood that nearly all the old officials were to go. All, in fact, whose services could be dispensed with. Not at all to my astonishment, among the rest came my old friend Dr. Scroggs, expecting to get something handsome for having printed the first editorial nominating Lincoln. I did not at all discourage him, but was not a little amused to hear him weighing the respective desirability of a Treasury Comptrollership, Auditorship, and the post of Examiner in the Patent Office. He did not care to take a consul's place for that would compel him to go abroad. I was not quite sure that he had an idea that he could hold office in Washington, or at least draw a salary, without entirely giving up his Champaign County practice and his fever and ague patients.

It was two or three days later that I worked my way into the White House and struggled as far as the bottom of the main stairway. The stairs were a sweltering jam but an usher at the top was managing to receive cards in some inscrutable manner. He obtained mine and it went in and in a few minutes Nicolay came to the banisters to shout my name while three or four eager patriots tugged at his coat tails. I hollered back.

"Do you wish to see the President?" he asked.

"No! I don't!" I shouted. "Tell him I'm here, 'cording to orders. That's all. He'll know what to do. I won't bother him."

I did not understand what a score of fellows found to laugh at in my reply to the great Mr. Nicolay, and it even seemed to please him. I hope it pleased Mr. Lincoln, and it was only a few days before I received notice of my coming appointment as Secretary to sign Land Patents.[12] After that, and even before actually receiving my commission, I was a marked man and worthy of much respect. I came and went from the White House, but the stairway was still corked. I did get up once or twice and got acquainted with Nicolay and Hay, but did not try to speak with the President.

I went to the Interior Department building for a look at my office and found it a pleasant one. At the same time I was aware that about four hundred of the old Secession clerks who were so soon to leave were armed and organized for some possible pernicious undertaking in the near future. There were other treasonable organizations in the city on the other side of the river in Virginia, besides such as were known to exist in Baltimore.

Washington itself was practically without a garrison. One battery of light artillery was posted near the Interior Department, one company of cavalry was camped near the Navy Yard and at the Yard were also a number of marines. There would have really been no army so to speak, if it had not been for five hundred office seekers who obtained muskets and cartridges from the War Department and camped in the East Room and corridors of the White House, to protect the government all night and to be ready to press their claims in the morning. The worst of that corps was, however, that whether a man was appointed or disappointed he became sick of war and ran away.

Hotter and hotter grew the excitement as the days went by, but for all the current events, the Peace Congress, the setting up of the Montgomery [Alabama] Rebel Government, the attitudes of foreign powers and a host of other matters, reference must be had to the several—I think there are several—historical accounts which have been printed. Nothing in any of those volumes, however, can include the black clouds overhead, the close, stifling atmosphere, the constant listening for thunder, and the suspicious feeling concerning all men, as to what they might do next, which made life in Washington what it was in the days when the Civil War was crawling on.

28

War

*I*f there was one thing, more than another, concerning which the people of the United States knew nothing of any consequence in the year 1861, it was war.

They had read about it and that was all, except for a few regular army men and a few more who could boast of having served in the war with Mexico. In the city of Washington, as in other cities, there were militia organizations, but none of these were worth much to the country just then. The "crack" corps was a company of select and eminent young gentlemen who regarded themselves as the pink of chivalry. Almost all of them were either from slaveholding states or were natives of the District of Columbia. As the prospect of hostilities grew darker, the secessionist captain of the Rifles resigned and went to offer his services to the Sunny South and more than half of his comrades in the militia business followed his example. This had a remarkable consequence for me.

Hardly was it known that I was appointed Secretary, before a fine young fellow came and told me that he was trying to get recruits for his company but that all the men he had tried were averse to taking commissions as private soldiers. The current notion appeared to be that what the country needed was an army of finely uniformed and highly paid officers. If, he told me, the President's secretary would set a patriotic example, he felt sure that the high pride of certain heroes would yield and they would enlist in the Rifles.

Of course I accepted the proposition and went in, but I did so with only a dim idea of the toughness of the job I had undertaken. The Rifles had been organized as an artillery company, as the red trimmings of its uniform witnessed and the fact that it owned a French bugler instead of a drum to wake it up in the morning. Its new commander was also an artilleryman, Captain John R. Smead, formerly of West Point, and with the fullness of regular army drill for recruits in his soldierly mind. A soldier he was, every inch of him, and he had a crack company under him, now that its gaps were filled up. Nominally of the District, the Rifles now contained picked men from Virginia, Kentucky, Indiana, Illinois, Missouri, New York, Connecticut, Ohio, Maryland, and elsewhere. The armory was about two squares west of the general Post Office and the weapons were what was called the Harper's Ferry pattern of rifle, the heaviest I ever saw and weighted also with a sabre bayonet of which it was proudly asserted that it was of the exact pattern and size of the old Roman Gladius with which so many men were killed. It was a good thing to split wood with or to break hard tack but it was not very murderous for any but the short ranges to which the said Romans were accustomed. The common sense of later military genius lightens the load of a soldier's iron and saves him needless fatigue.

Other companies of District militia were forming. Three of them were grouped as the Third Battalion, D.C. Rifles, and our commander, while retaining his position with us, became Major of the battalion of which ours was Company A. Captain Smead did not have much confidence in his other companies and the work fell mainly upon us. One of them was a company of all sorts and the other was entirely German "Columbians." We were put upon duty at once but I was allowed to go the Land Office and sign some thousands of delayed land patents. Piles of them were military warrants issued to soldiers of the War of 1812, and for the first time I became aware that the American armies in that skirmish with Great Britain must have numbered over a hundred and fifty thousand men. The historians are all at sea on that point and it is no wonder that poor England was compelled to take a return ticket and get out of the United States. It is barely possible that some of that land went to the Home Guard.

Things were getting thicker and the day came when we were informed that we were to be sworn into the service of the United States although no call for troops had yet been sent out by the general government. It put into my head a very natural question of personal duty and I decided that I must see Mr. Lincoln about it and that was by no means an easy thing to do, in those crowded days. I thought I could do it, for one of my official privileges as private secretary had come to me. The post of Patent Secretary had not before that time been held to include the higher rank, but my case was somehow understood to be an exception. Some days previously, on a visit to the White House, I had met out in front of it old Edward Moran, the antediluvian doorkeeper, and he halted me with:

"Mr. Secretary! I've something for ye." He was holding out something for me to take and he added: "I've been getting some new latchkeys for the young gentlemen. I don't know what's become of the keys we had. May be they've gone south and mean to come back, some day, and open the door."

Two of the keys were bright and new, but one was old and tarnished.

"There's one for Mr. Nicolay and one for Mr. Hay and one for yourself. That's the 'owld' one, that belonged to the lock when it was put on."

"That's the key I want, Edward," I said. "Give Nicolay and Hay the new ones." And I had the traditional antique in my hands.

"It's like meself," said old Edward. "It can open the door as well as ever it could."

When, long afterwards, I left my private secretary duties behind me, I kept that key and whenever I visited Washington I enjoyed the joke, if it was one, of visiting the White House and astonishing the doorkeepers by walking right in without any help from them. The lock remained until some time in the second term of President Grant. I still have the key which has opened the White House door for so many presidents and their officers.

Armed with my bit of brass and almost wishing I had more in my face, I went upon my important errand, early in the morning of the 12th of April. I went upstairs and looked into the official rooms but they were as empty as I had expected to find them.

A bit of topography will help just here. Along the full length of the second story of the house, runs a broad hall, with rooms of various sizes and uses on either side of it. Beginning at the eastern end, on the right is a somewhat narrow room which was soon to become my own. On the left is the Private Secretary's room, or there was, of the same size. Next to that was a large room, "The President's Room," from the building of the house until a later day than mine. Opposite to that is a large chamber, then used by Nicolay and Hay as a sleeping room. Then comes the grand stairway and beyond are other rooms. Just beyond the stairway, the hall is cut off by folding doors and another pair like them cuts off the part of the hall which is over the western wing of the house. On the left, northerly, is the library, and I had ventured in that far when the further folding doors slowly opened. It had been a sunny morning, outside, if it were not that every soul in the land was waiting for news from the Rebel siege of Fort Sumter. Not a shot had yet been fired, except at the steamer *Star of the West*,[1] but a sort of pall hung over Washington and it seemed to me as if there was the gloomiest kind of shadow in the White House.

Slowly opened the doors and very slowly came forward Mr. Lincoln, leaving them open behind him. All beyond was the "family" part of the house. He was bent until he almost appeared to stoop and he was looking straight before him, as if gazing at something in the distance or like a man who is listening intently. Just in front of the library door, I stepped before him and dared to say:

"Good Morning, Mr. Lincoln!"

He stood stock still, for a moment, looking down into my face, but the expression of his own did not change. He may have been listening for the sound of guns in Charleston harbor. I was astonished, almost alarmed, for there were deep, dark circles under his eyes and they were vacant.

"Why, Mr. Lincoln," I exclaimed. "You don't seem to know me!"

"Oh, yes, I do," he wearily responded. "You are Stoddard. What is it?"

"I wish to ask a favor," I said.

His lips contracted, for that was about what everybody he met was saying to him, just then, and he asked, in an almost petulant manner:

"Well! What is it?"

"It's just this, Mr. Lincoln," I said. "I believe there is going to be fighting, pretty soon, right here, and I don't feel like sitting at a desk in the Patent Office, or here either, while any fight is going on. I've been serving with a company, already, and if it's ordered on duty I want to go with it."

"Well, well," he interrupted, with a very different expression of face. "Why don't you go?"

"Why, Mr. Lincoln," I said, "only a few days ago, I took a pretty big oath to obey your orders, and now I'm likely to be asked to take another to obey somebody else. I don't see how I can manage them both without your permission. I may be ordered to service outside of the District of Columbia." He half smiled as he cut me short, right there.

"Go ahead!" he exclaimed. "Swear in! Go wherever you are ordered to go."

"That's all I want, Mr. Lincoln," I said and I was turning away when he called me back to add with some emphasis: "Young man, go just where you're ordered! Do your duty." Something else that I have forgotten ended with: "You won't lose anything by this."

Off I went and he went on into his office, having granted really the first favor I ever asked of him.

As nearly as I can count it, that was just four hours after the firing of the first "Sumter gun," and he may have heard the report of it as he was coming out to meet me, but it was many hours before any regular news of it reached Washington. Then came Sunday, but the President's Proclamation, which went out to the country that night, was dated as on Monday the fifteenth [of April].[2] While the people of the North were reading it in the morning papers, the National Rifles, with myself among them, were being sworn in, in front of the War Office, the first company of volunteers sworn in at the beginning of the Civil War. None of the other boys had to go and ask the permission of the President.

It was almost unlucky for us that we were so trusted a company, for it brought upon us an extra allowance of hard duty, over and above the severe drill called for by the martinet notions of our West Point captain. I was particularly overburdened, for I had patents of importance to sign both at my own office and at the White House. Here I was all the while getting better acquainted with Nicolay and Hay and liked them both. As to the nature of our duties, they were largely as guards at important points for there were continual rumors of secessionist conspiracies to seize the city. How true all of them were, I do not know, but remember one evening when we were drilling on Ninth Street and at the same hour an unarmed battalion of secessionists was drilling.

One of the points to be guarded was the Long Bridge over the Potomac. In the middle of the channel was a draw, wide enough for the passage of large vessels. This draw was left closed all day, for the passage of teams and men, but was regularly opened at sunset and a guard of ours or some other company was set at the edge of it. At the same hour, shortly, a similar guard of the Virginia Militia was set at the southern side of the draw and I obtained a clearer idea of how near the war might be when I stood guard on the Union side, rifle on shoulder, with a Secessionist rifleman standing in like manner within short range across that narrow barrier of water. In the daytime, the Virginians would fall back to the mudhole village known then as Jackson City, in the swamp on the southern shore.

There was a tavern there and one fine day a large squad of our boys disobeyed the orders which commanded them not to cross the bridge in uniform or with arms. They went over pell mell, captured the Virginians on duty, and compelled them all to march to the tavern and swallow unlimited mint juleps. Next day, the Alexandria papers were boiling over at this invasion and violation of the sacred soil of the Old Dominion, but their wrath broke down when their own militia responded by defying the Rifles to come and try it on again, daily. Major Smead's angry reprimands prevented that and the Virginia boys did not get any more julep. The Major also sat down on me severely when I acted as the spokesmen of a chosen squad who had agreed to go with me and take down the secession flag which was then waving over Arlington House. He explained that the State of Virginia might declare it an act of war and that it would be a fool's errand, useless, in any event. He was entirely correct, but what did I and the other volunteers know about war?

The hardest guard duty I ever had on the bridge was one night when a bitterly cold rainstorm came blowing fiercely up the Potomac, for we had no shelter. Sleep was impossible and in the intervals of guard duty I tried to console myself with fishing. I caught some bullheads, a garpike, and a very miserably long, thin eel that tangled up my line.

Another uncomfortable night was when I could not leave my post at the Treasury building front and had to do my sleeping upon one of those magnificently wide stone slabs in front of the portico. It was a hard bed. Perhaps as hard was the bed I had one night in the middle of the main street of Georgetown. The pavement was of cobblestones of about a peck measure each and it was impossible to lie down with those for bedfellows for any length of time, tired as I was. Another bad feature of the case for me was a strong idea in my mind that the President's secretary must set a good example. Therefore, whenever Major Smead or General Stone[3] came into the armory and called for volunteers from among our overwearied fellows for any special duty, it was my place to be on my feet and call out "Here!" before any other fellow. It speedily obtained for me a laughing soubriquet, for the sergeant on deck would immediately respond, "Stoddard! Number One!" Well, it was no disgrace to be known as Stoddard Number

One. Speaking of General Stone, he ought never to be forgotten, for the inestimable services he rendered in saving the national capital in that hour of doubt and danger. Not long after the war began in earnest, he was put under a cloud, severely, unjustly criticized for the errors he did not make at the defeat of Ball's Bluff, and his military career was ruined by jealousies and some politicians.[4] That was after I had returned to the White House and one day, in the middle of his troubles, I met him on Fifteenth Street, by the Treasury. He was looking downcast and his head was bent. I stepped in front of him and saluted and said:

"General Stone, I want to say something to you. You don't remember me."

"Oh yes, I do," he interrupted me, heavily, "I remember you very well. You are Stoddard Number One. What is it?"

"Well, General," I responded, "our boys of your old command are white mad about this matter and I want to say, for myself and them, that you have our utmost and undiminished confidence and esteem."

"Thank you, my dear fellow! Thank you from the bottom of my heart!" was all he could say, but his lip was trembling and he turned away with his hat lifted and walking as straight as an arrow. I'm glad I did it. General Stone afterwards attained the rank of Pasha for services to the Khedive of Egypt, but New Yorkers will remember him better as the engineer who set up the Bartholdi statue of Liberty.[5]

Dangers were thickening around the city of Washington. The Northern States were preparing to send on their seventy-five thousand militiamen but none of them had as yet arrived and the Montgomery Rebel Government was as busy as a bee in a sugar barrel. We Rifles were all but worn out with extra duty and there came a night when two-thirds of us were lying on the floor in the armory, about used up. I was not yet asleep and lifted my head at the sound of conversation in the doorway. There stood General Stone and Major Smead, talking hurriedly with one of our lieutenants. In a moment more the voice of the latter rang out: "Twenty picked men wanted, for special and dangerous duty!"

I was on my feet like a flash and the next I heard was: "Stoddard Number One! Taken!"

The rest followed rapidly, although I believe that some were rejected as being manifestly unfit to go. We were ordered to take forty rounds of cartridges each and not a word was said of our destination but we all knew that something extraordinary was to the fore.

In those days, what was known as "the Island," between the city and the Potomac, was cut off by a narrow canal. It contained the Smithsonian Institution and a [great] deal of fever and ague. In the middle, opposite the Institute was a draw footbridge, for communication of science and the city. Our squad went at a quick pace down across Pennsylvania Avenue and met with no warlike opposition except from a snoop who demanded of Lieutenant Webb where in Heaven we were going at that time of night. Then he lay down and swore gently to himself, for Webb was a good hitter. In a few minutes more we were filing across the footbridge, as if we were to storm the Institute. On we hurried through the grounds and their scientific shrubbery and we were soon within a hundred yards of the river bank, where was a low bluff, beyond which was known to be the ferryboat pier and wharf.

"Halt!—Load!—Silence!—Fix bayonets!—Forward, double quick!— Charge!" Over the bluff we went, at a run, and there just reaching the pier end was the well-known passenger steamer *St. Nicholas,* from Alexandria.

"Forward! Board her! Silence!"

Hardly was a hawser around a snubbing post before we were over the rail and pouring into the saloon of the steamer. On either side of it were long ranges of staterooms and not a door of them was open.

"Men! Ready there! If any man puts his head out of a stateroom, put a bullet through it!"

"Thank God!" exclaimed an agitated voice near me.

It was the captain of the boat, explaining to Major Smead, or somebody, that the staterooms were full of armed secessionists and he had feared that if they captured his boat it would be condemned as contraband of war. Not a head made its appearance and when, an hour or so later, all the passengers were permitted to land, not any offence could be charged against one of them and no arrests were made. Virginia had not yet seceded and no acknowledged state of war existed in that vicinity. Nevertheless, we were a proud lot of pirates, for we had captured the first steamer ever captured in any of the waters of the United States. It was the first naval victory ever won at sea by riflemen and it was the first also of the War.

Next day, after a long sleep, I wrote a graphic account of the affair to my brother Henry, and, much to my surprise, the whole column-long letter was printed in the Syracuse daily papers and copied elsewhere. It was a new kind of fame for me and it sounded loudly until some other affairs sounded a thousand times more loudly. Then it was forgotten, but if the Washington part of that conspiracy had not been in this manner disconcerted there is no telling what the results might have been.

The skies were growing darker. State after state was "going out" and the Montgomery government[6] was raising an army. Sumter had fallen. The whole North appeared to be in a comatose condition so far as real war was concerned, although some of the states, New York, the New England states, and some others were gathering their quotas. Maryland seemed to be in the hands of the rebellion and Baltimore was as secessionist as Richmond.

The first reinforcements to arrive were the Pennsylvania Fifth Volunteers, a disorganized mob without discipline or arms and not fit to stand guard. News came that the New York Seventh was on its way and there were serious doubts of its ability to cut its way through the barrier of foes which now isolated Washington. It was not to pass through Baltimore but around by way of Annapolis and the Junction, nine miles from the capital, as I remember. There it would be in danger of attack and there was a Rebel plan to seize the railroad and the Junction and stop the Seventh.

Our battalion was ordered to go out and hold the post until its arrival. Five hundred secessionists were said to be marching out of Baltimore at the hour when we started and I do not know whether they did so or not. The second, or "Dutch" company, was sent along the railway as scouts and we soon went past them for they were in no hurry. Our third company was not fit for this duty just then. We carried a carload of rations for the coming New Yorkers and Washington people said goodbye to us as if we were a forlorn hope, going to destruction. The train did not run a race but it landed us at the Junction and we garrisoned the station house. It was a poor fort but it might do and we were about seventy strong. We were waiting anxiously for events when suddenly a long line of gray uniforms made its appearance to the eastward and some of the boys shouted:

"There come the Rebs! Now for it! There are the Baltimore men!"

"Nonsense!" roared Major Smead. "Don't you see the flag?"

My impression is that we all admired the elegant silken banner of the Seventh and we at once began to bring out the provisions of which the reinforcements were really in great need. How they did eat!

Our return to Washington was a triumph, the city was much safer, and the next day the President reviewed the Seventh.[7]

About that time I had a surprise in the altogether unexpected arrival of my brother Henry. I was only half glad that he had come for I did not wish him to be a soldier. Our ranks were full and he could not enlist in the Rifles. It was a puzzle, for I could not let him go off by himself. The problem was solved by getting him a uniform and permitting him to serve with us as an unenlisted and unpaid supernumerary. We did the same thing for one of the "Fighting McCooks,"[8] a brother-in-law of our Lieutenant Davis. Henry soon became a prime favorite, for his social qualities were of a high order and he was such a handsome fellow!

Washington was as secessionist as ever, and it did seem as if all the young women at all the pianos were drumming southern music. You could hardly pass a house without hearing the "Bonnie Blue Flag" or "My Maryland" or something, but the prime favorite was "Dixie." It has a weird, uncanny ring in it, for me, to this day. It died out of Washington suddenly.

About the next full regiment to get through Baltimore, after the attack there upon the Massachusetts Sixth,[9] was the New York Twelfth, and it was a very full regiment indeed. I heard that it was twelve hundred strong. I was on duty on Pennsylvania Avenue when the magnificent corps came in. It was formed at the depot and then it came sweeping down the avenue, full company front, flags flying, bayonets gleaming, and my heart gave a great thump for it meant safety to us overworn fellows who had held the city. It had a large, splendid brass band and at that moment it struck up and the gallant boys swung forward to the tune of "Dixie." Oh, how much marching music I at once discovered in that much-abused lilt. On went the regiment and the band played nothing else until in front of the White House, where Lincoln waited to review them; they struck up "Hail Columbia."[10]

The Girls declared, in deep disgust, that the blessed Yankees had stolen their music and they did not play "Dixie" any more.

The political course to be taken by the State of Virginia was in no manner of doubt but the people were not to vote upon the Ordinance of Secession until May 23. Until that date, therefore, the Virginia militia might gather unhindered for no cause of war legally existed. On the Sunday before the eventful day, I took a furlough and went for a look at the White House. It wore a deserted look. My latchkey let me in and I went upstairs. I went from room to room and all were empty, for Mr. and Mrs. Lincoln were at church and I don't know where the boys were.[11] In my room were many patents awaiting my signature but I left them on my table and walked over to Nicolay's room to be greeted by a shout from a distinguished, but now forgotten, Colonel Ellsworth of the Zouaves.[12]

He was a great favorite of the President and as much at home there as I was. We were talking war and the future when I picked up a carbine which stood in a corner and began to put Ellsworth through the manual of arms. As I did so, my orders brought him close to the south window. His movements had the precision of a machine and when the order came to "take aim," the carbine went forward recklessly. It went through a pane of glass and I ordered him to shoulder arms. When the others came in, we had a story to tell them of an assassin among the bushes out yonder who had doubtless mistaken Ellsworth or me for the President and had attempted assassination. Perhaps the yarn would have lasted longer if Ellsworth could have kept his face straight, but the fun ended and he and I went to our quarters to prepare for the invasion of Virginia.

The President wisely took the vote of Virginia for granted, and he was as ready for immediate action as if he had seen the ballots counted. Already a number of militia regiments were encamped in the vicinity of Washington and others were on their way. All day on the fatal 23rd there were preparations going on and in the afternoon our company was posted on the bank of the Potomac, near the head of the Long Bridge. Our first duty was the gathering of boats, in case any crossing might be done by water. They were large fishing boats some of them, and when Major Smead came to inspect us he was accompanied by a number of much uniformed officers. He rode a light colored nag and the boys laughed when I remarked to them:

"Boys! The war's come. Death on the pale horse."

I believe Smead was in the habit of finding out what I was up to, for he drew rein and inquired the meaning of the fun.

"Nothing at all, sir," I said, as I touched my hat. "I was only saying how glad I am that these are seine boats [from which fishermen cast "seines"—large nets with floaters on one side and weights on the other, to keep them vertical in water—ed]. I'd hardly like to risk any of the men in a crazy boat."

Small as the wit was, they all laughed and I heard him remark: "That fellow's worth his weight in gold. He keeps up the spirits of the men, and some of them need it."

He was all wrong if he meant our fellows, for they were doing finely. I think it was nearly nine o'clock when we were ordered to fall in and form column[s] of twos. We had been given the post of honor, the right of the line, and we were the first Union soldiers to invade the Sunny South, on the night when the war nominally began. We went across in a prime moonlight and were then informed that we were to be thrown forward on scouting duty, because so many of us were acquainted with the country. I said, for one, that I knew every inch of the Alexandria road and it got me an extra errand, that night. On we went until we reached the foot of the hill upon which Fort Albany was afterwards erected.

Here we halted to load and rest and as we did so, a strong party of horsemen, supposed to be Rebel cavalry appeared on the hill. They surveyed us for a minute and then galloped away without any battle. Then the word was "forward" for a distance and we were halted again. Our commanders had some idea of the neighborhood of hostilities and were disposed to move with caution. At that time there was a wide reach of swamp along the sides of the Alexandria Turnpike. It was bushes and reeds, then a couple of hundred yards of water and then more dense bushes. It was desirable to know if there were enemies in the really strong position offered by the other end of that long causeway. A column attempting it recklessly might be mowed down by marksmen in the bushes.

We were halted in a double line and Major Smead explained the matter. He told us that scouts trying the position might be marching to certain death and that it was too dangerous duty for him to order men upon. It was as a forlorn hope and he must have volunteers. Every man willing to volunteer was to step one pace to the front at the word of command and he would pick from the volunteers. The men were standing at right shoulder shift and at the word "Forward!" every last soul of them stepped out as if on parade. No cheering was allowed but there was a puzzle until Second Lieutenant Matthews said to the Major that he would go if he might pick his own men, four of them. His offer was taken and I must say I felt a thrill of pride when his first name was called out:

"Stoddard Number One!" But I was not so well pleased when his next call was for "Stoddard Number Two." Two more were taken and forward we went. Then it quickly came to pass that the brave lieutenant was a greenhorn. He did not know the ground. He spread his men, right and left, and they were quickly lost in the bushes and he was stranded with them. I had but one stupid idea and that was the causeway. Probably it was a good thing for me that I was a solitary man and not a squad or a company. On

I went, walking lazily, until I reached the opposite end of the viaduct. On either side of me, ten yards ahead, were thick bushes and I saw the military reasons for considering that a pokerish place. Then I heard a considerable number of rattling clicks and I knew very well the sound made by a gun lock in cocking.

I was within short range of Virginia riflemen, supposed to be good shots but I was well aware that they would not wish to have their presence discovered, not just for the fun of killing one man. So I stood still and turned to look back as if listening. I wish I knew to whom I am indebted for a long, shrill whistle that came at that moment from our end of the causeway, for I was able to nod my head and take it for a recall signal. I strolled listlessly away, whistling as I went, and I was greatly pleased with one personal discovery. I had always had an idea that I might be nervous under fire or in a tight place in actual war. Now, on the contrary, I knew that I had not felt the quiver of a nerve and I had at once a better opinion of myself.

I went back and made my report and was thanked at the head of the column for heroic service but I never saw that adventure in the Associated Press despatches. At all events, it was now necessary to halt for reinforcements and for somebody to turn that position. How it was done I don't know, but believe the riflemen in the bushes considered themselves discovered and skedaddled. We were halted to rest at the roadside and before long there came swinging by the splendid column of the Twelfth New York. Following them were two New Jersey regiments and one from Connecticut and our scouting duty was over for the night. We marched back and when we drew near the end of the bridge, there were our old friends of the New York Seventh, hard at work throwing up earthworks. Some of them showed us their blistered hands and I advised gloves.

It was in that night that my friend Colonel Ellsworth, was killed, murdered, at Alexandria.[13] All the country felt bad about it but his most sincere mourners, perhaps, were in the President's household. It was only a few days later that I obtained leave go to go the White House to sign some patents and of course I went over into Nicolay's room to see him and Hay. The room was crowded with visitors, mostly distinguished, and I knew some of them. Among these was my old Syracuse friend, General Elias W. Leavenworth, formerly Secretary of State of New York. We were talking over old times and war times and we drifted toward the south window. I had but just spoken of Ellsworth when, as I turned, I saw a freshly put-in pane of glass, still bearing the marks of the glazier's fingers. It was the pane that had replaced the one broken by the bright young soldier only a week ago and I said goodbye to Leavenworth and went out.

The next military duty of any importance performed by the Rifles was in camp at Tennally Town in Maryland. We were provided with tents and we were only too well supplied with everything else. Near that camp was a ferry and route supposed to be used by Rebel spies and mail carriers. If that were not true, one of the sentries on guard at a path among the woods was killed, one night, and in those days a man was of more importance than afterwards.

Next night, it was my duty to patrol up and down that lonely and brush-bordered place of danger. I did not mind sentry duty in the daytime but I believe I was an alert kind of watchman during my four hours of weary tramping up and down and I was not sorry to be relieved. My successor was an entirely newmade American from our German Company. He had his instructions and to these was added by the boys the information that he might expect to be assassinated. Just how long it was I cannot tell, but the shades of night were still deep among those woods when our camp was startled by the crack of a rifle. The drum beat to arms and the squad on duty dashed bravely in among the trees after the supposable corpse of the massacred sentry. They found him still alive, standing behind a tree, reloading his rifle and ready to swear that he had killed some Rebel or other who had come creeping in upon him through the bushes. Reinforcements having arrived, a search was made and there indeed was the body of the imprudent intruder, a really fine, fat hog who had rooted his unwise way too near to the end of a brave volunteer's deadly rifle. Dead he was and he was also duly cut up for army rations.

We had grand times in camp, for the neighborhood was full of Union people who admired us. Just as we had our tents in flowery and evergreenery ornamentation we were compelled to move them to avoid sleeping on the damp, damp soil of Maryland. I remember one curious incident that gave me a new idea of soldier life and stern discipline. One of our fellows was a reckless young fellow from New York whose family was rich and let him have too much money. One morning we were astonished to learn that he had been found asleep on his post as sentry and was in danger of the death penalty. I had seen him marched to his post and an idea occurred to me. I at once made my way to battalion headquarters. There stood Major Smead, stern and silent, with several important military men. I walked up to him and saluted, saying that I had something to report.

He was evidently interrupted, annoyed, and his response was gruff: "What is it, sir?"

"If that man is court-martialed, I wish to be called as a witness."

"What for, sir? What can you know about it?"

"He was drunk when he was put on post, sir. The sergeant had no right to put a drunken man on guard duty. Of course he went to sleep. That's all."

"Thank you sir!" exclaimed the major. "That ends it. Stoddard, you have relieved me of a terribly disagreeable matter!"

No more was heard of the death penalty but the culprit stood a long term of guard duty on the head of a big barrel.

Our camping was ended by a sudden call to arms at the beginning of a woefully hot day near the end of June. The Rebels were reported preparing to cross the Potomac near Edward's Ferry and we were to be thrown forward to check them. Other troops were to follow fast but we were to make a forced march and seize the position. We made the march at the rate of over four miles an hour, losing a man a mile by sunstroke among our three companies.

Among those who fell and were left till the wagons picked them up was my brother Henry. I believe he never fully recovered from that shock, although he seemed to do so. We reached a bluff near the ferry and threw ourselves behind the ridge with our rifles over it, but the Rebels had fallen back and all their lives were saved. Next day I was ordered to take a carryall and convey Henry and three others back to Washington. The end of our three months term of service was near and I was willing to get back to the White House.

29

A New Life in Washington

On my return to the city, I at once secured a good boarding house and went to the Interior department concerning patents. A large pile had accumulated and I began to sign the President's name at the rate of about nine hundred times per diem.

During my three months of military service I had been a close student of war affairs and had really learned something. I kept up the study from that day forward and it led me to make the acquaintance of a large number of army and navy men of distinction. It has since been of value to me in my literary work. In social matters I had done more than at first I was aware of. For instance, it was natural for me at the beginning, to go to a Baptist church. It had not been an over loyal concern and I had not liked it. Moreover, it was now taken, with nearly all the others, for hospital purposes.

I think it was at an earlier day than this that a member of Trinity Episcopal Church came to me with the story of the brave and splendid stand for the Union which had been made from the pulpit by that noble Christian man, Rev. Dr. Charles H. Hall of Trinity church, Episcopal. All his Secession parishioners had left him in a body and all their pews were to be let on a day named. I was there to bid, with a determination to get the pew of Jeff Davis if possible. The said Davis was then engineering the Confederacy and he afterwards did much for it in both ways.[1] I was just one minute too late for his pew but obtained a good one, well forward in the left middle aisle. Soon I became a personal friend of the Doctor and am so to this day, for I did not leave him, even when long afterwards, I gave up my pew to oblige somebody with a larger family, I forget who it was.

Before long came the battle of Bull Run and it has not at any time been half-described as to its Washington effects. That week in July was a strange experience, but I was not among the disheartened fellows, for I had an idea that it was what we needed to wake up the people to the reality of this thing. I had from the beginning expected a long, hard war.

The Rifles had returned from upper Maryland after a curiously unmurderous campaign, and I went to see Major Smead as to what we were to do concerning further service. He was good enough to me, personally, but he strongly expressed his determination never again to "command a company of gentlemen." He had failed to make West Pointers of several of them. I did not see him again for a long time but one day I met him on the Avenue, patrolling with three or four army officers. Every man was a Major, for they were quartermaster and the like. I took them all to Gautier's, then the Delmonico's of Washington, and gave them the biggest dinner the place could get up. It was a jolly time, but the next I heard of poor Smead he had been killed by a cannon shot while handling his battery bravely at the Second Bull Run battle. Of course, I went to the White House and it was but a few days after my return that I received orders to transfer myself to the correspondence desk in the northeast room which I was to occupy thenceforward.

At first, I had to make visits to my old office to sign patents but that was ended by an order to have them all sent up to the White House for my presence there was needed hourly. It was one curious indication of the great change which was making in the machinery of the government. In quiet days, one private secretary had been enough and the law provided for only one, with the vast salary of twenty-five hundred dollars per annum. That post was now held by Mr. Nicolay. The Private Secretary to sign land patents was appointed under a law passed in 1836 when Andrew Jackson swore by the Eternal that he would not scrawl his name over any more blessed parchments. The salary of fifteen hundred had been a big one in those primitive days but it was not so now. John Hay was, practically, Assistant Private Secretary, and in order to provide him with a salary he was appointed a clerk in the Interior Department and drafted to the White House for special duty. His pay at first was fourteen hundred and it was afterwards raised by making him a staff major and then a colonel in the army, with full pay and allowances for quarters, horses, and rations. He actually did do some military duty with marked credit to himself. In after days, the increasing work on our hands did compel Nicolay to call for occasional clerical assistance but nobody but myself was ever allowed to meddle with the duties at the first assigned to me, for reasons which may soon appear.

The northeast room was not narrow and it was long. Its south door opened into the great hall, and the Executive offices, as I have said, were over the way. In the middle of the eastern side of the room was a big fireplace with an extensive marble mantel. I hope no vandal of improvement has dared to remove those huge brass andirons or otherwise to destroy that antique of the nation.[2]

My desk, in front of the door, had at its right, in front, the door into Nicolay and Hay's bedchamber. It was a huge, flat table desk, full of capacious drawers for documents. As for stationery and the like, the economies of the Republic had refused to increase the annual appropriation since the days of John Adams, and it remained at two hundred and fifty. I had to buy for myself every pen and every sheet of anything but document paper that I used while I was in office and Nicolay and Hay had to scramble for themselves. The other expenses of the house were eked out in one way and another but they were always calling for more and not getting it, like so many Oliver Twists.

In the far corners, by the north window, were two upright desks, old and apparently somewhat infirm, over which John Hay claimed supervision and he now and then sat down at one of them, but most of his time had to be spent in Nicolay's room for his peculiar abilities quickly began to manifest themselves. He was a born diplomat if ever there was one and he was a right-down good fellow.

He and I struck up a kind of queer partnership. Neither of us could dance worth a cent and we engaged the dancing services of a Professor Marini to remedy the defect. It was a laudable endeavor but it shortly broke down under the pressure of official duties which would come in at dancing hours and upset the professor's appointments. Hay may have afterwards become a good dancer but I never did, although I mastered schottisches and broke down at waltzing.

Our next enterprise came out of the fact that Hay was a poor horseman. The War or some other department had assigned a pair of large bays to the White House "for special duty," that is to drag the Executive cab to the Capitol when the Private Secretary was going there with a Presidential Message, that he might get there quickly and not be robbed on the way.

So another requisition was put in for saddles, for horseback messages, and Hay and I began to take morning rides. That lasted some time, but we found it too fatiguing in hot Washington weather. I had had twenty times as much previous practice as he had and he admired the ease of my seat. He did not know how really uneasy I found that army saddle. Our next undertaking was more in the line of duty. Both of us knew some French and so did some of the many Europeans who came to the White House, diplomats, army men, tourists, and others, but it was needful for us to know more. It was especially necessary for me to be able to read the large number of letters which came to my table in that official tongue. So we called in a really good teacher, a Professor Marix, a Russian Jew whose pronunciation had the St. Petersburg improvement upon the Parisian dialect. We really did pretty well with that matter and the Professor boasted of me that I was the only man he ever knew who acquired a perfect knowledge of the French language in thirty days. I think he was willing to take some credit to himself and to leave out of account any previous work of mine under Professor Mixer at Rochester University. Hay and I got on well together, as we do to this day, and it was not long before he was down with a brief attack of Potomac fever. I took care of him and when he got out at the end of it I heard him say that he could not have been more assiduously watched if his own mother had been with him. I was used to sick people.

My relations with Mr. Nicolay were, from the first, of an entirely satisfactory character, but my assignments to duty came through him from the President himself. In after years I saw little of Nicolay, but a few months before his death he sent me a very cordial letter of remembrance and friendship which I was glad to get.

For all strictly historical matters I must leave everything to the books, but there were some queer things at my desk. Among other curiosities in my drawers were all the recommendations for appointments to chaplaincies and brigadier generalships, which I was directed to sort and analyze and file. There was fun in many of them. A curious idea appeared to have entered the minds of many men that if a fellow had made good speeches and torn around actively in the presidential campaign, he was therefore the right man to head a brigade on a field of battle. If he had done well with a flour mill or a country store, he must know all about war and be ready to use up any mere West Pointer on the Confederate side. Mr. Lincoln and I had some small fun over those papers.

The chaplaincies were not so funny, for it did seem as if all the preachers that their own churches were tired of were eager to obtain major's pay, rations, and a uniform. Some of the consequences were so disgusting that Mr. Lincoln one day exclaimed to me, "Why, Stoddard, I do believe that the chaplains are the worst men we have in the army." The whole system was given up after a while. The volunteers were now coming forward fast enough but the great difficulty was to find competent officers for them. Henry was now in pretty good health and it was time to set him at work. Hardly was he back in Washington before a senator, a friend of ours, offered to obtain for him an appointment as second lieutenant but both Harry [Stoddard's nickname for his brother Henry—ed.] and I knew that the army was no place for him. He was, however, a well-trained and remarkably efficient bank clerk and bookkeeper and there was the Treasury. The increasing needs of war finance were largely increasing the demand for clerks, but the politicians were ready to offer ten times as many as could be employed and to fight hard for their nephews and other nominees. I determined to get Harry in and his application was duly registered but as yet I had not developed any influence. I was of less consequence than even a mere Congressman in the eyes of the appointing officials.

Secretary Chase[3] was at this time so busy that a large share of the appointing power really fell into the hands of one of his most active subordinates. I did not wish to ask a favor of Mr. Lincoln, so I went to the Assistant Secretary. He was polite and kindly, of course, but he was able to paint to me vividly the pressure he was under from the politicians and assure me of the all but utter impossibility of granting my request. Things looked a little cloudy for Harry but I too was a little of a politician.

Mr. McSmith, if that was his name, was a relic of the old time, retained mainly because of his ability and because no green hand could have done his work. That was a credit to him and so was his loyalty and his readiness to serve his country, but he had one misfortune. He was from Savannah and had originally been appointed as a citizen of Georgia, at a time when it was well for an applicant for office to hail from below Mason's and Dixon's line. It was not so now and the Senate committees were only too rigidly scrutinizing all nominations sent in, with reference to that very matter. Every rejection opened a door for somebody else and Mr. McSmith knew that he had his watchful enemies. So it came to pass, one day, that a list of Treasury nominations lay upon my table, all but ready to go to the Senate.

Every name was down in good handwriting, with the State and previous residence set opposite in due order. All were filled up except that of my impossible friend Mr. McSmith. I saw the blank and I saw something else: I was ready to say to Mr. Nicolay that I would run over to the Treasury and have the blank filled up before sending in that batch of nominations. He ordered me to be quick about it and so I was, for a President's Private Secretary could not be detained one moment in an anteroom. He must be seen at once, no matter who else had to wait. I showed my list as sweetly as a bit of maple sugar but as soon as I gently suggested "Georgia?" his susceptive mind added the word "Rejection!" and he began to hum and haw in a dissatisfied manner. He even changed color.

"May I ask," I said, "how long you have lived in the District of Columbia? That is not a seceding state, is it?"

"Just the thing, Mr. Secretary! Just the thing! But can you—"

"I will fill it in now, Mr. McSmith, and I will see that the nomination goes to the Senate this morning, before anybody—"

"All right, Mr. Secretary! By the way! I have found a place for your brother. Send him around right away. It's a twelve hundred dollar—"

"Thank you, Mr. McSmith. I must hurry now and get this in. I'll speak about your nomination to some of my friends. My brother is just the man for that place. He has the highest recommendations, you know."

There they were, on the paper before him, and I smiled blandly as I picked it up and went out into the hall, where Harry was waiting for me. He was duly appointed and he was at his Treasury desk when the Senate confirmed Mr. McSmith of the District of Columbia. He and his very excellent family became close friends of ours and he was really an exceedingly valuable Treasury official. So was Harry, for his appointment was in Secretary Chase's own office before many days went by, and he was duly promoted from grade to grade. Speaking of appointments for merit, the irregular volunteer whom I had saved from court martial for sleeping on post had "influence" behind him and obtained a commission as second lieutenant of marines. He at once drew upon his doting father for one hundred and fifty dollars to buy a horse. The draft was honored but the young warrior did not take any horse to sea with him.

Before long my sister Kate came on to join us and we made up quite a family.

30

The War City

here was war now, all along the lines, east and west. But the attention of the nation, if not of the world, was concentrated upon the City of Washington and the Army of the Potomac. Of course, the White House was a place of frequent resort for army correspondents and the local news-gatherers.

Among the first of the newspapermen to make himself pretty well known to us was a bright young fellow from Ohio by the name of Whitelaw Reid.[1] We all liked him very much and friendships sprung up which lasted through after years. He was in due time well known as a New York editor and also attained diplomatic appointments abroad. In those days, we considered him as decidedly the best fellow of the whole lot.

As for myself, at an early day I received an invitation from my Uncle Bright, of the *New York Examiner & Chronicle*, to write news letters for that journal. I was glad to do so and the success which I attained led to my subsequent staff connection with the *Examiner* during many years.[2]

Speaking of newspapermen and distinguished editors, I must not forget my old friend Dr. Scroggs. He lingered in Washington until all the important appointments, such as he was adapted to, had been filled and then he sadly went back to Champaign, declaring that Stoddard had robbed him of his pay for printing the nominating editorial. Not long after I returned from the army, the Congressman from our district, a good friend of mine, came to me to say that there was a fight over the Champaign post office between the doctor and his rival editor, Mr. Crandall. He remarked that that appointment properly belonged to my disposal rather than to his and asked me to decide. I had to laugh but promptly responded that Scroggs and his paper lived in Champaign while Crandall and his paper lived in Urbana.

"Make it a question of locality," I said, "and give it to Scroggs."

So the doctor got the post office instead of being tied down to a mere Comptrollership of the Treasury at Washington—or a place in the Cabinet.

The business of Private Secretary, per se, was generally pretty well absorbed by Nicolay and Hay, but there were odd days, first during Hay's illness, when I had to go over and take Nicolay's place in the opposite room. That gave me more than a little instruction. Among other things, I learned that the House and Senate did not recognize any individual but knew the Private Secretary only by the practical fact of his bringing a message from the President. It was therefore an important day for me when I proudly appeared at the doors of the Houses and was led in to be loudly announced to the Vice President and the Speaker as "The President's Private Secretary with a Message!" From that hour onward, by rule, I was free of the floor of both Houses. That privilege was afterwards continued to me during several administrations, but a day came when the Democracy was again in power and Randall of Pennsylvania was Speaker of the House.[3] I went to Washington on business which compelled me to see a friend of mine, a Congressman from Ohio by the name of Garfield.[4] I went up to the Capitol and found at the door a new king who knew not this Joseph. He sent in my card, however, and in a minute or so Gen. Garfield came striding out to exclaim in some surprise: "My dear fellow: Why didn't you come right in? I can talk with you at my desk. I can't stay out here."

I kindly explained to him the difficulty in the way and he replied: "You stand still a moment. I'll fix that!"

So he wrote something on a card and sent it in to Randall, whom I knew pretty well but who had not liked me much, and in less than no time, out came a messenger to hand me a perpetual pass in and out, signed by the Speaker at the request of Gen. Garfield. I have that card in my box now and am proud of it as well as of a number of letters which came to me from Garfield, for whom I had a peculiarly warm feeling, for reasons which I may write down hereafter. He was then the House leader on the Republican side and afterwards was murdered for the crime of being President in the days of the political lunacy.

Among other incidents of my official life at this time was the discovery that fifteen hundred dollars was a small tightness for a man attempting to hold such a position as had somehow drifted under me and was lifting me up into larger expenses than might have been those of a clerk now or of even a Secretary in Andrew Jackson's time. It was therefore something worthwhile when a New York banker whose friendship I had acquired told me that two thirds of the up and down movements in stocks and gold were caused by false rumors or by misunderstandings of the course of current events. He proposed that I should keep him advised of the true state of affairs, as far as I could, and he would open a stock and gold account for me. I was just the man for him and there was nothing in my position or sources of information which rendered it improper. It happened that my early guesses at truth were singularly correct and my bank accounts grew rapidly, both in New York and Washington. There was no manner of secrecy about my varied speculations. President Lincoln laughed at them. One day, however, a gentleman who loved me not was at Mrs. Lincoln's afternoon reception and struck me a deadly blow by remarking:

"Madame, I understand that your favorite Secretary has been quite successful on the gold market. He has cleared half a million!"

"Has he, indeed?" she exclaimed. "I'm so glad to hear it. I wish he may make a million! I think a great deal of Mr. Stoddard. Glad of his good luck."

He subsided and that very evening she warmly congratulated me on my good fortune next morning, advising me, however, not to lose all my money.

Before my sister came on and even afterwards I had one bit of experience which I must not forget. A gentleman of some means and with affairs before Congress and the departments had opened what might be called a select political boardinghouse not far from the Executive mansion. I had made his acquaintance and was cordially admitted to the golden number of his distinguished "day boarders." I dined there pretty regularly until, for some reason or other, he gave up keeping hotel. I had a regular place at the dinner table. At my left was regularly a gentleman who was Speaker of the Maine House of Representatives and who was in Washington to look out for the volunteers from Maine and for other New England affairs. I formed a strong liking for him and a friendship sprung up between us which lasted to the day of his death. His name was James G. Blaine[5] and he afterwards became pretty well known in national politics. On my right sat a prominent Treasury officer, a capital dinner table companion, by the name of Hugh McCullough [sic]. He also was afterwards nationally well known.[6] Just beyond Blaine sat Senator Anthony of Rhode Island and with him also my friendship was lifelong. Other Senators and great men came and went and I was sorry when at last the thing broke up, or down.

At about this time a curious incident came. I went to New York City on business, going and coming in the uncomfortable sleeping cars which were then running, and was away from my desk only a full day. When I came to my office in the morning, there on my table lay a heap of letters, all duly cut open but very few of them otherwise dealt with. I went on with my work for an hour or two before Hay came in, with a most rueful countenance.

To understand the predicament he was in, I must explain a little. At the outset, he and Nicolay were to take their meals at the President's table. Ward Hill Lamon, appointed Marshall of the Supreme Court,[7] was to have general charge of the White House, assisted by Mrs. Lincoln's friend, his wife. Hill, as we called him in Illinois, might have done well enough if he had had less government in him and had let the household affairs alone. In less than a fortnight he discovered that Mrs. Lincoln proposed to be mistress of her own house, wherever it might be, and Hill had no more tact than a drill sergeant. So he went out and the Commissioner of Public Buildings came in.[8] He was also a very fine man but he did not know enough to restrain himself from giving orders directly instead of through Mrs. Lincoln. His house power went to grass and she in some disturbance of mind transferred much of the load to my shoulders. That was the beginning of the process by means of which malicious people were afterwards able to speak of me as "Mrs. Lincoln's secretary."[9] At all events, I understood her thoroughly and formed a much higher opinion of her real character than a lot of foul-mouthed slanderers permitted to go out to the country. To retrun to Hay and his trouble.

"Stod!" he exclaimed. "I'm in the worst kind of fix! You know how it is. Nicolay and I are out with Madame. She is down on both of us. Now! You were away, yesterday, and I tried to help you along on the mail. I had seen how you did it and so I turned a whole pile of them over on their backs and sliced them open with a paper folder, before I saw the address on one of them. Then! O my soul! There they are! About a dozen of 'em are for Mrs. Lincoln and won't she give it to me!"

I was lying back in my chair and laughing, for he put it in first-rate style and it really looked awkward.

"What shall I do about it?" he woefully demanded.

"Don't do anything," I told him. "Shut up and say nothing about it. I'll take the letters and go down and see Mrs. Lincoln. She won't know but what I opened them myself. I can make it all right." He evidently did not believe I could and he awaited the result with some anxiety. Down I went to the Red Room and sent for Mrs. Lincoln. In she came and asked me what on earth was the matter.

"Bad conduct of this here impertinent paper-folder," I told her. "Opened a lot of your letters, just because they were mixed in with the others. No fault of his, either. He didn't know they were there. Stupid fellow."

At first she laughed heartily but then her face grew sober.

"Mr. Stoddard," she said, "read them all. I want you, from this time onward, to open every letter or parcel that comes in the mail for me. You know my sister's handwriting and hers are the only exception. No! You may open hers, too. They accuse me of correspondence with the Rebels. I want them all read!"

She was blushing an angry crimson, too, and I did not know the meaning of it until I read some of the infamous things which the political ghouls were sending her. The President's own mail was bad enough but it did seem too bad for the nasty devils of the enemy to torment his unoffending wife. She had good reasons for wishing her mail winnowed. So I went back and told Hay that she was going to appeal to the President and have him discharged, but he looked so badly that I let him up and told him the new arrangement. After that I had the mail to myself for nobody else would touch it if it could be avoided.

I doubt if there was any spot in the United States in those days, outside of a battle field, that was more continually interesting than was the correspondence desk of the Executive Mansion. I took pains at one time, to strike an average of the number of daily arrivals, other than newspapers, and was surprised to find that it was not far from 250. These were of every imaginable character, with quite a number that could not be reasonably imagined.

The newspapers themselves were interesting. The majority of them contained marked columns, editorials, or letters and that sort of thing, abusive, complimentary or advisory, which the authors fondly hoped might reach the hungry eyes of the President. They did not do so. At one time he ordered me to make a daily digest of the course and comments of the leading journals, east and west, and I made one. It was wasted work and was discontinued, for Mr. Lincoln never found time to spend one hour upon those laborious condensations. He remarked to me, that it was of no consequence, after all.

That is, I understood that he had no need for anybody to edit him.

The letters were a study. Large packages of documents were all the while coming, relating to business before one or another of the departments. Some were in law cases. Some were in relation to claims. In any event, it was my duty to know where they properly belonged and to endorse them with the necessary reference from the President, favorable or otherwise, or perfunctory. I seemed to myself to know exactly what he would say about it and my decision was never found fault with except in a few cases and in these I was approved, as I remember it. There was a river of matter relating to appointments to office and these too were referred, except such as belonged in my custody.

The very much larger number of the epistles belonged in one or another of the two tall waste baskets which sat on either side of me and their deposits were as rapid as my decisions could be made. It had to be swift work and one day there came a funny incident in that department of my judicial capacity. It did seem to me as if the foulest blackguards on earth had made up their stupid minds that they could abuse the President through the mails and they tried to do so. Added to these were the lunatics. I imbibed an idea that whenever any man went "clane wud" [crazy—ed.] he sat down and wrote to the President. Well, one day I and my paper-folder and my wastebaskets were hard at work. While we were at it, in came a portly, dignified, elderly party and sat down near me while he was waiting for an audience with Mr. Lincoln, to whom his card had been sent in. He appeared to be some kind of distinguished person, maybe a governor or something of that sort, and he watched me with an interest which evidently grew upon him. He became uneasy in his chair and then he waxed red in the face. He himself may at some time have written letters and at last he broke out with:

"Is that the way you treat the President's mail? Mr. Lincoln does not know this! What would the people of the United States think if they knew that their communications to their Chief Magistrate were dealt with in this shameful manner? Thrown into the wastebasket! What does Lincoln mean? Putting such an awful responsibility into the hands of a mere boy! A boy!"

I had been all the while watching him as he fired up and I had an uncommonly dirty mail that morning. I had therefore put aside as I opened them a number of the vilest scrawls that infamy could put on paper. He had risen from his chair and was pacing up and down the room in hot indignation when I quietly turned and offered him a handful of the selected letters.

"Please read those, sir," I said, "and give me your opinion of them. I may be right about them. Do you really think, now, that the President of the United States ought to turn from the affairs of the nation to put in his time on that sort of thing?"

The dignified party took the awful handful and began to read and his red face grew redder. Then it was white with speechless wrath. Perhaps he had never before perused anything quite so devilish in all his life.

"You are quite right, sir," he gasped, as he sank into his chair again. "Young man! You are right! He ought not to see a line of that stuff! Burn it, sir! Burn it! What devils there are!"

He may even have admired me but I returned to my work and he fidgeted around the room until the messenger came to summon him to his audience. I do not believe that he entered any complaint concerning "that boy," but he was correct about the responsibility, for it was a big one for any fellow, old or young.

It included many of the applications for pardons and all of these were at one time in my keeping. I remember some of them and what became of them. There were those who grumbled at Mr. Lincoln's strong objection to any kind of capital punishment and his tendencies toward mercy for all sinners. I may have been one of these. There came, one day, a pile of influential petitions on behalf of a southwestern guerilla of the most cruel sort. He was unquestionably a red-handed murderer but the movement in his favor was a strong one. It included even loyal politicians and next day a gang of big men of several kinds came up to see the President about it. They spoke of the high character of the papers in the case and these were sent for but they were not in my possession. They may have been duly referred and transferred to the War Office, as was sometimes the custom. Inquiry was made there but the papers could not be found. The delegation went its way and that application for pardon was hung up. So was the woman and child killer who was the most interested party in the case and hardly had that fact been telegraphed before all the missing papers arrived at the White House. I think Mr. Lincoln did not more than look sidewise at me and I am sure he made no verbal commentary.

There may have been other exceptional instances of the power of the paper-folder but I have forgotten them. I have not forgotten, however, the almost daily communications from "The Angel Gabriel," who professed to write in blood that appeared to me more like an inferior variety of cheap red ink. Besides, the angel mixed his inspiration terrifically and some of his work would have read well in *Puck*.[10] One day there came a really curious paper which afterwards perished with my collection of autographs in Arkansas. It purported to come from the spirits of a score or more of the old worthies of the Republic and it was certainly a strong and dignified document of advice and encouragement which would not have disgraced any of them. It was signed with the signatures of George Washington, John Hancock, John Adams, Benjamin Franklin, Thomas Jefferson and others, as perfectly as the most expert forger could have done it if he had traced the names over the printed copy of the Declaration of Independence.

It was a queer thing and so were all the letters from simple people who wished that the President would kindly step around among the several departments and attend to their business for them. Even inventors asked him to see about their patents and hurry them up. One of these, however, came from a curious party in Tolono, Illinois. He stated that he had invented a "cross-eyed gun." It was a two-shooter with diverging barrels and he proposed to form a regiment of cross-eyed men who could march up the Potomac and clean out the Rebels from both sides of the river at once. He averred: "I know enough of cross-eyed men to make the regiment and, by thunder, Mr. Lincoln, I'm cross-eyed enough to be their colonel."

As to some other matters, I believe I really did do a number of helpful things for honest ignorances by my references and recommendations and suppose they attributed it to that good man, Honest Abe. Mr. Lincoln laughed well over the cross-eyed letter, but there were many over which he could not have laughed. I was forbidden to show him any of the many threatening epistles. The idea of assassination was in the minds of blood-thirsty men from the beginning, but those who really meant murder were not likely to write any warning of their intention.

There were letters of another sort. I will only mention one. It was an intensely patriotic and eloquent letter, telling the President of one woman who was praying for him and for her country. I read it thoughtfully, for every here and there the paper was blistered, as if drops of hot water had fallen upon it. The writer had lost her four sons in the battles of the war and she was now alone in the world. Mr. Lincoln also was alone when I took that letter in and laid it open before him. I stood still, for a moment, saying nothing, and then I left the room for I saw a probability of more hot water. I could not see very clearly, just then, either.

3-1

Guns and Things at the White House

t the outset of the war, one of the important problems before the Administration was the procuring of guns and ammunition for the armies it was gathering. A large quantity of the weapons and so forth which had been accumulated in former days had somehow been transferred southward before the outbreak of hostilities and the Confederacy obtained the benefit of them.

With the general perplexities of the War Department I had nothing to do but a part of them speedily drifted into my northeast room. Every proposed vender of condemned European firelocks was possessed by the idea that he might make a sale of them if he could induce the President to overrule the decisions of the Bureau of Ordnance. In each case of that kind, I was likely to have a specimen gun deposited in the corner. At the same time came to the front a large number of inventors, and some of them had practical ideas and some had not. That tide continued almost unto the end of the war and not by any means without good results. At the first, however, I had an opportunity for studying quite a number of out-and-out cranks.

I remember in particular one enthusiastic party who had invented a curious kind of far-shooting rifle the weight of which required it to be mounted upon a spider wheel as high as your shoulder. Oh, how that genius did abuse the President for his inability to appreciate the spider-wheel gun and for his general bad management of the war.

Then there were other curiosities, one after another, until my room looked like a gunshop. On my table at one time were specimens of steel cuirasses, designed for the loading down of our volunteers on forced marches in hot weather. We might well have wished them to be worn by Stonewall Jackson's "Foot Cavalry" on their way to some of the mischief they did us by getting there first. Another item was a devilish kind of hand grenade, made to burst on striking and to scatter bits of iron in all directions. It would have been a terrible thing at close ranges, if the enemy would only stand still to let it be thrown among them. Swords were on hand in several patterns and so were various descriptions of cannon. As to the cuirasses, Mr. Lincoln decided that he would not take them unless the inventor would put on one of them and let some rifleman practice on the thing to be sure that it was bullet-proof. The trial was never made that I know of. Mr. Lincoln was really deeply interested in the gunnery business and he was not at all ignorant concerning war and weapons. In fact, he had ideas of his own which were far in advance of some which were entertained by a few venerable gentlemen in the War Department, relics of old wars and forgotten skirmishes.

As to cannon, I was studying them and made trips to the foundry at the Navy Yard to study the processes of their manufacture. One of the results of this was a lifelong friendship with Admiral Dahlgren, then in command of the Yard.[1] He taught me a heap of things and I invented a boat gun which he did me the honor to approve of. It consisted of steel bars wound with steel wire and soaked in a bath of melted brass to convey the explosive force laterally and so forth and the idea was afterwards made extensive use of but I got no credit for it. Speaking of inventions, while in Champaign I had invented a new printer's chase. It was the first improvement upon the chases used in the old Franklin press and involved many new ideas. I obtained a patent for it which now rests among my old papers. I had then no time or opportunity to do anything with it, if I had known how, and the whole thing got away from me but that chase is the basis for many now in use in the power presses of today. I had also invented a news and book paper-folding machine but had then no time to perfect it and it passed out of sight. To return to guns and Abraham Lincoln, among the new patterns in my room were several which seemed to promise good results and I knew that he was taking an interest in them but did not know how much, until one evening when I was at work over a pile of letters and was dimly aware that somebody was coming in. I looked up to exclaim:

"Ah! Mr. President!" which was not my ordinary salutation.

"Stoddard," he said, "they say you are a pretty good marksman. I want you to be here early tomorrow morning; say half-past six. We'll go out to the Mall and try some of these guns. I can get a better idea—"

I do not remember my next saying but a talk on guns followed which was so interesting—to me—that it kept on until he was called to his late dinner in the other side of the house with a sharp reminder that he was to have distinguished company. That did not mean me.

The Mall is the wide grassy slope from the White House grounds to the Potomac and at that time it was badly littered with rubbish. Out in the middle of it was a huge pile of old building lumber. This was just the thing to set up a target on. I was at my room good and early, and I did not have to wait long before in came the President.

"Well," he remarked, "you didn't keep me waiting. Now, you take that thing and I'll take this and we'll go right along."

The weapon assigned to me was a breech-loader made over from an old Springfield smoothbore musket. The new arrangement was a kind of screw twist, and was fitted somewhat loosely. It carried the old cartridges, of which he brought a supply. His own gun was a well-made affair, resembling the Spencer carbine.[2] I think it was rifled. So the Commander-in-Chief and the White House division of the Army of the Potomac marched away to the Mall, discussing guns and war as they went.

"Mr. Lincoln," I remarked, "General Ripley says that men enough can be killed with the old smoothbore and the old cartridges, a ball-and-three buckshot."

"Just so!" he responded. "But our folks are not getting near enough to the enemy to do any good with them, just now, I reckon we've got to get guns that will carry further."

The entire field of breech- and muzzle-loaders was run over and I found that he was strongly in favor of the new movement in small arms. A hundred yards was paced off and a target was set against the lumber. We took turns in firing and I soon discovered two things. One was that the old Springfield barrel carried first-rate, and the other was that Mr. Lincoln was anything but a crack shot. I afterwards learned from Hill Lamon that he never had been.

It did not exactly irritate him but he remarked: "Stoddard, I declare! You are beating me. I'll take a good sight this time—" and down he went to level his piece across one knee.

Now he had forgotten one thing, and I already knew that there was trouble coming. There were stringent military orders out, forbidding all kinds of firing within the city or camp limits. Washington was then little better than a fortified camp. There were guards set everywhere and one had been posted on the avenue at the entrance to the Mall. It consisted of a very short corporal and four men and it was now coming after us at a double quick and it was swearing but I did not deem it my duty to stop Mr. Lincoln's long squint over that breechloader. The guard came within talking range just before the piece went off.

"Stop that firing! Stop that firing!" shouted the corporal and I am compelled to say that his additional remarks did not cause me to suppose him any kind of Sunday school teacher.

"Bless you! You ——! Stop that firing!" But at that moment the gun went off and the corporal was within a few paces when the President slowly uncoiled himself and rose to his feet. He looked like a very tall man and he may have looked even taller to the angry little warrior who was putting out a hand as if to take him in charge and hive him in the guardhouse. I think the other soldiers were first in catching the joke, if it was one, but Mr. Lincoln was now looking smilingly down into the face of the corporal and that had undergone a sudden change. It seemed to me as if all their lower jaws went down together but not one of them said another word right there. It was "bout face" in a twinkling and they set out toward the avenue at a better pace than they had come with. I only heard, as they went, some confused ejaculations concerning the preposterous fact that "We've been cussin' Old Abe himself!"

He too was laughing, as well as I, he in his half-silent, peculiar way.

"Well, Stoddard," he said, "they might have stayed to see the shooting."

That was all there was of it, except that the old Springfield, with its loosely fitted twist, had almost kicked my shoulder out of joint.

Among the other ornaments of my room were the first models of the turtle tinclad gunboats which were to be the right arm of our forces in the coming campaigns along the rivers of the West.[3] These all owed their adoption to Mr. Lincoln, against the opinions of pretty good army men. More important still was the decision he made in the matter of the *Monitor* ironclad, the cheesebox on a raft, which was so scornfully treated by the wisest fellows in the Navy.[4]

I was not present at any of his examinations of the new invention but I was not ignorant, afterwards, of what he did to secure it for active service. Meantime, it was in charge of a gentleman named Cornelius S. Bushnell and he was let into the northeast room on his arrival. My talks with him there resulted in a personal friendship which lasted to the end of his life. He was a splendid fellow. Through him it was that I became interested in the financial affairs of the Pacific Railway enterprise and formed my friendships with Thomas C. Durant[5] and others of the strong men who carried that wonderful undertaking to success.

My interest in war matters of course led me to wish some information about forts and earthworks, and I obtained a little. After I had seen a few, I was better able to understand pictures and ground plans of all sorts of defensive construction, the general principles being much the same all around.

One of my excursions at an early day took me out to the camp of General Wadsworth of New York[6]. It was just then a difficulty with many of our new brigadiers that their pay and rations made them richer than they had ever been before. Some of them were really men of property and they were launching out in a ridiculous manner, so that the headquarters displays were anything but popular with the rank and file of the army. At the headquarters of "Wadsworth of Geneseo," ex-governor of New York and said to be worth his millions, I had half expected to find military magnificence. On the contrary, I found that he had engineered a stinging rebuke to some of his newly rich neighbors. His quarters were in an old farmhouse and he had put into it nothing but camp furniture, although his elegant lady of a wife was with him. All was of the plainest kind; and when I came to the long, plank dinner table it had no useless cloth to cover the wood. The fare was only the regular army rations very well cooked. There was no silver to be seen, although I had heard that his home mansion abounded in that bright metal.

In due course, it was in order to drink the President's health, at the general's own call, one of his official household being present. When it was so done, was there any flowing goblet of brigadier champagne? No! Only a black bottle with some whiskey in it was brought to me, and the swarm of visiting officers obtained nothing better. The whole thing was admirably done and I afterward received an impression that he and a few others like him had done much to put away the unadvisable extravagance of men not quite so rich as they.

From the beginning of my career at Washington, my social position had been all that I could reasonably have asked, if not a little more. It was continually making demands upon my valuable time. At this date, the Winter of 1861–62, I was expected to be in attendance upon Mrs. Lincoln at all her public and private receptions and also at the regular weekly public receptions of the President. At the occasional absences of either Nicolay or Hay, I was also expected to leave Mrs. Lincoln to her own resources and take the vacant place on one side or the other of the President. After the arrival of my sister Kate, she became a great help to me in some of these matters, for Mrs. Lincoln took a fancy to her and liked to have her assistance at receptions.

My brother Henry was a fellow of unusual social abilities, and before long he was taking a similar position with Miss Kate Chase, and it was somewhat fun—considering that the Treasury beauty and the White House Madame were most of the time at war—to see how benignly he worked himself into the good graces of Mrs. Lincoln also.[7] I believe she had a sufficient sense of humor to appreciate what I called his unfathomable impudence. John Hay did, anyhow, and he and Henry were good friends. He was always a welcome visitor in the northeast room, whenever his really severe and responsible duties at the Treasury gave him an hour off to come over for a chat with the private secretaries.

Among the friends whom I made at an early day were the Shermans[8] and I valued them exceedingly. During that first Winter, Miss Mary Sherman, niece of the great Ohio Senator, came to the capital for the season and on her first evening "out" I was introduced to her by my friend Miss Clara Harris. My acquaintance with Miss Sherman soon became of a most agreeable character. I was with her frequently. After that, we were regular epistolary correspondents during several years, and I fully appreciated the rare ability and high personal character which she has since exhibited as the wife of the commanding general of the Army.

Several of the Harris family were now on hand. I now discovered, by way of John Hay, that upon hearing of my probable appointment, Senator Ira Harris had written a splendid letter about me to the President. On my way to Washington, I had visited at his house in Albany as of yore. I remember being almost shocked at the unceremonious way in which he helped me carry my trunk upstairs, laughing heartily at my protest, asserting roundly that there was no snob in him. His older daughter, Clara, was a kind of society queen. She afterwards married her stepbrother, Henry Rathbone, and thereby follows one of the saddest of sadly tragic stories.

My old chum, Will Harris, had graduated at West Point and was now an officer of artillery, stationed at Fortress Monroe. I saw but little of him, therefore. My cousin Enoch Stoddard of New London was now an army surgeon and could come to see me but once. Two of the Stoddard Morgan boys were in the army, and so were a number of others of our family connection. I became more and more interested in the Union Pacific Railway enterprise. It had been one of the leading features of the Republican Party political position and now the deep earnestness with which the President watched its progress had my entire sympathy. One of the consequences of this was that I shortly found myself invited to attend various organizational and other meetings of capitalists and railway men in New York and I had great times at some of them.

One of these social-financial gatherings was an all-evening affair at Judge Roosevelt's, then, if I remember correctly, the most prominent member of the family which has provided us with our admirable president at this later day.[9] I liked him very much indeed. Another was at the house of a pretty well-known drygoods merchant named Alexander T. Stewart and the acquaintance then began with him had some funny consequences at a then far future.[10] There were several other gatherings which I need not mention. Oh, what remarkable men I did fall in with.

Among them was an exceedingly good-looking fellow whom I liked very much. He had invented improvements in sleeping cars, for which I was grateful to him, and was trying to get them introduced into the several railway systems. He and I had more than one good railway ride together and I believed that he would make it out, for he had great energy and was an adept at meeting and persuading intelligent men. I saw little of him in later years but whenever we did meet he was as cordial as I could ask. His name was George M. Pullman and in the course of time he accumulated property.[11] Then he was poor.

Another of the railway men with whom I then formed a lifelong friendship was that wholehearted, magnificently energetic man, Dr. Thomas C. Durant, of whom I can never think without longing to shake hands with him again. One of the first fellows to turn up after I was settled in the White House was my old friend Hop Strong. He had married his young lady "Quail," Minnie Hoyt, and was not disposed to become an army man. He was wild after government contracts, without any distinct information as to precisely what the army might be most in need of. I think he was interested in a very remarkably impenetrable steel cuirass, for military clothing in hot weather or upon forced marches. He also brought in specimens of several lots of guns of which, I, as a rifleman, could not exactly approve. I could have wished the Confederates to be armed with them. I did obtain for him and one of our Rochester friends contracts for leathern infantry equipments and the like, and for artillery carriages and harness to be made by a Providence concern, but wish to register the fact that I had no interest of a pecuniary nature in these or in any other army contracts, from the beginning of the war to the end. All I ever made by any of them was a splendid lot of Havana cigars that was sent to me anonymously but which bore a strong, very strong, and high-flavored family resemblance to some fine Cubans which I had sampled from the pocket case of a gentleman from Rhode Island. I admit smoking the cigars but do not think I had been bribed.

Hop Strong was visionary in business affairs, although I was not sufficiently experienced to perceive it at once. I was much attached to him and wished to assist him, but he cost me too much, altogether, in the course of time. He next came in with a newly invented arm and leg, for the expected cripples of the coming campaign. I was making money and put in enough to set that patent surgery going, only to lose every cent of it through the joint worthlessness of the inventor and his invention. Hop also brought to me a really valuable patent paint and I sunk several thousands of dollars in trying to make a whistle out of a pig's tail, the "pig" being the paint man and his tendencies toward the nearest rumship. I did several other costly things for Hop, but he only got me into scrapes of one sort or another and I had to give it up.

On the whole, all my business, official, social, and otherwise, appeared to be in an extraordinarily active condition during that opening period of the great conflict for the Union, but I must not leave out some of the incidents which are in the nature of illustrations.

One evening in the earlier days I was at my desk, over my correspondence, when the President came in, with a large portfolio under his arm. I produced some letters which I had wished to show him, if I could.

"Not now," he said, as I told him about them. "Come! I want you to go over to Seward's with me. Bring along that—"

It was to be seen that he was intensely absorbed by something or other and I took up the portfolio which he had laid down on my desk, without inquiring what could be taking him to the house of the Secretary of State at that unseasonable hour, or why he did not rather send for the Secretary and make him come to the White House. I did not even ask him whether or not we were likely to be out late. The fact was, there were times when no wise man cared to ask Abraham Lincoln any questions. This affair might be none of my business, but a worse case for any curious party to pump for information than Abraham Lincoln had not then been invented.

Out we went and downstairs, and when we reached the front door we found that it was raining. The door had been opened for us by old Edward Moran and he, too, saw that it was raining. He began to look quizzical and to rub his hands with invisible soap, as was his custom.

"Edward," said Mr. Lincoln, "go up to my room and bring my umbrella. It stands in the corner, by my desk."

Edward went and Mr. Lincoln stood in the doorway, as absorbed as ever, gazing out into the darkness as if he wished he could see through it. Back came Edward and he brought no umbrella but he washed his hands with peculiar diligence while he dryly reported:

"Your Excellency! It's not there. I'm thinking the owner must have come for it. Just a minute, sir. I'll get another."

He very quickly did so, but his small joke and his way of making it had broken the Executive ice sufficiently to bring out a laugh and to make the situation somewhat easier for me. We walked on under cover of a queer old rain tent that certainly was neither young nor handsome and the President shortly had a story to tell.

"Old Edward!" he said. "Well, there's fun in him. Did you ever hear the answer he gave to President Fillmore?"

I never had heard a word of it and he went on to tell:

"The way of it was this. Just after President Taylor's death, when Fillmore succeeded him, Fillmore needed to buy a carriage. Some gentleman here was breaking up housekeeping and had one for sale and Fillmore took Edward with him when he went to look at it. It appeared to be a pretty good turnout, but Fillmore looked it all over carefully, and then asked Edward: 'How do you think it would do for the president of the United States to ride in a second-hand carriage?'

"'Sure, your Excellency,' replied Edward, 'you're only a second-hand president, you know.'"

"Fillmore used to tell the story himself," said Mr. Lincoln, and then he had other pleasant things to tell, and I discovered part of what our business was to be at the house of the Secretary of State. I even learned whom we were to meet there. We had but a short distance to go and we went in with small ceremony, for Mr. Lincoln was expected—if I was not.

We were shown into a large room at the right of the hall, half office, half reception room, and I put my portfolio down on a long center table. There was a log fire blazing in the fireplace. We did not have to wait long before the hall door opened and in came Mr. Seward, accompanied by Major General John A. Dix, ex-governor of New York, ex-United States Senator, ex-minister to England, ex-Secretary of the Treasury under Buchanan, to whom had recently been assigned the military district including Maryland, West Virginia, and some other doubtful regions. He was a short, slightly built man, and one of the most perfect gentlemen I ever met, so far as manners or anything else might be concerned. The President expressed his pleasure at meeting the General, introduced me as his private secretary, and then began decidedly the most important conference I had attended, up to that date, for it included the entire policy to be pursued by the Administration with reference to the Border States and the Union people of the South, a subject concerning which General Dix held pronounced ideas of his own, to the forcible presentation of which the President listened with profound attention. So did I. Dix had been regarded as the stiffest Union man in President Buchanan's Cabinet, and from him had gone out the then famous order. "If any man attempts to haul down the American flag, shoot him on the spot!"

It was a late hour when the conference terminated, but my part in it had been limited to the production of papers and maps from my portfolio, and neither of the other gentlemen present had annoyed me with questions as to my views upon the important questions before us or upon the line of policy which we then and there decided that the government was thenceforth to pursue. On the whole, however, I inwardly agreed with them. The President and I went out into the rain again. I noticed that he appeared to feel relieved but that he was still thoughtful. So was I.

"Mr. Lincoln," I ventured to ask. "What do you think of General Dix? I never saw him before, but I've heard a good deal about him."

"Neither did I," replied Mr. Lincoln. "This is our first interview. What do I think of him? Well, if I am to judge by what he has said tonight—by the advice he has given—General Dix is, I should say, a wise man. A very wise man!"

I recall that at the parapet of the stone wall of the walk near the White House portico, the President stood still for a whole minute, it seemed to me, and stared southward as if he were trying to look across the Potomac through the dark. He could not have seen anything more than ten feet away, but I kept still until we went on into the house. He went into his office and shut the door and I carried my portfolio into my own room. It had been a wonderfully interesting evening, but I had not the slightest idea that I had really formed a permanent acquaintance with General Dix, or that one day his memory of that first meeting would be to me a matter of exceedingly great importance.

I can hardly help laughing when I look back to another of those social incidents. It was the great dinner party given to a number of visiting journalists and politicians from the North and West by Colonel John W. Forney. The colonel himself was a prominent politician and journalist. He was the editor and proprietor of the *Philadelphia Press* and the *Washington Daily Chronicle* and was at the same time Secretary of the Senate, an office of much distinction. I had formed a warm friendship for him at an early day, but for some unknown reason both Nicolay and Hay were at the time a little out of his books. He had a big house on Capitol Hill and he determined to give the biggest political dinner that it would hold. He really needed to have it stretched a peg or two. When the evening appointed came, his dining room for the occasion went all the way through the two large parlors and the adjoining rooms and the upstairs spaces took the overflow.

It was a distinguished company when it assembled. It included military and naval men, Cabinet officers, Senators, Congressmen, editors, and all sorts of incidental celebrities. But the gallant colonel had invited his guests in the most patriotic and political and liberal way, without any reference whatever to his own personal acquaintanceships, and had failed to agree with himself beforehand upon any regular plan of operations. I saw the point as soon as I got in, and that was at an early hour. Some of the celebrities were gawking around as if they had lost their way and I at once followed Colonel Forney's example, greeting every man I met as if he were a long-lost brother and offering to introduce him to his new neighbors. I had indeed met a great many of them at the White House. My next discovery was that the other private secretaries were not to come and that I was really the sole representative of the National Executive. I did not intend to make myself prominent, but the fates hurled distinction upon me in a most unexpected manner.

The dinner got itself going, nobody knew exactly how. Perhaps the waiters and the soup did it. I didn't. It was not long, however before it was time for the patriotic oratory to begin. The guests were swarming miscellaneously around and among the refreshments when Colonel Forney came hastily to me, with dismay in his face, and exclaimed:

"My dear fellow! You must help me out with this! I don't know half of 'em and I don't know what to do next. You're the only man here what knows everybody. Can't you set 'em going? Call out somebody."

I overcame my naturally retiring disposition, and at once stepped to my proper place at the head of the long table, as being really the host himself and the oldest dignitary present. Perhaps the most distinguished literateur present was Morton McMichael of the *Philadelphia North American*, but it was much more to my purpose that he was distinguished as an unsurpassed dinner table orator. I called the crowd to order, therefore, and then, with a brief eulogy upon him and the press and the flag and that noble bird, the eagle, I introduced McMichael and announced that he would respond to the first patriotic toast, which may have been "Our Country," for all I can now remember. I selected it on the spot, as I did others which were to follow and the men who were to respond. I made a Cabinet Minister take care of the toast to the President and completely escaped any oratorical display of my own. Which was good of me. The speeches made were really splendid, and the affair was a grand success. Colonel Forney could hardly express his gratitude and I could hardly tell myself how I had gotten out of my sudden scrape. I think it was after two o' clock in the morning when I wandered into the wine room. I had wisely abstained from stimulating and was as clear as a bell.

An astonishment was waiting for me right there, however, for against the wall were piles of bottles, stacked up like cordwood for a hard Winter, and I exclaimed: "Good heavens! Forney doesn't expect them to drink all that!"

Of course, he could not have done so. It would have been preposterous on his part—for my next glance told me that every last bottle was empty, although it had been full when that dinner began. Not long afterwards, I was laboring down Pennsylvania Avenue with a Cabinet Minister on one arm and a pair of great men just behind me, and the patriotic story of the evening did not cease until I had landed my heavy and eloquent friend at the top of a flight of stairs. He explained the situation of this and other countries to the very last. I took one good lesson from it all, nevertheless: "Never drink wine at a big dinner party."

Not long afterwards I was at another distinguished "high" and there was a splendid lot of women, young and old, in the drawing room, by themselves, while the financial and political grandees at the table were slow and I was silently aware that no "president," like myself, was needed. My place was at the right of the host and next to me sat an exceedingly distinguished Senator who was said to do his best oratory when he had just come into the senate chamber from one of the "cloakrooms." He was a first-rate good fellow and was talking well, but before long he turned in his seat to gaze admiringly at me, who had said nothing, and remarked: "Stod-d-dard, my b-oy ! Hic! One of us has been drinking. You ort not to ever drink at er dinn'r party. Jes' sho, my b-oy!"

I turned to my host to say, in the kindest manner: "Mr. Z., if the senator is right, you ought to excuse me. I'd better go up into the parlors. But I'm glad he's entirely sober."

I was excused and so I got off without disputing the great man and without missing a really good time upstairs, although I frankly informed my handsome hostess and the girls of the manner of my escape.

The trouble in this direction was that the city of Washington had been born and educated on the old Southern plantation hospitality plan. Every house was a barroom and so were most of the public offices. All over the city, drinking went on almost without cessation. In the Capitol itself, the refreshment rooms and the committee-rooms were so many rumholes, and the celebrated "Hole in the Wall," near the Supreme Court, was really no worse than were several others. When a fellow made a social call, he was almost sure to be bored with a bottle. There were a few notable exceptions, beginning with the President's house, but it would now serve no good purpose to specify the other temperance houses by name. I will add, however that at Mr. Lincoln's own table, I have seen him smell of a highly recommended glass of champagne and put it down without drinking.

The fact that he was a total abstinence man was well known in Illinois, but not so well elsewhere. Of that fact I received a somewhat peculiar illustration that first Fall. Very naturally it was understood all over the country that the Executive Mansion was a place of necessarily expensive hospitality. It may have been with this idea in their heads that several of his admirers in New York clubbed together to send him a peculiarly fine assortment of wines and liquors without letting him know precisely from whom it came. It was an altogether unexpected kind of elephant, and Mrs. Lincoln at once sent for me in a good deal of a quandary as to what she was to do. We went down to look at it, in the basement where the Express men had left it, but all that I could discover was that the assortment was miscellaneous. I remember remarking that the generous donors did not seem to have left out anything that they could think of.

"But, Mr. Stoddard," said Mrs. Lincoln in evident dismay, "what is to be done? Mr. Lincoln never touches any and I never use any. Here it all is, and these gentlemen—what is to be said to *them*?"

I had to laugh at her discomfiture, but advised that the only course I could see was to acknowledge the gift in due form, to the only address that was provided. As for the wines and liquors, she had better send them to her favorite hospitals and let the nurses and doctors take the responsibility of their future.

"That's what I'll do!" she exclaimed, and that was the end of it, for she was positive that her husband would not allow all that stuff to remain in his own house.

At the great public, official reception which was afterwards maliciously described as "My Lady President's Ball,"[12] though it was not at all a dancing party, there were wines furnished with the refreshments, out of deference to established custom, but that was an exceptional case.

Now, as to that "Ball," I had some fun with it. It was a rigidly formal, official affair. The invitations were limited to certain species of men and women. Senators, Congressmen, Judges of the Supreme Court, members of the Cabinet, generals and high naval men, for there were then no admirals, [and] members of the diplomatic corps, made up quite as large a mob as the White House had room for. But from all over the country came to prominent Washington men urgent applications for invitations, as if these were but free tickets to "the Greatest Show on Earth."

To have granted any of these requests, by favoritism, would have given just offence to the multitude who could not be gratified. The first applicants to be disappointed and to get mad about it were the local representatives of the great northern journals, nearly all of whom appeared to consider themselves sufficiently official or military or naval or judicial or diplomatic to be entitled to tickets. Nicolay and Hay were masters of the situation, but for some reason, perhaps because it was disagreeable and I was young, it was shunted over upon my shoulders, in part, and I found all explanations in vain. A certain number, of course, could be admitted as "reporters," but when I mentioned that fact, the fat was all in the fire. In the language of one excited scribe, "If we cannot come as gentlemen, we will not come at all!"—which was hard upon any fellow who ceased to be a gentleman when he became a reporter. I was in my room one day, when Nicolay sent Hay to see me, in hot haste. Two of Mrs. Lincoln's favorite Congressmen, one of whom was my old friend Caleb Lyon, of Lyonsdale, New York,[13] and the other, my especial friend Gen. Daniel E. Sickles,[14] had asked for tickets for two New York literateurs, an editor of the *Herald*, a daily paper, and Mr. George Wilkes of the *Spirit of the Times*,[15] both of which journals had been anything but complimentary to Mr. Lincoln.

"Stoddard!" exclaimed poor Nicolay. "I can't do anything. It will make all sorts of trouble. She is determined to have her own way. You will have to see to this. She wouldn't listen to me."

"Give me the tickets," I said, "and I'll attend to it."

Down to the Red Room I went, and there were present all the parties to the case. Mrs. Lincoln was smilingly inspecting the cards which she had sent for under the pernicious beguilement of Dan Sickles and Caleb Lyon. They also smiled at me, as I came in.

"May I see you for a moment, Mrs. Lincoln?" I said, and she could see that I was boiling over, wild mad about something, furious but restraining myself, and she followed me into the Blue Room at once.

"What is it, Mr. Stoddard?"

"Mrs. Lincoln! Oh, but won't I give it to Dan and Caleb!"

"Why? What for? What have they done?"

"Why, Mrs. Lincoln, I suppose you have a right to *know*. They have demanded of Mr. Nicolay invitations for those two fellows in there that have been abusing you, personally, and Mr. Lincoln, like pickpockets. If we are to give out extra cards, we had better send them to our friends, not to our enemies. Besides, it would offend some of the best friends we have. I wish you would put your foot down on this and stop it. They can't have the invitations"

"Of course they can't!" she said. "I'll go right in and tell them so."

"And I'll give Sickles and Caleb a wigging!" I declared.

Into the Red Room she went again, to say very firmly: "Gentlemen, Mr. Stoddard, who has absolute charge of this business, tells me that I cannot give you the invitations. I am sorry, of course, but I must abide by his decision."

There was no help for it and they had to give it up, but I did have an interesting little mill with Caleb and the General in the vestibule. As for Mrs. Lincoln, I had felt sure of her. She never really went back on me and she was wide awake to any attack upon her husband. Nicolay and Hay were ready to pat me on the back when I went upstairs and they expressed much wonder as to how I did that thing. At all events, in this case as in some others, all the ugly part of it fell on me and sometimes I was not making friends as fast as you might think.

The only other tellable incident which I remember, connected with that party, was felt by me at the time as of vast importance. It was the singularly good-natured way in which Secretary Seward chaffed me for an awful international blunder that I made in misunderstanding my instructions and leading him and his whole Diplomatic corps, marching solemnly behind him, through the wrong door, so that they wandered away out into the vestibule.

32

A Very Busy Year

The administration of public affairs by Abraham Lincoln actually began on the day of his nomination for the presidency. From that day forward, he became an important factor in all the political movements in the United States and also in some which apparently belonged across the Atlantic.

All the country and a large part of the outside world began listening and waiting to discover what there might be in him. The interest deepened and his actual administrative work increased enormously upon his election, although it would even then be months before he could take the oath of office. Nobody understood him as yet, and as for myself I was but dimly aware of the manner in which I was studying him.

I got a better and better idea of him as I went along, so that I appeared to myself to know, as if by a kind of instinct, precisely what he would do in any given matter. At all events, I referred papers to Departments and bureaus and officials, with remarks and recommendations, or put untellable quantities of stuff into my wastebaskets, with the most supreme calmness, and not once was my decision overruled, not even when a western murderer, a guerilla, was hung in consequence, while his advocates were trying to engineer his pardon.

If I was beginning to understand Mr. Lincoln, I believe he understood me perfectly well, or he would not have placed such confidence in me. He must have seen how entirely I was devoted to him and to the correct performance of my duties. I think I did not understand myself very well. I was really only a very green, energetic sort of fellow, who was fast growing into a knowledge of the ways of a new world which was itself growing along in the mistiest kind of semi-darkness. Nearly all the men and women whom I met, great or small, conveyed to me the idea that they were at sea, or at least were lost in a fog. I could see into it only a little distance myself, but I could see Mr. Lincoln.

The year 1861 was exceedingly busy, but it was a time of the confused, perplexing reorganization of an entirely shattered government. It cannot be too distinctly understood that the old Republic had temporarily disappeared and that all men evidently expected Mr. Lincoln to assume the undefined powers given to the President in emergencies by the unwritten clauses of the Constitution. He became practically dictator, by the common consent of the people, and was therefore not unjustly held responsible for the results of all sorts which were crowding upon us.

I did not see much of him, and for that matter, nobody else did. Nicolay and Hay never entered his office except on business, and they both performed admirably well their manifest duty of keeping out of it as many intruders as they could, high or low. The Winter passed slowly, with the armies apparently almost inactive in their camps and with general dissatisfaction all over the country, as well as a wonderful and increasing amount of utterly devoted patriotism.

Opposed to this was also the tremendous natural reaction which called itself the Democratic Party, although the Old Democratic Party was pouring recruits into the army and many of its leading men were among the staunchest supporters of Mr. Lincoln and of whatever he might see fit to do. The Democratic Cave of Adullam was gathering its clans rapidly, however, and the Republican Party itself was greatly in need of a more thorough organization all over the country. Not only was it new, but a large part of its effective membership was in the army. How the work of reorganization was to be accomplished was ingeniously pointed out to us by our good friends the enemy.

Even before the war, and much more so after it began, the whole South had been honeycombed with political secret societies. One of these was known as The Golden Circle,[1] and it was well understood that it had its branches all over the North. How many other such vipers were wriggling in and out among the anti-Administration elements of the loyal states was more than any one could guess and as for myself I had somehow let my imagination loose in guessing at them. Evidently this devil might be fought with his own kind of fire and several organizations of Union men took form in some of the seceded states. One of these, of which I was afterwards a member, grew to considerable strength in the Southwest. Its outside name may be called the Loyal League and it was more than Masonic in its secrecy.

In West Virginia, for similar reasons, a secret affiliation called The Union League was beginning to make itself useful and Mr. Lincoln saw that this kind of usefulness might be extended as well as increased. When or how he took the matter up, he did not take the pains to come over to the northeast room and tell me, but I remember noting that Judge J. M. Edmonds, the Commissioner of the General Land Office and a close friend and counselor of the President, was making an unaccountable number of shut-the-door visits to the Executive office. He was one of the shrewdest of long, hawk-nosed, twinkle-eyed, sharp-smiling old men, and was said to be the best-informed and most capable politician in the country.

Well, one day he came loping over from Lincoln's room into mine and I was glad to see him, for I liked him particularly well.

"Stoddard," he said. "Good morning. I want you to come down to my room in the Land Office at about seven this evening. Don't tell any one you are coming. Not even Mr. Lincoln."

I told him I would be there, and then half wondered why Mr. Lincoln should send me on an errand which he wished me to conceal from him and not to let him know that he had sent me. At all events, I went at the hour appointed and did not notify the President that I had obeyed him. It might be that here was something that he wished to conceal from himself.

At that hour, the Interior Department building was closed and the watchmen at the doors would not let in even a known clerk without special orders or a permit in writing. At the north door, however, was a guard with a list in his hand, and my name was on it, for he let me in without speaking and I went up to the Commissioner's room. It was large, it was badly arranged, it was sadly in need of some brooms, but it soon had in it over a dozen men, perhaps more than a score, including several of considerable importance—like myself.

Very soon, and before any talking was done, we were all solemnly sworn not to tell that we were there or what we were there for. We were to be and to allow all others to be as ignorant of that meeting and its doings as Mr. Lincoln himself. Then we went to work upon a plan which was all ready for operation, not appearing to require any discussion, and we organized

The Union League of America. The only remaining relic of it that I know of is the Union League Club of New York City which grew out of one of its earlier Councils.[2]

That night, among other things, it was decided to organize a dozen Councils in the City of Washington itself. The construction of Number One was assigned to Judge Edmonds, and of Number Two to myself. He was at once a success, of course, and I did gather a wonderful crowd in Number Two. What was especially wonderful, also, [was that] they elected me its president and I was thenceforth called upon to preside, once a week, over a packed assembly, more than half of which consisted of Congressmen, Senators, Cabinet officers, their assistants, department clerks, and army officers. It imparted to me a queer feeling of advanced age and increasing dignity.

As for the League, it spread with feverish rapidity all over the North. In order that it should do so, large funds were needed, for traveling agents and the like, the hire of halls, all sorts of things, and we had started our machine without a dollar. It was apparently a difficult financial problem, but it was unexpectedly solved. A number of army contractors became members of our Washington councils and they speedily became liberal contributors. So did they also become successful bidders for army and navy contracts but I was never able to perceive any real connection between the contemporary successes. There may have been none, but a good man who put in a hundred thousand dollars obtained so heavy a line of army supply contracts that he was afterwards driven into bankruptcy by an unexpected rise in prices of the materials he had joyfully agreed to deliver. But the treasury of the League was full.

I wish to recall some points concerning the creation of our present system of finance and paper money, for all that we now have is a direct result of the Civil War and its financial requirements.

At the outset of the war, there was absolutely no gold coin in circulation in the United States. Almost the same might have been said of silver coin, since what little we had was altogether insufficient for ordinary trade purposes. Also, whatever we had, of either metal, was steadily disappearing, owing to the demand for foreign exchange, all such balances being for the time against us.

Cotton, with the proceeds of which our foreign accounts had previously been balanced, had ceased to be an important feature in the exchange market. Added to this were the timid hoardings of coin and the pernicious offerings of the silversmiths of two and afterwards even four or five percent premium for silver, for manufacturing purposes. The State banks were said to be increasing in number, but they were by no means improving in character. It was upon this state of things that there now came a tremendous government requirement for an unlimited circulating medium.

The day came when the administration tyrannically declared its power, under an Act of Congress, to issue legal tender for its expenses without any reference whatever to such a fiction as a gold reserve or any visible promise to pay—except that what was on the paper—and that was something which called for patriotic faith. Vast was the outcry of the antiques, including all the original Andrew Jackson men, who loudly averred their unswerving attachment to a "specie basis." But the new currency flowed out like a river, in spite of them, and every man in the country took all he could get of it, even after it went down to little more than half its face in gold value.

It was near the very beginning of this paper flood that some dry joker trifled with the feelings of a large number of his fellow countrymen. Out in front of the White House was a respectable railed enclosure known from ancient times as Lafayette Square. In that day, it had in its center what purported to be a life-size bronze statue of the great Frenchman, but I had sometimes dreamed of him as a larger man. It had been there long and the rain and shine had entirely changed the color of the garments of the noble-hearted friend of George Washington. He was now, therefore, anything but a stylish or handsome hero. Well, one morning, a Washington daily paper announced in conspicuous type that "The Original Greenback" would be on exhibition in front of the White House at nine o'clock. Admission free to all.

The announcement was of interest, even to me, for I knew that editor and had conversed with him upon financial subjects the previous evening. So I went and preempted a post of observation in the portico and awaited the results. Just before nine o'clock these began to come. One column of free Americans marched up Pennsylvania Avenue from the east and another of like character from toward the setting sun. As each of them reached a White House gateway, it wheeled and marched in and advanced steadily to the front of the Executive Mansion. On arriving there, each citizen in turn came to a halt and turned to gaze admiringly at the emerald-rusted statue of Lafayette, facing the other way in the middle of the "square."

He did so because of a small boy who was ready to point out to him The Original. Then it was an interesting undertaking, for a student of human nature like myself, to note the rapidly changing expressions of so many countenances. Also, many of them made remarks of an exceedingly varied and often vigorous, if not eloquent, character. I did not keep any count of those two processions but believe that all their membership were ready to consider this as a strictly mercantile transaction. It was a complete sell.

From the beginning of the greenback era, with it's well-known characteristics, I may as well step right forward across the intervening time to the day when it became only too plain that no more legal tender currency could be put out without dropping the entire mass to something like the fate of the old Continental currency which disappeared altogether at the end of the War for Independence. It was almost as plain that no more government loans could be floated, largely on account of the many reverses suffered by our armies and the dispirited condition of the nation. In this emergency, the National Bank scheme was brought forward. As is well known, it proposed a loan of four hundred millions of dollars, with the privilege to the takers of the bonds of employing them as a basis for banking, including the issue of bank notes as money.

The entire scheme was bitterly opposed, even by many sincere patriots, especially by all the old-fashioned "Jackson Democrats." These gentlemen discovered in it a resurrection of the United States Bank which had been done to death by Old Hickory. There was an all but desperate state of affairs created, after several of the preliminary votes in House and Senate had appeared to indicate the probable defeat of the bill. The entire organism of the government was threatened with financial paralysis and already the pay of the soldiers was in danger of getting behind hand as badly as in a former day had that of George Washington's Continentals. Moreover, there was to be discerned an increasing jealousy among many legislators of what they called "The interference of the Executive with the Constitutional powers and freedom of the Legislative branch of the government."

There came an evening when a number of leading statesmen, Republicans who were most strenuously opposed to the Bank Act, were all invited to attend an important meeting of the Central Council of Twelve of The Union League. I was a member of that important body, as well as honorary Grand Corresponding Secretary, and the meeting was to be at the rooms of Judge Edmonds in the General Land Office. I think that only select members of the Grand Council were present, but there was a rare lot of intelligent statesmen and they had wonderful reports to hear of what the Union League was doing and could do, especially in their own states and districts. It was, indeed, as if we were proud to show and explain to them how very much we could do for them at the next election. Judge Edmonds was a capital hand at lucid explanations and I have never heard anything done better. They listened with intense interest and then, as the still time floated by, they found themselves led on into a discussion of the needs of the treasury and the absolutely imperative need for the four hundred millions of dollars provided for by the Bank Act. Of course, I cannot imagine why Edmonds now and then appealed to me, on point after point, or how, at last, I came to be faced so sharply by Senator Timothy Howe, of Wisconsin, as spokesman for himself and other recalcitrant anti-bank men. He and I had been good friends, however, and he was a genuine patriot. I can pretty well recall, now, one of the fag ends of that controversy, and how deeply, or ridiculously, I felt that the fate of all the banks to come, or not to come, depended upon me and upon my ability—or cheek—to give convincing answers.

"Well now!" he said, at last. "I did not so understand it. If I could only be assured that the President felt so deeply about it, personally. I did not know that his views were so positive—"

"The President, Mr. Senator," I replied, "is always cautious, and wisely so, about saying or doing anything which might be construed as Executive interference with the independence of the Legislature."

"Of course he is!" exclaimed Howe. "But then! I had no idea! Do you mean to say, of your own knowledge, that he regards—that he has said—or that he would look upon any man who voted against that bill as a public enemy?"

"By no means, Mr. Senator," I at once responded. "Do not misunderstand me. I have said nothing of the sort. He has said nothing whatever nor would he assume such an attitude. Far from it! He would only feel and would be compelled to say that the men who defeat the bill are cutting off pay and supplies for the armies in the field; starving the soldiers; forcing the abandonment of campaigns; preventing enlistments; acting as reinforcements to Lee and as supporters of Jeff Davis. That is all I meant. Of course, he would not influence in any way."

"That'll do, sir!" rasped the Senator. "That'll do. I do not want to hear any more. He shall have his bill! Judge Edmonds, is there any more business for us to attend to?"

That was about all, but somehow, every enemy of the Bank Act went home that night in company with a fellow who believed it the only salvation of the army and the country besides being a blessing to the whole world. Many long years afterwards, however, I discovered that Mr. Howe had really never forgiven me for my anti-Jackson raid upon his patriotism.

I suppose I hardly need to say that my duties in the Red Room, in care of Mrs. Lincoln's receptions, brought me in contact with a large variety of remarkable people. So did the President's public receptions, at which also I was on duty with the Lady of the White House. On the whole, nevertheless, I must give the palm to the old northeast room for rare studies of human character or the lack of it. As to the latter, I must not fail to record one remarkable specimen.

He was pointed out to me at a later day as being probably the worst man in the United States, but the first time I saw him he was in the hallway, waiting to obtain an interview with the President. He was of medium height, with long, silvery white hair and the most sanctimonious of faces. He was dressed in shining broadcloth, with a white necktie of voluminous folds and a diamond pin, a new silk hat, and a costly overcoat. From his outfit, he might have been a doctor of divinity and he may have imagined that he had taken in an old hawkeye of a criminal lawyer like Abraham Lincoln, for he did get into the office. He had not quite done so. The next day, he came again and for some reason I was standing at the door of my room when I saw him suddenly emerge from the Executive Chamber with the likeness of a large and propulsive boot just behind him. I asked no questions and cannot say how it was that I was so very quickly thereafter down in Willard's Hotel, gazing into its gorgeous barroom. There, at the bar, had gathered a splendid array of "sporting men," as they would have called themselves, and with them, as sleek and unabashed as ever, was the white-haired party whom they addressed as "General." There were glasses out and as he lifted up his own he rolled up his pious eyes and exclaimed, sonorously: "Brethren, let us drink!"

Speaking of sporting men, Washington City had always been a favorite field for the gambling fraternity. The legends were many concerning the card-playing propensities of some of the old-time statesmen, and quite a number of those now on hand were well known faro and poker players. There were old and all but famous gambling houses which were in full blast but to which the entree was not easy to obtain. Smaller and meaner resorts were open to all who came, but only "gentlemen" with long purses were welcome in the grand and costly-luncheoned hells. There was a great increase in the gambling mania as greenbacks grew more plentiful and easier to get hold of. I found, too, that the old custom of "making the game interesting" still obtained at private parties, whether of whist or euchre. I was fond of whist but did not care much for either euchre or poker. A sort of club rule generally prevailed of making a limit of not to exceed five dollars a corner at whist and two-and-a-half at euchre.

Partly because of the legends and partly out of curiosity, born of my studies of human nature, I visited the really celebrated Joe Hall's and some of the other hells, a number of times. I was much interested in what I saw but could not entirely understand why any fairly good mathematician should go crazy over that particular method for throwing away his money. At Joe's, which was decidedly the best specimen den, I saw, on one occasion that was not more remarkable than another, among the distinguished crowd in the elegantly furnished rooms, Baltimore and northern businessmen, planters, judges of courts, lawyers, prominent members of Congress, army contractors, and the like. One of the faro dealers came to me to ask if I saw any army paymasters, commissaries, or quartermasters. He said that fighting generals, if we had any, would not be out of order, but the War Office had sent a notification that they must not admit any government officers, not even from the Treasury, whose duties put them in charge of public money. I was able, after a brief search and after sending a man out, to assure him that his coast was clear and that he was free to plunder anybody I saw there. They never plundered me and I do not think I was cut out for a gambler. In fact, I was more than once sarcastically informed that I was about the coolest young party in Washington and was inquired of as to whether anything on this earth could excite me. I remember that on one occasion a well-known banker was told by a friend that he believed he had met me on Pennsylvania Avenue, but he was not sure.

"'Well,' said the banker. "Was he walking fast?"

"Ye-es, pretty fast, seemed to be in a hurry."

"Doubtful. Did he have a cigar in his mouth?"

"No. He didn't."

"That's all. You didn't meet Mr. Stoddard. Not if he was in a hurry. He never was. And no cigar, either."

That too was at a time when John Hay was almost angrily telling me that he considered me a kind of miracle of hard work and that I could do more without showing it than any other man he had ever seen. He abused me, also, for being what he called "statuesque" and always inclined to strike attitudes and take positions, but I replied that the latter was just what we were wishing the army would succeed in doing.

33

Wartime Enterprises

*I*t was a brain-busy time. All the wheels of activity were rolling on diligently, swiftly, except the wagon wheels and artillery wheels of the Army of the Potomac. These, indeed, were so quietly resting in their lazy camps that the whole country had grown weary of reading in the newspapers the stereotyped announcement that "All is quiet on the Potomac."

The vociferous response of "On to Richmond" had also become a stereotyped re-print. From what has already been set forth, it may be imagined that my own brain was pretty well occupied, but there was still room in it for the formation of many plans and the development of a number of curious undertakings. Speculation in stocks and gold, especially the latter, was all the while running insanely wild in New York and other financial centers, and I formed an idea that it was almost true patriotism to be what was called a "bear" in gold. I therefore went in, a little at first and then deeper. I had good correspondents, was not by any means a bad judge of the changing situations and their effects upon the markets. On the whole, I succeeded pretty well, rarely making any important losses, except in stocks. I had not the least idea that there was anything wrong in it for a fellow in my position, and made no secret whatever of my transactions.

My leading associate in New York was a banker named Edward Wollf, "Wollf & Dike." He was a German by birth, of good family, highly educated, and we formed a strong personal friendship as well as business alliance. Not a great while after our first meeting, I was called upon to make a flying trip to New York to attend his wedding with a daughter of Mr. A. M. W. Ball of Elizabeth, New Jersey, the author of "Rock Me to Sleep," in its original form. Afterwards there was a long newspaper controversy as to the claims of a then pretty well-known authoress, but I had seen the entire original from which the published verses were selected and was well convinced that all the fair poetess had to do was to change them somewhat, so, for instance, that she, a beauty of eighteen, might the better ask "time to Smooth the few silver threads out of my hair, etc.," as the old gentleman had done, more appropriately. It makes me sad, now, to think of the end of it all. Years later under the pressure of disasters, Wollf went temporarily insane and committed suicide. I attended his funeral.

But about my speculations. Strange as it may seem, there were those who did not like me. Many of them. I was too positive to be popular.

The fact was that all sorts of men were dipping into the great gambling river of Wall Street. My own dippings were made alongside with those of senators and statesmen, not one of whom thought of concealment or supposed that he was doing anything which his position forbade him to do. We were all under the excitement of a tremendous fever to which none of us had ever before been subjected. I think, however, that the first strong impulse toward speculation came to me from my expense account, which was unpleasantly increasing. A salary of fifteen hundred dollars was sadly inadequate for a fellow who had upon his hands so many costly affairs, public and private, and who, by reason of his brother and sister, was really a man of family. Harry cost me something, but Kate cost me a great deal, for her social position had its imperative demands of many kinds and I was altogether willing to meet them.

I now come to the story of my exceedingly curious vacation, in the early Fall of 1862. I was well entitled to a vacation and I went to the President about it. I even told him what I proposed to do with my outing and he smiled kindly, audibly. The state of affairs was this. Our army under Gen. Ambrose E. Burnside,[1] had captured the most important points of the North Carolina coast, including New Berne, the mouth of the Neuse River, Fort Mason, etc. I had learned that the Navy Department was greatly in need of tar, turpentine, and other naval materials, and especially of white oak timber, seasoned if possible, for the new gunboats that were to be constructed. I had also learned that large quantities of crude turpentine, ready for distillation, were lying on the banks of the Neuse, a little way up, and also much tar. Moreover, there were large rafts of white oak and some pine.

I consulted with the Navy Department and agreed to let them have all this stuff at regular contract prices, if they would send me a tug to New Berne, by way of the Albemarle Canal and Sound, then reported clear of interference. What I did not know was that at that date there was a vicious jealousy between the two departments, War and Navy. I arranged for capable assistants and for the sending down of a shipload of supplies for the proposed trading, in a keel chartered by other parties.

Mr. Lincoln gave me a rousing letter of introduction "To all officers of the Army and Navy" and with it a special pass as his private secretary, ordering all human beings met by me to give me a lift. Then I bought a new blue suit, which might indicate rank on land, water, or otherwise, and went to New York to find a passage to North Carolina.

Down on the Hudson River front, I learned, was the office of the Commissary in charge of transportation, and I went to see him. He was of the high rank of Major, but I did not at all know how high that might be until I got into his office and waited humbly outside of a railing until my turn came to have him turn in his chair of state and cast his august eyes upon me. I had never before seen such concentrated authority and dignity in my life and felt like a black beetle in the presence of a king. It was awful! I modestly stated my desire for transportation and was at once sternly overwhelmed by the assertion that there were altogether too many "civilians" obtaining passages to here and there and that no more such unmilitary wickedness would be allowed. This was from a chap who had never drilled an awkward squad, nor with one, and had never been anything more warlike than a grocery clerk. I strengthened myself, however, and faintly held out to him some pieces of paper. One was from the Secretary of War and one from the Secretary of the Navy, and both were mandatory, but he had hardly feasted his mighty eyes upon them before he was asked to gaze upon another manuscript containing the words "My Private Secretary" and "Abraham Lincoln."

He had roundly asserted that there were no vessels of any kind going to North Carolina, but he suddenly remembered something, just as he jumped out of his chair and stood up tall to bow to the Secretaries and the President as represented by this civilian in the new blue suit. There was a steamer to start for New Berne that very afternoon, and the great men could have a stateroom all to themselves, as there were no other passengers. I assented and went on board with a curious idea of the amount of politeness which could be suddenly knocked into one great man by three or four others.

It was a pretty little craft, whose name escapes me. She was of about six hundred tons' burden and all her inwards were burdened with supplies for the army. Her staterooms were on deck and there was only one of them besides those required by the officers. Her other passengers consisted entirely of an enormous deckload of baled hay for the horses under General Burnside. That is, under his cavalry and artillery.

I had been at sea before, for I had fished for bluefish off Point Judith in rough weather and I had put into my bag a dozen lemons for use in case I should feel symptoms of sea-sickness—though I did not really believe I would. Old sailor, you know. Well! We went away from New York and out upon the briny deep finely enough. I spent most of my time on deck, gazing at the Atlantic and getting acquainted with the Captain, a right good fellow, and his crew.

The nights followed the days, for the hay was in no hurry, and my lemons did well by me, but as we drew near the ugly point of land known to the maps as Cape Hatteras, we ran into the heel of a tremendous gale which had been mean enough to blow from the east and toward the continent of North America. It was not so much the wind, you know, as it was the awfully rough, chopping sea, some of its grown-up billows long legged ones, that played the ancient Henry with our top-heavy steamer. How she did roll! We were driven so near the land, the long, low, miserable sandbar between the ocean and the Sound, that we could see across it, and away ahead of us we could dimly discern the low-nosed outline of the Cape. I crawled forward, holding hard the rail, to where the Captain and mate were holding on with steady grip, and I inquired of him:

"I say, Captain, what are we to do?"

"Do?" he responded, courageously. "Why, I'm going to keep her this side up, most of the time, if I can. Kind o' doubtful."

"Can you round the Cape?"

That was what we had been trying to do, for hours, and the boat had seemed to make hardly any headway against that sea. If she should fail, we were to be smashed against the Cape, as so many other unlucky craft had been and the hay would have been lost. But the captain was staring landward and after a minute or so of silence he turned to me, pointing westward with outstretched arm and a resolute face.

"Do you see that there sandbar? Well! If I find I can't steam it round the

Cape, I'm going to head this boat for that bar and run her up on shore as far as I can. It's our only chance. Through the breakers."

I was looking at them and I must say that they were a credit to the gale and to the ocean. They were tremendous. He further remarked that he believed he could do it and save some of us—perhaps.

All steam was on, however, and after another hour or so of doubt and of considering the breakers, we did round the Cape, but we passed it so nearly that I was in some uncertainty whether or not, after all, it might not decide to come on board. Beyond that, all was plain sailing and in due season we were pointing our nose toward the wretched gap in the bar known as "Something or other Inlet." We could hit it and did so, but a short distance to the left, when we went through, was the dismasted hulk of a large ship, three-master, which must have struck at high water, so very high and dry was she driven upon the bar. She was not broken up. We saw no signs of occupancy, but she was a striking commentary upon our own captain's notion of the right way to escape the breakers.

Steaming across the Sound was nothing and then we were tied to the hitching posts of a long, dingy-looking wharf in the ancient harbor of New Berne, at the mouth of the Neuse.

It was a large town, rather than city. It had been a cotton port, of course, with some trade in tobacco and lumber and wheat, but its main celebrities were tar and turpentine. Here were said to be the largest turpentine distilleries in the world. Not knowing if that is true, I will assert that they were indeed very extensive and so were the dreary forests of tar pine that spread away into the interior for I do not know how many sandy miles beyond New Berne.

My first duty after landing was to call upon the commanding general [Burnside—ed.] and pay my respects. On presenting my credentials, I found that I had made the acquaintance of one of the pleasantest men I had ever met. It was an acquaintance that afterwards became even more agreeable when he came to Washington as United States Senator from Rhode Island.

His headquarters were in a quiet frame dwelling house and he came out into the piazza to welcome me. I had looked for army style, and here it was, for the Major General commanding this Department was arrayed in a plain sack suit of white flannel, no signs of war on it, but just the right thing for the weather we were having. He was all smiles and good humored, took especial care in providing me with proper quarters. These were with a brigade paymaster and thereby was to hang an adventure. My next call was upon Governor Stanly, the Military Governor of North Carolina,[2] but I had already sent out my emissaries after crude turpentine. He entered into my plans with spirit and expressed a hope that I might be able to do something to stir up industries for the benefit of the people of the state as well as for that of the Navy Department at Washington.

He did more than to say pleasant, encouraging things. As Military Governor, he was a kind of autocrat and he at once turned over to me the largest turpentine distillery in New Berne. It was a tremendous affair, fitted up with huge brazen retorts in which were coiled up the worms and there were all sorts of appliances in perfection. I had other interviews with my good friend General Burnside, and he heartily approved of my enterprise. In one thing I seemed to be fortunate. There were quantities of crude turpentine already in New Berne, waiting patiently for a cash purchaser, and within twenty-four hours from the signing of the order giving me possession there were charges in all the retorts of that distillery. I felt good when I saw the great clouds of black smoke going up from it and looked forward to grand things. Nevertheless, all the material on hand would last but a few days and then I would have to wait for my tug and for supplies from up the river. These, I was again informed, were quite sufficient to carry the concern along. In the meantime, I might as well take a vacation and I took one.

It was taken on this wise. Out along the coast a number of miles and with a view to the protection of the harbor, the United States had constructed, long before the war, the very respectable fortress known as Fort Mason. It had been captured by Burnside's men and was now held by a considerable garrison of Union troops. It was nearly time for these to receive a large amount of pay and back-pay and two paymasters had been assigned to that duty. One of them was the very pleasant gentleman with whom I had quarters and he invited me to go with him and inspect the fort. We had formed almost a friendship and I gladly accepted.

While the paymasters were getting ready and my distillery was using up its last crude turpentine, I employed my time on general inspection duty. One of my first visits was to the battlefield, the curious peninsular isthmus of an affair along which our troops had charged when they stormed the Confederate works and captured New Berne. I wondered, at first, how it was done with so comparatively small a loss in killed and wounded and made up my mind that the shooting had not greatly resembled the work done at Bunker Hill.

But I learned something. All the ground in front of the breastworks, except for a short distance, had been left covered with a fairly thick growth of small-bodied second growth tar pine trees and through this forest our men had made their rush, partly protected by it from a storm of rifle balls. But there was one thing more. The Confederates had forgotten the order of Putnam at Bunker Hill. Hundreds of bullet marks on the pine trees testified that in the excitement of the moment the men behind the breastworks had fired too high. Very few of the shots were low enough, as "Old Put" had known they were likely to be. Then our men went over with the bayonet and all was done.

Another visit, oddly enough, was to the two army graveyards and here I found another subject for investigation. It led me to halt on the street a Confederate Colonel, prisoner of war, fine fellow, with whom I had become acquainted.

"How is this thing?" I asked. "You didn't lose half as many men as we did in the fighting. Your troops are all acclimated and you ought not to have had so many in hospital. But look at the difference in the death rate, as testified by the graveyards. I can't understand it."

"Come along with me," said the brave fellow, with a saddened face. "I can explain all that to you."

He led me on to what I now remember as a large, wooden, white-painted church, with a tall steeple, which had been occupied by our army for hospital purposes. On entering, he turned to the right and we were in a cheerful room, of moderate size, over the door of which were the large lettered words "Christian Commission." Here were two or three men and women at work among all the appliances that the warmhearted people of the North could think of as likely to do any good to their Boys in Blue when they were sick or wounded. I studied the place a little, thinking.

"Come on!" he said, and led me out across the church portico into a similar room on the other side over the door of which was "Sanitary Commission." Here was in part anything the wide world which the Christian Commission had failed to send.[3] I studied the matter and felt a warmth at my heart and a queer feeling in the corners of my eyes, but he said again, "Come on!"

Then we entered the main room, in which so many congregations of good people had worshipped God in the days of peace. There were no pews in it now. In their place were long rows of narrow, iron camp bedsteads, white-covered, pillowed, beautiful, and around and among them passed to and fro on noiseless, slippered feet a lot of angels, male and female, nurses, surgeons, assistants, with here and there a visitor bending low and whispering to some white sheeted form upon a bed. One of them was an old woman, kneeling, sobbing. What for?

"Do you see this?" asked the colonel, sadly. "Well! Our poor fellows had nothing of this kind. No surgeons to speak of. No Christian Commission. No Sanitary Commission. No such supplies. Our officers did not treat their men like men. More like dogs! When one of our men was badly wounded or sick, and went into one of our hospitals—well, it seems to me that hardly one in ten came out again. It wasn't quite so bad as that, but when ten of your men come in here, nine of them get back into the ranks again. Ours are out yonder in the graveyard."

We walked slowly out and I had learned a great lesson concerning the old-time wars and their horrors, as well as concerning the change which has somehow been wrought, even in wars, by the coming of the Christ into the hearts of men and women.

I think it was the next day that our money-carrying expedition set out for Morehead City, across a little arm of the sea from the point of sand on which Fort Mason had been built, with a pine swamp behind it and not much else than swamp between it and the rest of the world, including New Berne. With this latter place it was connected by a one-horse railway from which all the steam engines and other rolling stock had been removed by the Confederates, long ago. In doing so, however, they had left behind them a large platform handcar and this was to be the chariot of our expedition. The motive power was to be furnished by a sergeant and four stalwart volunteers, armed, while the passengers consisted of two Pay Majors, one clerk, one Presidential Secretary, elected "colonel" by the soldiers, and the greenback treasure was in a large, ironbound wooden box, securely locked.

I think we must have set out at a late hour, for the shades of night were falling fast when our machine pulled up at an army outpost, where an officer came out of a shed to meet us. He was a kindhearted man, for he informed us that all the pickets on the line of that railroad had been swept in by the roving bands of the Confederates the previous evening. They had been replaced and other precautions had been taken, but he cautioned us that it would be well to be prompt in answering any hails we might hear, on penalty of being fired into at short range, for the picket boys would be unusually wide awake. We all determined to be so and our train went on out of that station. At that hour, up from the wide and rolling sea, so near at hand, came a fog so dense that you might have leaned against it, and a kind of night was upon us. Also, not many minutes later, upon us came falling water. I can't say it was a storm of rain, for the water seemed rather to fall in blocks, each of them of about my size. I had experienced rains, on the prairie and elsewhere, of which I had had a high opinion, but this thing beat them all and I knew why vessels sometimes filled and foundered in the neighborhood of Cape Hatteras.

We were now out beyond solidities and were running along through a swamp, with occasional gleams of open water on either side of us. It was very dark, and the passengers and other people were peering nervously around them into that dense gloom but they did not see anything. Pretty soon, however, they heard something.

"Halt!" came hoarsely from a solid mixture of air, water, and peril many paces in advance of us, at the left.

"Picket!" exclaimed the sergeant. "We must halt and give the counter-sign, or we'll be fired into. There won't be any trifling this time."

There was none, for the power ceased working, the brakes were applied successfully and one of the men stepped off into the swamp, nearly waist deep, to answer that hail as it ought to be answered. He shouted, too, and he even told who we were, but no further utterance replied to him and the darkness grew deeper. We waited, prudently, until one major declared that it would be safer to run and run we did, the power doing wonderfully well, but before we had speeded a mile there came to our ears once more that hoarse and threatening "Halt!"

Again we obeyed, and again the eager soldier sprang out into the morass to answer the hail. He waded and he swore but it was of no use. It was decided by all of us that this picket also had hidden away in the dark to avoid capture by the enemy. For a similar reason, we again set forth, but our troubles and dangers traveled with us. Those loud-voiced North Carolina swamp frogs halted us five times before we really answered a United States army demand from an outpost at the end of our journey. Here, however, a kind of explanation was given by a galoot who remarked that every picket on the line knew the sound of the wheels of that handcar and wasn't going to come out of his cover on account of it. He knew it wasn't a Confederate car.

How large a seaside watering place Morehead City might be, it was impossible to ascertain right away, but I had heard that it had had a deal of popularity before the war. Elegant residences had been built there by rich planters and others from the interior and even from the North and the neighborhood of the fort and its garrison had aided it. It contained, however, but one large hotel, by no means a poor affair, and to this we directed our drenched and weary way, trying to forget the frogs and the war in a prospect of supper and a fire, for a sharp wind from the rude Atlantic was giving us all the shivers. Alas, it happened that the one hotel was owned and still occupied by a curious character, one of whose most pronounced idiosyncrasies was intense loyalty to the Cause of the Sunny South and a corresponding hatred for everything belonging to its ruthless invasion by the barbarians in blue. On our arrival at the hotel, therefore, we were informed that he could not or would not give us any supper, nor would he kindle any fires in his ample fireplaces, nor would he allow us rooms for the night. All his rooms were locked up and we could not get into them and he was out of wood, anyhow. We were in a quandary, for General Burnside had issued strict orders concerning all treatment of the North Carolina civilians by the troops under his command, but I was not and when one of the dripping volunteers came to me and whispered:

"Colonel! Don't tell them majors, but I found 'er axe in ther woodshed. We might find some wood, if you'd say ther word."

"Get some wood!" I ordered, in my capacity of independent colonel, "and make a good fire in that fireplace!"

More than one of the gallant boys may have found axes, for more than one of them suddenly disappeared, while I remained to expostulate with the obdurate hotelkeeper. We were prepared to pay well for all we could get, and he was bound to take us in, under the provisions of the Hotel Act, but it was all of no avail until I turned to my friends and said: "Well! It's of no use. We are forbidden to employ force, but the boys have their rations with them. They can camp in the kitchen. If they find anything there to cook with, they are entitled to use it."

Just then, a pair of brave volunteers were piling fuel in the fireplace and the landlord stared at them angrily, but another volunteer put some glasses on the table and both majors appeared to have brought their flasks with them. I think one of those canteens was of glass and would have held an alleged quart. A glass was filled for the landlord and he drank solemnly but it failed to mollify him, but the blaze was springing up in the fireplace and he may have heard a noise in the kitchen, for he arose to his feet and made some indistinct remarks to the effect that his hotel could do its own cooking. He must have had a cook at hand, for we really did get a good supper. Paid for it at watering-place prices, too, but there his subservience to the conqueror ceased. He would not give us any rooms and we might camp where we pleased.

"Major," said I, "I know where I'm pleased to camp. Come on boys."

The brave volunteers followed me, like one man, and I led the way upstairs. Here were the usual long corridors, with rows of doors that all were closed against such brutal tourists as we were. The landlord also had come up, with an inquiring expression on his face, and as I paused before one of those doors and beckoned to a volunteer, he demanded: "Colonel! What are you going to do?"

"Why," I benevolently responded, "you said you could not open any of these doors. I can! I found a key down in the woodshed."

The brave volunteer was stepping forward with the axe in his hand, ready to put it into that lock and see if it fitted, when Mr. Landlord suddenly roared "Hold on!" and in his right hand appeared a whole string of keys, of the ordinary shapes and kinds. In a moment more the doors began to come open and we had no more trouble about camping. But just before we finally went up again to our very good beds I called one of the men aside. I had noticed suspicious appearances of polish and even of elaborate carving upon some of the firewood. Whence came it?

"Colonel!" responded the gallant soldier. "Don't ye tell either o' them there majors, but did ye see that mighty good lookin' house, jest along the road there, a ways? Well! Colonel! I reckon that when that there Reb that owns it gits back inter it agin, after the war, he'll have a heap o' trouble a gittin' up sta'rs."

They may or may not have burned the entire stairway, mistaking it for yellow pine firewood, of a high quality. Such are the ways of war!

The morning came and I was up early. So was the landlord, who absolutely appeared to have taken a fancy to me. I cannot say whether it began with the fact that he was paid so well, at a time when other angels were like tourist's visits, few and far between; or whether his exceedingly bitter

Confederatism had been sufficiently manifested and might go to sleep; or that he found me in his sandy soiled garden, pacing along one of the walks in company with his pet, a tame lame-winged seagull, a bird that I discovered to have something like the born genius of Old Man Howe's pet crow, away down on the Embarrass River prairie in the days of long ago. He was a companionable bird but I had to part company with him, eat my breakfast, and then go over with the paymasters to the fort. This was to me intensely interesting, for I took with me a friendly officer and boned him for a full account of the somewhat remarkable manner in which it had been taken, from the landside, its elaborate defenses having been planned with wise reference to a possible attack by a European foe, sitting in warships out upon the water.

As soon as all was over, the soldiers paid, the fort inspected, the seagull and his landlord revisited, we all handcarred it back to New Berne in safety, not even a frog molesting our march through the swamp. Nevertheless, there was news for me at New Berne. I learned there that there was to be no steam tug for me, and therefore neither white oak nor turpentine for the Navy. The War Department had its reports from its officers in McClellan's army that the tug might be captured while in the Albemarle canal, and might then be mounted with heavy guns and employed to bombard them, if they should march down in that direction, which they were pretty sure never to do.

It occurred to me that our vast army might safely have risked the loss of one tug, for it was not running many other risks, just then, but I had to give it up. The new gunboats were afterwards built, indeed, but of green, unsuitable timber, which did not last very long. My shipload of stuff did not lose anything, for I was informed that it was all sold easily. On the whole, I had had quite a vacation and it had not cost me much more than I could reasonably have spent at Newport, for instance. My return to the North was made on the large, fine steamship, the *Helen S. Terry*, and I had a good stateroom but spent most of my time on deck. The fact was that we struck into another storm off Hatteras and the gay boat under me learned to perfection the art of rolling her way through a gale in the character of a corkscrew. On my way down, I may have been too much interested in the surrounding scenery to have time for getting seasick. At all events I had not suffered to speak of, but now, deeply as I was attracted by the size and grandeur of the gigantic billows of the mad Atlantic, I was the sickest Private Secretary you ever saw and vowed that if ever I went to sea again I would avoid Hatteras and corkscrews. On arriving in Washington, I was speedily head over ears in an accumulation of work which was waiting for me in my northeast room.

34

About Mr. Lincoln

I shall make no attempt at bringing out of my treasure house these things new and old in any kind of chronological order. Let it be enough that my memories are now drifting through the Autumn and Winter of the good year 1862. I had long since succeeded in organizing what was known as "The Washington Club," for social purposes, as the one really good restaurant in the city did not offer by any means the desired facilities for political and other assemblies. We secured for it a good four-story, brown, front-residence building, and many were the remarkable gatherings held there before it gave way to time and tide and my own absence.

For my own residence I obtained a lease for a year on Louisiana Avenue, and in it my sister Kate not only kept house for Harry and me and for three of our friends who boarded with us, but also kept a kind of open house for visitors we were willing to show hospitality at our own expense. I found open house an expensive affair and was glad that my business operations, as a whole, were proving profitable—for all the outlay fell upon me and the board charged to Harry and the three favorites was a small figure.

About Mr. Lincoln? Well, I saw him every day, as he went in or came out of his office room, and I now and then had talks with him, but he was generally the most absorbed and unconversational of men. The fact was that he had a great deal on his mind, including office-seekers and the United States of America, with an occasional load put on by the decayed but still troublesome monarchies of downtrodden Europe. I think I was unconsciously making a study of him for future uses and really understood him pretty well.

He was invariably kind and cordial in his treatment of me, but, of course, Nicolay and Hay saw a great deal more of him, day after day, than I did. The two houses of Congress did not know a Private Secretary of any president except by the solemn fact that he came to them with an Executive Message. This kind of carrying was in the hands of Nicolay and Hay and they kept an official cab to do it in. Well, a day came when neither of the other boys was on hand, I think it was in the latter part of '61, and Mr. Lincoln sent for me. I was glad to take my papers and pay my own car fare, without waiting for any White House cab. It was a big adventure when I reached the Capitol, to have the door of first the House, and then the Senate, fly willingly open and hear the doorkeeper announce "A message from the President." That was me. Then the Speaker in one case and the acting President of the Senate in the other was bound to stand up and rap with his gavel and make a similar announcement, loud enough for everybody to hear him.

As to army affairs, the collections of specimen weapons on or about my table and against the walls of the northeast room, continued in considerable varieties. I believe that in my earlier reminiscences I set forth the manner in which the President and I tried the breechloading rifles. It was a funny affair and it had its practical consequences, but he was now occupied with something more than the manufacture of new weapons, or even new armies, for the non-use of the armies already in existence was greatly troubling not only him but the nation.

The troops were technically declared to be "in the field" when it would have been nearer the truth to say that they were in camp. This was more offensively true of the Army of the Potomac than of any of the forces in the West and General McClellan[1] was rightly or wrongly held accountable for the fact that his soldiers were dying in fever-smitten camps rather than on fields of battle. There came an end to the inactivity, at last, in the long series of bloody engagements on the Peninsula,[2] which came of course after the Confederates had been given abundant time for complete preparation, instead of being struck at once, before they were entirely ready. Those fights were largely in the nature of drawn battles, fought to cover a retreat which had also been prepared for. The entire Peninsular campaign had turned out a failure and its general was in Washington in a state of only half-suppressed war with President Lincoln. There was an external appearance of a temporary truce, but some collision or other was evidently not far away.

With reference to my own perception of this fact I will put here an incident which I recall as occurring at a later date. I was in the President's room one afternoon, when nobody else was there, and I ventured to make remarks concerning the commander of the Army of the Potomac. I may even have expressed strong opinions and asked questions, for I brought out the emphatic rejoinder:

"Well, Stoddard, I will say, for organizing an army, for preparing an army for the field, or for fighting a defensive campaign, I will back General Mc-Clellan against any general of modern times—I don't know but of ancient times either—but I begin to feel as if he would never get ready to fight!"

That was one trouble with the very capable commander. Another was his inability to comprehend the fact that he was not yet the President of the United States. Yet another foible was his failure to perceive that he had no supervision of political questions, or constitutional law or amendments, or the great war of races. I liked him, personally, for there was a vast amount of dash and energy in him. I had seen him dashing on a fine horse, at full gallop, attended by a wonderfully brilliant staff, in which were counts and dukes and even princes, as well as the best kind of American officers. They all rode well and allowed him to keep just a little ahead of them. It was a muddy day and they all were in brilliant uniforms upon which spatters of the red clay soil of Virginia might easily suggest the bloody stains of the unfought fields in which none of them had ever been killed.

There came an evening, a dark one, not long before the army was called upon to march up the river to Antietam Creek and meet the invading force under General Lee, when a fine opportunity was given me for understanding the real nature of the truce between the civil and the military powers of my beloved country. I had them both under my mental microscope for an entire evening and it was one of the most interesting studies that I ever went into. I was studying all the while, too. I was sitting at my desk. The hall door was open and I was so absorbed in some epistle or other that I heard no sound of anyone coming in to interrupt me until a low voice at my shoulder said to me:

"Leave that and come with me. I am going over to McClellan's house." I arose at once but did so without any reply whatever, for there was something in Mr. Lincoln's voice and manner which seemed to forbid any remarks on my part. I do not know that he appeared to be taller than usual, but there was a world of dignity hanging about him and, with it, something or other that was not to be instantly interpreted. He did not give me any portfolio or papers to carry but I quickly gathered an idea that the President, the constitutional Commander in Chief of the Army and Navy of the United States, was going to call upon the general in command of the Army of the Potomac, attended only by his "official staff."

He was arrayed in a black frock uniform and I in a neatly fitting sack suit which carried no epaulets. Neither of us wore either sash or sword and we did not glitter. Down and out we went and the distance to be traveled was not long. He did not utter one word, nor did I, but I was strongly impressed with the fact that there was something or other on his mind. All the while a kind of rebellious feeling was growing within me, for I inwardly growled that the President ought to have sent for his subordinate, commanding him to come, instead of in this way or any other going to call upon him. All that could be said, or thought, however, was that this was Abraham Lincoln's way and it was not to be disputed by a mere "staff," like myself.

The house was reached and entered and we were shown into a well-furnished front parlor. Put it square in shape, with the usual fireplace and mantel and a center table. I went over to the right and sat down in a chair but the President took a seat in the middle back. He was calm, steady, even smiling, but in half a minute there was no room there at all. Only Abraham Lincoln, filling the place brim full.

Our names had been carried upstairs, I knew, but long minutes went by and I felt the hot blood surging into my cheeks, hotter and hotter with every moment of what seemed to me a disrespectful waiting time. Not so the great man over there beyond the table, for he was as solid as ice and pretty near as cool.

Then, for the hall door was open, I could hear a sound of a kind of preliminary rattle at the head of the hall stairway. Then a kind of jingle, mingled with slow footsteps, began to descend the stairs. It was the great general himself, in full uniform, followed by his chief of staff, General Marcy,[3] and an army colonel. The jingle came from their dangling swords and they were certainly a very impressive trio to be confronted by so plain a pair as we were. They were brilliant and we were not. General McClellan may have thought that he had come downstairs to formally receive the President, impressively, hospitably, dignifiedly, or anything of that kind, but that was where he was altogether mistaken. He had entered that parlor to be received there, very kindly, by President Abraham Lincoln, who somehow had taken possession and was the only man in the room. I had passed out of sight but was watching, with a growing sense of being a bigger staff than the other. The conference began almost immediately, for a kind of réport of the situation and of plans was plainly called for. It was given, in a masterly way, for McClellan was a thoroughly scientific soldier and knew perfectly well how to present his side of the questions at issue. He was a man of nerve strength, too, and I admired him, as he went on into what was made more and more evidently a grand wrestling match, with the control of the armies for the prize of the winner. Also, the future control of the political situation or field and the next presidency of the United States. That important point was really settled before the wrestle was over, for it was a long one.

Lincoln listened well and said little, at first. Then, a word at a time, he began to open, expanding visibly as he went on, and the match became intensely interesting. Grapple after grapple, tug, strain—down you go! Perfect accord, perfect good will, perfect good manners, not a trace of excitement on either side. There was, in fact, a mutual yielding of all the points under discussion, but at the end of it they had been all yielded by General McClellan, with the grandly courteous assistance of that handsome, polite, and capable chief of staff, General Marcy.

I had sat still and internally refused to give up anything, for I was the brilliant and capable staff of the Commander-in-Chief. Silence was my stronghold, and I held it tenaciously. A close came, and Mr. Lincoln and I were ceremoniously shown to the door. The parlor we left behind us was still, to my mind, full of Mr. Lincoln, although he had walked out, and other men might now appear to be there. Never before had I so fully appreciated what I had read about as personal power or magnetism, or personified human will in its highest development. The will of Lincoln had been stronger than that of McClellan.

We went back to the White House and I do not think that either of us uttered a word until I saw the great man safely enter his office and close the door behind him—that he might be alone with his purposes for the country and the future. What one of those purposes was nobody on earth had any idea until a later day, but it was quite enough to make him wish to be alone with it—and with God Almighty—for yet another grand wrestling match, that night. It may have taken all night, for all I know, but he won it. Not many days afterwards, General McClellan led his forces up the valley to the battles of South Mountain and the Antietam.[4] Both were reported as victories and General Lee was driven back into Virginia, but there was believed to be a fault, somewhere, in the very fact that he was permitted to get away. However that may be, the echoes of our really first great victory in a contested field were still reverberating over the country and finding their sonorous way back to Washington, when, one afternoon [a few days later—ed.], as I sat at my table and my letters, John Hay came hastily in with a sheet of foolscap paper in his hand and a white sort of flush on his face. There was something the matter with him as he put down the paper before me.

"Stod," he said, "the President wants you to make two copies of this right away. I must go back to him."

I took the paper and some fresh sheets and went at it, mechanically, in the ordinary course of business, as cool as a cucumber. Then, as I went on, from sentence to sentence, word to word, I wrote more slowly and with a queer kind of tremor shaking my nerves.

Then I looked up from my work and listened, for far away, nearer, near, I could hear the sound of clanking iron, as of breaking and falling chains, and after that the shouts of a great multitude and the laughter and the songs of the newly free and the anger of fierce opposition, wrath, fury, dismay. For I was writing the first copies from Abraham Lincoln's own draft of the first Emancipation Proclamation.

These went back to his office, care of John Hay, and the original remained in my drawer, with a secret purpose on my part to "smouch" it, until one day John came for it, to send it to Chicago, for uses at the great patriotic Fair there, and for subsequent burning up in the great fire.[5]

35

The Long Winter of 1862

There were a great many other things taking place in my neighborhood in the Fall and Winter of 1862, but most of them were of more interest to me at the time than they would now be to anybody else in the telling. They may be allowed to rest untold.

One little occurrence has always seemed to me to have an element of fun in it and I will put it in. Some time after the city received its additional garrison from the Peninsula and elsewhere, the general in command of the political fort issued a very stringent precautionary mandate. The occasion of it was a big fire which consumed large quantities of hay, straw, wagons, sheds, supplies, and withal, a number of Union Army horses. The fire was said by some to have been maliciously kindled by Confederate sympathizers or agents, but the more probable theory pointed to a carelessly thrown-away cigar. Therefore the order went out with an all but hysterical prohibition of smoking in or near "any of the public buildings." Strictly construed, it would have forbidden Members of Congress to smoke in or near their incombustible "cloak rooms," and burning tobacco would have been shut out of the Treasury.

It was just getting dark one evening. I had been to dinner and was returning to my endless toil at the White House. This was now under strict military supervision. At each of its Pennsylvania Avenue Gates, and elsewhere, there were regularly posted sentries, one on foot and one on horseback. No passwords or countersign were required of those who came or went, but it was supposed to be now assured that the Executive Mansion and its inmates were not to be captured and carried off to Richmond in the night.

I drew near the eastern gate, with my mind busy with matters of vast importance, when I was aroused to this present world by a fiercely gruff: "Put out dot cigar!"

"What?" I exclaimed, in bewildered forgetfulness of the fire and the orders, but a rifle and a sabre bayonet came suddenly in view and behind it was one of the most zealous patriots you ever saw.

"Put out dot cigar-r-r-r!" came again, husky and stern with authority.

To avoid, it might be, sudden death and then military arrest, I dropped my nearly exhausted weed, but just then I heard something else.

"Mr. Secretary!" came loudly from the mounted guard whose horse was stepping around in the gateway while the rider was rocking back and forth in the saddle in what appeared to be a kind of fit. Then he wheeled his gallant beast alongside of me to say, as well as he could:

"It isn't an hour since Germany halted Stanton,[1] right there, just as he did you!"

"Did he make him throw away his cigar?"

"Well, he did. Stanton all but ran against him, in the dark, and Germany shouted at him: 'Put out dot cigar!' till he gave it up. But that wasn't all. Stanton laughed, but he hadn't more'n got out of sight before old Seward, he came along, and he's almost always a smokin'"

"Did he halt Seward?"

"You bet! He pointed his frog sticker at him and yelled, 'You put out dot cigar-r!' 'I guess not!' said Seward, and he was going right on, through the gate, but he had to halt and stand still and no kind of explanation was worth a cent. Out it had to go before he could pass in."

"Stanton and Seward, both?"

"That isn't all, though. Seward got away without being prodded, but a few minutes later along came old Ben Butler,[2] as large as life, and he was swinging right in. 'Halt! You put out dot cigar!' shouts Germany and Ben halted. 'Are those your orders?' he asked. 'Does is my orters. Put out dot cigar!' 'Orders are orders,' said Ben, as his cigar went over the fence, 'and they must be obeyed. There it goes.' You ought to ha' seen it and heard it."

The cavalryman made his story good in the telling and then he chuckled back to his post, but I did not hear any horse laugh. I made the best of my way to Mr. Lincoln's room and felt that I was doing him good for I never heard him laugh harder.

"Seward, and Stanton, and old Ben?" he said. "Well, I reckon I'd better send for the officer on duty and tell him to let up a little. The orders against smoking do not include this part of the camp."

The officer came, a young captain, and he may have been glad of an unexpected private interview with Father Abraham, for all the reprimand he received was some good-natured fun. Out he went, grinning, and there was no more peril at the gates for smokers.

Speaking of Butler, he was a character that ought not soon to be forgotten. He was an original and made his mark upon the time in several ways. One of them was his memorable declaration that all fugitive slaves were to be retained, as fast as captured, for they were manifestly "Contraband of war" since they might be used in various ways against us by the enemy. They were dangerous, particularly, because of their probable employment in shoveling hostile dirt for the making of forts. He did not send back any that came within his lines. The night of the forbidden cigar, he was in the ordinary rig of the Army, but I never saw him wear quite so much uniform as he did when, in 1861, he came up to pay his respects to the President as a commander of Massachusetts militia. He then wore the full uniform of the Bay State militia Major Generals, and a wonderful disguise it was, with a vast amount of sash, mountainous epaulets, and a scythe sword with a railway curve in it. The cocked hat was also a curiosity of war, or peace.

By the way, it must be remembered that the Army of the Potomac did not come up from the Peninsula in one body, under the immediate command of General McClellan, but by consecutive installments, each of which, as it came, was absorbed, apparently, by what was called "The Army of Virginia," under General Pope,[3] an officer who had gained an enviable reputation in the West, only to come east and lose much of it by being asked to put together a lot of not altogether easily fitted fragments and to handle them as if they were a unified army. There were ugly things in the air as to the probable action of some of the personal friends and admirers of General McClellan, who declared that this was but an underhanded way of cashiering or retiring him without cause and without a court martial to sit on his head. Put it in here that all this was before Lincoln and I had our wrestling match with the old commander of the disappearing Army of the Potomac.

It was a day or so after the Second Battle of Bull Run,[4] as it was called by some people, had been fought and lost. Our Army had fought well, as it always did, but the day had been out of joint and the net result was terribly discouraging. One thing which made it more so, was a venomous rumor that General Pope had not been loyally supported by several of his corps commanders, supposed to be discontented partisans of the displaced McClellan. I was in my room, at my desk, but the silence around me was not disturbed by the usual throng of visitors, for the President had denied himself to all but what might be called "disaster men." That is, Nicolay was at his desk in the other room, and Hay was mourning around, somewhere, as he always did after bad news, for his Patriotism was fairly a burden to him. I saw Stanton come in and go out, and then Mr. Lincoln had a session with General Halleck,[5] a man with a very cloudy face who threw a curious nod at me, through my open doorway and for what I don't know, for I was not an army corps commander with McClellan tendencies. Halleck went out, studying the carpet pattern as he went, and I picked up some letters but then I dropped them, for an agitated voice just across my table exclaimed:

"Bill! I want to see the President!"

I looked up with sudden astonishment, for there were few men then living—there are fewer now—who were at all accustomed to call me by my Syracuse and Homer name. It required a second look to be sure that it was my brother Harry. True, I was aware that he had gone out [in charge of a] detachment of Treasury clerks who had volunteered to go over the Potomac and aid in caring for our altogether too-many wounded soldiers. But then, his ordinarily correct rig had the general suggestion that he had stolen it from some tramp, after the said wanderer had been in the hands of some robbers and the police.

Moreover, there were bloody stains on it, here and there, and so there were on his face, from which he had evidently mopped away the perspiration with powder-stained hands or a sooty handkerchief. Take him all in all, he was a fine representative of a lost battle, and he eagerly repeated his demand. Of course, I asked him why, and then he told me a strange story of how, after many other war experiences, he had been picked up among some wounded men at a roadside by Major General Sumner, an old friend from Syracuse, who had taken him to Major General Slocum, another old Salt Pointer, and how the two of them and another had conducted him to a large tent in which there appeared to have been held a kind of impromptu, volunteer, extraordinary, remarkable Council of War, into which general after general came drifting, somewhat as if he had been sent for and was angrily glad to come.

Henry had been ordered by General Sumner not to take down anything in writing, but to sit back of the other great men and hear and remember every word any of them might see fit to say, especially keeping track of ranks and names. One of his characteristics was a remarkably retentive memory and probably not anything of importance escaped him.

At the end of it all, as the assembly crumbled away, General Sumner led him out and repeated to him an assertion which he had made when he found him at the roadside: "You are just the man we wanted. Your brother is Lincoln's Private Secretary, and you can get to the President when nobody else might be able to do so. The regular army despatches must tell one story, but you have heard another and it cannot be transmitted now by any army officer, in writing." He seemed to have said more, cautionary and so forth, but that was the sum of it and Harry loyally refused to tell me any more of his report intended for the President. In I went, to see Lincoln's face cloud discontentedly as I came, but in a moment more he stood up and exclaimed, with intense interest:

"Stoddard. Bring your brother right in!"

I did so and very quickly the army messenger was closely closeted with the Commander in Chief and was telling him the professional opinions of that conclave of military leaders. Harry had reached Washington curiously enough. By Sumner's orders, an upset artillery wagon had furnished him with a barebacked mule, upon which he rode as far as the wharf at Alexandria. There a startled Quartermaster gave him a steam tug, on which he was the only passenger, and so he had engineered his way to the White House, and into it by help of Old Edward.

Then the President's bell over my head rang out a sharp summons and I hurried over to see what advice I could give, under the circumstances.

The President had written something on a card and gave it to me.

"Take him to Stanton and then to Halleck. They must see him at once."

"Bill!" said poor Harry. "Then I want to get something to eat, and take a bath, and change my clothes. I've had the worst kind of time."

He looked like it, but when we reached the War Office that card of Lincoln's carried us right past a crowd of men in shoulder straps and uniforms, and even through a mob of waiting Legislators and Bureau men. Henry was in with Stanton quite a while. Then they came out together and went across the passage into General Halleck's office. Just what took place there and what influence it had upon the subsequent conduct of the war, I do not know, but at last the scarecrow from the lost battlefield was set at liberty to go and rest and wash and eat.

Away back of all this, which comes to memory more easily because it is closely connected with things to come which are on top in my mind, there were several occurrences of a somewhat personal nature which are wintertime history. Some of them were curious, too, and I will try and freeze them in, seeing how nearly I came to being frozen, myself. Before beginning on them, however, I must refer to the fact that there afterwards took place the memorable court-martial of Major General Fitz John Porter,[6] who had been one of the men in the tent with Harry. Long years after, here in Madison, I made the general's acquaintance and related to him the account given me by Henry. He was much interested and soon afterwards I received from him a letter, now among [daughter] Margaret's autographs, in which, as in our conversation, he expressed the opinion, from a somewhat clouded memory, that the council of war was held in the headquarters tent of General Pope himself, but that Pope had not been in it at the time. Porter's own remarks had been among those which were in this manner conveyed, verbatim, to the President, the Secretary of War, and General Halleck. It was a curious piece of business and shows how many unexpected things may happen in a great battle.

My first interesting Winter incident took me all the way back to Champaign [Illinois] and *The Gazette*. On leaving that concern, I had settled my small outstanding accounts, and Kate's, from the advertising accounts then outstanding, and there still seemed to be much money due me. I supposed this was all right with Doctor Scroggs and continued my apparently friendly relations with him while he was in Washington, in sad doubt whether or not he was to receive foreign or domestic appointments with big salaries. Even when the Congressman from our district came to me and asked to whom the post office was to be given, "Crandall or Scroggs? It is one of your appointments." I at once replied "Scroggs" and he was made Postmaster of Champaign. That done, he turned tail on me and repudiated all my settlements, leaving me sadly in debt to my old neighbors, on account of the very newspaper and man I had built up.

It was therefore necessary for me to run back and settle and I put some money in my pocket and did so. At the same time I had in my mind another errand, growing out of the conduct of a runaway New Jersey cashier of a bank in which one of my New York business associates was interested. The banker's name was Sam Hallet and he eventually failed, chiseled me of a large sum, and was shot in Omaha by a railway man who asserted that he also had been chiseled.

I reached Champaign, paid up, was well received by everybody, had a good time, but did not go to see the repudiating doctor. There always had been a screw loose in his organization, making him difficult for me to manage at any time, and he finally died in a lunatic asylum. It was good to see my old friends but that being done I set out for home with an eye for that cashier, of whom I had somehow heard that he was temporarily boarding at the Canada end of the Niagara Suspension bridge, just out of reach of an executive agent of New York courts. That was a place, it was said, where the boarding houses were doing well.

I checked my baggage forward to Syracuse and landed at the Canada side with snow in my eyes, for a terrific blizzard had struck that region. I found, too, that the town was built on a steep sidehill, for in stepping from one of its curbstones I went clean out of sight into a snow bank, out of which I clambered only to shortly be informed that my financier had gone over to Lockport [New York].

There was an unpleasant interruption of railway traffic and time might be of importance. I therefore determined to cross the Suspension Bridge on foot and take my chances for a train on the other side. It was a ticklish thing to do, for the wind was blowing at so many miles an hour and perhaps more. At about the middle of the bridge I had a magnificent view of the vast chasm beneath me and of the white and foaming cloud under which I might suppose the falls to be. It was magnificent, beyond all description, but I had my best view of it lying down and holding on while the fierce gusts swept over me and the wire-drawn structure under me shook and trembled in every limb.

The combined roar of the cataract and the hurricane made a kind of storm music I had never heard before and am in no hurry to hear again. I did manage to walk and crawl until I was once more in my own country and there I found a train about to leave for Lockport. I was one of a sardine box of belated passengers and the cars did stop at the town where the Erie Canal makes its great climb, or descent. I even found my absconder and obtained some small satisfaction from him. Then there was an adventurous train about to set out eastward and I went on board. The storm had now tired of living in Canada and had come across the line, bringing all its Winter baggage with it. The wind blew from all directions but particularly in the direction of that train. The consequence was that somewhat more than halfway to Rochester we were "stalled" in an enormous snow bank and could neither go ahead or pull out. I was informed that no less than six other locomotives were in like manner shut in before morning, in the attempts that were made to come to our rescue.

Oddly enough, the supply of fuel was none too large. We brought it all into the one sleeping car and anxiously awaited day and developments. It was a long and uncomfortable night, with the blizzard all the while making desperate efforts to get into those cars or turn them over. The engineer had been frozen dead at his post and the conductor was badly frostbitten, but there were no other human casualties. Dawn came, at last, and with it a most hospitable invitation from the people of a large and prosperous looking farmhouse at no great distance, to come over and get a good, hot breakfast. Almost at the risk of our lives, we passengers, among whom, fortunately, there were only a few women, managed to climb through or over the intervening drifts and reach the house, except some women to whom their provisions were to be brought by the men. Oh, what angels were those kindly people in that beautiful Winter home, and how well the buckwheat cakes and the bacon and eggs did taste. It was a splendid work of humanity and charity on their part and when it was done and we settled for it, we had only two dollars apiece to pay for buckwheat cakes. I could have bought them for less than that at Delmonico's but then where would have been the sweet charity to fellow beings in distress?

Relief did come, but I did not stop at Rochester for more than a few hours, at that time. I hurried on to Syracuse, to find my father's affairs in such a fix that I was compelled to draw down my bank account unpleasantly to get him out. He had been endorsing again and he had too many dear old friends who were ready to tell him sweet stories of how well they were doing. Besides, he was not yet out of his old woods that had grown up around the costly building of the Baptist Church.

On I went to New York and then to Washington, not having been gone long but having seen, learned, and lost a great deal. I was really glad to be back among my letters and documents, even if some of my experiences obtained for me a laugh from John Hay. I had not by any means proved myself a first-class diplomatist, such as he was.

It was not a great while after the assembling of Congress that I made the acquaintance of a most remarkable character named George M. Willing. He was of an old Philadelphia family, after which one of the streets of that city is named, and he had been educated for a physician. He was still somewhat scientific but had lived a roving and adventurous life as a mining explorer and mountain wanderer. He was now in Washington as a Delegate from the somewhat informal gathering of borderers and Indian fighters who were petitioning Congress to have a certain or uncertain expanse of plains and mountains set off into a new territorial organization.

On that account he had the temporary privilege of the floor of the House of Representatives and it was there that I found him, apparently as much at home as if he had ridden into a gulch on a bronco. He charmed me in many ways, one of which was his enthusiasm as a miner and his readiness to tell wonders of the future and the past. He had a theory as to the nature of the intra-montane and extra-montane system of mineral deposits, especially of gold. He also believed in precious stones, of which he had a few specimens to show, and he was the first man I had met to announce the American existence of tin-stone, of which so much use is now making. He was a tall, well-built man, with hair and eyes and face which made him look like an Indian—and like one did he walk and talk.

One peculiar incident may serve to illustrate him after a manner. His bill for the new territory was before the House. It was about to pass but the committee reporting it had gone all ashore as to the name which they were to give it. Dr. Willing was in one of the seats and a little girl, daughter of a friend of his, had been playing with him. She ran off across the aisle and he called after her in a loud whisper: "Ida! Ho! Come back to me!"

It was the next instant that the chairman of the committee came to bend over and ask him, "That was the name that you and your associates had selected?" Without the quiver of an eyelash, Dr. Willing promptly responded, "Idaho!"

"And what is the meaning of it?" asked the committee. "It is an Indian word," calmly replied the imperturbable Delegate. "It means Gem of the Mountain."

The beautiful, romantic, poetic title took the committee unanimously, it went into the bill, the Territory was organized and now it is a state and its name is the only monument to the memory of George M. Willing. Long years afterwards, some galoot printed an atrocious attempt to trace the name to some dialect of the Shoshones, a tribe that was ever in the habit of wearing "gems," for the greater part taken from the heads of their neighbors. I replied in the *Tribune* and the matter went to a then-celebrated Indian tongue scholar of New London, Connecticut, who reported that the word could not have meant anything in any red lingo known to him. There it rested and my account was never afterwards disputed. I wonder if Kentucky really means "The Dark and Bloody Ground," or if the Red Stick Creeks or the Choctaws or some other poetic clan were the first to murmur gently, "Alabama," and thereby softly utter, in their accustomed way, "Here We Rest." We do!

Well. Willing had his collection of ores to show. He found them in eastern California and Arizona, after a journey thither all the way down from The Dalles of the Columbia River in Oregon, on the same mule, exploring for his Heart of the Mines all the mountain ranges and passes and narrowly escaping the loss of his scalp and mule.

It was almost a matter of course that he was now nearly out of money in spite of several valuable mining finds which were now in the hands of other men. I gazed a great deal at his collection of specimens and then took them over to the Assay Office of the Philadelphia Mint to have them analyzed and reported on. Certainly no more fascinating report was ever given to dazzle the eyes and agitate the mind. I at once advanced funds and proceeded to organize The Willing Mining and Exploring Company, to send the Doctor to Arizona and California to set the great Golconda in operation. He went, with a picked gang of ancient miner men, and they spent the following season in locating and opening and experimentally working a number of claims. At the end of that season, I was the owner of thousands of running feet of "lodes," some agricultural preemptions and the like, but the Apaches were then in the ascendant in Yavapai County and all of our party, with the single exception of Dr. Willing himself, had lost their scalps.

He came again to the East and I again went in with him. Another expedition was made up, with a Philadelphia banker named Simpson as leading capitalist and manager, and once more much work was reported done with good results, but again the red men took up the hatchet and the scalps, and poor banker Simpson was among the slain. I will not say how much worry that enterprise and the doctor himself cost me in later years, in the Bradshaw Gold and Silver Mining Company and otherwise, but it all ended, at last, when I could do no more and when the doctor died suddenly, of heart disease, at Prescott, Arizona. It was a wonderful dream and I have no doubt of his sincerity. One of our lodes is said to be running now and the others may be waiting for somebody to come and re-discover them. Good bye!

36

Forward March

I was thinking of the night when President Lincoln and I went to Ford's Theatre to see the celebrated actor Hackett play Falstaff.[1] He had made himself more famous in that than in any other character. I was sitting at my work one evening when the door opened and Mr. Lincoln came in. He had perfect right to do so and he said to me, at once:

"You are here? I reckoned I'd find you here. I am going to the theater, to see Hackett play Falstaff, and I want you to come with me. I've always wanted to see him in that character. Come to my room. It's about time to go."

For some reason or other, not uncommonly arising, I was already in evening dress and had no objections to make—nor preparations. We went over into his office and I believed that he was all the while trying to put away from him any and all of the load of thoughts which appertained to that political shop. If he had landed his cares upon the Cabinet table it would have been stacked ten feet high.

I do not now remember anything else that took place until we were seated in the Executive box at the theatre. The chair in which he seated himself could not have been many inches from the spot upon which it stood, [two] years afterwards, when the assassin Booth crept behind him and fired the cowardly shot which cut off his usefulness in the hour of its culmination. My own seat was at his left, near the door by which Booth entered, and all the while I was studying Lincoln rather than the play, in spite of the masterly manner in which the great actor was rendering Shakespeare's ideal.

The fat liar of Prince Harry's gang seemed to be there as a living rascal rather than as any kind of fiction. He made me think of some fat rascals, one in particular, whom I knew in Washington. They may have been his descendants and were a credit to their ancestor. There were some persons, even then, who criticized the President severely for his heartless wickedness in ever going to a theater, listening to music, or any such frivolity at a time when the affairs of the nation required him to sit in a corner and weep whenever he was not signing commissions for office seekers or listening to delegations of solemn functionaries, clerical or other, who came to advise him upon the conduct of the war and upon his own conduct and that of his generals and of Congress. They were represented at Ford's that night in a peculiar and offensive manner which would have given them complete satisfaction. The house was crowded and there were many soldiers in uniform who had obtained furloughs, perhaps, that they might come and hear Hackett and have an evening's relief from the dull monotony of camp life.

Besides these there appeared to me that there were present an abnormal number of opera glasses, all of which, from time to time or even all at the same time, were aimed at our box—either at Mr. Lincoln or at me and I believed that I was really escaping from most of them. As for him, he did not care a cent for that kind of telescope. In fact, I believe he was becoming hardened to both remarks and staring.

Hackett, if I remember correctly, had not yet made his appearance when there came a brief and unexpected experience. One of the President's oversensitive critics had a seat away back toward the entrance and his soul, if he had one, was moved within him. He arose upon his feet, or hoofs, and shouted out something like this:

"There he is! That's all he cares for his poor soldiers—" and other words were added which I cannot now recall.

The President did not move a muscle but another party, also in uniform, was instantly up, declaring vociferously that:

"De President haf a right to his music! Put out dot feller! De President ees all right! Let him have his music!"

There was a confused racket for a few seconds and then the luckless critic went out of the theater, borne upon the strong arms of several boys in blue who agreed with their German comrade as to the right of Abraham Lincoln to as much theatrical relief as they themselves were.

Somewhere about these days, without date, the smallpox was raging with some severity, taking generally the shape of varioloid, and it brought me an odd experience. One morning the face of my family physician came into my house a little clouded, to inform me that it was his duty to revaccinate every soul of us, whether we had ever been poisoned in that way before or not. I had been and thought it a useless precaution but he insisted and to my surprise my arm swelled dreadfully and I felt sure that I was thereby made entirely secure. Blackly so. My scab had peeled and my safety had come before the President himself was taken down with the varioloid.[2] Some of his enemies averred that it was the larger kind of smallpox and that his fatal case was only concealed from the public for war purposes.

All the other members of the White House family were visited by the President's own doctor and I was compelled to show my arm. I am not sure that it was not punched again. I am inclined to think it was, in his zeal for the public good. I do remember that we boys held mournful consultations over the idea that all the country would go to ruin if Abraham Lincoln should die of the dread disease, or any other. But it came to pass, as he was convalescing, that he was informed of my ironclad condition and sent for me. I went right in and attended to whatever the business was, telling him how glad I felt that he was doing so well and adding now, at least, he was safe from office seekers. He might do well, afterwards, to have his office in one of the smallpox hospitals. His laughing reply contained the information that one eager hunter had already replied to his doorkeeper.

"Oh, that doesn't matter. I'll see him. I've been vaccinated."

As to the hospital experiment, he almost sadly declared that the office seekers would only wait until they had been vaccinated and would then come buzzing back around him like so many greenhead flies.

A word more here. That was in the room beyond the library and in a later day it was taken by President Cleveland for his own private office and place of refuge. It was in that room that I sat with him, hour after hour, talking over the story of his life, his early struggles with poverty and so forth, Fayetteville, New York, Buffalo and so forth, and preparing the materials not only for his own biography but for that interesting historical novel, *Crowded out o'Crowfield,* not only the boy of which, but Governor Plowfield himself, are Grovers. When it was printed in book form, after a run in *St. Nicholas,* I sent him a copy and among my autographs somewhere is his letter of acknowledgment, for he actually read that boy book from end to end.

I wish to go back, for a moment, to Ford's Theatre and the President. I had expected that he would be intensely amused by the conduct and conversation of the redoubtable Sir John and that I should have the pleasure of seeing him laugh, a feat which we, his office boys, wished much that he would perform more frequently. I was curiously disappointed. I watched his gloomy face in vain for any sign of a smile although he paid the most ceaseless attention to every word and movement of Hackett, that is, of Falstaff. At last the truth slowly dawned upon me that Mr. Lincoln was not there for the purpose of being amused. He had not come to laugh and therefore did not do so. His intention was rather a deep study of human nature as rendered by the great poet and his capable interpreter behind the footlights yonder. He was reading a man and men as was his lifelong custom, or habit. Looking back through my long portrait gallery of the leaders of men, I cannot find one other who was, in my opinion, so keenly capable of meeting another human being as a book to be opened and read on the spot, nearly through.

There were many interesting occasions and occurrences that seemed to tread upon each other's heels and that do so now as I look back upon them, but the next important arrival from among them rises in my memory as a terrible, great, black cloud. It came rolling across the Potomac and into the White House from the lost battlefield of Chancellorsville. John Hay brought it into my room to say to me:

"Stanton says this is the darkest day of the war. It seems as if the bottom had dropped out."

The Army of the Potomac, after its weary history on the Peninsula, had been reinforced and put under the command of Fighting Joe Hooker,[3] a general with whom I afterwards had a pleasant personal acquaintance. It is of no use here to put in any mention of the difficulties and jealousies, even of the asserted military errors, which were at the time said to have interfered with the efficiency of that magnificent army. It is enough to say that it fought the battle splendidly, heroically, and that it was defeated, as many a gallant army has been. The losses on either side were severe. I recall those of the Confederates at about twelve thousand, "killed and wounded," and those of our army at about seventeen thousand, "killed, wounded, and prisoners." The figures were appalling and not every man who read them paused to consider that our opponents had lost far more than we had, proportionately to the number of men that either side was able to spare without ruin. In one view, that desperate fight was a disaster to the Confederate cause.

It is to be doubted if they ever recovered from that and from their previous victory, a costly one, at Fredericksburg. Later on, their Southern army was all but shattered by its sad success at Chickamauga. It was never again the same force. But that was an awful day in Washington. It almost seemed as if the White House itself had been transferred to the battlefield. We could not hear the died-away thunders of the artillery nor the rattle of the musketry, but instead of these were the groans of the wounded, the dying, and the sound of the picks and spades of the burying parties. Added to these, in the minds of all, were the wails and the mourning which would quickly come down from the North and, mingled with these, would be the sounds of despair and the unsuppressed curses of the unreasoning people who would surely hold Mr. Lincoln and his administration responsible for this one more lost battle and for its dead.

I remember that upon my table, that very day, lay a perfect mass of letters, from friends and foes, telling the discontent, the anger, the despondency, of the American people, and I had not dared to tell the President one word of their contents. The whole city was kind of dead, that day. Men and women went hither and thither as usual, if they were compelled to, but there were no crowds lingering around the telegraph bulletins. Men came and looked at them and shook their heads and walked away. At the White House it was as still as if there were a coffin in the house. I believe that some of those who were permitted to come in did so on tiptoe as if walking too heavily might awaken the dead. Not many were allowed in, or had a mind to come. Cabinet officers, leading statesmen, army officers on duty, despatch bearers, but all others were stopped at the door, if they reached it. Perhaps it was because my heart was so full of the letters which would surely come to me in due season, after Chancellorsville,[4] that I cried like a child over some that I read that day, from mothers who had lost sons, for instance. My mail was a large one. I had been hindered greatly by other duties and it had accumulated, not but what it often compelled me to toil on into late hours.

I had been out to my dinner, long ago. I do not know what had become of Nicolay and Hay. My door was open, however, and at last I saw men come out of Lincoln's office and walk slowly away. I can recall Seward, Halleck, Stanton, but after they had departed I believed myself to be alone on that floor of the Executive Mansion except for the President in his room, over yonder across the hall. It was then about nine o'clock for I looked at my watch. It was so silent that I could hear it tick. It seemed as if the rooms and hall were full of shadows, some of which came in and sat down by me to ask me what I thought would become of the Union cause and the country.

Not long afterwards, a dull, heavy, regularly repeated sound came out of Lincoln's room through its half open door and found its way into mine. I listened, listened, and became aware that this was the measured tread of the President's feet, as he walked steadily to and fro, up and down, on the further side, beyond the Cabinet table, from wall to wall, and thought about Chancellorsville, its wounded and its dead, and about the nation and its thousands of broken hearts and about the days and the battles which were yet to come. He must have been listening to a great many weird utterances, as he walked and as he turned at the wall at either end of his ceaseless promenade. Ten o'clock came and I was still at my papers but whenever I paused to endorse one of them or to consider its destiny, I could hear the tread of the feet in that other room. Eleven o'clock came, and it had not really ceased for a breathing space. It had become such a half heard monotony that when, just at twelve o'clock, midnight, it suddenly ceased it was the silence itself that startled me into listening more intently. I did not dare to go and look in upon him, but oh, what a silence that was.

It may have continued during many minutes. Lincoln may have been at his table, writing, but there was a strong, strange impression upon my mind, I know not why, that if I had then looked in I would have seen a strong man kneeling down by one of those chairs. God was with him, anyhow, for He was then and there dealing with that man, helping, caring for him and for the nation.

Then the silence was broken and the sound of the heavy feet began again. One o'clock came and I still had much work before me and Lincoln did not seem to me to be even pausing at the walls. At times his pace quickened as if under the spur of some burst of feeling or impulse of angry energy. Two o'clock came, for I again looked at my watch, and Lincoln was walking still. It was a vigil with God and with the future and a long wrestle with disaster and it may be with himself—for he also was weary of delays and sore with defeats.

It was almost exactly at three o'clock that my own long task was done and I arose to go but I did not so much as peer through the narrow opening of the President's doorway. It would have been a kind of profanity. At the top of the stairway, however, I paused and listened before going down and the last sound that I heard and that seemed to go out of the house with me was the sentry-like tread with which the President was marching on into the coming day.

I went home weary enough but did not go to bed. I remember taking a bath and then a breakfast at Gautier's restaurant, on the avenue. My table was still heavily loaded and I knew fresh duties were at hand. It was therefore not yet eight o'clock when I was once more at the White House, letting myself in by my latchkey. It was a bright, sunlit morning, without a cloud in the sky. On reaching the second floor I saw the President's door wide open and looked in. There he sat, near the end of the Cabinet table, with a breakfast before him. Just beyond the cup of coffee at his right lay a sheet of foolscap paper, covered with fresh writing, in his own hand. I do not now recall how, before I came out, I received so strong an impression, amounting to knowledge, that upon this paper he had written his instructions to General Hooker to rally the army, to take fresh courage, and to fight again at the earliest opportunity. They were really the orders under which General Meade[5] shortly took Hooker's place and marched on to Gettysburg. That long night vigil and combat and victory ought to be recorded forever in the most sacred annals of his country. I knew it had been a victory, for he turned to me with a bright and smiling face and talked with me as cheerfully as if he had not been up all night in that room, face to face with—Chancellorsville.

It was now beginning to be plain to the minds of many men that the Civil War was approaching a kind of climax. The Army of the Potomac was undergoing a process of reorganization and the country had responded nobly to the President's call for "Three Hundred Thousand More." You may have heard or read the song of that title that was so thrilling:

If you look up all our valleys
Where the growing harvests shine,
You may see our sturdy farmer boys
Fast forming into line;
And a farewell group stands weeping
At every cottage door:
We are coming, Father Abraham,
Three hundred thousand more.

One day its author, a middle-aged, farmer-looking man, came to the White House and was taken in to be introduced to the President. I went in with him, as did the other secretaries and half a crowd of statesmen and militaries, and we heard him sing his song to Mr. Lincoln. He did it very well, too, and it was a good thing for the country.[6]

I do not now remember the exact date at which the Draft Act went into effect to aid the popular tide of patriotism,[7] but when the District of Columbia lists were made out, I found myself listed with the rest, for there was really no favoritism. So was Harry, but we were neither of us drawn when the fearful lottery wheel was turned.

The air was getting hotter, thicker, and the clouds overhead were dense with the smoke of burning powder. The armies of the West and Southwest were everywhere busy, for Grant had been rushing along and was now tightening his terrible bulldog grip upon Vicksburg.[8] Then came the announcement that the Rebel War Department had determined upon the capture of Washington. It was to be done, it was said from two directions, one by way of upper Maryland and one across the Potomac, lower down, so that our forces would be divided and so more easily beaten. The President called upon the North for its uniformed militia to reinforce the Army of the Potomac and the call was answered in a manner which stripped a city like New York of all its fighters except its policemen. Then came the facts.

> The hills of Maryland echoed back
>   The invader's ceaseless drum,
> For Lee was over the border,
>   And the day of wrath had come.

Such a state of mind as the capital was in can better be imagined than described and all the Secessionists in it were beginning to raise their heads and hopes and smile visibly at their abolitionist tyrants as they passed them on the streets or met them in social gatherings. Now, it had always been the custom in Washington, as in some other American places, to make a great fuss over the Fourth of July.

As the national anniversary drew nearer, the excitement concerning the aspect of military affairs grew worse and worse. The latest news from Grant was badly mixed in the minds of panicky men and all the old women of Washington were of the opinion that it would soon be in the hands of the Confederates, whether or not those awful men would sack it and murder its helpless inhabitants. It was said that more of them than usual decided suddenly that they needed visits to northern watering places.

So high ran the discussion of the propriety of celebrating the Fourth under such discouraging circumstances, that a great and crowded public meeting was held in one of the largest halls of the town for the purpose of considering the matter. To the astonishment of the timid, the tone of that meeting was in favor of celebrating, in spite of a vigorous, dolorous, declamatory opposition. The meeting having decided to celebrate, the next question was as to the proper committee of arrangements and here there was a break, for the Mayor was a Secessionist and the customary masters of civic ceremonials were largely sympathizers with Robert E. Lee and his invading army. Name after name was called and begged to be excused. I was not there and had not given the matter a thought, but many fellows who knew me were there and among them was a chap from Illinois with a peculiarly stentorian voice and he arose to his two, or six, feet to shout my name in full as his nomination for Chairman of the Committee. Another man got up to ask him for any reason why such a man, not a known citizen of Washington, should be selected for that undertaking.

"Why?" came back the basso profundo response. "Why? Because, sir, if he is made chairman, by God! He will put the thing right through!"

The nomination was promptly made, on that endorsement, backed as it was by a storm of cheers from all the Department clerks, soldiers, and other old citizens who were in the hall. The first I heard of it was the next morning, and as soon as I read the names of my associates also duly elected I knew that I was expected to be the Committee, with autocratic power to do all the work and pay all the bills. That promised to be an affair of some importance and I became financial. Then, too, I was again surprised to find how readily the bankers and other businessmen, of several kinds, became patriotic when the President's secretary called upon them for a little love of country. They came down and were not at all afraid of Lee. It was on my mind to think whether or not the Illinois roarer had this in view when he set me up. My next trips were to Masons and Odd Fellows, who were in the habit of making an appearance on such occasions and they were all ready to put on their aprons and cocked hats. Then came the twelve Councils of the Union League, and I was sure of the last man of them. It happened that the officer in command of the District was my old Rochester friend, General Martindale,[9] and he shouted at me:

"My boy! Yes. I'm going to move a whole division and some cavalry and artillery up the river and I'll take them all on to your Procession. Give you a band of music, too. Flags! Hurrah! Pitch in!"

I then went to a well-known western statesman and asked him to be the orator of the day. To my astonishment, he drew himself up, dignifiedly:

"No, young man!" he solemnly responded. "This is no time for empty Fourth of July celebrations. The country is in too much danger and our people are too nearly brokenhearted." More trash than that was sent at me and my blood was up.

"Mr.——!" I roared back. "You're wrong! We will not give it up. I will tell you, sir! There will be a Fourth of July celebration in Washington, this time, if we can hear Lee's cannon all the while and if we adjourn from the speaker's stand to the trenches, to defend the city!"

I strode away indignantly, but what I had said to him pleased me so much that I repeated it upon the first opportunity. That came right away, for another great public meeting was held and a heavy committee was appointed to wait upon Mr. Stoddard and represent to him the state of popular feeling and request that he at once abandon the untimely attempt at disturbing in this way the troubled souls of Washington. I gave them the answer, eloquently, again liking the sound of it, and went ahead. It was easy to find a plucky orator of the day. As to the place, the broad Mall below the White House, toward the Potomac, was practically under my orders and there the grandstand was erected. I also had the Marine band. Mrs. Lincoln was backing me in all such matters. I did not speak to the President about it but did not dream of doubting his approval.

Well, the day came and before it I went wildly short of gold in New York, so sure did I feel of a good result all around. The procession was formed under good, military direction. Its tails were away at the City Hall and the Capitol when its head, and I, were at 14th Street. All along the line, the division of infantry stood at parade rest. The cavalry led the van. The batteries of field artillery brought up the rear. It was universally declared to be the grandest Fourth o' July procession that had been seen in Washington since the city was founded. The crowd on the Mall was tremendous. The music was good. So were the speeches. So had been the subscriptions to such an extent that all I had to pay out of my own pocket was the really tremendous bill charged by Gautier for the fine dinner I gave to the Committee, the orators, the city officials, and the distinguished guests, after the doings wound up.

The best of it all was that good news from Gettysburg and Vicksburg[10] came tumbling in upon that celebration, to make it cheerful, and that the price of gold was tumbling at a rate that made my dinner bill of small account. I noticed, however, that all bills for carriages and the like, big ones too, came in before dark and it was explained to me that never before had such things been actually footed on the spot by any committee, the rule being that the bill holders had to hold them until a fresh appropriation could be smuggled through the Board of Aldermen, and that was sometimes dilatory.

On the whole, I was proud of my feat and had no idea that it actually made enemies for me. It was rough on the city, you know, and on all its great men, to have so grand an affair gobbled by a mere boy from Illinois, one of Lincoln's hirelings, and not a Southern man at all.

37

On Assignment by the President

I do not now recall anything of especial personal interest which followed quickly upon the heels of the great Union victories, east and west. I only know that what with excitement and overwork and Potomac River malaria, I found myself out of order. I went, therefore, to my good physician, Dr. Lieberman, who had but one druggist in Washington that could read his Russo-Germanesque prescriptions, and stated my case.

"O!" he replied. "Ees dat all? Den I tell you. You no wand Pheesic, pheesic, pheesic, pheesic. All you neet ess to get away up Nort unt go to de seashore unt lie on der sant unt keeck oop your heels unt do notinks. Den you comes back anoder man. I geef you a donic. Dots all."

So, armed with his advice and the tonic, I applied for a furlough and obtained it. My brother Henry did the same, but he was bound for Syracuse and I for the shore of the beautiful blue sea.

So far, all was well, but we timed our departure from Washington without any knowledge whatever of the things which were about to occur. So sadly do intelligent men sometimes neglect the future. There had been dark rumors of the excited state of feeling in New York City with reference to the enforcement of the coming Draft for men, but no great attention had been paid to the matter in government circles, owing to the confident assurances of peace given by men in office and by such apparently good authority as the *Tribune*—Mr. Greeley.

Henry and I went on in the night, for coolness and to save a day, so that we reached the Astor House very early in the morning of the very day when the outbreak began which is known as "The Draft Riot of 1863."[1] However it began, it shortly was nothing but a bursting up of the criminal classes of the great city, for the workingmen of New York are neither thieves nor murderers. We took our breakfasts and walked out in front of the hotel. Not a word of any uprising had been heard, even then, but I saw a cart driven rapidly along upon which lay a Negro, while a small mob of ruffians appeared to be trying to drag him off. I saw another Negro chased and maltreated in another direction and the air was full of direful exclamations and prophecies.

At first I did not understand the matter but the truth dawned upon me as my blood rose hotter and I went back to my room. There was my pistol belt, knife and all, and the weapon was of heavy caliber. Henry had none, so I gave him mine and we went hastily to Maiden Lane, where the gun stores were, to get me a new outfit. I was just in time, for hardly had I buckled on my longer barreled heavier shooting iron, before all those stores were closed by order or the police and by the fears of their owners that they would soon be looted if they were open. We had plenty of ammunition, but where we were likely to use it we could not guess. The idea was in my mind that any mob would be likely to plunder the money men and so I led the way toward Wall Street. When we reached the corner of the Sub-Treasury, there upon the steps was General Ward B. Burnett, organizing a company of volunteers that appeared to promise to be a good one. I knew of him that he had commanded the First New York volunteers in the Mexican War and was accounted a brave, capable officer. That was the man to serve under and we at once fell into line, recalling our soldier experience in the Rifles.

To my astonishment, at my right was an old Geneva College Alpha Delta Phi acquaintance from Buffalo, named Lee, a very handsome fellow, and who should stand at our left but Hop Strong, ready for a fight. The General swore us in, gave us instructions, looked very cool and determined but a little bloodthirsty, and we were posted. That is, we were put temporarily in charge of the Treasury, under the impression that there was to be an immediate attack upon it. I will not need to explain here how completely the city was stripped of its uniformed militia by the call to Gettysburg nor how numerically inadequate were the brave and efficient police to operate over so wide an area as that mob soon provided for them. Neither can I go into any detailed account of my own personal experiences.

The air was hot, sultry, full of smoke from many fires. The crowds of rushing men. The frantic women. The contradictory rumors. The swift marchings here and there. The smoky glimpses of the horrible mob. The weariness. All is now to me as the dim figures of a disordered, nightmare kind of dream which never had anything to do with real life. I will only say that later in the day we were transferred to the portico of the Customhouse, to keep company with a wide-mouthed mountain howitzer, filled to the lips with grapeshot, that stood looking angrily down in the middle and seemed to be begging for a mob to come so that he might be reasonably touched off. He would have swept those steps badly if he had been fired.

I think it was that first night that I slept on the floor of the hall in the Metropolitan Hotel, on Broadway, for a few hours, after much tramping around, I can't say just where and don't care. Before the end of that hot day, stronger men than I, seasoned policemen, were utterly prostrated with the heat. Harry had long since given in and set out for Syracuse. Hop had disappeared. Somewhere in the hours of that next night, I believe it was, I found I could do no more, and was "invalided" by the General. I had really done my duty and afterwards a great many others did the same and the mob was put down. I do not remember just how long I watched the subsequent proceedings, the clouds of smoke and all that, but I saw enough, cloudily, to never forget what a robber's mob might be and the interest stuck to me until years later, I set myself at work and wrote and printed *The Volcano under the City*.

In my belief, the larger part of its truly ferocious, inhuman atrocities, had for their inspiration almost unlimited rum. The countless gin mills of every grade were at the mercy of the half-crazy devils who drank their fill and went out to destroy. It may have been of some importance that large numbers of them fell before this enemy and did no more harm after they were dead drunk. Something similar has recently been noted among the vodka-maddened Jew killers in crazy Russia. The worst mob-leader there was De Vodka or Von Whiskysky.

As soon as I could get away from the prostration of the Riot days, I too was on my way to Syracuse, but I did not remain there long. In fact, I went there by way of Homer and spent days in looking around upon the old, familiar places. I saw some of my boyhood's friends but not many of them were to be found, somehow. I went up into Shearer's woods, where I used to hunt squirrels and tap the maple trees for sugar sap. I went all over the old pasture lots and the orchards. I visited the Osborn homestead and looked in upon the room where I was born. Then I prowled around the village and over the new cemetery to which the remains from the old graveyard had been removed. I saw the millponds where I had done my first fishing and swimming. Then I took the Syracuse train with a full heart. All the Syracuse people were good to me and I had an opportunity for using a considerable sum of money in helping my father out of one of his customary "endorsement" difficulties. I never saw that money again and do not care to say anything more about it. I would have gone to Rochester but more than one of the persons I would have most earnestly wished to see had gone on into the other country.

My next destination was New London, and here I had really a restoration time. I saw many relatives, but particularly my Stoddard grandfather and grandmother. The old gentleman was failing fast with old age, but his wife was as bright as ever. They were in the farmhouse at Noank and I once more caught fish in that cove. She took me right into her heart and told me stories of the old times, even before the Revolution.

No changes awaited me on my arrival at the capital, unless it was in the fact that both Nicolay and Hay were entitled to some sort of vacations and that I was more frequently called upon to take Nicolay's desk and act as big Private Secretary. On the whole, I think he was much better qualified for it than I was. He was older, more experienced, harder, had a worse temper, and was decidedly German in his manner of telling men what he thought of them. I was more reticent and Hay more diplomatic, but now and then Hay could express his inner opinions very well. He did so, sometimes when I read to him sundry poems, in return for a number of pretty good ones of his own that he came and read to me. It is on my mind that I admired his productions a number of sizes more than he did mine. We were the best of friends, nevertheless, and I recall his daily association with great pleasure.

The Summer and Autumn drifted away and the Winter came and all things went along in the usual way: receptions, parties, debates in House or Senate, dinners, speculations, patents, army news, daily meetings with remarkable persons in my northeast room and elsewhere. It was all a sort of wonderful phantasmagoria routine, a kaleidoscope full of statesmen, generals, rascals, battles, dissipations, hard works, and at the end of it I was down with the typhoid fever. It was a pull of weeks and I got up too soon, only to go down again. We had given up our brownstone front on Louisiana Avenue the previous Spring and now Kate went north and I got well alone. Henry had been promoted, from time to time, until he was now in the highest grade of Treasury clerks.

It was a bright Spring morning when I at last mustered strength to walk to the White House and take a look at my long-neglected table. Hay had done much for it but it was just then a hay-mow of unopened correspondence, waiting for my hand and paper-cutter. It was a Sunday morning and both of the boys were absent, so I wearily strolled across the hall into Lincoln's room. For a wonder, he was actually lying down upon the sofa on the easterly side of the room, with his hands folded over his head and looking as if he did not care two cents for the past, present, or future. He half arose as I came in and told me to bring a chair. I did so and received a warm handshake and kindly inquiries after my bodily condition. He was all geniality and I had an inquiry on my mind.

"Now, Mr. Lincoln, what sort of man is Grant? I've never even seen him. He has taken hold here while I have been laid up. What do you think of him?"

Lincoln had once more stretched himself out on the sofa but now he half rose on one elbow, laughing in his silent, peculiar way.

"'Well, Stoddard," he said, "I hardly know what to think of him, altogether. I never saw him, myself, until he came here to take command. He's the quietest little fellow you ever saw."

"How is that, Mr. Lincoln?" I said. "I had another kind of idea about him. Quiet?"

"Why," slowly responded the President, "he makes the least fuss of any man you ever knew. I believe, two or three times, he has been in this room a minute or so, before I knew he was here. It's about so, all around. The only evidence you have that he's in any place is that he makes things git! Wherever he is, things move!"

I had a number of other things to say before I boldly put in: "But how about Grant's generalship, Mr. Lincoln? Is he going to be the man, as commander of the Army of the Potomac?"

The President now suddenly arose to a sitting posture and his long forefinger was aimed right at me as he responded: "Stoddard, Grant is the first General I've had! He's a General!"

I did not quite understand him, for I knew, or thought I knew, what had been his estimates of others—McClellan, Burnside, Meade, Hooker, etc. "How do you mean?" I asked.

'Well!" said he. "I'll tell you what I mean. You know how it's been with all the rest. As soon as I put a man in command of the army, he'd come to me with a plan of campaign and about as much as say, 'Now, I don't believe I can do it, but if you say so, I'll try it on'— and so put the responsibility of success or failure upon me. They all wanted me to be the General. Now, it isn't so with Grant. He hasn't told me what his plans are. I don't know and I don't want to know. I'm glad to find a man who can go ahead without me."

"He took his own gait in the West, Mr. Lincoln," I replied, "and he came out pretty well, that's a fact; but he hasn't proved, yet, that he can handle the Army of the Potomac and beat Lee on his own ground."

The President was sitting up straight and his face had put on his story-telling expression, with something of fun in it.

"Stoddard," he said, "you see, when any of the rest set out on a campaign, they'd look over matters and pick out some one thing they were short of, and they knew I couldn't give 'em, and tell me they couldn't hope to win unless they had it, and it was most generally cavalry"—and at this point he again held in for another long, quiet fit of laughter, through which it was now dawning upon me that his lying here so contentedly upon the sofa this Sunday afternoon, was all along of the vast relief he felt at having the Army lifted from his shoulders by someone who appeared to be able to carry it while he lay down for a bit of rest.

He went on: "Now, when Grant took hold, I was waiting to see what his pet impossibility would be, and I reckoned it would be cavalry, as a matter of course, for we hadn't horses enough to mount even what men we had. There were fifteen thousand or thereabouts, up near Harpers Ferry, and no horses to put them on. Well, the other day, just as I expected, Grant sent to me about those very men; but what he wanted to know was whether he should disband 'em or turn 'em into infantry. He doesn't ask me to do impossibilities for him and he's the first general I've had that didn't."

Long years afterwards, a friend of Grant's told him this story and he quietly remarked: "Well, it gives about my idea of the truth of what they call Lincoln's interference with military plans. He never interfered with me, from the beginning to the end."

There was a sad sequel to that. Other things were also told him and he said to a member of his old military staff, "I must have Stoddard up here to dinner. I'd like to have a talk with him."

So it would have been, for he was in the habit of fulfilling his intentions but before any invitation could be sent, the banking house of Grant and Ward went down and he had no more a house in which to give dinner parties.[2] Then came the long struggle, the heroic death-grapple with his terrible disease, and the end. I always appreciated Grant, but, to my mind, his greatest service to his country, second at least to no other, was his service as military dictator, or rather as Tribune of the People, in the dark, stormy confusion of Andrew Johnson's impeachment days, when all the country turned to the strong, stern man in whom it had put its uttermost confidence, with the old Roman injunction repeated:

"See thou to it that the Republic suffers no harm!"

When I wrote that 1863 wound up without any notable incident, I must have been sleepy, for I look back upon the Black Thanksgiving as one of the most interesting things that I ever saw or did. Even before I tell that, however, I am reminded of the afternoon when Mr. Lincoln called me over into his office to serve him for the people of the United States and Europe while he read to me an important manuscript. You see, it was a new one, of the fit of which he was not quite sure, and he wanted to try it on me.

"Sit down over there," he said, as soon as he had taken a chair to the easterly side of the Cabinet table and placed upon that several sheets of closely written foolscap paper. "I can always tell more about a thing after I've heard it read aloud, and know how it sounds. Just the reading of it to myself doesn't answer so well, either."

So down I sat, across the table from him, and kindly offered: "Do you wish me to read it to you?"

"No, no," he replied, "I'll read it myself. What I want is an audience. Nothing sounds the same to me, when there isn't anybody to hear it and find fault with it."

"I don't know, Mr. President," I said, with all the humility he knew I hadn't a drop of, "that I'd care to criticize anything you'd written."

He did know that I had criticized everything I got hold of that he or anybody else had written, but all he said was: "Yes, you will. Everybody else will. It's just what I want you to do. Sit still, now! And you'll make as much of an audience as I care for."

That was complimentary and all the while he was himself making criticisms on his own work, with a pen and a grin. He began and he read well, pausing, now and then to think and to look across the table and see how

I was being affected. I concealed my thoughts artistically but it was really a long and very important document. It was a letter, since famous, to all mankind by way of certain eminent citizens of Illinois who had been criticizing his Negro and other policy.[3] I listened for all the world, therefore, and felt largely cosmopolitan but it was done at last.

"Now!" he said. "Is there any criticism that you want to make?"

"Well!" I said. "I was thinking, of course, it's as nearly beyond criticism as it well could be, but there's one place . . ."

"What's that?" he said. "Take the paper and show it to me." I did so and ventured to find my faulty spot.

"Why, Mr. Lincoln," I said, "some people will find fault with this—'Nor must Uncle Sam's Web-feet be forgotten. At all the watery margins they have been present. Not only on the deep sea, the broad bay, and the rapid river, but also up the narrow, muddy bayou, and wherever the ground was a little damp, they have been and made their tracks.'"[4]

Lincoln was laughing silently when I began and loudly when I ended.

"That's it, is it?" he exclaimed. "I reckoned it would be some such place as that. I'll leave it just as it is. I reckon the people'll know what it means."

"That's about the only fault I find," I said, "but I never saw a web-footed gunboat in my life. They're a queer kind of duck."

"Some of them did get ashore, though," he said, with another laugh. "I'll leave it in. Now I know how it's going to sound. That'll do. I shan't want you any more, this time."

We did have more talk, about other things, but when that letter was printed there were stacks of literary geniuses, everywhere, who made the same criticism that I did—but not in the hearing of Mr. Lincoln.

Now, to go back to the Thanksgiving. The regular proclamations had been sent out by the President and the State Governors and all over the land the usual preparations were making. Probably the South was doing something, but there was one lot of southern people for whom this might be regarded as their first great Thanksgiving Day, if they were to keep it as one. Over the borders and through the army lines, from the beginning of the war, there had been a steady tide of colored fugitives, men, women, and children. To these in many places were to be added those who had been practically freed by the advance of our army lines, without any formal assertion of the fact prior to the Emancipation Proclamation.

Before the war there had been a large colored element in the District of Columbia, slave and free. To this was now to be added on any great occasion, all the colored folk of Maryland within reach. More than either of these in free enthusiasm if not in numbers were the Contrabands who had flocked in with an apparent notion that they were safer the nearer they were to the Gub'munt an' Marssa Lincum. They could not all be provided at once with either employment or palaces, but army rations could be assigned them and a place for a kind of corral was given them. It was wide, large, extensive and it was only a mile or so north of the city limits. Around it had been put up a high plank fence and in it had been constructed many not uncomfortable shelters. Nobody knew, unless he was a quartermaster counting rations, just how many were the regular settlers in this Africa, but the number began to swell as soon as it was made public that a lot of kindly abolitionists were intending to give here a tremendous Thanksgiving dinner.

I had heard of it, of course, but had given it no special attention, although I sympathized heartily with the idea. I heard more on the afternoon before the Day, when into my office marched my friend Senator Pomeroy of Kansas[5] to provide me with details and say that I had been selected to deliver the address of the occasion. He was to open with a few remarks and then I would have full swing. I was taken so far aback that I asked him why he had not waited till next morning, in order that I might have abundant time for preparation. He would not take "No" for an answer, however, and I returned to my work. I did not have a moment to give to my proposed speech until next day, as I walked, all alone, out in the direction of the Contraband Camp, with a curious conviction that I had a peculiar job before me. Some help came when I recalled the fact that every member of my audience had probably attended "camp meetings" and was familiar with holler it loud oratory—and no other kind.

When I reached the camp, it was a sight to see. All along the sides were the barn-like dining halls, except at one point on the west where had been built a large, high platform for the guests, the speakers, and the ample brass music, to be heard by all. Upon this elevation were already gathered Senator Pomeroy, other abolition statesmen who were not to speak, the Colored Methodist Bishop of the Diocese, and a number of abolition women of great zeal, enthusiasm, and intelligence. Some of them were very good looking and all were there to encourage me.

I had trusted that the senator's remarks would use up lots of time but they did not, for he had no pretension to oratorical eminence and only read a short sermon from manuscript notes. Then the band worked hard for several minutes and my time had come. I stepped forward and oh, what a sight it was. Some men said there were ten thousand before me and some let it off at five thousand, but the latter figure must have been exceeded. I did not try to count them—that wonderful sea of dark faces, turned toward mine. I only began to feel a strange fire running all over me and in an instant I had fortunately forgotten myself altogether, which is always the best thing any orator can do, if he is to do anything else well.

Besides the senator, the Bishop and one more colored man had spoken briefly, but neither of them had touched the idea which had burst into my mind. At that date there had been no important urging of so wild an idea as that of putting arms into the hands of escaped slaves, African barbarians who could not be turned into soldiers. Whenever a small mention of it had timidly crept out, it had been hooted down, as at the least an insult to all white volunteers who had been conscripted or had paid three hundred dollars apiece not to go a soldiering. Here were the slaves set free, but it was in me to say little or nothing about their past. It was better to lead them on into the future they were escaping toward, but had not yet quite reached. As I did so they grew more and more excited and I found myself getting wild. However, I was leading them on in the direction of a thought which had come to me and at last I asked them whether having received freedom they were willing to fight for it. Other men were shedding blood for them; were they ready to give life and blood of their own? Would they fight, if called upon? I put it as best I could but my voice was drowned in a great tumult. I shall never forget the lurid faces, the fierce, guttural exclamations, the half frenzied shouts and yells.

"Gib us dem guns! Let's hab dem bay'nets! We'll show, ye, Marssa! We's ready! Whar's de guns?"

Women all but shrieked. Men swung their arms as they yelled and all the throng pressed nearer. It was the old, terrible, savage, African fighting fire let loose within them, and a surge of it had risen angrily into me, making me fit for the occasion, as I otherwise would not have been. Then it was over, and I sat down after shaking many hands. The band played. The dinner eating began as the swarms went for it. Then at last a queer idea came to me. I had been introduced as Lincoln's secretary and loud applause had welcomed his name. That was it. Senator Pomeroy, the old fox, had put me there as if to represent the President, and who should say how many of my audience half believed they had been listening to their all but adored Liberator? Well! I walked back to the White House in a train of thought, as if I had taken an undue responsibility, for which I might be called to account. Not so. Often enough, afterwards, I was spoken to about that address, but Mr. Lincoln himself never gave me any trouble, although this was before he announced his purpose of arming the colored men. Sometimes I have believed that he did not think less of me for so curiously assuming statesmanship and, it might be, "compromising the Administration." Bah!

38

Year of Decision, 1864

itting here at my Blick [typewriter—ed.], I can recall nothing to prevent me from at once returning to the Summer of 1864. All my business operations had been more or less interrupted by my long illness, but the one thing most apparent was my need of outdoor air for as long as might be. I was no longer fit for close confinement and late hours. So I put things in order as best I might and looked around me. I need not detail the many considerations, official and other, which led me to determine upon a prolonged inspection of the armies in the west and south.

Mr. Lincoln approved and I was provided with abundant passes and letters of introduction, endorsing me as his Secretary, entitled to go everywhere and be well-received by everybody. One idea included a visit to New Orleans and word thereof went to Admiral Porter,[1] eliciting from him a pretty long letter of official and personal proposed welcome. I was not to be able to avail myself of his cordial, sailor-like hospitality, much to my regret, for my final determinations led me in another direction.

I went to New York first and rested a few days, completing my arrangements of all sorts, one of which included ample remittances to my father. I do not now recall the date of the marriage of my brother Charles, but he wrote me about it and about an opposition to his marrying so young. Believing it best for him, I replied with a check for a hundred and on it he got married right away.

I think that my next observations were briefly taken in Cincinnati, Pittsburgh, and Louisville. Thence to St. Louis, where I met a number of old acquaintances and some new ones that interested me greatly. Among the latter, to my extreme delight, were General Frank P. Blair,[2] Colonel Kit Carson,[3] the celebrated scout and Indian fighter, and a whole crowd of their like, with whom I spent at least one pleasant evening, hearing their wonderful yarns and acquiring a remarkable acquaintance with the Indian sign language, which they used liberally all the time and kindly explained to me wherever it required explanation.

From St. Louis I went down the river in a steamboat that gave me a stop at Helena, and all the way I was industriously studying the throng of remarkable characters on board, beginning with the Negro roustabouts and not neglecting the planters, army men, wanderers, speculators, gamblers, cut-throats, and professional thieves of all sorts. The whole collection was nuts and honey to me.

At Memphis I was admirably well received by General Washburn,[4] in command, and saw the whole city, gathering some information which was to be of value to the general. Here I did not linger long but found a queer sort of steamer bound up the White River, with army supplies, rascals, and other cargo. It landed me at Duvall's Bluff, but I was in a reduced state of health, so much so that when, for some reason or other, all sorts of men came to tender me important testimony upon varied matters, I had to hear them lying down. They were of all ranks, from a brigadier down to a private, refugees, quartermasters, and sons of Satan. I was deeply interested in their reports, also in the fact that the Rebs had carried away all the rolling stock of the one-legged railway from thence to Little Rock and that I would have to make that journey on a handcar. I had a mattress put on the car and a strong guard was given me to prevent seizure by accidental guerillas.

We set out in a morning and I was soon on good terms with the sergeant of the guard. He belonged to a cavalry regiment and it was one which was previously indicated to me with reference to an important subject which I was to inquire into. The main thing which I acquired from him was communicated in reply to a leading question.

"Sergeant," I said, "what did you and your boys do with the gang of guerillas you captured last week? You didn't bring 'em in."

"Well! No, Colonel, we didn't," he frankly responded. "I don't mind tellin' you 'f you won't say no more 'bout it. Our officers is all right but folks at the east mightn't understand it. You see, thar was 'leven of 'em, wust kind o' grillers—an' we didn't fetch 'em in."

"I know you didn't," I told him, as he sort o' hesitated and took another bite of Virginia plug. "But did they get away, or did you let 'em go? What became of them? I won't say a word."

"Well! Colonel!" he bit from the plug. "This was the way of it. Thar was a'leven of 'em. Wust kind. Do ye see that neck o' timber, 'way off yonder? Well, 'twas jest byant that that we took 'em. You see, we had plenty o' rope along an' so we jest let 'em all go. Thar was trees handy."

Precisely what that meant I will let out in the report which I afterwards made to the President. We reached Little Rock in safety and I put up at the Anthony House and at once began to receive an unaccountable stream of visitors, most of whom I had never heard of but all of whom became imbued somehow with the idea that it was their duty to tell me all they knew about everything in the Department of the Southwest. In a few days, I was well enough to call upon General Fred Steele,[5] in command, and by him I was well treated. I obtained much information from him and his staff. I also obtained an insight into the composition, or uncomposition of the new loyal State Government which had a decisive influence upon my own plans for the future. That is, it made some plans for me to carry back and tell to Mr. Lincoln. On the whole, I enjoyed my visit in Arkansas and heard more army yarns than I had ever before heard in the same number of consecutive days. When all was done that could be done, I took a steamer down the Arkansas, back to Memphis, St. Louis, Cincinnati, and Washington, leaving that steamer at Memphis and doing much of the rest of the way by rail, not by muddy water.

Speaking of Kit Carson and the Indian trading remarkables at St. Louis, puts me in mind of some of my previous experiences in Washington in relation to the Red Men of North America. I will also insert that I took a deep interest in all the diplomatic and other Indians who came to us from Mexico and studied every man of them on account of Montezuma.

Whenever delegations of copper-colored magnates came on from the West for pow-wows with their Great Father at Washington, I was sure to be on hand for an investigation of them and for as many personal acquaintances as I might be able to make. I gathered heaps of information from them and from the scalplocks upon their war-leggings, some of which had stories to tell, as not by any means all the locks were from heads of dark hair. Added to these were my studies at the Smithsonian Institution, among the collections of Catlin and other Indian historians. Included were original specimens of all the household, wigwam, hunting, warring, cooking, clothing, and other implements and properties of Indian manufacture, from a wide variety of tribes.

On reaching Washington I went to the White House and was all but astonished by the promptness with which Mr. Lincoln summoned me to his room for a report and a private conference. I quickly learned from him, however, that there were at the moment several important "cases," under Executive consideration, which called for precisely the testimony I was supposed to be able to give. If I remember rightly, he was at his desk and was leaning forward at me when the conversation began, but that he did not sit still while I was talking. Not all the while.

"Now, Stoddard," he began, "you've been all through the West. Tell me what you think of it. Tell everything."

He didn't mean "the West," but the affairs of our armies in the parts I had been examining. So I replied:

"Well, Mr. President, I've been down as far as Memphis, and up the White River, and across to Little Rock, and down the Arkansas and up to St. Louis . . ." I need not try to recall all I said, nor his cross-examination on some points, but at last he plumped me with:

"But! About the stealing!"

"Well," I told him. "There's a great deal going on, there's no doubt of that. But General Washburn's an honest man, honest as the day, and so is General Steele. The charges are lies," and I could tell why I said so.

"I'm glad to hear that," he said, with strong emphasis. "I like Washburn. I never saw Fred Steele, but I've always liked him and I like his brother here in Congress. I'm glad the charges are false. How about that corn?"

He referred to a matter of which much had been made in various ways.

"Well," I replied, "there's almost a joke there, but Steele had nothing to do with it. He doesn't know what became of that corn. I went and saw where it was attended to. When our army marched in, the Arkansas River bottom plantations were mostly in corn instead of cotton. Finest standing crops you ever saw. Sixty, seventy bushels to the acre and more. It was put in to feed the Confederate army with, but it's been fed out to ours, all the way down to New Orleans."

There had been many things said about corn stealing and he had been talked to about it but a grin was growing on his face when he said: "Go ahead. How did they get it?"

"Right through the regular contractors," I told him. "You see, the contracts called for so much corn, to be delivered so and so, up and down the rivers, the Mississippi, Cumberland, and so on, and the contractors lived up to their agreements to the letter. It did not specify where they were to get the corn from. The corn they harvested in the Arkansas valley was good corn and it cost them something. They had to pay the boys a dollar a day for husking it, just as if they had been in Illinois or Ohio, instead of in Arkansas and in the Army. Their officers gave 'em short furloughs, changing 'round to give as many of 'em a chance as they could. Nobody knows what the contractors paid for the army wagons and mules that hauled the crops to the river landings so it could be delivered on board the steamers. There was a heap of it. Some people would call it stealing, but it's a puzzle whom they stole it from, and the boys won't say a word. They took their dollar a day and called it all right. It was next thing to taking a trip home."

The President mused for a moment before he said:

"Corn intended for the Rebel army. The guerillas would have taken it or destroyed it, if it hadn't been stolen for our army—"

"I don't know," I said, for the mention of guerillas brought us at once to another part of my report. Loud and bitter had been the accusations made against the commanders in the South and West as to their asserted cruelties in dealings with the very irregular troops that went by the ugly Spanish name. On the other hand, terrible indeed had been the accounts of the atrocities committed by these land pirates, as useless as wolves to the regular armies of the Confederacy and as pitiless as hyenas to their noncombatant victims, the helpless people of the infested states. He was quite willing to hear what I had to say.

"There are not so many of them as there used to be," I told him. "You can see that from the army reports. When any are taken, nowadays, either they get away or the boys just let 'em go."

"What's that?" he exclaimed, perceiving that there was a large cat of some sort hidden under that meal. "Just tell me what you mean!"

"Well," said I, "I got it from the boys themselves. There was about a dozen of them taken, red-handed, over on the White, while I was there, by a squad of Clayton's cavalry.[6] I asked a sergeant of that squad what became of them and he said they happened to have plenty of rope and so they let 'em go. Didn't report 'em to Clayton or anybody else. You see, if a man is sitting on a mule with his hands tied behind him, and if one end of the rope that is noosed around his neck is drawn a little taut to a limb of the tree he is under, then if the mule—or if it's a horse it's all the same—gets a cut from a whip and runs away somewhere else, it lets the man go. He needn't be reported. Now, if instead of this way he is left entirely free, and is told to clear out, and nobody says anything till he reaches the line at fifty yards regular starting distance, why, then, if nobody makes out to hit him, at fifty yards and over, he gets away and there's no use in reporting him, to make trouble for the General or the War Department, if there are charges of murder or arson against him. That is one reason why so few guerrillas are heard of here, nowadays. But there is no doubt about Steele's honesty or Washburn's."

I had entirely satisfied him concerning a number of troublesome southwestern matters, concerning which he really knew a great deal more than I did and had apparently been told a great deal more than was true or even reasonable lying, as an old lawyer like him was entirely able to see. He did not tell me a word of what he knew that I did not, but remarked:

"That will quiet all that matter. I'm glad to hear it. It'll quash that whole indictment. Yes, if you really wish to settle in Arkansas, you can have the Marshalship, as soon as the organization is made. But I want Stanton to hear your report, just as you've made it to me. He'll be as glad as I am to dismiss those charges. Go right over to the War Office and see him."

"The difficulty about that is," I replied, "that he won't see me. There's always a perfect jam outside of his office, and inside, too . . . he doesn't like me too well, anyhow."

"Yes," he said, "he will see you. Take that. He'll see you at once."

He wrote a few words on a card and I took it with me with an increasing idea of the immediate urgency of my testimony. On reaching Stanton's place there was all the customary throng outside, but I sent in my bit of pasteboard by a messenger and, much to my astonishment, he made his appearance without delay.

It seemed to me that the whole pack of statesmen, army officers, contractors, and other miscellaneous members of the densely respectable mob in that narrow hall of the War Office made a sudden, grasping rush at him, but he was a vigorous man and he escaped them. He did not exactly collar me, but led me quickly out of their reach and into a little cupboard of an anteroom at that end of the hall. It had a frowsy, war-worn, time-worn brick-red sofa under its one dirty window, and upon this he sat down beside me to hear my interesting story.

He poked many lawyerlike questions at me and obtained a vast amount of reliable information with extraordinary rapidity, for I also helped him much. He appeared to be as greatly pleased as Lincoln had been and it occurred to me, as it does now, that I was in this way filling in chinks or vacancies in the previous testimony of other men, if not giving him desirable cause for believing that they had lied to him. I had just about wound up and was feeling more than ordinary admiration for the Great War Secretary when an officer stepped in from his own room, by the side door, and handed him one of the yellow tissue or fly paper slips upon which the army despatches were usually duplicated. He took it with a growl but his eyes widened largely as he glanced over it and I do not assert that he swore joyously. His face turned fiery red, anyhow, and he handed it to me.

"Read that, Mr. Secretary!" he shouted. "Read that! Hurrah! Take it to the President. Show it to Mr. Lincoln! It's the turning point of the war! It's the beginning of the end! No more work in this office today. This is enough!"

I read it. It was Phil Sheridan's first announcement of his victory over Early,[7] in West Virginia, when he "sent him whirling up the Valley," and it was the very thing which was a military necessity at that date. The despatch was snatched out of my hand and up sprang Stanton. Out into the hall he dashed, waving it over his head as if it had been the American flag. The swarm recoiled rather than rushed at him but in among them he dashed on, absolutely dancing up and down, with no bricks in his pockets, while he roared out the glorious news, with comments of his own to fill up all the omissions left by Philip Sheridan. There were all sorts of yells and shouts but Stanton handed me the yellow paper again and all but upset me as he repeated his order to "Take that to the President!" It is on my mind that he actually called him "His Excellency," but nobody would believe me if I should say so. Not anybody that knew Stanton.

I tell you what, though. I actually ran most of my way to the White House and in and up the stairs, and I was out of breath when I was arrested, by Hay and Nicolay and some statesman or other and I do not know who else besides. Old Edward was in the procession which formed behind us as we stormed into the President's room. Now! We did not disturb his nervous system a hair. He took the despatch, though, read it through, and I told him the condition into which it had thrown Stanton.

"Boys," he said, "That'll do. I feel as Stanton does. We'll shut up shop for the rest of today."

That may have been a cunning device of his for sending us all out of the room and away from national affairs, for although the White House at once had an appearance of having shut itself up for a season of mutual self congratulation, I had an idea that its next hour of loneliness was shared with the President by Stanton, Seward, Halleck, and two or three old boys in blue uniforms. I hope they had a good time but as for myself, I invited Nicolay and Hay to dine with me at the Club and we three did well by our dinner, making also patriotic remarks concerning Philip and his West Virginia army.

The most important event then about to come to pass was not of a military character. The National Convention of the Republican Party was soon to assemble at Baltimore to select candidates for President and Vice President and to declare its opinion of the present administration. It would seem, to anybody now looking back, that there was only one opinion to be expressed by anybody, but the truth was altogether different. The entire course of events from the beginning of the war had inevitably bred a multitude of critics, criticisms, angry discontents, fierce personal disappointments, [and] genuine sore-heartedness, and the President was staggering under the accumulated load of all the defeats, errors, blunders, and positive misdeeds of his military or civic subordinates. He even had to bear all the popular disapproval of some things which had been done by Congress and of many which had never been done at all but which were entirely the creation of newspapers, their army correspondents, and of the innumerable viperous race of malignant slanderers, reinforced largely by that other great, loudmouthed clan which may be described as the sputtterers, chatterers, and empty-head rattlers.

At the outbreak of the war, the two wings of the old Democratic Party may be said to have completely folded themselves. That party disappeared in the smoke of the battles but left behind it a sufficient quantity of political ruins for the foundations of a new party which assumed the same name and which grew by the mischiefs which it fed on. I need not here go into any analysis, more than this, of the really tremendous opposition to the Lincoln Administration. It included a great Cave of Adullam[8] into which had wandered thousands of good Republicans, although, as Lincoln quoted to a party of his visiting friends, their number of active or important men was "about four hundred."

In order to give any idea of my own connection with the National Convention or its deeds, I must go back one year to an event that can best be told, in this relation. When the Union League was founded, I was made one of its central Council of Twelve, its executive, and I was re-elected at the end of my year, keeping also the post of Grand Corresponding Secretary, all the important penwork of which was necessarily performed for me by a clerk in the Interior Department, under the direction of Judge Edmunds, who from time to time gave that man the pens of as many other clerks as were required for the really tremendous performances of the League headquarters.

It came to pass that the Annual Convention, or elective, representative Grand Council of the League, was convened in Washington in the Summer of 1863. It was composed of leading men from all parts of the country, governors and the like but even for convenience sake, the State and Local Councils had generally named their Senators and Congressmen as their delegates, so that a more distinguished crowd of Americans could hardly have been gathered than was that same Grand Council. As to numbers, it just about seated itself in one of the smaller public halls, and there were no outsiders, every man present being as firmly sworn to secrecy as if he had been a Lodge of Free Masons or a camp of the Golden Circle with a rope around his neck.

Into this body, especially from Missouri and Kansas, through governors, Senators and Congressmen, poured a compact and exceedingly able company of the bitterest enemies of Abraham Lincoln. My own seat was on the platform, in front and at the left of the presiding officer, Judge Edmunds. There I was compelled to sit in squirming silence, while exceedingly eloquent men arraigned the President and his Administration, appearing to make out a case of sins of commission and omission sufficient to hang the whole rotten, incapable, worthless, criminal, futile concern. Perhaps the most bitterly eloquent and convincing speech was made by that strange character Senator Jim Lane of Kansas,[9] but another like it had been spoken by Governor Carney, of that state and two of the other great men had put their feet into my drawer of preserved letters in the northeast room. That drawer was opening all the while they were speaking and so was a hot tide of indignation in all the veins of my organism, for as yet not a voice had been raised, not one word had been spoken, in defense of the President.

The entire Convention appeared to be swept away and the pending resolution condemning the Administration and its head and calling for a new party deal, seemed sure of being passed almost unanimously. Carney had made his last cursory remark and had hardly seated himself before I was on my feet in front of the Chair, just boiling. It is of no use now to attempt a paraphrase of any fiercely indignant arraignment of those men for condemning the President for deeds he had never done and for others which they had themselves advised, in writings then in my possession, or in words uttered in my presence or to my sure knowledge. You may be aware that I am never exactly an orator and have usually no faculty for "putting things," but whether you believe it or not, I did "put" them, that night. One Senator actually got out from under my pointing finger and retreated into an anteroom. I think I described him as a direct agent of Jeff Davis, Robert E. Lee, and Satan and Slavery and the Confederate Rebellion, and other words of that kind, freely spoken.

I sat down at last and the Chairman laid before the Council a substitute resolution, endorsing the Administration and providing that the Grand Council do now adjourn, to meet one year hence at the time and place provided for the assembling of the Republican National Convention. To the astonishment of some of the opposition leaders, this resolution passed with but nine dissenting votes, not one other orator opening his mouth, for or against it. There was a kind of queer silence. Then I was myself utterly astonished, for the moment the adjournment was declared, a perfect mob of great men pushed around me to congratulate me upon my star and spangled speech and its national consequences. Sunday School! The first man to grab my hand and thank me for convincing him against his will was Senator Jim Lane of Kansas, declaring, loudly: "Henceforth I am an unquestioning supporter of Abraham Lincoln. I was cheated!"

That was glory enough for one evening but there were no newspaper reports of it. Years afterward, however, men who met me here and there averred that they had been in that council and praised me for my angry oratory. I do believe it was the best speech I ever made and it shows the importance to any orator of being wild mad and of not caring two cents what he is saying, so long as it is true and he can find in him the right words to say it with.

One year passed away and the Annual Grand Council was to meet in Baltimore, according to its resolution of adjournment, one day earlier than the Republican National Convention. It was well understood, however, that it would be a much more numerous body than before and that nearly all its members, man for man, were also members, delegates duly appointed, to the great Convention itself. Its meeting, therefore, would be neither more nor less than a vast preparatory caucus, held in secret, in which the work of the Convention would be discussed, cut out, and practically decided beforehand. I was only an outside delegate to either body, except that I was to sit on the platform of the Grand Council as one of its silent ornaments. I had it in mind that the silence would depend upon circumstances, but I was not to be needed. I had in hand some work of my own.

Mr. Lincoln had told me that in order to make my Arkansas appointment go smoothly, I ought to have some endorsements from the loyal representatives of that state and other Border States. With that in mind, I had gone to work and identified myself with the Border State delegations, as one of the leading men of Arkansas, and we were all pulling together, for I told them we must have the vice president named from among our own men, in place of that unnecessary statesman Hannibal Hamlin, of Maine, who had never appeared to admire me and who had been, whatever else he had ever been, a sort of fifth wheel to the Administration coach, not at all necessary to the preservation of the American people. They agreed with me enthusiastically and I put my prospective finger upon Andrew Johnson of Tennessee, little thinking of what a mess I was preparing for the future of my country. It sometimes requires only a small match to set a big barn on fire, but then it was the fire and not the match which was responsible for the discomfort of all the rats which were deprived of their homes when the barn burned down.

I here absolutely disclaim any blame for the conduct or misconduct of the Johnson Administration. Wilkes Booth did it when he murdered Lincoln, and a number of other men, including Andrew Johnson himself,[10] were vastly more to blame than I was. Things were looking more and more squally as the day appointed drew near, for the Cave of Adullam was sending out tempest blasts which it mistook for trumpet blasts and all over the country the critics of Mr. Lincoln were blowing their whistles, of all sizes, from that of a sore-throated locomotive down to little screeches which came from hole and corner men who had failed to obtain offices, Post and other offices and who yelled like post mortems just risen in a hot place. Some of the worst attacks had come from leading Republican journals or from prominent Republican politicians, in and out of Congress. The set day came but before its sun arose I was in Baltimore, going from hotel to hotel and getting acquainted with such delegates as I had not met before, but one of the curiosities of the time was how large a proportion of them I had already taken hold of, in the Capitol, in the White House, or elsewhere. It was at that time and afterwards my belief that I had at least shaken hands with almost every prominent American, as well as of some whose prominence was nothing for them or me to be at all proud of.

When the Grand Council of the Union League of America assembled for its portentous session, the evening before the Convention day, it was a troubled and excited body of men, a little more than half afraid to tell itself what it was about to do, and all of the other half afraid to actually make up its mind and do it. It was in order for business at an early hour and all smaller affairs were rapidly swept out of sight in preparation for the discussion of the Presidential nomination, or rather of an expected resolution denouncing Lincoln and of another endorsing his administration and demanding his renomination. The hall was large, well lighted, and it contained a rarely distinguished gathering of eminent citizens of this illustrious republic.

My place was upon the platform and there I was, in solemn dignity, well aware that I was not one of the expected orators of the evening. At the same time I was troubled greatly by the consciousness that all sorts of angry eloquence were swelling within me and surging up in my throat. All the preliminary exercises were rushed through with small ceremony, for every man present was nervously opposed to delay. There was none. Hardly had the chairman announced that general business was in order before a western senator whom I will not now name sprang to his feet and began a furious denunciation of Abraham Lincoln personally and of his evil administration generally and of his satraps, sub-tyrants, satellites, corruptionists, vampires, serpents, failures, mistakes, blunders, incompetences, and fools. He was a splendid speaker, a lawyer with experience in criminal courts and able to do all that was to be done for the sure conviction of the vile prisoner at the bar.

He wound up eloquently and patriotically and was followed by another orator of the same sort in even a more vehement tirade and appeal to this body to save the nation from four years more of these intolerable evils. Another followed, then another, and the very air seemed to tell that it was red hot against the ruined dictator whose eternal condemnation had been pronounced. If at that moment a vote could have been taken, it is and at the time was the opinion of all good judges, the result would have been disastrous. I felt like springing down upon the floor, but I was not needed. To my utter astonishment—to my momentary disgust—I was shut off. Up in a place near the front center arose the tall, lank form of Senator Jim Lane of Kansas. Now, thought I and others, Lincoln will catch it, red hot. There was a pin-drop silence while he stood still and deliberately stared around him into the faces of men and then enlarged his scope of vision as if he were studying that crowd with more than a little contempt for it. His attitude and manner were absolutely insulting, but he began and for years afterward I could remember most of that speech.

Its opening phrases were something like this, but much better:

"For a man—or men—great orators, to arise here and bid us look upon the bleeding wounds of our suffering nation; to arouse in hurt and aching hearts the hot sympathies which all of us feel; to thus bring up to its utmost tension the heartstrings of our patriotism; this requires no great eminence of oratorical power. For them then to pervert and mischievously mis-direct the tides of feeling which they have in this manner set loose—this is no triumph of oratory. It is the accustomed trick of the political charlatan. . . . For any man to take such an assembly as this, hot-hearted, angry, utterly convinced already and prepared for action, already settled in its will and in its purpose of condemnation, and bid it face the other way—compel it to reverse its decision and march onward upon the very path it had abandoned—that would indeed be a triumph of oratory. I am myself no orator, as these men are, but that feat is precisely what I am now about to perform, for you must hear me."

The terrific insolence of this opening I cannot render nor the absolutely fierce contempt for all "the oratorical agents of Jeff Davis now present" with which he went on. I do not believe that the celebrated border ruffian and single-hand knife fighter ever came so near old Cicero before or afterwards. I was in ecstasies, for he all but cursed Lincoln's enemies in the name of God. His last words were something like these:

"We must renominate Abraham Lincoln. We must do it here, tonight for the Convention tomorrow will but formally register the verdict which we shall here pronounce. If the Convention shall name any other man, at this juncture, it will but at the same hour nominate Jeff Davis; declare DisUnion; perpetuate the Confederacy; and for us it will elect the wasted blood of our dead, the defeat of the Union cause—Ruin! Ruin! Ruin!"

Quite a large number of extensive verbal expressions had escaped him from time to time as he went on, and when he sat down the Lincoln resolution was promptly substituted for the other and was adopted with only nine dissenting votes, all oratorical. The Council adjourned from the hall to the hotels and streets and I joyfully adjourned with it, dashing around from crowd to crowd to hear what was going on and saying. Only here and there were groups of grim and silent men who stood and looked into each other's faces in the dissatisfied attitude of guns which had been fired off without hitting anything worthwhile. Even if they had any more powder, it would be of small use for them to load up again in preparation for more blank-cartridge shooting in the Convention next day. It is true, as the record shows, that they did some small firing, but all who listened could perceive that the ammunition used was a little damp, even if unaware of the precise manner in which its explosive force had been taken out of it.

The Convention was really a grand affair and in it were large numbers of distinguished men who were entirely unaware of the fact that the Presidential nominating vote had already been taken and counted. I will not attempt a picture of the Convention but when its perfunctory edict was announced it declared nine votes for General Grant and all the rest for Lincoln. The next business was supposed to be the renomination of Hannibal Hamlin for Vice President but here the confident expectationists were disappointed. There were really several other likely candidates and it quickly appeared that there was no immediate choice. Now, I will say that I had somehow strengthened my idea that Lincoln did not want Hamlin and that he had a leaning toward Johnson.

My memory is that a boy named John Hay played the diplomat in the matter. I received an idea from him that it would not do for Nicolay or Hay to express any wish of the President in the matter, but that another person might act with proper prudence.[11] That is precisely what I did and I could not now be qualified as to how many delegates received, directly or indirectly, the idea that they were instructed confidentially to comply with the President's wishes. It was a narrow affair, even then, and Andrew's nomination was entirely due to the Arkansas and other Border State men among whom I was sitting—or moving around. It was done and the glory or anything else of the achievement may by me be partly shouldered over upon that handsome young diplomatist Hay. I did hear something, however, which prevented me from reporting to either him or Nicolay. It was as well for them to remain in ignorance, for they might have ignored me and that would have been bad.

It was now time for me to get ready for the West. My appointment was given me and my first commission dated on my birthday, September 24th, but I received another after my confirmation by the Senate. I had many things to attend to in Washington and New York and among them were the affairs of my sister Kate and my brother Henry. I will not say just why I assented to Harry's assertion that he could not remain in Washington; one reason in my mind was that he was not fit to stay there alone. The fact was that he had not been the same man since his fiancée in Syracuse threw him over. I remember crying like a child when I saw what a break it had made in him. So I told him to come on after me as soon as he could and I would take care of him, somehow, I did not exactly see how, but believed I could do almost anything.

All was ready, at last and I remember John Hay telling me that Nicolay expressed his regret at my departure in this form: "John! What'll we do with the Madame after Stod goes? Heaven! You and I can't manage her."

She did not love him and John's diplomacy had entirely failed there.

My last interview of any consequence, in Washington, presents itself to my mind with a mournful vividness. It was necessary for me to say goodbye to Mr. Lincoln, but I had not the least idea that it was an eternal farewell to the man I loved so well. He sent for me, and Old Edward led me away on to the room on the left at the end of the upper hall, the same in which he had lain with the varioloid and in which I afterwards conferred with Grover Cleveland. The President lay on a sofa, apparently very weary, but received me in a most fatherly way. He expressed his strong good wishes for my success in my new career, for the restoration of my health, and so forth. Then he talked about the future of Arkansas, the Rebel states, and of the colored people. He had already given me letters of introduction, army passports and the like, and I will try to recall as nearly as I may the last words spoken to me by Abraham Lincoln.

"And now, Stoddard," he said, half rising on the sofa, "there's just one thing more I want to say. The war is nearly over. Just when it will end, I can't say. But it won't be a great while. Then the Government forces must all be withdrawn from all the Southern states. Sooner or later, we must take them all away. Now, what I want you to do is this: Do all you can, in any and every way you can, to get the ballot into the hands of the freedmen.

We must make voters of them before we take away the troops. The ballot will be their only protection after the bayonet is gone, and they will be sure to need all they can get. I can see just how it will be. Will you?"

I said anything I could say to assure him of my intentions and then took my last look into his deep, sad, almost prophetic eyes, that were so weary of all they had been compelled to look upon and into during the long years through which I had been with him. If, not long afterwards, I took an even offensively prominent part in caring for the future of the colored people of Arkansas, I did so in fulfilling my promise to Lincoln and to this day I am not ashamed of it. There is on my mind a dim memory that he was not at that date publicly uttering his mind upon this subject and there may have been good reasons for his prudence which are now nobody's business. But this was the thought that was uppermost in his heart and mind in the hour when he said farewell to me and there is a kind of jewel in it. It belongs in regular sequence to his earlier declarations, including the Emancipation Proclamation and his Illinois letter about the arming of the blacks. I am glad I've made this small record of it.

39

Notes from the Southwest, and the Death of Lincoln

The war was indeed slowly drawing on toward its now inevitable close, as Lincoln had said, but the Confederates still had large armies in the field. They had lost the coast lines, the Mississippi, and other great rivers, but there were terrible battles yet to be fought. They had but nominally been driven out of Arkansas and that state was still somewhat debatable ground. Its interior was largely in the hands of roving bands of guerillas that were a curse to all kinds of people and were fit only for merciless killing.

The Mississippi River itself was in a curious condition. Its levees, entirely neglected during several years, were broken down at many places. It was notable that the lower levees were in better condition than the upper and sometimes acted as dams to produce a "set-back," so that the floods above were worse than ever before. So serious was this hydraulic experiment that I remember one great flood when all the Arkansas lines were under water, almost if not quite back to Bartholomew Bayou and the Sunk Country.

My first duty [as Marshal of the Eastern District of Arkansas] was to pay a visit to the Statehouse, where, to my great satisfaction, I was welcomed by the Hon. Henry Clay Caldwell, recently appointed United States District Judge, by whom I was duly sworn in and placed in charge of the Statehouse.

I found the Statehouse an empty shell, for when the Confederates marched away they destroyed or removed every article of furniture or equipment with the utmost care. It was a brick building, large in the middle to accommodate the halls of the State Senate and House of Representatives, and having wings on either end for other offices. The middle was of two stories and the wings of one. Around was a large open space with recollections of fences at its edges and with many good trees. It made good camping ground, now and then, for soldiers or refugees, and it was crossed in all directions by well-worn cattle—or human—paths. The Marshal's office was in the southerly wing. It was a large, high-ceilinged room, oblong, with two big deep-seated windows, in front, and one at the end. At the middle back was an enormous fireplace, and its chimney served also for the like kind of cavern in the Clerk's office, a precisely similar room, in the rear.

In one corner I found the most remarkable "safe" I ever saw, and somebody had preserved its antiquely tremendous key. It was of the "old kind," brassmounted, and of such is the primitive idea of how to beat a burglar. It would have kept out a good cracksman about ten minutes, if he were at all lazy, but it was good enough against the non-experts who were likely to hunt for its deftly hidden keyhole. I arranged to get my meals at the Anthony House, and then it was needful to look out for sleeping matters, as that hotel was temporarily overcrowded and I was not attracted by its crowd or landlord. It was altogether another specimen of the ancient hostelries of the Sunny South in the days befoh de wah. The Army helped me out, for I easily obtained an iron camp bedstead, linen sheets, and a pair of heavy gray blankets. This apparatus I set up in the Clerk's office, adjoining my own, and procured from the quartermaster a liberal allowance of cordwood for the respective fireplaces. Of course, I did get one night's lodging in a queer coop of a room at the hotel, but was not hungry for another roost in that hole. So I fixed things as well as I could, including fires to drive away a great, cold, foggy dampness which had settled over Little Rock and concentrated its worst qualities in and around the Statehouse.

The head of the Treasury Office was a rare specimen who had been "running the nicest little game" of faro and roulette down near the Chicago stock exchange when police interference nipped his career in the bud and he [decided] to serve his beloved country as a Treasury Agent to whom had belonged the custody of considerable amounts of seized or abandoned property which now had to be turned over to me. Whether or not he turned over to me all the property he had taken possession of was a question for the astronomers.

Another piece of valuable property that I at once fell heir to was a remarkable relic of bondage days who went by the name of "State House Jack."

Short, thin, black as coal, exceedingly respectful, sometimes even truthful, and conscious of his title to all that lot of public buildings, Marshal and all. How long he had lived in it, nobody knew, but he was a friend of his own race and he had filled with free Africans all the outbuildings and as much of the main structure as had not yet been taken over for other purposes. The big point of that, I soon found to be, [was] that contrabands without other visible, responsible employment were likely to be set at work on the fortifications in return for the army rations they were regularly receiving. State House Jack was free of the pick and shovel and so, shortly, were all his constituents, and I never knew how many dark parties were actually registered as "Colonel Stoddard's niggers."

"Colonel?" Yes, that came right along as a matter of course, for an army rank was almost a necessity under some circumstances and any man in Arkansas "befoh the wah" had been a titled magnate of some sort. I was told that there had once been an exception but that he was killed for putting on airs and trying to set up for something distinguished and exceptional.

I had come with an idea that I might possibly do something in cotton operations and had obtained for myself and others a number of what were called "permits" for that purpose. It was the desire of the Government to get out as much Reb cotton as was consistent with military operations, for the material was greatly needed. I sympathized with the authorities in that matter and did a great deal, first and last, to meet the public needs and my own. Not to go into particulars, however, I may say that really the biggest thing I accomplished in cotton was to have about a thousand bales of my "permit" burned up for me by a Rebel horde down near the Texas border.

My profits on that line were a large hole in my pocket. I still had some money and was disposed to use it, but I could obtain none from anybody for the restoration of the Statehouse offices to a state of usefulness. I had to furnish them myself, with the aid of the Quartermaster and some army carpenters, and all my outlays were dead beat. It was not long before my brother Harry made his appearance. He was made chief clerk of the Seventh Army corps, with a salary of $1,800 and a fine, responsible position. He became immensely popular.

There came a night in the Spring of 1865 when Henry and myself lay down as usual upon our camp beds in the Marshal's office in the old Statehouse building. The night was warm and one of the windows was open. The previous evening we had heard of the attempt upon the life of Mr. Seward and of his dangerous condition, and had been talking about him, for to myself he had been always a kindly friend for whom I had a strong personal regard. It was in the early dawn, or a little after sunrise, that I found myself suddenly sitting up in bed, listening. In a moment more I knew why, for there came booming in through the window the sound of a heavy gun. Henry was also now awake and the first exclamation made by either of us was, in some form, "What? An attack by the Confederate army? That's from a fort!" "Impossible!" I exclaimed. "None of them are near enough. Hark!"

One minute, another gun, one minute more, another ominous report, and I was on my feet at the window.

"Minute guns, Harry," I said. "Seward is dead. Get up. We must go out and get the news." Just then there was a loud bang at the door and when I opened it the bewildered, excited face of Captain Redmond looked into mine as he shouted:

"Marshal Stoddard, President Lincoln is assassinated!"

Away he went and we were left to stare at each other as bewildered and as excited as he had been. We began to dress and it happened that the only black clothes we had were our dress suits. These were put on, therefore, without discussion, and we walked out into the Main Street. The first man we met was Mr. Jacks, the newly elected Union Congressman from the northeast district. He was a short, sturdy, rough-looking man, but he walked along, swinging his hands, weeping bitterly and swearing like a pirate. He did not speak a word to us for he went by, staring at the ground. Not many yards further, we met a tall, portly man, well dressed, who had been Confederate District Attorney and an intense Rebel. In one hand he was carrying a tremendous bowie knife and in the other a huge red silk handkerchief with which he was mopping his face, for he too was weeping—and swearing furiously—exclaiming:

"Damn them! This is the worst blow that could have fallen upon the South at this hour!"

We passed him without speaking and at no great distance beyond we were near a row of small houses occupied by the colored people. Men, women, and children were swarming out of them but all appeared to have been struck dumb. They were busily tying bits of black cloth, of any sort they could obtain, upon the doors and windows of their houses.

A little further and I saw a squad of angry men in blue with their knives out, pursuing a fellow who took refuge in a dwelling when I called them to "Halt!" receiving from husky voices the explanation:

"Why, Colonel, he ought to be killed! He said it was good enough for him! Good enough for him!"

Killed he would have been if they had not been halted, but hardly had that incident passed before another squad of volunteers came running to me to shout at me that "Old Bernays is opening his liquor store We told him not to but he's taking down his shutters."

"Go and tell Bernays to shut up," I replied. "No stores will be open in Little Rock today. Tell him he will get his orders from the Provost Marshal pretty soon. Every bar must close."

I had no real authority but took for granted the sure action of General Reynolds and the soldiers took care of the obedience, for if "Old Bernays" had not obeyed they would have cleaned him out. I myself went on to head-quarters to obtain the facts of the matter. It was the third or fourth day after the assassination, I think, owing to the delay in getting telegraph despatches from Memphis to Little Rock. The quarters were thronged with military men and prominent civilians and before long a surprise came to me that somehow or other did not surprise me, perhaps because nothing on earth could have done so, just then. Little Rock had been a great headquarters of the Masonic Fraternity. They had there a "Masonic College" and nearly all the old citizens, of any good standing were members of the order, including neighboring planters, etc. Somehow or other, the leading Lodge had won for itself the title of "The Reb Masons" and it had the finest hall in the town. It was from this body that I received an invitation to attend a "Lodge of Sorrow," to be held in the hall at noon, and to deliver an oration.

I went and found the hall crowded. I made an address which was received with evidently sincere and intense interest by an intelligent body of men who saw and felt that in the murder of Abraham Lincoln the really best friend and protector of the future interests of the defeated South had been taken away. I finished my address and walked away to my office, weary and sick at heart.

The loyal state officers and representatives and senators had been only nominally friendly for it was in the air that I might be in their way in any subsequent political operations. I can even suppose that they suspected me of ambition and of being on too good terms with the old secesh element which I failed to condemn as they did. Therefore, in preparing for a tremendous public meeting at the State Representative chamber, that evening, a long list of speakers was selected and announced and my name was not upon it. I was not wanted and other men were to avail themselves of the political occasion. I did not at all care to attend but went and lay down, after supper, to grieve for Lincoln. I had not yet had time to consider how great a change this loss of my best friend was making in my own position and in my future course in life. I was not asleep, nevertheless, when several men, one of them a U.S. Senator, came hurriedly in to stir me up. The hall, they said, was packed to suffocation, but "the boys" would not allow any other man to speak until they had heard from me.

Every effort of any orator on the list had been angrily shouted down, for the boys in blue had no political aspirations and knew their own minds. I arose, wearily enough, and with some difficulty I was wedged through the crowd to a place on the platform. Behind me were flags in crape and many men. Before me was a sea of mournful faces, and a kind of inspiration came upon me. Just what I said, during the hour that followed I never tried to recall but when I at last sank back upon my chair it was of no use for the chairman of the meeting to announce another orator. The boys had heard what they wanted to hear and with one accord they marched slowly, thoughtfully, out of the hall, leaving it almost empty. It was a most impressive sight to see those bowed heads go—a greater tribute to Lincoln's memory than anything that I or any other man could have uttered in words.

The next morning, to my next surprise, Judge Caldwell came and asked me to write upon the Court records the memorial tribute he deemed the event to require and there it is to this day. So the death of Lincoln became a thing of the past but his memory hardly seems so, he has left behind him so much that still is living in the history of his country.

Afterword: Picturing Lincoln

Editor's note: Stoddard's original manuscript continued for more than two hundred additional pages, carrying the author from war-torn Arkansas to a new life in New York.

But save for one long passage, his most historically important revelations were behind him. Besides, by 1906, when he resumed his memoir-writing in earnest, like many men his age the author possessed more precise recall of his early days than of the more recent events of his long life. Stoddard told the rest of his story, he conceded, in "kaleidoscopic" form, acknowledging that "at this distance of time, the almanac begins to resemble the records of the Continental congress" (original Stoddard manuscript, 505).

We know that, saddled with his and his brother's debts, Stoddard at first harbored postwar hopes of becoming "a planter as well as a politician" (531), even while facing "ten times more personal peril [from bandits, unreconstructed Confederates, and guerillas] than any soldier in the Southwest—most of whom were no longer in any peril whatever from any hostile forces" (532). "Money was scarce and land was a drug" (536), and Stoddard, only twenty-eight, felt for a time that if he withstood the rigors of Arkansas he might become one of its Senators by the time he reached thirty (555). Instead, malaria struck him down, and "almost dead and assured by doctors that I could not possibly live thirty days" (559), Stoddard left the Southwest and headed north, his funds depleted, his possessions gone, and his "Arkansas ambitions . . . a thing of the gloomy, disappointing past" (559). America's—and Stoddard's—war was finally over.

Stoddard chose not to throw himself on the mercy of the new president, convinced that Andrew Johnson "had never quite forgiven me for my atrocious conduct at Baltimore in forcing upon him his nomination for Vice

President, which was the cause of all his subsequent troubles." Stoddard convinced himself that "but for me he would never have been President and would never have been so dreadfully impeached" (561). He does manage one more visit to the White House, in 1866, using his trusty old latchkey to let himself in—security apparently no more rigorous than in Lincoln's day, assassination notwithstanding.

Stoddard's manuscript went on to trace his emergence as a New York writer, a career that blossomed despite his refusal—a decision he implied that he regretted—to accept an offer to become assistant editor of *Harper's Weekly* (574). Stoddard recalled at one sad point that his old trunk of letters and "priceless" autographs went up in flames (596)—making his ability to recollect his presidential years in their absence all the more remarkable.

The onetime White House secretary had yet to publish his first book on Lincoln, but he had one more major contribution, of the nonliterary kind, to make in preserving the sixteenth president's memory. When his upstate New York friend, artist Francis B. Carpenter, turned to him for help in convincing a stubbornly indifferent Congress to acquire his famous Emancipation Proclamation painting in 1877, Stoddard rose to the challenge [see pages 63–64].

The picture had long been well known and well regarded. The giant, fifteen-by-nine foot canvas had been exhibited throughout the country to such frenzied acclaim that, in Pittsburgh, the painting aroused public fervor "to such a pitch that, once at least, the exhibition room had actually to be closed." An 1866 engraving became an instant bestseller.[1] Yet Carpenter had been unable to convince the public, or their representatives, that the picture deserved permanent, public display. The artist yearned for the recognition—and the money—he thought he deserved. Stoddard came to the rescue, lobbying and testifying before Congress to convince House Democrats and Senate Republicans to accept the gift of the picture—an unexpectedly difficult challenge.

He told the detailed story, since unpublished, near the end of his voluminous manuscript. Reprinted here as an afterword to his book, it serves as a fitting coda to the autobiography of the presidential secretary who helped preserve Abraham Lincoln's memory in picture as well as word.

*M*ore than one effort to obtain Congressional action had failed, for lack of time at the session's end, but Carpenter was not discouraged. He came to see me one day and told me that he had secured a loft in New York City and had set up his canvas there for final touches before conveying it to Washington. This was truly an alarming announcement and I hurried over to see what he might be up to. There it was, and my worst fears were realized. He asked my opinion of his "improvements" and I responded:

"Yes, the picture is all there, but where is Lincoln? You have gone to work and painted him out."

That was what he had done. He had been smoothing and regulating and making him better-looking until all that was left was a sort of caricature of the Lincoln I had known. Frank replied in utter dismay with all sorts of questions but I ordered him to get his step ladder and his crayons. Then I made him climb the ladder and go to work. A darkness under the simpering eyes. A renewing of the wrinkle in the forehead. A reproduction of the furrow under the lower lip. A readjustment of the chin. Putting back the lost wart on the right cheek. In fact, he had to undo about all that he had been doing. It seems as if Chase and Seward also required amendment and he had actually softened poor Stanton. As for Caleb B. Smith,[2] he never recovered and his portrait is dead, or at least sick, to this very day.

It was not long after that before the canvas was actually on exhibition in Washington and I was there to urge it upon Congress. It was in the last days of Grant, and somewhere along here, there was a great renewal of the furniture and so forth of the White House. The work was done by a gang of vandals in whose disreputable hands most of the priceless relics of the time-honored building disappeared. I went after some of them but learned to my dismay that even such things as Lincoln's desk, at which so many presidents had sat, and the cabinet table and Andrew Jackson's chair, and my own old desk, had gone for sale at some second-hand furniture concern. The old brass locks were no longer on the front door and no trace of them could be found. My latch key would not fit the new lock. In spite of that, it was needful to see President Grant and to get him to take an interest in the picture. It was not a reception day but that was of no consequence. I went and was let up into the private secretary's room and had no reason to be displeased with my welcome. He even sent in my card and the response was gracious. The President would not come out but he would meet Mr. Stoddard in the library.

In I went and there he was, looking finely, and we had talk about the picture. Much to my gratification, he took an interest in it and promised to come down the next day and see it for himself. No doubt he meant to keep his word, for he was in the habit of so doing, but the Secretary of State and some pesky national affairs intervened and he could not come. Neither could I linger long in Washington to force upon him another appointment. I did succeed in cornering Montgomery Blair, with whom I had always had a pleasant acquaintance, and he willingly went with me to look.

It was while he and I were commenting upon the figures and faces that a singular memory came flashing into my mind. I had been the only other person present in Lincoln's room when Blair came to pay his last, formal good-bye on leaving the Cabinet, in the old days.[3] There he was now, in the picture, standing on the very square yard of carpet, near the end of the table, on which he had stood when he made his last, unsmiling bow and turned to walk out. There had also been no smile on the face of Lincoln, for although they parted nominally as friends, neither of them was at all satisfied with the conduct of the other and that fact was in their faces when they parted.

Now, many years later, a great change was taking place in the management of national affairs. General [Rutherford B.] Hayes[4] was elected President by the narrowest majority on record, and after a contest which only failed of something like a revolution because Grant was on deck and because he made energetic remarks as to what might be his duty in case of any threat of civil war or armed resistance to the decision made at the polls. At the same time, however, the Democrats had succeeded in obtaining a majority in the House of Representatives, not in the Senate, and the former body was not untruly said to be under the control of a battalion of "Rebel Brigadiers."

The leader on that side on the floor of the House was, beyond question or dispute, the former Vice President of the Confederacy, Alexander H. Stephens of Georgia,[5] and a right good sort of man he was. On the Republican side, just as autocratically, was my splendid-looking and heroic friend James A. Garfield of Ohio, Chickamauga, and some other interesting places. Mr. Blaine afterwards said of him, in a sad eulogy, that his speeches on the floor at this era, if collected, would be found to contain in condensed and perfect form the entire political and war history of his time. No man knew better than did Blaine the value and extent of the oratorical and other services of the statesmen who had served with him during his own long and eventful career in the national legislature.

The course of pictorial events must be kept in series, or outline, lest they might become mixed up with something else and fail of their exceedingly picturesque effect upon this descriptive canvas. Susie [the author's wife] and I were at home in our house on Willoughby Avenue one evening, when we were surprised by a call from Frank Carpenter. Not but what he had been there often, but that now he was accompanied by a remarkably handsome woman of perhaps fifty, and a large, important story to tell us.

The lady introduced to me by Frank Carpenter was Mrs. Elizabeth Thompson. She was a widow and the possessor of considerable wealth. She was also patriotic and a strong personal friend of the artist, to whom, as I afterwards learned, she had advanced considerable sums of money for his wild theatrical undertakings as the promoter of the genius of Mr. Mackaye,[6] the actor who undertook to improve, if not to reform, the American stage. Susie and I went to one of his performances and I made a sad mistake when asked for my criticism on the performance. I innocently replied to Frank:

"Good! He has fine points, but he might have done better if he had selected a better play. What on earth made him take that thing?"

Alas! for my poor judgment. The play was one which the actor had written himself, with an idea that it would enable him to bring out the more brilliantly not only his genius as an actor but his other genius as a new Shakespeare. The whole thing was a financial failure and the worst of its losses fell upon Carpenter. As for Mackaye, he was a cousin of my old and intimate friend and longtime roommate, Henry G. Mackaye, by whom he had long ago been introduced to me.

The cause of the present interview was that Mrs. Thompson had agreed to pay the twenty-five thousand dollars for which I had fought in Washington and that she would then make the United States of America a clean present of the picture of the Reading of the Emancipation Proclamation, if the national legislature could be induced to accept the gift.

Inquiries had thrown doubt upon even that question, and Frank and his lady benefactress now came to me to ask me to go on again to Washington and secure the acceptance of the great canvas for permanent placing in the Capitol. Susie was in doubt about it but consented, and I made my arrangements accordingly, for Congress was then in session and there was no time to lose. I remember that part of my preparations carried me to a tiptop tailor, that my personal outfit might not throw any cloud upon the work of art, for recent events had compelled me to be economical in the matter of dress. At that date the picture was already in Washington. Rutherford B. Hayes was President, and with him I as yet had no personal acquaintance. Randall of Pennsylvania[7] was Speaker of the House and I could suppose him to have forgotten me, although I had met him often enough in wartime. As was said, Alexander H. Stephens was leader of the Democratic House, Garfield was the leader on the Republican side, and the Senate was pretty strongly Republican but all the while in the worst kind of bad humor over its unfortunate position as a kind of chained bear unable to get a good grip of its opponents. All it could do was to put in a sharp scratch now and then without having reach enough to hug that "Resurrection of the Confederacy" to death.

It was a day of exceedingly bitter political feeling, for the Democracy, with one voice, declared itself to have been robbed of the Presidency. It was an article of the Democratic faith to believe Tilden was the rightful President and Hayes a usurper. At the same time there was an abundance of other old bones for the angry orators on both sides to gnaw upon, from day to day, and the debates in both houses contained large quantities of eloquence which had in them a disagreeable smell of the used-up gunpowder of the Civil War. This, it appeared, was not the brand of which Lincoln once declared that "Some kinds of powder can't be burnt but once."

All preparations having been made, I was in Washington, at a quiet place near the depot. The picture had been inspected and was found to be in good condition, without any more destructive improvements. Then my first next duty was to go to the Capitol and see General Garfield, to stir up all the art enthusiasm and pictorial patriotism there might be in him. On reaching the outskirts of the House of Representatives, time was taken for a survey of its present exterior and a discovery, without needless clashing with the doorkeepers, that my privilege of the floor as Private Secretary of the tyrannical dictator who had crushed the Sunny South had passed into the forgotten past. It did appear that at each entrance there stood an ex-Confederate soldier, instead of the old doorkeepers whom I had known so well. I saw two or three angry word-collisions between them and parties who were less prudent than myself and doubted their probable appreciation of me. So I went around to the main front entrance and sent in my card to General Garfield. In a minute or so he was out, to shake hands and to inquire:

"What did you call me out for? Why didn't you come right in?"

"Why, General," I responded, "there's a new king risen who knoweth not Joseph. I am no longer in the majority."

"I can arrange all that!" he exclaimed, and he quickly began to write something on a card. He sent it in by a messenger and only a few minutes later, the messenger returned with the perpetual card of admission, signed by Speaker Randall "'at the request of Gen. Garfield." From that hour onward I was as free of the floor as if Lincoln had been a Democrat and I his Democratic secretary.

This time it was needful to go on in with Garfield and to sit with him at his desk while he attended to various legislative duties while I tried to explain to him the new situation. It was of no use, for he was intently watching important bills and had to be frequently on his feet.

"It's of no use, Stoddard," he said, at last. "You'll have to come to my house this evening. We can talk it all over there, at our leisure."

So I got out and went over to the Senate, to study the many changes that had there taken place. Perhaps a majority of my old friends were gone, but quite enough were left to give me some courage. There were many other things to see and do and the Senate was finished so far as one day's work would do it. Memory seems to say that it was not until the next evening that I had my appointment at Garfield's house, and at the appointed hour I was there and with him in his private room to hear him talk gloomily of our prospects for success.

"The fact is, my dear fellow," he said, "this is a rebel House. It is controlled by the dead Confederacy. It will not listen for a moment to any commemoration of the Emancipation Proclamation or of Lincoln. Why, the leader on that side of the House is the Ex-Vice President of the Confederacy. He would at once put his foot down."

"General Garfield," I exclaimed. "What if Mr. Stephens would consent to support a resolution for the acceptance of the picture?"

"Impossible!" he shouted back. "He would never do so."

"General Garfield, if Alexander Stephens will promise to second the resolution, will you have the courage to present it? May I tell him so?"

"Tell him? Why, yes. You may tell him so from me. But he won't." Some other things were said and he drew up the required Joint Resolution with diplomatic care so that its wording should not give offense.

There was a carriage waiting for me at the door and, thus armed, I rode to the National Hotel, where Mr. Stephens had his quarters. Prompt admission followed the sending up of my card; and in a minute more I was with one of the most remarkable men of his day. He was a short, slightly made man, with an intensely intellectual countenance. I was at once reminded of the traditional duel in Georgia. The story goes that he had challenged a giant of a statesman, whose name escapes me. His antagonist was a fighting man but objected to the shooting match as unequal, since he himself would furnish so large a target and the size of his proposed adversary would make it difficult to hit him. "All that can be remedied," replied Mr. Stephens. "You can chalk out my size on him and any shot that hits him outside of that line needn't be counted." Somehow or other, that settled the fight. Many will recall the remark of Mr. Lincoln, when he saw Mr. Stephens taking off a tremendously long and ample surtout overcoat, that, "I never before saw so much husk taken from so small an ear of corn."[8]

He was all cordiality and was interested in what I had to say to him, as one of Lincoln's secretaries, about his own former personal friendship for Lincoln when they were in Congress together. He spoke strongly, even eloquently, of the life and services of the dead president, of his known good will for the South, and of the great misfortune his murder had been to the Southern people. From that it was easy to lead on to the Emancipation Proclamation and here was a surprise, for Mr. Stephens genuinely approved of that measure and believed the removal of slavery a good thing for the people whom he represented. He was patriotically anxious for a removal of all remaining sectional bitternesses and a restoration of a complete Union. All this was the tone and thought of an able and broad-minded statesman, well worthy of the confidence universally given him, but it did not reach my point yet. It was necessary to talk to him about the picture, which he was desirous of seeing, and then to relate the several previous efforts to secure its adoption by the nation. He was not too deeply interested, not even when I told him of the generous offer of Mrs. Thompson. But I remembered something I had heard about his temper.

"I have heard all you have said, Mr. Stephens. I do not doubt your sincerity, but the sectional feeling is still venomously strong. Besides, one sad effect of the war seems to have been that the gentlemen of the South are no longer the men they were. They have lost their chivalry and some, even of their best men, appear to have lost the courage of their conviction."

"What, Mr. Stoddard? What do you mean by that?"

I forgot to say that he was a cripple and was sitting in his go-cart chair, in which he was every day carried to the Capitol and in which he was accustomed to wheel around in front of the Speaker's desk while directing legislation and making speeches. Just at this moment, the go-cart was wheeling rapidly all around the room as if it were excited.

"Why, Mr. Stephens," I mildly and sadly and almost penitently responded, "here is this picture, a memorial of a great event in the history of the nation; an event equally momentous to the North and the South; an event the consequences of which must endure as long as the nation endures; and the meanly sectional feeling on the Democratic, the Southern, side of the House of Representatives, is so strong that it cannot be placed among the pictorial archives of Congress. What is more, a woman, a patriotic, noble-hearted woman, comes and offers it as a free gift, and the gentlemen of the South, the boasted chivalry of the Confederacy, scornfully throw it back in her face, like gentlemen! What is more, as for courage, you yourself have expressed to me your approval of Emancipation, of the Proclamation; you have told me of your strong personal friendship for President Lincoln in whose house the painting was made and whose earnest wish was that it should become the property of the nation, and yet you dare not favor a proposition for its acceptance."

"I dare not? Mr. Stoddard, what do you mean?"

"What do I mean, Mr. Stephens? I mean just this. General Garfield himself is ready to offer a resolution for the acceptance of the picture. He has actually drawn up such a resolution. I have it with me. But General Garfield told me it was of no use to offer it in the face of the sure opposition of Mr. Alexander Stephens, on behalf of the dead Confederacy."

"Show me that resolution!" The go-cart chair had been racing at a rate of so many miles a minute. He took and read the resolution and paused at a table to take a pen and make one solitary amendment, to which I readily assented as a manifest improvement in diction.

"There, Mr. Stoddard! You tell me that General Garfield will offer it if I will not oppose it. Go back to him and tell him that if he will offer that resolution in the House tomorrow morning, I will second it!"

Again the chair was wheeling, while he said all that he had to say in response to any approving and soothing remarks on my part, and then I left the room aware that I had added one more to the many scores of notable interviews into which my curious meanderings had brought me. The carriage was at the door and it was driven at once to Garfield's house.

He was still up and there was nobody else in his room when I went in. I had heard that there was fun in him but did not know how much, and his face grew longer, impatient-like, as he noted a kind of shade on my own. Down I sat and somewhat tiresomely told him, inch by inch, the story of my long, interview with the Confederate Vice President. The effect was wonderful. Here was I, telling him how the support needed had been promised, and there on the sofa, with his legs drawn up and kicking, was the hero of Chickamauga, laughing as if he could not stop. But he did stop, at last, and he even said some things which I chose to accept as personally complimentary while he examined the amended resolution and agreed to present it for the approval of the House in the "morning hour." I left him feeling pretty well, but as memory brings up his parting remarks, it appears that in them was a vigorous declaration of his admiration of what he may have called my dauntless courage, but which had really been nothing but a high order of human nature and genuine diplomacy. Perhaps John Hay might have done it better, but at all events it was a good thing for the nation and for Frank Carpenter and Mrs. Thompson. I saw them both that evening, before I went to bed, and they were quite as complimentary as Gen. Garfield.

True to his promise, the general offered the joint resolution in the morning, and when, to the astonishment of many people, it was vigorously seconded by the venerated Democratic leader, it was passed by an all but unanimous vote, only one man, from Texas, retaining enough of the unchivalric war spirit to say nay. So far, all was well and it only remained to obtain the assent of the Senate. This was by some expected as a matter of course but there was a large lion in the way.

The matter was formally referred to the Library Committee of the Senate and the chairman of this committee was a gentleman who had pragmatical features in his character. In the first place, apparently, was the curious idea he entertained that he knew something about art and that this might be best exhibited by detrimental criticisms upon whatever might at any time be brought before his committee. (The same idea is to be noted among a long procession of art critics outside of any legislature.) He was a man of great ability, nevertheless, and would have proved a steep fence to climb if he were left in the way. There was one other point in him worse than the other.

Senator [Timothy] Howe[9] had an old grudge against me, personally. He had been a hard money Democrat before the war, Jefferson and Andrew Jackson and Anti-Bank and all that sort of thing. Therefore, on principle, he had been strongly opposed to the National Bank plan of Secretary Chase and President Lincoln. He could not swallow it, if he tried, until I calmly suggested to him, personally, that in defeating that plan for raising money for war purposes he would be reinforcing Lee's army, starving our own, compelling the abandonment of campaigns, engineering defeats, directing the disbanding of our volunteers, and offering an easy triumph to his friends the Confederacy. Other kindly things had been added and Senator Howe voted for the Bank Act with something like rheumatism creeping up and down his hard money back. But he had never forgiven me for my rash eloquence and I knew that he would now be after me with a sharp stick. So I went and cut some sticks before going into his committee room. There was the committee and the room was pretty full. So was he and so was I, for he looked at me with eyes in which there was more criticism than affection. He began to ask questions and make remarks, one of these to the effect that although the picture was apparently offered as a free gift, before long the giver or her representatives would probably be before Congress with some claim or other for compensation. It was a hard shot and I replied, most respectfully:

"Now, Senator Howe, I had expected some such objection as that from you and I prepared for it. I have with me a detailed statement of Mrs. Thompson's property and income, and am prepared to prove that this gift does but cover her real estate income for ninety days. She is not likely to come to you for reimbursement. I will read the . . ."

"No! You need not, Mr. Stoddard. I do not care to know anything about her income. But there is a graver point than that. This bill, for such a purpose, should have been first offered in the Republican Senate and not in a Democratic House. It is an insult from you . . ."

"No, Sir!" I exclaimed. "I thought of that. I was well aware of the different character and patriotism of the two Houses. I knew the difference in the respect they were likely to pay to a last request of President Lincoln. I saw that my chances were better among the gentlemen of the South. You are even now assuring me how much better this memorial of the abolition of human slavery was likely to fare in a Democratic House than it can in a Republican Senate. The patriotism and public spirit . . ."

"Stop there, Mr. Stoddard!" roared the senator, with a queer look on his face as if he were trying not to laugh. "We will report the resolution favorably and we will show you that the Emancipation Proclamation is as highly honored by a Republican Senate as by a Rebel House of Representatives."

There was some other skirmishing, but Timothy and I had had out the Bank Act fight and he did the right thing by the picture. He sent it in well, without any reference to me, and it here also had but one opposing vote. That was from Senator Edmunds of Vermont,[10] who was also a tenderfoot art critic and may have been a personal friend of Caleb B. Smith, whom Frank had murdered in the picture.

The grand work of putting that work of art in its new home was by no means yet completed, and I had some other fish to fry. One was to get for Mrs. Thompson a "special passport" of honor for her proposed trip to Europe, and the other was to secure for her an especial interview with President Hayes. Both of these objects might best be obtained through the then Private Secretary at the White House and he, poor man, had no acquaintance with me, nor I with him. So I went one morning, and sent him in my card. Of course I was sent for and he received me with politeness, but there was a straw in his hair. He intimated, in pretty direct English, that he had never before heard of me as one of President Lincoln's Private Secretaries.

"Oh," I said to him. "I suppose Nicolay and Hay can settle that. I will have them call upon you and explain my position with President Lincoln."

"I shall be very happy to see them!" he replied. "Neither of them has as yet done me the honor to call upon me."

Instantly the cat was out from under the meal. He was not on smooth terms, in his own mind, with the relics of the Lincoln dynasty. I cordially bowed myself out and went on down Pennsylvania Avenue, while he went out also to take a carriage and convey an Executive Message to Congress at the Capitol. There is a tide in the affairs of men. Halfway down the Avenue, whom should I meet but Nicolay and Hay, walking arm-in-arm and as good as pie. I had a cow to pick with them, after exchanging greetings and being congratulated upon my brilliant success with the painting.[11] They had not done the right thing by the Private Secretary of President Hayes, and so grave a breach of courtesy ought to be repaired at once, as he had just been complaining of it to me. Seemed hurt, you know. They said they would go and fix it up all right, for both of them were great sticklers for official and diplomatic courtesy. So on they went and an hour or so later I was again in the White House with my new friend the secretary, to tell him that Nicolay and Hay had promised to call upon him without any delay whatever.

"Why, my dear sir, they have already done so. I found their cards on my table when I came back from the Capitol. They were prompt, indeed."

That settled the matter. My status was fixed with President Hayes and I had kindly messages to take to Nicolay and Hay. Also, the passport was promised and soon obtained. And an evening was set for the formal reception of our crowd in the Red Room by the President and Mrs. Hayes.

That evening came and we were all there, and Mrs. Hayes took possession of Frank and Mrs. Thompson. She was a splendid-looking woman, and her husband a very handsome man. You do not often see as fine looking a pair. There were others present to join in and I had an opportunity of the best sort to absorb President Hayes. I did so, to the end of the interview. I had worked hard for his election and believed him to be about as thoroughly honest a man as I had ever known. There was a great deal in him too, and his critics have underrated him. He was not so big a man as Lincoln, but made a tiptop president. At a later day I became even better acquainted with him. He alighted in the White House at a singularly trying time, with the House dead set against him and a thousand other impediments to anything like independent usefulness. On the whole, though, I think the best-looking part of that Administration was Mrs. Hayes.

That ordeal over, the next thing was to prepare for a grand public presentation and reception of the picture by Congress, both Houses melting into joint account for that purpose in the hall of the House of Representatives. The day was set and here again the friendship of General Garfield came to my assistance. So did that of Mr. Stephens of Georgia, for whom I was cultivating an increased appreciation. Each agreed to deliver speeches on the occasion. That was to be the jewel of the whole affair.

It was really something tremendous. The picture was hoisted back of the Speaker's chair and the light on it was good. So was everything else. The galleries were crowded with male and female brilliancy. So was the floor outside of the rows of desks. There was no room for anybody else in that splendid hall except in the front rows of seats reserved for the members of the Senate on their arrival. Elegant armchairs had been placed in the open area in front for the artist and his party. Mrs. Thompson was looking her best and that was saying a great deal, for she was both handsome and dignified. The plan that nearly caged me was that on the entrance of the Senate I should be discovered standing up with Mrs. Thompson in front of the crowd, facing it and ready to introduce each man as he came to the giver of the national prize gift. I saw trouble ahead but also saw my old friend Governor Banks,[12] bright and smiling as ever, and went for him instantly.

"Governor Banks! I'm in a fix. Of course, I know all these senators. Known 'em from childhood, but I can't recall the names of more than half of them. You must come to the rescue or I shall break down."

He laughed merrily at my dismay and came forward like the hearty man of good will that he was. He too was handsome and he stood by me like my next of kin and helped me out with the long procession of Senators and Congressmen which to blind eyes appeared to be presented by him and the former Private Secretary of President Lincoln. That was what all the newspapers of the country named me in the report of the affair sent out through the telegraphic despatches of the Associated Press. The way that happened so universally was this. At the head of the Washington Bureau of the Associated Press was my old friend Gobright[13] and he had never been an admirer of Nicolay since the latter failed to appreciate him in the old war times. It was his hand that sent the current despatches, and he put me in on top.

General Garfield made a magnificent speech of reception and so did Mr. Stephens. It was exceedingly picturesque all around and not the least remarkable feature of the occasion was the Vice President of the Confederacy wheeling around vigorously in his chair and eulogizing Abraham Lincoln.[14]

All was now over and we went back to New York but when, not many days later, I came to settle accounts with Frank, I discovered that his money had already parted company from him and that only a moderate sum remained for me. It was partly on that account that he afterwards undertook to paint for me a portrait of Susie and one of [daughter] Sadie, but the times were against him. He had lost his grip and his industry, after his great trip to England with another gift picture,[15] and he died without doing anything more than to lose for me some highly valued photographs.

But there is the picture to this day, and I am glad that it fell to my hand to have so much to do with its placing on the wall of the Capitol.[16]

Post Impressions
Eleanor Stoddard

y memories of my grandfather are, of necessity, few, since he was leaving his life as I was starting mine. The only images that I can recall were his sitting in an armchair or reclining in his bed in a big house in Madison, New Jersey, that belonged to my uncle. The chair was covered with aging brown leather and had a hole in one arm with straw sticking through. His pipe tobacco was held in a canister beside the chair, and I can smell it now.

Grandpa Stoddard was very old and very deaf and had a nicely trimmed gray beard. I am sure I never spoke to him. When my infant brother John was placed on his bed and crawled over to pull his beard, the old man laughingly shouted, "Take him away!"

He died when I was four. On growing older I became aware that he was distinguished as a secretary to Abraham Lincoln, had had exciting adventures in Arkansas, was a great marksman, had written a number of books for boys, and had suffered much sadness in the loss of his wife and three daughters to TB. All of these events were long ago and had little effect on us kids except that my mother read some of his grandfather's books to John at bedtime. They were stirring tales.

Our library contained two heavy volumes of William O. Stoddard's typewritten autobiography, a copious narrative put together for his children as he approached the age of seventy. I did not read it until the late 1980s after I retired and found much of it new and fascinating but often hard to follow. He had had an unusually eventful life, and he seemed to be trying to capture his memories, one after the other, before they faded away. He wrote rapidly, like a reporter, but in the midst of a vivid description of one episode he would be reminded of a person or incident in another, and these digressions would interrupt the flow. He failed to supply the reader with enough dates, and he had a habit of citing an incident on one page and then referring to the same incident many pages later. He made innumerable references to historical figures that I only dimly recognized.

My uncle, William O. Stoddard Jr., deeply admired his father and undertook to edit his story in a truncated version mostly related to his association with Lincoln. This book, entitled *Lincoln's Third Secretary,* reads like a novel, recasting my grandfather's elaborate descriptions into punchy script that speeds the tale. Published in 1955, it serves a story-telling purpose but omits hundreds of pages of historical background and the sense of first-hand experience that can only be conveyed by the original words in their full-blown context.

Uncle Bill was convinced that almost no one would have the interest and patience to wade through the whole story; he saw the chief strength of his father's account as centered on his memories of Lincoln, and that might have been the case fifty years ago. But nowadays more and more readers are showing their eagerness to learn all they can about the Civil War president and the people surrounding him. Research into a growing body of sources has broadened the historical perspective and whetted our curiosity to understand the origins from which the various participants in the wartime saga may have sprung.

My grandfather's narrative touches on a number of significant events in American history, expanding on existing accounts or giving information not previously known. Spanning the last sixty years of the nineteenth century, his story provides a glimpse of the life styles and social attitudes of the times. It shows the upbringing and education of a young man from the eastern seaboard who sought his fortune in the western prairie lands and whose audacity propelled him into the role of secretary to Lincoln during the Civil War. His recollections move from wartime scenes of Washington through tense encounters in occupied Arkansas as the war was ending and on into the turbulent economy of postwar New York City.

I have studied the descriptions William O. Stoddard gives of himself at different stages in his life in an effort to visualize him and detect his underlying character. It seems that he started out with some exemplary family role models and an excellent classical education. He was clearly endowed with innate energy and curiosity that led him to seek knowledge and develop skills, both physical and intellectual. He made many friends and enjoyed life enormously.

He had little trouble making decisions, sometimes hasty, that led him on to new adventures. He seemed to leap from one new experience to another, sometimes just keeping himself afloat. But he was fortunate in possessing what we now would call a "marketable skill"—he could write. In fact, he loved to write, from an early age sending articles to newspapers and publishing one himself (one issue). He was a prodigious worker, driven to describe whatever his eyes had seen, his ears heard, his senses felt.

As he grew into manhood, he was motivated by a keen interest in public affairs, a hatred of slavery, and a devotion to the service of Abraham Lincoln. Appointed as a Federal marshal in war-disrupted Arkansas, he was working to maintain order in that recently surrendered state when the President was shot. Here the author's outlook changes abruptly, and so does the tone of his narrative. He knows that the loss of his "best friend" has altered his expectations and the course of his future.

With hopes shattered, my grandfather moved north, suffering from recurring bouts of malaria and dysentery, struggling to stay alive. Miraculously regaining his health, he found a new footing in New York City, where he wrote for newspapers and pulp fiction publishers. He became a churchman, married, and started a growing family. He invested in a number of dubious enterprises while finding himself assailed with pleas for help from his three brothers and his sister, now a "single mother" with two children. He referred to himself as "Issachar, a strong ass crushed under a double burden."

In the midst of these cares this man maintained his impetuous nature, plunging into one money-making scheme after another, some involving his own inventions. He was devoutly religious, beginning with immersion in an icy baptismal font in a Baptist church in Syracuse at the age of eighteen. He joined the Tabernacle Baptist Church in New York City, where he taught Bible classes and met Susan Eagleson Cooper, his wife-to-be. I believe he was able to bear up under his stressful work as a writer, his tenuous business endeavors, and continuing family demands because of his religious faith.

I am struck with the appalling conditions of public health in those days. It is no wonder "Stod" contracted typhoid in polluted Washington, or malaria in Arkansas, and even in the New York area disease was rampant. He had moved his family to Morrisania in the Bronx for a more rural environment where in 1876 my grandmother gave birth to her fourth child, Henry. During a thunder storm a sewer pipe burst under the house, flooding the cellar with foul water and the house with noxious odors. The mother contracted a lengthy fever and almost died, and the newborn baby lasted only a day or so. The author speaks of his resulting ill health and approaching deafness.

The family was forced to move from home to home around the city for financial or health reasons even as relatives appeared, seeking rescue. By 1887 the head of the household was responsible for supporting five children and an ailing wife (a sixth baby had also died). He turned to a serious career of writing books for boys, as well as stories for *St. Nicholas* magazine, a number of which were later expanded in book form.

This magazine was edited by Mary Mapes Dodge; its authors were outstanding writers and included Robert Louis Stevenson and Louisa May Alcott, among others. The illustrations were wonderful. I later read some of my grandfather's stories and articles and especially loved one about the circus, entitled "Shows of Men and Animals and How They Are Moved About."

Always able to find publishers, author Stoddard was less able to find a salubrious environment. Living in a damp house, Susie suffered hemorrhages from incipient tuberculosis. The family doctor advised my grandfather to move his wife out of the city for the sake of her health. They explored northern New Jersey, and discovered Madison, thirty miles west of the city, to which they moved in 1894.

In the middle of the eighteenth century this town began as a small settlement in the woods centered around a Presbyterian church. During the Revolutionary War military skirmishes took place in the region. The townspeople entertained Colonial officers from an encampment nearby, and some of the soldiers are buried in the local cemetery. After the war the village kept growing because of its strategic location, and the building of a railroad to the east in 1837 increased opportunities for trade with nearby towns and urban centers.

By the time the Stoddards arrived, Madison contained banks, schools, stores, five churches, a Methodist seminary, and a number of wealthy landholders with big estates. The town was known as The Rose City thanks to the presence of thirty-five commercial greenhouses whose business thrived on the soil and climate and nearness to the affluent New York market. The family settled in to stay, but within two years both daughter Sarah and wife Susie had succumbed to tuberculosis. My grandfather joined the Presbyterian Church and commented on "the hands and hearts that went out to me in the deepness of that shadow." He remained a faithful member of the church for the rest of his life.

Certain traits in his character emerge from his widely ranging account of himself. A downside of his nature was his inability to manage money. His sister Kate commented that her brother, having made quite a sum of money during the war, "wished to use it again and lost all and more." She implied that he could have profited from his time in Arkansas if he had been a better businessman. He lost his investments there, and a number of subsequent ventures did not pay out.

A positive trait, however, was his apparent ability to get along with people. He seemed to be a canny judge of other men, including politicians, and he relished social interaction. He enjoyed exchanges with many kinds of people, from wily congressmen to "nigger" helpers, from financiers to artists. He could trade threats with ruffians and outlaws and managed to keep them at bay. He could be tactful and tolerant with difficult women like his stepmother and Mary Lincoln. But, of course, he is telling the story, and he has a good opinion of himself that never wavers.

His narrative could be seen as egocentric except for a saving grace that appears in the author's genuine affection for others. He does not show hostility. He expresses honest admiration for friends and colleagues, great affection for Lincoln, and a love of family members that bursts out in frequent asides throughout the text. But running like a thread through the story is a sense of loss that accompanied these loving attachments.

In the course of his life, my grandfather loses his mother, his beloved sister Julia, his idolized president, his three brothers, two infant sons, and later, his wife and three daughters to the scourge of tuberculosis. As he enters on the final stretch of his memoir, he laments the loss of his little grandson Tom. A sigh of sadness often pervaded references to this family on the part of the next generation when I was listening.

My father, Ralph, the youngest child, lost his mother at the age of eight, and was brought up mostly by his sister Margaret, who was ten years older. He remembered a rather stringent upbringing with no money to spare. His father continued to publish books at a rapid rate, but the royalties came sporadically. This son later commented ruefully on the small recompense for so much creative work. As the next century began, however, the presence of William Jr. and his family in the same town was reassuring, and when Margaret married and brought her husband into the household on Central Avenue, daily life could become more comfortable.

We knew that Grandpa Stoddard often said, "The Lord will provide." In the final years of his life, his children provided, and he could feed on a rich harvest of memory and the veneration of his fellow citizens.

Chevy Chase, Maryland
March 2006

Notes
Index

Notes

INTRODUCTION

1. Among them are *Inside the White House in War Times* (New York: Charles L. Webster, 1890), *The Table-Talk of Abraham Lincoln* (New York: Frederick A. Stokes, 1894), and *Lincoln at Work: Sketches from Life* (Boston: United Society of Christian Endeavor).

2. The original, created on Stoddard's Blick typewriter and bound in two leather volumes, is in the collections of the Detroit Free Public Library.

3. According to the town historian, a silent movie theater opened in 1912 on Central Avenue in Madison, New Jersey—the same street on which the elderly William O. Stoddard lived—"so there's a good chance he went to a movie." Eleanor Stoddard to Harold Holzer, October 17, 2005.

4. In 1990, the city of Syracuse unveiled a "Jerry Rescue Monument," to honor the white residents who broke into the local jail and freed the captured black man before he could be sent back into slavery. See "Jerry Rescue Saw Two Races Work Together for Good," letter to *Syracuse Post-Standard*, August 23, 1990.

5. Although historian Michael Burlingame—see *Inside the White House in War Times: Memoirs and Reports of Lincoln's Secretary* (Lincoln: University of Nebraska Press, 2000), viii—suggested that Stoddard graduated with his class in 1857, the autobiography notes that he was granted a B.A. in absentia in 1858, and an M.A. in absentia in 1861.

6. Douglas L. Wilson and Rodney O. Davis, eds., *Herndon's Informants: Letters, Interviews, and Statements about Abraham Lincoln* (Urbana: University of Illinois Press, 1998), 365, 770.

7. *Central Illinois Gazette*, May 4, 1859, also in Burlingame, ed., *Inside the White House*, ix.

8. "How Lincoln Chose a Secretary": William O. Stoddard, in an interview with a representative of *Success Magazine*, undated clipping in the Lincoln Museum, Fort Wayne, Indiana.

9. Ibid.

10. New York *Evening Post*, September 21, 1858, quoted in Edwin Earle Sparks, *The Lincoln-Douglas Debates of 1858* (Springfield: Illinois State Historical Library, 1908), 319.

11. "How Lincoln Chose a Secretary."

12. Ibid.

13. Stoddard to William H. Herndon, December 27, 1860, Abraham Lincoln Papers, Library of Congress. "I do not wish to inflict any more letters upon Mr. Lincoln," Stoddard wrote in this correspondence with Lincoln's law partner, indicating he had sent others previously—letters that have not been located. Worried that Lincoln would simply give him another of the many federal jobs within his power to confer, Stoddard added: "Should he honor me with his confidence I will set about the duties of my office with a degree of enthusiastic pride in their performance which I could hardly fill in another position. While I have reason to fear that I shall really need some position—you know how lucrative a business editing a country weekly is—there is no office with twice the net profits which would so highly gratify me as the one in question."

14. See Lincoln to James C. Conkling, Roy P. Basler, ed., *The Collected Works of Abraham Lincoln*, 8 vols. (New Brunswick, N. J.: Rutgers University Press, 1953–55), 6:406–10. Although Lincoln entrusted former Springfield mayor Conkling ("one of the best public readers," the president believed) to read his letter aloud at the city's Union rally, he was "mortified" when the letter got "botched up in the Eastern papers"—a measure of its importance to the chief executive. Ibid., 414, 430.

15. William O. Stoddard Jr., ed., *Lincoln's Third Secretary: The Memoirs of William O. Stoddard* (New York: Exposition Press, 1955), 134–35.

16. Stoddard, *Lincoln at Work*, 72, 75–76, 81; Stoddard Jr., *Lincoln's Third Secretary*, 107–8, 194.

17. Stoddard to Hay, August 13, 1875, John Hay Papers, John Hay Library, Brown University. According to Stoddard's amusing recollection, once Lincoln's purported preference for Johnson circulated among the delegates, "the very general response [was], 'well, he ought to have his way in such a matter, and they've abused him about enough. I don't mind going for Andy, myself.'"

18. Quoted in Burlingame, *Inside the White House*, vii; Burlingame, ed., *Dispatches from Lincoln's White House: The Anonymous Civil War Journalism of Presidential Secretary William O. Stoddard* (Lincoln: University of Nebraska Press, 2002), xxiii.

19. Nicolay was paid $2,500 per year, and Hay at first received $1,600 (some $2 per week more than Stoddard, at $1,500 annually), later raised to $1,800. See

Harold Holzer, *Dear Mr. Lincoln: Letters to the President* (New York: Addison-Wesley, 1993), 8–9.

20. Burlingame, ed., *Inside Lincoln's White House,* 105.

21. William O. Stoddard, "Shielding Lincoln from Personal Abuse," *Rochester Alumni Review* (October-November, 1924), 7.

22. Stoddard was commissioned on September 24, 1864, but not until January 27, 1865, did Lincoln and Attorney General James Speed formally send his name to the Senate for confirmation. As usual, Stoddard had to wait for his reward. See *Collected Works of Lincoln,* 8:242.

23. "Recollections of Kate Stoddard Gibson," typed, unpublished journal in possession of the Stoddard family, 22–23. Harris's daughter and future son-in-law were the Lincolns' guests at Ford's Theatre on April 14, 1865, the evening of the president's assassination.

24. Stoddard to Hay, April 22, 1865, John Hay Papers, John Hay Library, Brown University.

25. Original Stoddard manuscript, 562.

26. "An Important Life: Happenings in the Eventful Career of W. O. Stoddard," ca. 1905, clipping in Eleanor Stoddard's archives.

27. Frances M. Stoddard, *Genealogical History of the Allen Family and of some of their Connections* (Boston: privately printed, 1891), 111–12.

28. "Wm. O. Stoddard Dies; Was Aid [*sic*] of Lincoln . . . ," *New York Times,* August 30, 1925; "An Important Life."

29. "The New Idria Scandal," *New York Times,* March 11, 1878. The Panoche Grande Quicksilver Mining Company was organized in July 1861, with McGarrahan deeding title in return for 40,000 shares. Other stockholders allegedly included such luminaries as Francis Preston Blair Jr., who reportedly held 3,250 shares.

30. *New York Evening Post,* March 11, 1878.

31. "The McGarrahan Claim," *New York Times,* April 14, 1878. A month later, the paper called it "the interminable case." See "The New-Idria Scandal," *New York Times,* May 22, 1878. In 1881, McGarrahan placed a claim on eight million acres of public lands. See "M'Garrahan's New Move," *New York Times,* February 20, 1881.

32. *New York Evening Post,* letter to the editor, March 12, 1878, clipping in the Brown University Library.

33. Stoddard to Hay, March 17, 1878, John Hay Papers, John Hay Library, Brown University.

34. The byzantine dispute was revived years later in 1892, when President Harrison vetoed a congressional bill aimed at McGarrahan's relief, sending the dispute back to the courts. See "M'Garrahan Loses Again," *New York Times,* January 30,

1892. William McGarrahan died in 1894, "forty years a petitioner at the National Capitol," his ancient claim still in dispute—and his last words reportedly a plea for recognition to his right to the Panoche Grande lands. See "Claimant McGarrahan Dead," *New York Times*, April 25, 1894.

35. Stoddard to Hay, February 12, 1885, March 25, 1885, John Hay Papers, John Hay Library, Brown University.

36. "William O. Stoddard, Noted Author; A Sure Shot," *Madison Eagle*, February 10, 1911.

37. *Madison Eagle,* January 3, 1896; original Stoddard manuscript, 600.

38. *American Authors: A Dictionary of American Literature* (New York: N. W. Wilson Co., 19[?]), 583.

39. Stoddard to John Hay, January 17, 1895, John Hay Papers, John Hay Library, Brown University.

40. Ibid.

41. Stoddard to "My dear Grandson Gordon," April 2, 1923, original letter given to the editor by Eleanor Stoddard.

42. "Secretary to Lincoln, 90, Confined to Room," *Madison Eagle*, February 13, 1925.

43. "Extreme old age" from William O. Stoddard, "Shielding Lincoln from Personal Abuse"; "I shall meet . . ." from Stoddard, letter to the Rotary Club, *Madison Eagle*, February 11, 1925.

44. William O. Stoddard, "The Half Told Story," undated typescript in the Detroit Public Library.

1. The Stoddard Family Tree

1. This account is altogether fanciful. According to the author's granddaughter, Eleanor Stoddard, "WOS is full of family lore that is quite inaccurate," including the assertion that "John Winthrop founded the Connecticut Colony by building a fort on the mouth of the Thames." There was "not a smidgen of evidence that the original Stoddards were dukes of Devon," according to later family research, noting that "once the reader gets past the first paragraph in the WOS biography he/she is on firmer ground." Following is Ms. Stoddard's account:

The first Stoddard to appear in New London was John Stodder, who may have come to Hingham, Massachusetts on the *Diligent* of Ipswich (Suffolk County) in 1638. We do not know how or why he came to Connecticut, but in 1651 and 1653 he received three grants of land on the east side of the Mohegan River; then he acquired two other pieces of land by deed in 1664 and 1665 also on the east side of the Great River. He signed these documents with an X, and they may be seen in the town hall in New London. His son John was executed in 1679 (having axed his neighbors for making noise on the Sabbath), and the name John was not used in the family until it was bestowed on one of WOS's brothers, but this name came from John Osborn.

2. The Revolutionary War general Israel Putnam (1718–90) saw action at Bunker Hill, New York City, Long Island, White Plains, and Philadelphia. The author's ancestor was Lieutenant Vine Stoddard.

3. The Panic of 1837 struck under Martin Van Buren's presidency. Hastened by an unfavorable balance of trade with England and a season of nationwide crop failures, the panic was triggered when New York banks suddenly refused to redeem paper money into silver and gold. The resulting downturn, which Stoddard called "the severest financial crisis the country had experienced since the days of the Revolution," lasted until 1843. See Stoddard, *Abraham Lincoln: The True Story of a Great Life* (New York: Fords, Howard & Hulbert, 1884), III.

4. Former New York State Supreme Court Justice Ira Harris (1802–75) replaced William H. Seward as U.S. senator from New York when Seward became Lincoln's secretary of state in 1861. Harris went on to become, in Mary Lincoln's words, "so kind a friend" that the Lincolns came to think of him "as if he was a relative." See Mary Lincoln to Charles Sumner, March 23, 1865, in Justin G. Turner and Linda Levitt Turner, eds., *Mary Todd Lincoln: Her Life and Letters* (New York: Alfred A. Knopf, 1972), 210. Harris' daughter, Clara, along with her fiancé, Major Henry Rathbone, were guests in the presidential box at Ford's Theatre on April 14, 1865, the night Lincoln was assassinated.

2. Childhood in Rochester

1. Whig candidate William Henry Harrison, a celebrated military hero, was elected president in 1840, handily defeating Democratic incumbent Van Buren, a New Yorker. Harrison died a month after his inaugural, and Vice President John Tyler succeeded him and served the remainder of his term. The rollicking Harrison campaign, which emphasized the general's log cabin origins, not political issues, was the first to inspire the proliferation of political broadsides, medals, tokens, textiles, and graphics. See, for example, Edmund B. Sullivan and Roger A. Fischer, *American Political Ribbons and Ribbon Badges, 1825–1981* (Lincoln, Mass.: Quarterman Publications, 1985), 27–49; and Bernard Reilly, *American Political Prints, 1766–1876: A Catalog of Collections in the Library of Congress* (Boston: G. K. Hall, 1991), 48–159.

2. Marco Bozzaris (a.k.a. Markos Botzaris, 1788?–1823) was a hero of the Greek war for independence who successfully defended Missolonghi against the Turks. His valor was celebrated in an 1825 poem by American writer Fitz-Greene Halleck (1790–1867), which Stoddard, a lover of poetry and admirer of Bozzaris, undoubtedly read. Stoddard's future chief apparently shared his interest. As president, Abraham Lincoln recited the Halleck verses for the benefit of fellow passengers

on an 1863 boat trip en route to the front. See Doris Kearns Goodwin, *Team of Rivals: The Political Genius of Abraham Lincoln* (New York: Simon & Schuster, 2005), 441; for the poem, "Marco Bozzaris," see Thomas R. Lounsbury, ed., *Yale Book of American Verse* (New Haven: Yale University Press, 1912), 12–13.

3. Boyhood in Homer

1. Before slavery fatally split the Union, the issue of protective tariffs was hotly contested and regionally divisive. Northern Whigs like Lincoln favored a high tariff to generate income for the federal government, protect factory workers from the rivalry of cheap imports, and increase domestic manufacturing. Southern Democrats preferred a free-market approach that increased global demand for the cotton crop. The Whig Party downplayed the issue in 1848.

2. Future Secretary of State Seward (1801–72) became governor of New York in 1839. He later entered the U.S. Senate, and by virtue of his "higher law" and "irrepressible conflict" speeches, warning against the spread of slavery, emerged as the leading contender for the 1860 Republican presidential nomination. Instead, Lincoln won the nod, and Seward—grudgingly, at first, but then loyally—joined the Cabinet.

3. Horace Greeley (1811–72) founded the weekly *New Yorker* in 1834, and merged it with the daily *New York Tribune* in 1841. He briefly toyed with the idea of supporting Democrat Stephen A. Douglas—not Republican challenger Lincoln—in the 1858 Illinois senate contest, and then opposed Seward for the 1860 presidential nomination. A leading voice for abolition early in the Civil War, he became the most famous newspaper editor in the nation—and in 1872, a presidential candidate himself, losing 56 percent to 44 percent to Ulysses S. Grant.

4. William Brewster (1567–1644) emigrated to America on the *Mayflower* in 1620, and became a church leader in the storied Plymouth Colony.

7. The Hill and the Woods

1. General "Mad Anthony" Wayne (1745–96) was a Revolutionary War hero, distinguishing himself at the Battle of Monmouth in 1778 and at the attack on the British garrison at Stony Point in 1779.

8. The Academy and the Shop

1. Artist Francis Bicknell Carpenter (1830–1900), a Homer, New York, native, worked at the White House for six months during 1864 to create a monumental history painting celebrating the first reading of Lincoln's Emancipation Proclamation to the Cabinet. Its 1866 engraved adaptation became one of the best-selling popular prints of the nineteenth century. Stoddard later helped the artist arrange the sale of his original canvas to the U.S. Senate. Some of the paragraphs in this section

were inserted from a later chapter in the manuscript. See Harold Holzer, Gabor S. Boritt, and Mark E. Neely Jr., "Francis Bicknell Carpenter: Painter of Abraham Lincoln and His Circle," *American Art Journal* 16 (Spring 1984): 66–89.

2. See Carpenter's memoir, *Six Months at the White House with Abraham Lincoln: The Story of a Picture* (New York: Hurd & Houghton, 1866). The artist later republished the book under a new title, *The Inner Life of Abraham Lincoln*, which infuriated the President's widow.

10. The Onondaga Street House

1. "Mr. Corning of Albany" was Erastus Corning (1794–1872), a wealthy manufacturer who in 1863 led a convention of anti-Lincoln Democrats that issued a stinging rebuke of the president's policy on civil liberties. In reply, Lincoln wrote a famous public letter defending his administration. Corning's descendants and namesakes went on to rule Albany politics for more than a century. See *Collected Works of Lincoln*, 6:260–69.

11. Hoyt's School

1. Andrew Dickson White (1832–1918) was a co-founder (with Ezra Cornell) of Cornell University, and its first president from 1868 to 1885. He served later as American minister to Germany and Russia, and chaired the U.S. delegation to the Hague Peace Conference in 1899.

12. The Bookstore

1. Not long afterward, freshman Whig Congressman Abraham Lincoln took the floor of the U.S. House of Representatives to denounce President James Knox Polk and the Mexican War, which most Whigs opposed. See *Collected Works of Lincoln*, 2:431–42.

2. Frederick Douglass (1817?–95) was a regional celebrity in upstate New York before he became the leading national spokesman for African American freedom and equal rights. Douglass founded the abolitionist newspaper *The North Star* in nearby Rochester in late 1847.

3. Samuel J. May, a Unitarian minister, reformer, and abolitionist from Syracuse, had been an admirer of Douglass since at least 1841. See William McFeely, *Frederick Douglass* (New York: W. W. Norton, 1991), 88.

4. *Harper's New Monthly Magazine*, founded in New York by publisher Robert S. Harper, became an enormous success, eventually claiming 170,000 subscribers.

5. *Uncle Tom's Cabin, or, Life Among the Lowly*, the 1852 book by Harriet Beecher Stowe (1811–96), became the best-selling novel of the nineteenth century, with fifty thousand copies sold in its first eight weeks alone. Its sympathetic portrayal of the

slave Uncle Tom, and frightening depiction of cruel overseer Simon Legree, fueled the abolitionists and infuriated Southerners. According to legend, on first meeting her in 1862, President Lincoln remarked: "Is this the little woman who made this great war?" See Don E. Fehrenbacher and Virginia Fehrenbacher, eds., *Recollected Words of Abraham Lincoln* (Stanford: Stanford University Press, 1996), 428.

13. THE NEW GARRET

1. Samuel Finley Breese Morse (1791–1872) sent the first telegraph message, "What hath God wrought?" on May 20, 1844. Stoddard may have miscalculated the landmark year here. Morse had to endure years of litigation before establishing his right to benefit from his invention, but by all accounts he enjoyed a prosperous old age.

2. In mid-nineteenth-century politics, the pre–Election Day publication of colorful electoral "tickets" became common practice among all parties. Apparently, Stoddard took the tradition a step further, using his access to a printing press to produce "tickets" to support his candidate for May Queen.

3. Mexican War hero Zachary Taylor won the presidential election of 1848 on the Whig ticket, winning New York with 218,603 votes. Democratic candidate Lewis Cass finished third in the state to former president, and New York resident, Martin Van Buren, running on the Free Soil ticket.

4. President Taylor served in office a bit more than "a few" months—fourteen to be precise, dying on July 9, 1850. His successor, Millard Fillmore, hailed from the nearby Finger Lakes region of upstate New York.

5. The Compromise of 1850, its obnoxious fugitive slave-catching provision notwithstanding, probably staved off secession and civil war for a decade. Senators Henry Clay and Lincoln's lifetime political rival, Stephen A. Douglas, managed it through Congress. Its other various bills held that: New Mexico and Utah territories could be organized, with the slavery issue there to be decided later, and locally, "consistent with the Constitution"; ended Texas's claim to western lands in exchange for federal assumption of the state debt; and ended the slave trade in Washington, D.C. Historian David M. Potter called the result "a truce" not "a true compromise." See Potter, *The Impending Crisis, 1848–1861* (New York: Harper & Row, 1976), 113.

14. THE CHURCH

1. The Democratic pro-slavery faction known as the "hunkers"—so named for their yearning for political patronage—opposed the "barnburners," the party's dwindling antislavery faction.

2. General Winfield Scott (1786–1866), a Whig, lost the presidency to Demo-

NOTES TO PAGES 104–11

crat Franklin Pierce in 1852. In an age in which presidential candidates traditionally stayed home and let surrogates speak in their behalf, Scott was much criticized for campaigning directly for the office (at first under the pretext of traveling to inspect the site for a future military hospital). Stoddard's lack of enthusiasm for the old war hero may be explained not only by the general's waffling on the slavery issue, but by the fact that Scott had defeated New Yorker Millard Fillmore, whom Stoddard admired, for the party's nomination. In November, many northern antislavery Whigs bolted to a new Free Democracy party, whose standard-bearer, John P. Hale, won more than 25,000 votes in New York. But even Scott's and Hale's New York votes combined were not enough to prevent Pierce from winning the electoral votes of Stoddard's home state. See Stefan Lorant, *The Glorious Burden: The History of the Presidency and Presidential Elections from George Washington to James Earl Carter* (Lenox, Mass.: Author's Edition, Inc., 1976), 212, 1064.

15. THE JERRY RESCUE RIOT

1. Daniel Webster (1782–1852) was one of the three giants of the U.S. Senate at mid-century—Clay and John C. Calhoun being the others—who achieved great national fame without ever serving as president. "Black Dan" was also a fabled orator, whose words, Abraham Lincoln believed, would "be read forever." See Michael Burlingame and John R. Turner Ettlinger, eds., *Inside Lincoln's White House: The Complete Civil War Diary of John Hay* (Carbondale: Southern Illinois University Press, 1997), 26.

2. Webster was instantly recognizable to most Americans from the widely distributed daguerreotypes, engravings, lithographs, and sculptures that had circulated nationwide. See James Barber and Frederick Voss, *The Godlike Black Dan: A Selection of Portraits from Life in Commemoration of the Hundredth Anniversary of the Birth of Daniel Webster* (Washington: National Portrait Gallery, 1982).

3. Robert Young Hayne (1791–1839) of South Carolina had engaged Webster in a legendary 1830 Senate debate on the Constitution, union, and federal authority.

4. At one typical antislavery meeting in Syracuse—perhaps this very one—dissidents threw rotten eggs at abolitionist orators. See McFeely, *Frederick Douglass*, 102.

5. John Brown's Raid on the federal arsenal at Harpers Ferry on October 17, 1859—though spectacularly unsuccessful, condemned by most antislavery leaders, including Lincoln, and shunned by Frederick Douglass himself—nonetheless agitated Southerners convinced that Northerners were intent on the violent destruction of slavery. Brown was hanged on December 2, leading some abolitionists to declare him "a martyr" and "a saint." See James M. McPherson, *Battle Cry of Freedom: The Civil War Era* (New York: Oxford University Press, 1983), 205–9.

16. Miscellaneous

1. In fact, the Republicans did not fully organize as a political party until 1854, and even then, many longtime Whigs, including Lincoln, did not rush to disengage themselves from their dying political organization. Lincoln joined the Republicans in 1856.

2. New York's "Exhibition of the Industry of All Nations" at the new Crystal Palace opened in July 1853. See Eric Homberger, *Scenes from the Life of a City: Corruption and Conscience in Old New York* (New Haven: Yale University Press, 1994), 216.

3. The Bowling Green statue of the British monarch was hauled down by angry colonists on July 9, 1776, and later, according to legend, melted down to make cannonballs for the Revolution. The act of defiance was memorably recorded in paintings and popular prints to symbolize American defiance. See Barry Schwartz, *George Washington: The Making of an American Symbol* (New York: Free Press, 1987), 34–35.

4. Stoddard confuses a famous story here. It was John Adams—the elder, not his son, John Quincy—who supposedly said on his deathbed, "Thomas Jefferson still survives," unaware that earlier on that fiftieth anniversary of American Independence, July 4, 1826, Jefferson had died at Monticello. Marie B. Hecht, *John Quincy Adams* (New York: Macmillan, 1972), 436–37.

17. Going to College

1. Edwin Vose "Bull Head" Sumner (1797–1863), the oldest corps commander in the Civil War, was so nicknamed because a musket ball fired in his direction early in his career had supposedly bounced harmlessly off his skull. He accompanied Lincoln on his inaugural journey to Washington in February 1861.

2. Henry Warner Slocum (1827–94) began the Civil War as Colonel of the 27th New York, and fought on the Peninsula, at Second Bull Run, Chancellorsville, Gettysburg, Chickamauga, and Chattanooga. His XX Corps was the first to enter conquered Atlanta in September 1864. Slocum later served as a congressman from Brooklyn.

3. Henry Alansan Barnum (1833–92) was wounded in action several times, captured by the Confederates, but returned to service to participate in William T. Sherman's March to the Sea. After the war, he became active in the GAR.

4. John Milton Hay (1838–1905), a Brown graduate, and later in life U.S. Secretary of State under Presidents William McKinley and Theodore Roosevelt, would soon become assistant secretary to President Lincoln, and Stoddard's colleague in the Civil War White House. Like Stoddard, Hay, together with senior secretary John G. Nicolay, went on to write about their martyred boss. Nicolay and Hay's ten-volume *Abraham Lincoln: A History* is still considered the "official" biography.

18. College Days

1. Isaac Ferdinand Quinby (1821–91)—not "Quimby"—attended West Point with Ulysses S. Grant (and finished fifteen places ahead of him in the Class of 1843). He ended his professional life as city surveyor of Rochester.

2. The book he refers to as his "Lincoln" was William O. Stoddard, *Abraham Lincoln: The True Story of a Great Life* (New York: Fords, Howard & Hulbert), 1884.

3. The pro-Democratic *New York World*—a longtime thorn in President Lincoln's side—not surprisingly supported New York governor Samuel J. Tilden over Ohio Republican Rutherford B. Hayes in the 1876 presidential election. Hayes's disputed victory ended postwar Reconstruction and curtailed African American rights in the South for a century. The federal government briefly closed down the *World* in 1863. Lincoln personally ordered General Ambrose E. Burnside to wire editor Manton Marble that the paper could resume publication a few days later. Robert S. Harper, *Lincoln and the Press* (New York: McGraw-Hill, 1951), 261.

4. William Harkness (1837–1903) became Astronomical Director of the U.S. Naval Observatory in 1894. He is credited with inventing the "spherometer caliper" and other scientific instruments.

5. Frances Folsom, twenty-one, married President Cleveland, age forty-nine, on June 2, 1886, at the White House.

6. Abolitionist Wendell Phillips (1811–84) was a leading associate of editor William Lloyd Garrison in the antislavery movement. After the Civil War, the tireless reformer took on the causes of penal reform, temperance, women's suffrage, and worker rights.

7. Major Henry Rathbone and Miss Harris were President and Mrs. Lincoln's guests in the state box at Ford's Theatre on the night of Lincoln's murder, April 14, 1865. Rathbone, who suffered a serious knife wound at the hands of assassin John Wilkes Booth, recovered to marry his fiancée in 1867, but later went insane and murdered her. He died in an asylum in 1911.

8. Former President Fillmore married Caroline Carmichael McIntosh on February 10, 1858, at Albany. They signed a pre-nuptial agreement under which Fillmore took control of the considerable fortune she had inherited from her first husband, Albany businessman Ezekiel C. McIntosh.

9. Philip J. Schuyler (1733–1804) of Albany had been a major general in the Continental Army, later serving as the first U.S. senator from New York.

10. The tribal name for Joseph Brant (1742–1807), an Anglican-educated Mohawk chief who joined the Tories during the American Revolution, and later fled to Canada, where the British gave him land.

11. Elwell Stephen Otis (1838–1909) went on to serve as military governor of the Philippines.

12. Margaret Fox (1833–93) and her sisters Leah Fox and Catherine Fox achieved great fame touring America and Europe as mediums who claimed they could contact the spirit world by means of table-rapping. After an investigation, Margaret admitted she was a fraud, but later retracted her confession and resumed her career as a spiritualist.

19. JUNIOR YEAR

1. The Kansas-Nebraska Act of 1854, authored by Senator Stephen A. Douglas of Illinois, effectively overturned the Missouri Compromise that for a generation had prohibited slavery north of latitude 36°30'. More important to Stoddard's future boss, Abraham Lincoln, "Nebraska" enshrined the idea of "popular sovereignty," under which white settlers in all new territories, North as well as South, could vote for themselves on whether to permit slavery or not. The law "aroused" Lincoln back into national politics on an anti-Nebraska platform after a long hiatus. As he would put it: "Popular Sovereignty, as now applied to the question of Slavery, does allow the people of a Territory to have Slavery if they want to, but does not allow them *not* to have it if they *do not* want it." See *Collected Works of Lincoln*, 3:18.

2. Although successful with New York voters, the first Republican nominee for president, the California explorer John C. Frémont (1812–90), lost the 1856 election to the pro-Southern Pennsylvania Democrat James Buchanan. Ex-president Millard Fillmore managed to collect more than one hundred thousand votes in New York under the Whig banner.

3. Republicans were frequently heard to complain that Irish immigrants were being imported into closely fought election districts to cast illegal votes for Democrats. The charge conveniently served to divert attention from Republican appeals to German-born voters, reflecting the party's wish to hold together its fragile new coalition, which included Nativists formerly loyal to the old anti-Catholic Know-Nothing party.

4. The Panic of 1857 began when the Ohio Life Insurance Company failed in August. The bankruptcy ignited a series of bank runs across the country, sending gold prices plummeting. Only the South, buoyed by the unchanging global demand for cotton, escaped the consequences of the downturn.

5. George M. Pullman (1831–97), then an upcoming Chicago businessman, went on to introduce lavish upper-and-lower train berths, amassing a fortune as head of the Pullman Palace Car Company. Lincoln's son, Robert T. Lincoln, served as its president from 1901 to 1911.

6. "Long John" Wentworth (1815–88), mayor of Chicago, caused Lincoln considerable political difficulty in late 1859 when he engaged in a roaring political feud with another Lincoln ally, Republican National Committeeman Norman

Judd. Lincoln wanted Illinois Republicans united behind his presidential candidacy. See Willard King, *Lincoln's Manager, David Davis* (Chicago: University of Chicago Press, 1960), 129–30.

20. GRAND PRAIRIE

1. Coles County, Illinois, was at this time home to Lincoln's beloved stepmother, Sarah Bush Johnston Lincoln (1788–1869). She resided on an eighty-acre farm there until her death.

22. PRAIRIE LIFE

1. As a young man, Lincoln, too, had once engaged in the apparently benign task of sewing shut the eyelids of unmanageable hogs. When a flatboat full of the creatures ran aground in New Salem, Lincoln scurried ashore to capture them and was forced to sew their eyelids shut to coax them back on board. Perhaps Stoddard and the president shared their common experiences when they met many years later. See Douglas L. Wilson and Rodney O. Davis, eds., *Herndon's Informants: Letters, Interviews, and Statements about Abraham Lincoln* (Urbana: University of Illinois Press, 1998), 457.

2. Stephen A. Douglas (1813–61) won his third term in the U.S. Senate in 1858 despite a serious challenge from—and seven memorable political debates with—Abraham Lincoln. Two years later, Douglas became the presidential candidate of the Northern Democrats, his chances for election doomed when Southern delegates bolted and nominated a presidential candidate of their own. That November, Abraham Lincoln defeated all his rivals to win the White House. Douglas supported the new president's efforts to resist secession, but after an exhausting speaking tour in support of the Union, he died in Chicago at the age of forty-eight. See Robert W. Johanssen, *Stephen A. Douglas* (New York: Oxford University Press, 1973), 868–72.

3. Lincoln was no statewide Whig leader at this time, but rather a committed member of the new Republican Party. Nor, to be accurate, did he "lose" re-election for a second term in the House of Representatives. Under a system of rotation under which fellow Whig aspirants agreed to serve only one term each, Lincoln did not seek a second term—although he likely wanted to do so.

24. FRONTIER JOURNALISM

1. David Davis (1815–86), a well-known judge during Lincoln's circuit-riding days in Illinois, served as his good friend's campaign manager during the 1860 presidential election. Lincoln rewarded his years of loyalty by appointing him an associate justice of the U.S. Supreme Court in 1862. After the president's death, Davis served as executor of Lincoln's estate.

2. Champaign County attorney William D. Somers often served as co-counsel with Lincoln when the Eighth Judicial Circuit Court convened at Urbana. See Albert A. Woldman, *Lawyer Lincoln* (New York: Carrol & Graf, 1994), 113.

26. SUPPERS, CHARACTERS, AND INCIDENTS

1. Stoddard seemed curiously unaware of the hotly contested 1858 Senate campaign between Lincoln and Douglas, even though the combatants met for one of their storied debates in nearby Charleston on September 18, 1858, and had met earlier at the town he mentioned—Freeport—on August 27.

2. Leonard Swett (1825–89) met Lincoln through their mutual friend and fellow attorney David Davis in 1849, and was for a decade one of the future president's closest and most trusted advisors. Swett never sought a political reward for himself, though he did lose an 1862 race for Congress against Lincoln's first law partner, John T. Stuart. In 1875, Swett prosecuted Mary Lincoln at the insanity trial that resulted in her commitment. It was Swett who said memorably of Lincoln that he was "a very poor hater." See Herndon, *Lincoln's Informants*, 166.

3. At the time Stoddard cites, Lincoln was already a Republican.

4. The Lincoln legal case that this account most closely resembles—the fabled murder of Jacob M. Early at the Spottswood Rural Hotel in Springfield (Lincoln successfully defended the accused, Henry Truett)—took place much earlier, in 1838, and involved death by gunshot, not shovel. See John J. Duff, *A. Lincoln, Prairie Lawyer* (New York: Rinehart & Co., 1960), 53–60.

27. LINCOLN AND A NEW BEGINNING

1. In fact, Lincoln had previously been endorsed by Jeriah Bonham, editor of the Lacon, Illinois, *Gazette*, on November 4, 1858. See Herbert Mitgang, ed., *Abraham Lincoln: A Press Portrait* (Chicago: Quadrangle Books, 1971), 129–30.

2. This is precisely the argument that Lincoln's eastern supporters employed to snatch the 1860 Republican nomination from front-runner Seward: that only a westerner could win the White House for the party. It is interesting that Stoddard, usually loyal to home-grown politicians like Millard Fillmore, seemed ready in this case, like many young New York Republicans, to award the party's top prize to Lincoln even if it meant disappointing a fellow New Yorker.

3. William H. Herndon (1818–91) was Lincoln's law partner for the final seventeen years of the future president's legal career in Springfield. Mary Lincoln despised him—and the feeling was mutual. Herndon exacted revenge after Lincoln's death by lecturing publicly about Lincoln's supposed first and truest love, Ann Rutledge. Although many of his claims of influence over Lincoln were exaggerated, Herndon remains a peerless source of information on his pre-presidential years, especially through letters received from and interviews conducted with Lincoln's

oldest acquaintances in preparation for his controversial 1889 biography, *Herndon's Lincoln: The True Story of a Great Life.*

4. Lincoln made Thomas McElrath appraiser for the New York Custom House. See Harper, *Lincoln and the Press,* 76.

5. The author's son, William O. Stoddard Jr., inserted a footnote into this section of his father's manuscript, along with the full text of the *Gazette's* editorial endorsement. The editorial runs within the text of this book; the footnote, reprinted here in full, reads as follows:

Note by W. O. Stoddard, Jr.

The story here told of the writing of the first editorial nominating Lincoln for the presidency had long been a legend in our family. It had in a way taken on an atmosphere of romance as a good story will when there is lack of confirming evidence. At the time of the writing these memoirs, we had nothing more than father's word for their correctness but we were accustomed to accept him at one hundred percent and did so in this case. However, it was a great satisfaction to us when documentary evidence was at length forthcoming. In 1908, *Lincoln the Citizen* by Henry C. Whitney was published, in the first volume of which appeared full confirmation of father's story and to our great satisfaction extracts from the *Central Illinois Gazette* including the editorial itself and also the personal note. I quote from Mr. Whitney's *Lincoln,* Vol. 1, Page 262 [The Whitney essay appeared as volume one of a nine-volume collection edited by Marion Mills Miller, *Life and Works of Abraham Lincoln, Centenary Edition* (New York: Lincoln Centenary Association, 1907).]

"The first newspaper that mentioned him as a Presidential possibility was the *Central Illinois Gazette,* published in Champaign, Ill., by J. W. Scroggs. On May 4, 1859, it printed the following articles, the first in the local column, the second in the editorial. Will O. Stoddard, Esq., afterward Lincoln's secretary to sign land patents, and later his biographer, wrote both articles, he being editor of the paper at the time."

It is sixty-four years since that editorial was written. Father was then twenty-four years of age. He is now (1923) eighty-eight. Young as he was he saw and knew his man. He sensed greatness. That was like father.

6. Actually, Stoddard was much more "nervous" about his prospects than he admits in his manuscript. Hearing no word from Lincoln about his hoped-for appointment—if there was indeed a lengthy letter of invitation from the president-elect, it has not survived—Stoddard wrote desperately to William H. Herndon in late December to inquire "what the indications are, if any" of his success, admitting: "'The President-Elect,' knowing so little of me, must necessarily, if he has

thought about the matter at all, have doubts as to my fitness for a post of so much responsibility, and hesitate about according to me the degree of confidence which a man must place in his 'private secretary.'" In some desperation, he even offered to "begin 'on trial,' as the Dutchman took his wife." Stoddard was not formally appointed until July 17, 1861. See William O. Stoddard to William H. Herndon, December 27, 1860, Abraham Lincoln Papers, Library of Congress; Stoddard's original presidential commission, copy in author's collection.

7. John Cabell Breckinridge (1821–75) had served as James Buchanan's youthful vice president from 1857 to 1861, and then ran for president as a Southern Democrat in the 1860 election. Though he did not appear on the ballot in four states, including New York, the 72 electoral votes he won nationwide were second only to the 180 garnered by Lincoln. (He received a total of 849,781 popular votes, placing third in the four-way race.) Breckinridge became a Confederate general during the Civil War, even though his home state of Kentucky remained officially neutral. He saw considerable action, and then served briefly as the Confederacy's last secretary of war, returning to Kentucky in 1869 after a brief exile in England.

8. James M. Mason (1798–1871) represented Virginia in the U.S. Senate from 1847 to 1861, resigning after his state left the Union. Named Confederate Commissioner to Great Britain, he and fellow diplomat John Slidell were seized on the high seas while en route to England on a British ship, then brought into Union territory and imprisoned. The sensational capture ignited a diplomatic crisis with Great Britain, which threatened to explode into war until Lincoln finally ordered the commissioners released. Mason went on to serve in his London post until the end of the war.

9. Joseph Lane (1801–81) the North Carolina–born U.S. senator from Oregon, ran for vice president of the United States on the Southern Democratic ticket headed by John C. Breckinridge in 1860. Thereafter he advocated the right to secede, earning him enmity in his adopted state and ending his political career.

10. Andrew Johnson (1808–75) was the Democratic, pro-Union U.S. senator from Tennessee. He left the Senate in 1862 to become military governor of his home state, then won the newly named Union party's nomination for the vice presidency in Lincoln's 1864 re-election bid. The circumstances of that selection have never been unearthed, and the president's role, if any, in the convention's decision still remains a mystery despite Stoddard's insistence, later in this book, that he was instructed by Lincoln to go to the convention and see to Johnson's elevation.

11. John George Nicolay (1832–1901) was a Bavarian-born Illinois newspaperman, later a clerk in the Illinois secretary of state's office, when Lincoln selected him to become his private secretary during the 1860 presidential campaign. Nicolay served as chief White House secretary from 1861 until March 1865, when Lincoln named him consul resident in Paris. He was on a cruise when he learned of the

president's murder. Later given exclusive access to Lincoln's papers by the late president's son, Robert, Nicolay and his White House colleague John Hay went on to write the popular 1890 biography, *Abraham Lincoln: A History*. Nicolay finished his government career as Marshal of the U.S. Supreme Court. For Hay, see n. 4, chapter 17.

12. The antiquated White House administrative budget allowed for only one secretary, so Lincoln had additional aides, like Stoddard, named to other government departments and "lent" to his staff. Stoddard was officially appointed to the Interior Department.

28. WAR

1. The merchant ship *Star of the West* left New York for Charleston, South Carolina, on January 5, 1861, carrying 250 reinforcements and supplies for the federal garrison at Fort Sumter. Four days later, the vessel was subjected to hostile fire as it approached the harbor, turned back, and returned to New York. Though the incident occurred before Lincoln assumed office, it was, in a sense, the opening salvo of the Civil War.

2. Stoddard here refers to the president's April 15, 1861, proclamation calling out the militia to suppress the rebellion, and convening a special session of Congress on July 4. See *Collected Works of Lincoln*, 4: 331–32.

3. Charles Pomeroy Stone (1824–87), a Massachusetts-born Union general, was in charge of security in Washington for the Lincoln inaugural in his role as inspector general of the District of Columbia.

4. Stone was charged with responsibility for the Union defeat at Ball's Bluff, October 21, 1861, though much of the blame likely rested with Colonel Edward D. Baker, who lost his life there—a grievous personal loss to the Lincolns, who had known the onetime senator for years and had named their late son Eddie after him. While Baker was lionized as a martyr, Stone became the scapegoat, and was imprisoned for more than six months. He briefly saw later action at Port Hudson, but then was mustered out of the service, his American military career over.

5. Stone was, more accurately, engineer for the installation of the foundation built to support the Statue of Liberty.

6. Montgomery, Alabama, served as the capital of the Confederacy until the seat of government was transferred to Richmond, Virginia, in May 1861.

7. President Lincoln observed the Seventh Regiment drilling in front of the U.S. Capitol on April 26, 1861, and visited the regimental headquarters the following day. See Earl Schenck Miers, *Lincoln Day by Day: A Chronology, 1809–1865*, 3 vols. (Washington: Lincoln Sesquicentennial Commission, 1960), 3:38.

8. Fourteen members of Ohio's celebrated McCook family served the Union during the Civil War, including seven sons of Major Daniel McCook, who enlisted

at age sixty-three and was killed in action, as were three of his boys. The Ohio Historical Society owns a fine 1872 Charles T. Webber painting of "The Fighting McCooks." See Harold Holzer and Mark E. Neely Jr., *Mine Eyes Have Seen the Glory: The Civil War in Art* (New York: Orion Books, 1993), 159–60, 162.

9. Riots broke out in Baltimore on April 19, 1861, when a pro-secessionist civilian mob attacked Union troops marching through the city en route to the defense of Washington. Four members of the Sixth Massachusetts Regiment lost their lives in the melee, along with at least twelve civilians. The violence seemed to validate Lincoln's controversial decision, two months earlier, to rush through that hostile city in unfamiliar garb that amounted to a disguise as he headed to Washington for his inauguration.

10. The Seventh Regiment serenaded Lincoln at the White House on April 27, 1861. See *Lincoln Day By Day*, 3:38.

11. "The boys" were Lincoln's mischievous youngest sons, William Wallace "Willie" (1850–62), and Thomas "Tad" (1853–71), who occasionally ran wild in the White House, to the dismay of the president's staff. Their older brother, Robert (1843–1926), was away at school during most of Lincoln's term in office. Willie's death in February 1862 cast a pall over the White House—family and staff alike.

12. Ephraim Elmer Ellsworth (1837–61), a onetime law student in the Lincoln-Herndon law office in Springfield, accompanied the family to Washington in 1861, already a celebrity with his Zouave Company, famous for its colorful uniforms and spruce military drills.

13. In 1861, Ellsworth raised a new company, the 11th New York Zouaves, and became its colonel. On May 24, he marched his men across the Potomac River to nearby Alexandria, Virginia, to remove a newly installed Confederate flag, clearly visible all the way to the White House, from atop the Marshall House hotel. Ellsworth tore down the banner, but was shot to death by the hotel's proprietor on his way downstairs. Devastated, the Lincolns gave him an East Room funeral, and the president lauded the first Union casualty of the war to his parents as "my young friend, and your brave and early fallen child." See *Collected Works of Lincoln*, 4:386.

29. A New Life in Washington

1. Jefferson Finis Davis (1808–89) was U.S. Senator from Mississippi before he left Washington to become the first and only president of the Confederacy—delivering one of those powerful Senate farewell speeches that Stoddard witnessed during his first days in the capital.

2. The interior of the White House was gutted during the Truman administration, but reconstructed according to original plans and pictures. With the president's office long since relocated to a new west wing, Lincoln's onetime official chamber and cabinet room had been re-designated the Lincoln Bedroom in

the Hoover years. Re-decorated by Mrs. Laura Bush in 2004, it contains a large bed purchased by Mary Lincoln, along with a copy of the Gettysburg Address in Lincoln's hand. See William Seale, *The President's House: A History*, 2 vols. (Washington: White House Historical Association, 1986), 1:386, 2:887, 1005–16

3. Salmon P. Chase (1808–73), had served as both governor of Ohio and his state's U.S. senator, and was considered a possible Republican candidate for president at the 1860 convention that instead chose Lincoln. Once elected, Lincoln made Chase his Secretary of the Treasury, but the Ohioan's presidential ambitions continued percolating, and when his barely concealed attempt to replace Lincoln on the ticket failed in 1864, he resigned from the Cabinet. Safely re-elected, a magnanimous Lincoln appointed Chase as Chief Justice of the Supreme Court later that year, in time for the newly robed judge to swear in Lincoln for his second term on March 4, 1865.

30. THE WAR CITY

1. Whitelaw Reid (1837–1912) was war correspondent for the *Cincinnati Gazette*, achieving later fame as the longtime editor of the *New York Tribune*. His descendants remained active in New York politics well into the twentieth century.

2. Stoddard wrote his columns from 1861 to 1864 under the somewhat deceptive pen name "Illinois." See Michael Burlingame, ed., *Dispatches from Lincoln's White House: The Anonymous Civil War Journalism of Presidential Secretary William O. Stoddard* (Lincoln: University of Nebraska Press, 2002), xi.

3. Samuel Jackson Randall (1828–90) of Pennsylvania served as Speaker of the U.S. House of Representatives from 1876 to 1881.

4. James Abram Garfield (1831–81) went directly from Civil War military service to a seventeen-year-long career as congressman from Ohio, the last four of which he served as Republican leader. Elected president in 1880, he served less than four months, dying—like Lincoln before him—at the hands of an assassin.

5. James G. Blaine (1830–93), a founder of he Republican Party in Maine, was a congressman beginning in 1863, later serving as Speaker of the House and U.S. senator. He was the unsuccessful Republican candidate for president in 1884, losing to Grover Cleveland.

6. Hugh McCulloch (1808–95) rose from relative obscurity as an Indiana banker to serve as Lincoln's Comptroller of the Currency from 1863 to 1865, then as Chase's successor as Secretary of the Treasury, a post to which he would return for another year's service in 1884.

7. Ward Hill Lamon (1828–93) served, to be precise, as Marshall of the District of Columbia, one of the few of Lincoln's longtime Illinois lawyer friends to receive an important appointment in Washington. Devoted to Lincoln's personal safety—the imposing Lamon often slept on the floor outside the president's White

House bedroom door, fully armed—he never forgave himself for being out of town when John Wilkes Booth attacked his old friend at Ford's Theatre on April 14, 1865. Lamon later purchased William H. Herndon's research files and published a *Life of Abraham Lincoln* in 1872, authored by a ghostwriter.

8. Stoddard may be referring to Benjamin Brown French (1800–1870), who served as chief marshal for Lincoln's inaugural parade, and was later rewarded with the post of commissioner of public buildings, which he held until 1867. He became a confidante of Mary Lincoln's, at whose urging he confessed to the president in December 1861 that the first lady had overspent a $20,000 Congressional appropriation to redecorate the White House. That news elicited a rare outburst of temper from Lincoln, who swore, "he would never approve the bills for *flub dubs for that damned old house!*" See Donald B. Cole and John J. McDonough, eds., *Benjamin Brown French: Witness to the Young Republic—A Yankee's Journal, 1828–1870* (Hanover, N.H.: University Press of New England, 1989), 382.

9. John Hay had no such relationship with Mary Lincoln, referring to her disrespectfully in his diary as "the Hell-cat." See John Hay to John Nicolay, April 5, 1862, in Tyler Dennett, ed., *Lincoln and the Civil War in the Diaries and Letters of John Hay* (New York: Dodd, Mead, 1939), 40.

10. *Puck* was one of the leading comic weeklies of the period.

31. GUNS AND THINGS AT THE WHITE HOUSE

1. John A. Dahlgren (1809–70) was commander of the Washington Navy Yard at the beginning of the war, becoming chief of the Bureau of Ordinance—and a close confidante of the president's—in 1862. Attaining the rank of rear admiral, he took command of the South Atlantic Blockading Squadron in 1863. But he is best known for developing the iron smoothbore naval canon that bore his name—Dahlgren Guns.

2. Patented by Christopher S. Spencer on March 6, 1860, the repeating rifle fired .52-caliber bullets. Although Lincoln ordered them manufactured for Union troops, they did not go into widespread use until 1863. See Faust, *Encyclopedia of the Civil War*, 708.

3. Light draft "tinclads," re-fitted paddle- and stern-wheelers designed for river patrols, saw much service during the Civil War. At least sixty were commissioned, and one served for a time as Admiral David Dixon Porter's flagship.

4. The USS *Monitor*—designed by Swedish inventor John Ericsson—was built in Brooklyn and rushed to Hampton Roads, Virginia, just in time to confront the previously invincible Confederate ironclad *Virginia* (or *Merrimac*) on March 9, 1862. Their epochal duel ushered in the age of iron ships and modern technology in naval warfare. Boasting a revolutionary, revolving gun turret, the *Monitor* was the first and most famous Union ironclad.

5. Thomas Cook Durant (1820–85) was a director of the Union Pacific Railroad for seven tumultuous years in the 1860s.

6. James S. Wadsworth (1807–64), a founder of the Republican party, served as a delegate to the unsuccessful Washington Peace Conference in early 1861, a last-ditch attempt to negotiate a settlement to restore the Union and prevent civil war. He became military governor of the District of Columbia in 1861 and died in action at the Battle of the Wilderness in 1864.

7. Mary Lincoln correctly suspected Kate Chase (Sprague), daughter of the secretary of the treasury, of conspiring with her father to promote his chances of replacing Lincoln in the White House in 1864. Mary's dislike for the glamorous Kate—the toast of wartime Washington—was no doubt intensified by personal jealousy of the younger, more glamorous Washington hostess.

8. John Sherman (1823–1900), served as U.S. senator from Ohio during the Civil War, and again from 1881 to 1897. His brother was Major General William Tecumseh Sherman (1820–91).

9. Theodore Roosevelt Sr. (1831–78), a New York merchant and pro-Lincoln Republican, was the father of the twenty-sixth president of the United States. To his son and namesake, the elder Roosevelt was "the best man I ever knew." President Theodore Roosevelt later became an ardent Lincoln admirer. See Theodore Roosevelt, *An Autobiography* (New York: Scribner's, 1920), 7.

10. A. T. Stewart's mammoth retail emporium in New York City was one of "shopaholic" Mary Lincoln's favorite stores. Wartime shortages notwithstanding, Stewart opened his lavish new store on Broadway in 1862, and soon employed 2,200 people, generating $50 million in sales in 1865 alone. "Next to the President," an English writer claimed, he was "the best known man in America." See Thomas Kessner, *Capital City: New York City and the Men Behind America's Rise to Economic Prominence, 1860–1900* (New York: Simon & Schuster, 2003), 35–36.

11. Pullman would also "acquire" Robert Todd Lincoln, the president's eldest son, who served as president of the Pullman Company from 1897 to 1911.

12. Mary Lincoln's February 5, 1862, White House reception proved "a brilliant spectacle," a Washington newspaper reported, but as the first lady's seamstress and friend Elizabeth Keckly recalled, "the brilliance of the scene could not dispel the sadness that rested upon the face of Mrs. Lincoln," who was worried about her sick son, Willie, who died a week later. See *Washington Evening Star*, February 6, 1862; Elizabeth Keckly, *Behind the Scenes. Or, Thirty Years a Slave, and Four Years in the White House* (New York: G. W. Carleton, 1868), 102.

13. Former one-term New York congressman Caleb Lyon (1822–75) had been a poet, author, and lecturer, and one of the organizers of the California territory (and designer of its state seal). In 1864, Lincoln named him governor of Idaho Territory.

14. Daniel E. Sickles (1819–1914) was a Democratic congressman from New York, best known before the war for shooting his wife's lover to death on a Washington street—and escaping conviction for the sensational murder on the then-novel grounds of "temporary insanity," with Edwin M. Stanton as his defense lawyer. Sickles became a colorful Union general and lost his leg at Gettysburg. Outrageous and flamboyant, he was a frequent visitor to the Executive Mansion, where in December 1863 he audaciously barked at Lincoln—then sheltering his sister-in-law, the widow of a recently fallen Confederate general—"you should not have that Rebel in your house." See Katherine Helm, *The True Story of Mary, Wife of Lincoln* (New York: Harper & Bros., 1928), 230–31.

15. The influential abolitionist newspaper became known as *Wilkes' Spirit*. See Harper, *Lincoln and the Press*, 123.

32. A Very Busy Year

1. George W. L. Bickley's Knights of the Golden Circle, a virulent anti-Lincoln society, was blamed by some conspiracy theorists for plotting the president's assassination. See William A. Tidwell et al., *Come Retribution: The Confederate Secret Service and the Assassination of Lincoln* (Jackson: University Press of Mississippi, 1988), 255.

2. In fact, Union League clubs still exist not only in New York, but also in Chicago and Philadelphia. Although the original headquarters that were erected in the 1860s are long gone, the newer club buildings retain their extraordinary collections of Civil War art, artifacts, and documents from the 1864 campaign. The New York club, for example, boasts Daniel Huntington's majestic painting of Lincoln delivering his second inaugural address, while the Philadelphia club's many treasures include Edward Dalton Marchant's 1863 Lincoln life portrait.

33. Wartime Enterprises

1. Ambrose E. Burnside (1824–81) succeeded George B. McClellan as commanding general of the Army of the Potomac, and then led it to disastrous defeat at Fredericksburg in December 1862. The Rhode Islander achieved his greatest fame by introducing the fashion for luxuriant side-whiskers, which thereafter bore a variation of his name: "sideburns."

2. Edward Stanly (1810–72), a North Carolina-born former Whig congressman who had migrated to San Francisco before the secession crisis, was summoned home to become military governor of North Carolina in 1862. Pro-Union, but not antislavery, he resigned and returned to California after Lincoln issued the Emancipation Proclamation.

3. The U.S. Sanitary Commission, a civilian-run charity organization founded in 1862, sent thousands of volunteers into the field to care for the sick and wounded

and help soldiers with their pay and pension problems. To raise funds, it held giant "Sanitary Fairs" in many northern cities. Lincoln donated to many such fairs during the war, and attended two of them himself—in Baltimore and Philadelphia—in 1864.

34. ABOUT MR. LINCOLN

1. George Brinton McClellan (1826–85) remains one of the most controversial figures of the Civil War. A West Point graduate, he succeeded Winfield Scott as Union commander in 1861, and transformed the bedraggled federal army into a well-trained fighting machine. Although popular with his troops, McClellan seemed perpetually reluctant to fight, and was openly insolent to Lincoln, telling his wife the president was a "baboon," an "idiot," and a "gorilla." His 1862 Peninsula Campaign proved a disaster, and Lincoln relieved him of command. Though the president reinstalled McClellan, who went on to win the bloody Battle of Antietam later that year, the general failed to pursue Lee's army as it retreated south, prompting Lincoln to dismiss him for good. In 1864, McClellan, who opposed emancipation, won the Democratic nomination to challenge Lincoln for re-election. The general lost the election decisively—garnering just 20 percent of the vote from the soldiers who had once held "Little Mac" in such high esteem. See Stephen W. Sears, ed., *The Civil War Papers of George B. McClellan: Selected Correspondence, 1860–1865* (New York: Ticknor & Fields, 1989), 85, 106, 114.

2. The Peninsula Campaign (March-August 1862) was General McClellan's long-planned "invasion" of Virginia from the eastern shore, where he landed more than 100,000 men. But he quickly went on the defensive, certain that he faced a superior force (in fact only 17,000 Confederate soldiers then stood between McClellan and the Confederate capital of Richmond, his goal). The campaign ended in a series of Union defeats, and McClellan withdrew in failure.

3. Randolph B. Marcy (1812–87) was not only General McClellan's chief of staff, but his father-in-law as well.

4. The Battle of South Mountain (September 14, 1862) was General McClellan's first, inconclusive, attempt to halt General Robert E. Lee's invasion of Maryland. Three days later, the Army of the Potomac met the Army of Northern Virginia at Sharpsburg (Antietam Creek), where the bloodiest single day's fighting of the entire war left 4,700 dead, and 21,400 wounded or missing—and Lee's army on the run. Though it was a costly victory, the Battle of Antietam gave Lincoln the military success he needed to issue the Emancipation Proclamation on September 22.

5. In fact, Lincoln donated the handwritten draft of his 1862 preliminary Emancipation Proclamation not to Chicago, but to an Albany, New York, charity fair, where it was purchased by abolitionist Gerrit Smith, who later sold it to the

state legislature. The document still resides safely in the New York State Library. It was most recently displayed in fall 2005 at the New-York Historical Society exhibition, *Slavery in New York*. Stoddard has confused this story with that of Lincoln's later donation of the manuscript of his *final* proclamation to the Ladies' Great Northwestern Sanitary Fair in Chicago in 1863. Though Lincoln won a gold watch for donating the most valuable item sold at that event, the document remained in Chicago, where it was destroyed in the great fire of 1871. See Mrs. A. H. Hoge and Mrs. D. P. Livermore to Lincoln, November 26, 1863, Abraham Lincoln Papers, Library of Congress; Alvin Robert Kantor and Marjorie Sared Kantor, *Sanitary Fairs: A Philatelic and Historical Study of Civil War Benevolence* (Glencoe, Ill.: SF Publishing, 1992), 172–74.

35. THE LONG WINTER OF 1862

1. Edwin McMasters Stanton (1814–69) had known, and rudely snubbed, Lincoln when they served as co-counsel at an 1855 trial in Cincinnati but became his loyal secretary of war in 1862. Of his intense, hard-working, often gruff, but highly effective Cabinet minister, Lincoln once reportedly said: "His bark is a great deal worse than his bite." It was Stanton who pronounced the unforgettable words at Lincoln's deathbed: "Now he belongs to the ages." See Fehrenbacher and Fehrenbacher, *Recollected Words of Lincoln*, 174; David Herbert Donald, *Lincoln* (New York: Simon & Schuster, 1995), 599.

2. Benjamin Franklin Butler (1818–93), a pro–Breckinridge Democrat who won his military commission as a "political" general" in recognition of his loyalty to the Union, won notoriety as military governor of conquered New Orleans. His order, declaring that the law would treat women there who defied his curfew as prostitutes, earned him eternal enmity in the South—where he was known as "The Beast of New Orleans." Butler later served as a congressman, governor of Massachusetts, and a splinter-party candidate for president. See, for example, C. Vann Woodward, ed., *Mary Chesnut's Civil War* (New Haven: Yale University Press, 1981), 385.

3. John Pope (1822–92), a Kentucky-born, Illinois-based general who was married to a relative of Mary Lincoln's, succeeded McClellan in command of the Army of the Potomac in 1862, but was soundly defeated at the Second Battle of Bull Run and promptly dismissed.

4. The Second Battle of Bull Run (August 29–30, 1862) was a triumph for General Robert E. Lee and a disaster for the North. A dismayed Lincoln, who was heard to cry out, "we are whipped again," blamed General McClellan for abandoning Pope at the Manassas, Virginia, battle. See Burlingame, ed., *Inside Lincoln's White House*, 37–38.

5. Henry Wager Halleck (1815–72) replaced McClellan as general in chief of the army in 1862, stepping down to the post of chief of staff when Ulysses S. Grant was promoted to lieutenant general and supreme commander in 1864. Known as "Old Brains," Halleck was a fussy, suspicious executive, a less-than-sterling field officer, and occasionally timid ("I will do no such thing," he once told Lincoln when instructed to relay an order to a commanding general in the field). At his best, he was a loyal officer and able administrator. See John F. Marszalek, *Commander of All Lincoln's Armies: A Life of Major General Henry W. Halleck* (Cambridge: Harvard University Press, 2004), 2.

6. Fitz John Porter (1822–1901) was, according to John Hay, "the most magnificent soldier in the Army of the Potomac, ruined by his devotion to McClellan." Porter was court-martialed for disobedience to Pope at the Second Battle of Bull Run, and dismissed from the service in 1863. He was not officially restored to the ranks until 1886. See John M. Hay to John G. Nicolay, August 1885, quoted in Ezra J. Warner, *Generals in Blue* (Baton Rouge: Louisiana State University Press, 1964), 379.

36. FORWARD MARCH

1. Celebrated actor James H. Hackett (1800–1871) was considered the greatest Falstaff of his age. Lincoln saw him play the role from *Henry IV* three different times in a single year: on March 13, 1863, at the Washington Theatre, again with his family on December 14 at Ford's Theatre, and, according to most sources, together with secretaries Nicolay and Hay at Ford's the very next night. It seems likely that Stoddard attended the December 15 performance along with the other White House secretaries, and did not go to Ford's Theatre alone with the president, as he remembered. See Earl Schenck Miers, ed., *Lincoln Day by Day: A Chronology*, 3 vols. (Washington: Lincoln Sesquicentennial Commission, 1960), 3:173, 227.

2. Lincoln came down with a case of varioloid—a mild form of smallpox—soon after delivering his Gettysburg Address on November 19, 1863. He took several days off and was not reported as "much better" for more than a week. Stoddard's recollections dovetail with a famous quote about relentless office seekers, attributed to Lincoln on his sickbed: "Now I have something I can give everybody." See Washington *Evening Star*, November 28, 1863; Jay Monaghan, *Diplomat in Carpet Slippers: Abraham Lincoln Deals with Foreign Affairs* (Indianapolis: Bobbs-Merrill, 1945), 344.

3. Joseph Hooker (1813–79) replaced Burnside as commander of the Army of the Potomac after the Battle of Fredericksburg. "Beware of rashness," Lincoln urged him, "but with energy, and sleepless vigilance, go forward, and give us victories." Hooker was genuinely inspired by Lincoln's message, but in May 1863,

led his troops to humiliating defeat at Chancellorsville. See *Collected Works of Lincoln*, 6:79.

4. The Battle of Chancellorsville (May 4, 1863) showcased Robert E. Lee's strategic superiority, and Confederate General Thomas "Stonewall" Jackson's brilliance in the field. The most meaningful result of the encounter, however, was that among its 30,000 casualties was the irreplaceable Jackson himself—shot by his own sentries.

5. George Gordon Meade (1815–72) succeeded Hooker, and within a week, commanded the army to its most celebrated triumph, at the Battle of Gettysburg. Lincoln believed that Meade should then have pressed his advantage and pursued Lee, and though Meade was never dismissed, he soon began reporting to Grant.

6. This may have been L. O. Emerson, who set the poem "Three Hundred Thousand More" to music in July 1862, after the verses were printed in newspapers in Washington, New York, and Boston, causing a mild sensation. See Kenneth A. Bernard, *Lincoln and the Music of the Civil War* (Caldwell, Idaho: Caxton Printers, 1966), 74–75. Stoddard recalled the verses inaccurately, so the editor has replaced them with the actual published words.

7. Although the Union began drafting troops as early as 1862, Congress passed the official Conscription Act on March 3, 1863.

8. Ulysses S. Grant (1822–85) is believed by many historians to be the greatest of all Civil War generals. Following early triumphs at Forts Henry and Donelson in February 1862, he triumphed again at Shiloh that April. Grant later placed Vicksburg under siege and accepted the city's surrender on July 4, 1863, just one day after Meade triumphed at Gettysburg, giving the city of Washington two victories—one east, one west—to celebrate on Independence Day. Grant, who later served two terms as president of the United States, finished his multi-volume memoirs shortly before his death. They are still considered the best recollections of the war, and among the greatest war memoirs ever written.

9. John H. Martindale (1815–81) served as military governor of the District of Columbia from 1862 until 1864, after controversial service with McClellan on the Peninsula.

10. The Battle of Gettysburg (July 1–3, 1863) was the most widely celebrated Union victory of the Civil War. Capping Lee's second invasion of the North, it ended forever the Confederacy's offensive war in the North. Though it was a decisive loss for the South, the war would go on uninterrupted for nearly two more years. The city of Vicksburg, Mississippi, fell to Ulysses S. Grant the same week.

37. On Assignment by the President

1. The New York City Draft Riots (July 11–13, 1863) remain the bloodiest civil disturbance in American history—save for the Civil War itself. Although

scholars are unsure of how many people died in the three days of fighting, newspapers reported many incidents of the torture and murder of African Americans, against whom the rioters, most of them Irish-born, directed most of their fury. The definitive books on the subject are Iver Bernstein, *The New York City Draft Riots: Their Significance for American Politics in the Age of the Civil War* (New York: Oxford University Press, 1990), and Barnet Schecter, *The Devil's Own Work: The Civil War Draft Riots and the Fight to Reconstruct America* (New York: Walker & Co., 2005).

2. The spectacular 1884 failure of ex-president Grant's brokerage firm, Grant & Ward—triggered by the thievery of his partner, Ferdinand Ward—wiped out the war hero's fortune, compelling him to surrender some of his many gifts to settle debts.

3. Lincoln's public letter, composed to be read aloud to an August 26, 1863, rally in his old hometown of Springfield, Illinois, featured his famous admonition: "You say you will not fight to free negroes. Some of them seem willing to fight for you . . ." By using the colloquial phrase to which Stoddard objected—"Uncle Sam's web-feet"—Lincoln hoped, as historian Ronald C. White has argued, "that his audience would see and be grateful for the now quite visible *tracks* that were leading the Union forces to victory." See *Collected Works of Lincoln*, 6:409–10; Ronald C. White Jr., *The Eloquent President: A Portrait of Lincoln Through His Words* (New York: Random House, 2005), 212. Lincoln's precise words were:

Nor must Uncle Sam's Web-feet be forgotten. At all the watery margins they have been present. Not only on the deep sea, the broad bay, and the rapid river, but also up the narrow muddy bayou, and wherever the ground was a little damp, they have been, and made their tracks. Thanks to all. For the great republic—for the principle it lives by, and keeps alive—for man's vast future,—thanks to all.

4. Lincoln asked that Conkling, whom he considered "one of the best public readers," read his letter "very slowly" at the "mass-meeting of unconditional Union-men." See *Collected Works of Lincoln*, 6:414.

5. Perhaps unbeknownst to Stoddard, Kansas senator Samuel C. Pomeroy (1816–91) wrote a memorandum that criticized Lincoln and urged Chase for the top spot on the 1864 ticket. Published in the press on February 21, the "Pomeroy Circular" caused the president temporary political difficulty, but in the end backfired because it helped rally the president's supporters for his re-nomination.

38. YEAR OF DECISION, 1864

1. Rear Admiral David Dixon Porter (1812–91) commanded the Mississippi Squadron from 1862 to 1864, and then led the Atlantic Blockading Squadron. The

adopted brother of naval hero David G. Farragut, Porter joined Lincoln, Grant, and Sherman for the president's final council of war in March 1865.

2. Francis Preston Blair Jr. (1821–75), scion of a prominent political family, became a Republican leader in Missouri, later a congressman and Civil War general. His brother, Montgomery Blair (1813–83), was Lincoln's first postmaster general.

3. Christopher "Kit" Carson (1809–68) was a fabled trapper and scout before the Civil War began, and later won additional fame as an Indian fighter in the Southwest.

4. The brother of Lincoln's Illinois political friend Elihu B. Washburne and a former Wisconsin congressman, Cadwallader C. Washburn (1818–82) likely owed his rapid rise in the Union military to his brother's close relationship with General Grant. The brothers spelled their family name differently.

5. West Point–trained Frederick Steele (1819–68) was the general who captured Little Rock in September 1863.

6. Stoddard is referring to the Fifth Kansas Cavalry, under Pennsylvania-born Colonel Powell Clayton (1833–1914), who later served as Ambassador to Mexico under presidents McKinley and Theodore Roosevelt.

7. General Philip Henry Sheridan (1831–88) made his famous ride from Winchester to the front on October 19, 1864, "cheered at every stop by men in whom new courage was kindled," and inspiring poets and artists to celebrate him for a generation. See Harold Holzer and Mark E. Neely Jr., *Mine Eyes Have Seen the Glory: The Civil War in Art* (New York: Orion Books, 1990), 159. A month before, Confederate General Jubal A. Early (1816–94) was defeated by Sheridan at Winchester.

8. See 1 Samuel 22:1–2: "David therefore departed thence, and escaped to the cave Adullam . . . and every one *that was* in distress, and everyone that was in debt, and every one *that was* discontented, gathered themselves unto him; and he became a captain over them: and there were with him about four hundred men."

9. James H. Lane (1814–66) was a pro-slavery leader in Bloody Kansas during the 1850s, elected as a free state U.S. senator as early as 1856 but unable to take his seat until 1861. Lane became an outspoken supporter of Lincoln and emancipation.

10. Andrew Johnson served as vice president for only five weeks before Lincoln's assassination thrust him unexpectedly into the presidency. Johnson's stubborn refusal to extend rights to former slaves in the South led to his impeachment in 1868. Acquitted, he served out his term, and later returned to the U.S. Senate.

11. Hay and Stoddard never agreed on which of them—if either—bore the responsibility (or credit) for igniting the dump-Hamlin movement at the Union Party nominating convention of 1864. "I cannot say positively that you yourself told me he [Lincoln] would prefer Johnson. I think you did. Anyhow, I got such an impression more or less distinctly, from you or Nicolay. Right or wrong, I went

in on it like a beaver." Stoddard to Hay, August 13, 1875, John Hay Papers, John Hay Library, Brown University.

AFTERWORD: PICTURING LINCOLN

1. See Holzer and Neely, *Mine Eyes Have Seen the Glory*, 78; Holzer, Boritt, and Neely, "Francis Bicknell Carpenter," 76–77.

2. Caleb Blood Smith (1808–64) served as Lincoln's first secretary of the interior, resigning in December 1862 to become a federal judge in his home state of Indiana. In Carpenter's defense, Smith died in January 1864, before the artist came to Washington to paint his Emancipation Proclamation canvas. Though he undertook to sketch the surviving Cabinet ministers from life, Smith, obviously, was unavailable.

3. Under pressure from the so-called Radical Republicans whose support he needed for re-nomination, Lincoln asked for Blair's resignation as postmaster general in 1864.

4. Rutherford B. Hayes (1822–93) won 250,000 fewer popular votes than Democrat Samuel J. Tilden (1814–86), in the acrimonious, hotly disputed 1876 presidential election, which ended in an electoral vote tie.

5. Alexander Hamilton Stephens (1812–83) was a Whig congressman from Georgia when fellow Whig Abraham Lincoln arrived in Washington to serve his one and only term in the House of Representatives from Illinois. Writing home to his law partner, the freshman from Springfield described his senior colleague as "a little skim, pale-faced, consumptive man . . . [who] has just concluded the very best speech, of an hour's length, I ever heard. My old, withered, dry eyes, are full of tears yet." Though opposed to disunion, Stephens later sided with Georgia when it seceded, and was elected vice president of the Confederacy in 1861. He subsequently feuded with President Jefferson Davis and returned to his home state. Briefly imprisoned after the war, he was returned to the House of Representatives in 1872. See *Collected Works of Lincoln,* 1:448.

6. James Morrison Steele Mackaye (1842–94) was a rising actor and impresario, soon to open the Madison Square Theatre in New York, where he introduced the concept of "intimate" playhouses to the city. He also wrote more than twenty plays. Stoddard probably saw him in his 1875 production, *Rose Michel.*

7. Samuel Jackson Randall (1818–90), a U.S. congressman since 1863, became Speaker of the House in 1876—the year of the centennial of national independence.

8. Lincoln made the remark about Stephens—or some variation of it—after meeting him again at the aborted Hampton Roads peace conference in Virginia in March 1865. General Grant remembered the president exclaiming: "Didn't you think it was the biggest shuck and the littlest ear that you ever did see?" See

Ulysses S. Grant, *Personal Memoirs of U. S. Grant,* 2 vols. (New York: Charles L. Webster & Co., 1885–86), 2:423.

9. Timothy Otis Howe (1816–83) represented Wisconsin in the U.S. Senate from 1861 to 1879.

10. George Franklin Edmunds (1828–1919) served in the U.S. Senate from 1866 until 1891, crowning his career by co-authoring the Sherman Anti-Trust Act in 1890. Twice, in 1880 and 1884, he was a contender for the Republican presidential nomination.

11. Nicolay had unsuccessfully championed Congressional acquisition of the Carpenter picture ten years earlier. See Nicolay to Francis B. Carpenter, January 22, 1866, Carpenter Papers, private collection.

12. Nathaniel P. Banks (1816–94), a former congressman, Speaker of the House, and governor of Massachusetts, had served as a Union major general during the Civil War, winning special distinction at the 1863 capture of Port Hudson, Louisiana. After the war, Banks served three more separate, non-consecutive terms in Congress.

13. Lawrence A. Gobright earned nearly $100 a week, a princely sum at the time, from various newspapers around the country for his wartime reports on the Lincoln administration. See Louis M. Starr, *The Civil War's Bohemian Brigade: Newsmen in Action* (New York: Alfred A. Knopf, 1954), 243.

14. New York publisher J. C. Derby called it a "sublime sight" to observe the onetime Rebel leader "in behalf of the United States, accepting a painting commemorating the downfall of slavery" on Lincoln's Birthday, February 12, 1878. Ironically, both Stephens and fellow orator Garfield emphasized preservation of the Union, not emancipation, as Lincoln's primary reason for resisting secession in 1861. See J. C. Derby, *Fifty Years Among Authors, Books and Publishers . . .* (New York: J. C. Derby, 1884), 490; *New York Times,* February 13, 1878.

15. Carpenter labored for a time in the 1870s on what he called his "Arbitration Picture," showing the signers of the 1871 Treaty of Washington gathered around a central table—very much in the style of the artist's *First Reading of the Emancipation Proclamation.* But though sketches for the work survive, the location of the original painting—if it was ever produced—is unknown.

16. Although Carpenter always dreamed that his Emancipation painting would occupy the Capitol Rotunda alongside the nation-affirming works depicting major events of the eighteenth century, his canvas hangs today over the west staircase of the Senate wing. Recently restored, it is still displayed in its 1878 gilt frame featuring the seal of the United States and rising suns at each corner. See William Kloss and Diane K. Skvarla, *United States Senate Catalogue of Fine Art* (Washington: U.S. Government Printing Office, 2002), 116–21.

Index

Unless otherwise indicated, women are indexed by maiden name. The note "*pl.*" indicates the presence of relevant plates in the gallery following page 156.

Harold Holzer, senior vice president for external affairs at the Metropolitan Museum of Art, is one of the country's leading authorities on Abraham Lincoln and the political culture of the Civil War era. A prolific writer and lecturer, and frequent guest on television, he serves as co-chairman of the U.S. Abraham Lincoln Bicentennial Commission.

Holzer is the author, co-author, or editor of twenty-nine books, including *The Lincoln Image* (1984) with Mark E. Neely Jr. and Gabor S. Boritt; *The Lincoln Family Album* (1990) with Neely; *Lincoln on Democracy* (with Mario Cuomo, 1990); *The Lincoln-Douglas Debates* (1993); *Dear Mr. Lincoln: Letters to the President* (1993); *Lincoln as I Knew Him* (1999); *Lincoln Seen and Heard* (2000); and *Lincoln at Cooper Union: The Speech that Made Abraham Lincoln President* (2004), which won a 2005 Lincoln Prize. In addition, Holzer has authored several Lincoln volumes for young readers, written nearly four hundred articles for popular magazines, scholarly journals, and newspapers, and contributed chapters to more than twenty books.

Holzer has appeared on documentaries aired on PBS, A&E, and the History Channel as well as on *The Today Show, The Charlie Rose Show, The News Hour with Jim Lehrer,* and many Lincoln-themed programs on C-SPAN. He lectures throughout the country and has organized Lincoln symposia and national traveling exhibitions of art of the Civil War era. He is also founding vice chairman of the Lincoln Forum and serves on the board of directors of the Ulysses S. Grant Association.

Holzer has won numerous prizes for his work—some of them repeatedly—including the Barondess Award of the Civil War Round Table of New York; the Award of Achievement from the Lincoln Group of New York; the first annual award from the Manuscript Society of America in 1996 for his use of original manuscripts in *Dear Mr. Lincoln;* and the coveted Nevins-Freeman Award of the Civil War Round Table of Chicago.

For more about the author, including his schedule of public appearances, visit www.haroldholzer.com.